The Intergenerational Effects of Adverse Childhood Experiences

The Intergenerational Effects of Adverse Childhood Experiences

Ripples on a Pond

Edited by

Richard Pates

Diane Riley

WILEY Blackwell

This edition first published 2026

Registered Offices
John Wiley & Sons, Inc., 111 River Street, Hoboken, NJ 07030, USA
John Wiley & Sons Ltd, New Era House, 8 Oldlands Way, Bognor Regis, West Sussex, PO22 9NQ, UK

For details of our global editorial offices, customer services, and more information about Wiley products visit us at www.wiley.com.

The manufacturer's authorized representative according to the EU General Product Safety Regulation is Wiley-VCH GmbH, Boschstr. 12, 69469 Weinheim, Germany, e-mail: Product_Safety@wiley.com.

Wiley also publishes its books in a variety of electronic formats and by print-on-demand. Some content that appears in standard print versions of this book may not be available in other formats.

Library of Congress Cataloging-in-Publication Data Applied for:
Paperback ISBN: 9781394282401
ePdf ISBN: 9781394282425
ePub ISBN: 9781394282418
Obook ISBN: 9781394282432

Cover Design: Wiley
Cover Image: Courtesy of Cleo Isabelle Pates

Set in 10/12.5pt Sabon by Straive, Pondicherry, India
Printed and bound by CPI Group (UK) Ltd, Croydon, CR0 4YY
C9781394282401_170726

CONTENTS

PREFACE

This book came about because both of us have spent most of our adult lives working with people who have suffered from the effects of childhood and other adversity, and we have seen the wide range of serious effects that they can have. We have both worked for many years with people who use alcohol and other drugs in different parts of the world and are well aware of the role ACEs play in substance use and dependence, both licit and illicit. We have also seen the impact that drug use can have on the children of people with whom we have worked. One of us has also worked extensively in children's homes, often with children who have suffered many ACEs, and the experience of talking to these children about their families makes you realise the intergenerational impact of events in the family's past.

We wanted to highlight the intergenerational effects of ACEs as well as the prolonged effects these adverse experiences can have, often lasting a lifetime and causing profound psychological problems. This is something not always recognised or appreciated, including by healthcare professionals. We also wanted to highlight the fact that it is not just events that happen in a family or some sort of abuse that can cause problems but also the impact of large events such as wars or natural disasters, including climate change. Preventing and dealing with childhood adversity should be everybody's concern in a caring society.

CONTRIBUTORS' BIOGRAPHIES

Gwen Adshead

Professor Gwen Adshead is a forensic psychiatrist and psychotherapist and Honorary Clinical Professor at the University of Exeter. She trained at St George's Hospital in forensic psychiatry, at the Institute of Psychiatry and at the Institute of Group Analysis. She is still working as a therapist with violence perpetrators, both male and female. She has a long-standing interest in attachment theory and how early childhood attachment insecurity can be a risk factor for violence, and she has studied attachment insecurity in women who abuse their children. Professor Adshead has published widely in both academic domains and for a general audience; her next book about trauma will be published in 2026. She was the BBC Reith Lecturer in 2024.

Saima Ali

Dr Saima Ali is a Senior Registrar in Forensic Psychiatry at West London NHS Trust and a Medical Education Fellow at South London and Maudsley NHS Foundation Trust. After completing her medical training at the Universities of St Andrews and Glasgow, she returned to London to pursue psychiatric training. Her current research interests include examining the role of gender in forensic mental health services.

Andrew Bennett

Andrew Bennett, MSc, Postgraduate Diploma and BA, is a former youth worker and drug service manager. He established one of the first syringe exchange programmes in the mid-1980s in the United Kingdom. He was the Managing Director at HIT, a national agency providing a range of drugs and other public health interventions from 1994 to 2006. During the last 20 years, Andrew has had a range of public health roles, including alcohol and other drugs, smoking, healthy weight, ageing, death, dying and loss, sexual health, youth violence and ACEs and trauma.

Sabine Bode

Sabine Bode, born in 1947, considers herself a child of peace but one affected by the long shadows of Nazi Germany and World War II. During the 90s, Sabine became concerned with the fate of German war children as adults and learnt how strongly this age group was kept in an almost total societal taboo. When working on her bestselling book on 'Die vergessene Generation',

The Forgotten Generation, 2004, Sabine found that 90% of the former war children rejected her enquiries, reflecting on the after-effects of war events. Many of them had developed an emotional numbness that helped them survive, keeping bad memories hidden. Bode's second book, 'Kriegsenkel' (war grandchildren 2004), focused on the children of war children. Since then, a grassroots movement has grown: war grandchildren breaking the silence of family history by asking their grandparents painful questions about war and Nazi past – a search to reveal family secrets and to work towards individual and societal healing.

Eric Breton

Eric Breton is a professor in health promotion at the EHESP School of Public Health and a researcher at the Arènes research unit (UMR CNRS 6051: RSMS team INSERM U1309). His research programme includes the evaluation of complex health promotion programmes. He is the co-editor of the first French-language health promotion handbook (3rd edition will be published in 2027) and the president of the Health Promotion Section of the European Public Health Association (EUPHA).

Line Caron

Line Caron holds a Master's degree in Social Sciences, specialising in Family Studies, and is a Practitioner in Applied Neuroscience. She is also an author, trainer and lecturer who developed the 'A Family Affair!' programme to prevent the intergenerational transmission of suffering related to family functioning, such as addiction, violence and anxiety.

Jiaying Chen

Dr Jiaying Chen is a Core Psychiatry trainee at Oxford Health NHS Foundation Trust. She completed her medical training at St George's Hospital Medical School and is pursuing her psychiatric training in Oxford. She has a budding interest in the impact of early childhood on mental health in old age.

Elodie David

Elodie David is a research assistant at the EHESP School of Public Health. She completed a master's degree in social psychology, specialising in the acquisition and management of knowledge and behaviours. From 2020 to 2023, she coordinated the PATTERN interventional research project, which aimed to evaluate the 'A Family Affair' programme presented in this book.

Mike DeGagné

Dr Mike DeGagné is President and CEO of Indspire, Canada's largest Indigenous charity. He has previously served as President and Vice Chancellor of Nipissing University. He is a member of the Order of Canada and a citizen of Animakee Wa Zhing #37 First Nation in Ontario. In 1998, Dr DeGagné became the founding Executive Director of the Aboriginal Healing Foundation, a national Indigenous organisation dedicated to addressing the legacy of

Canada's Indian Residential School System, a role he played until its closure in 2013. His career includes working with the federal government in the management of Indigenous programs and as a negotiator of comprehensive land claims.

Amy Johnson

Amy Johnson is a Senior Lecturer in Criminology and Psychology at the University of Worcester. With over a decade of experience in domestic abuse research and intervention, she specialises in working with marginalised communities, embedding lived experiences into practice and policy. Her PhD explores the interplay between housing and domestic abuse, focusing on multiple disadvantages and street homelessness. Having worked across the criminal justice system and third sector, Amy integrates practical knowledge into her teaching, shaping future approaches to criminology and social justice.

Lauren Jones

Lauren gained her BA in Linguistics from York University and an MSc in Language Pathology from Newcastle University before working in the NHS as a Speech and Language Therapist. After facing mental health challenges, she was diagnosed with Complex PTSD and later ADHD. Believing in the need for preventative, proactive mental health care, she completed a second MSc in Psychology at Nottingham Trent University (NTU), founded Chime to Thrive, and co-founded Staywell Derby CIC. She began a PhD at NTU exploring mental health diagnoses through a Social Identity and Survivor Research lens. However, she fell ill with Myalgic Encephalomyelitis before completion. She is now a very content full-time mum to Quinnley and wife to Jonathan; they have a cockapoo called Dexter.

Alison Knight

Alison Knight has been a lawyer, registered childminder, charity fundraiser, teacher and bestselling novelist. Her novel, *Mine* (now republished as *Lily's Choice* under the pen name May Ellis), was based on the final months of her parents' lives before their deaths in 1969. She says that writing it was the best therapy and helped her to finally understand the trauma from an adult's perspective rather than her confused and frightened child's view of that time.

Gaynor Madgwick

Gaynor survived the Aberfan disaster in 1966, where 116 young children and 28 adults died, including her brother and sister. She was one of a family of 6 children, aged 8, sustaining physical and emotional trauma and spent 3 months in hospital.

Aged 12, she had received no psychological support and was compelled to write a diary and poetry in her time of emotional trauma, suffering in silence, continuing to write until she was 16 years old, then aged 30, revisiting her earlier writings, her debut book 'Aberfan, struggling out of the darkness' was published.

Twenty years later, Gaynor was desperate to find answers and gain some closure, interviewing her parents, her four siblings, royalty and members of the church. Doctors, soldiers, rescuers, survivors and others, to reflect on her earlier writings and ask the questions that haunted her but she had not dared to ask for 50 years.

Her second book, 'A Story of Survival, Love and Community' was published in 2016 for the 50th anniversary by Y Lolfa. Gaynor's book is the only one written by a survivor, as a child and adult looking at the tragedy through the eyes of a child and adult. Lord Snowden's forward and the introduction by Vincent Kane are powerful.

She is the proud mother of three children and six grandchildren.

Deirdre McConnell

Deirdre McConnell has worked for thirty-five years with troubled children in a wide range of educational settings, as an art teacher, Local Authority 'behaviour needs' consultant, art psychotherapist and clinical supervisor. These young people's innate intelligence and creativity have always inspired me to try to create opportunities through which they can grow and learn that they are esteemed and valuable human beings with enormous potential. I presently lead a team of arts therapists in One Education, which was set up in 2011 to lever school improvement. I am undertaking doctoral studies at the University of Sheffield. The working title of my thesis is: *'Silent Revolution: School-based art therapy unlocks creativity and transforms lives'*.

Michal Miovský

Professor Michal Miovský, PhD, Clinical psychologist and psychotherapist. From 2016 to 2018, he was the president of the International Society of Addiction Journal Editors (ISAJE). In 2016, he became a founding member of the International Consortium of Universities for Drug Demand Reduction (ICUDDR). In 2021, he became a member of the board of directors of the International Society of Substance Use Professionals (ISSUP).

RG: https://www.researchgate.net/profile/Michal_Miovsky.

Adam Nicholls

Adam Nicholls is a Formerly an Assistant Psychologist within NHS and secure children's care, Adam later advanced into analytical leadership roles across health and justice. He now serves as a Senior Analyst, specialising in advanced modelling and strategic analytics, and sits on the International Advisory Board of the Journal of Substance Use.

Richard Pates

Professor Richard Pates is a Consultant Clinical Psychologist who has worked in Wales all his working life, firstly setting up services for drug users in Cardiff and running that team, and after retiring from the Health Service, worked in a secure children's home, which catered for the most troubled children and now works in a consultant capacity for a small company that runs four children's homes. It was working in these homes from which he got his interest in ACEs. He is a visiting professor at the University of Worcester in England and Charles University in Prague. He has a doctorate in clinical psychology, and he is the Editor of the Journal of Substance Use.

Diane Riley

Dr Diane Riley (BA, MA, PhD) is a psychophysiologist and consultant who has worked in Canada and internationally for many years in the areas of development, security, addictions, harm reduction and mental health. She specialises in the areas of trauma, drug-related problems and criminal justice, and has worked extensively with young people, women and marginalised populations. She has been an advisor to international organisations such as United Nations agencies for many years. Diane has taught at several universities around the world and was an Assistant Professor in the School of Public Health at the University of Toronto. She was a founder of the Canadian Foundation for Drug Policy, the International Harm Reduction International (HRI) and YouthRISE, and was on the board of UNAIDS, the Canadian HIV/AIDS Legal Network and a number of other organisations.

Diana S. Lesme Romero

Dr Diana S. Lesme Romero is a Clinical Psychologist and Senior Professor at the Psychology School, Universidad Católica 'Ntra. Sra. de la Asunción'. She coordinated drug use prevention programmes for eight years in a civil agency and co-authored five books on families, psychological development, adolescence and violence prevention. She serves on the Board of Directors of ICUDDR (2018–2025) and ISSUP-Paraguay (2023–present).

Liliana Templos-Núñez

Liliana Templos holds bachelor's and master's degrees in psychology from the National Autonomous University of Mexico, where she is currently a PhD candidate in Psychology. She specialises in clinical and psychosocial approaches to mental health and substance use, with a focus on trauma-informed care. Certified in Motivational Interviewing by the Florida Node Alliance (NIDA, United States), she has taught and supervised at institutions like the National Institute of Psychiatry. She currently works in research and training at Centros de Integración Juvenil.

Anna Tsiboukli

Dr Anna Tsiboukli is a Psychologist (AFBPSS), Senior Lecturer of Lifelong Learning, Group Dynamics and Adult Education at the School of Education, National and Kapodistrian University of Athens, Greece. Prior to that, she was the Director of Education at KETHEA, Greece. She served for six years on the Board of the International Society of Addiction Journal Editors, and for twenty years, she was co-editor at the scientific journal Exartiseis.

Maya Lasker-Wallfisch

Maya Lasker-Wallfisch is a Psychoanalytic Psychotherapist, Author and Educator. She is particularly known for her work with second-generation perpetrators. She divides her time between Berlin and London.

Part 1
Introduction to ACEs

Chapter 1

CHILDHOOD ADVERSITY – INTERGENERATIONAL EFFECTS

Diane Riley[1] *and Richard Pates*[2]

[1] Independent Consultant, Ontario, Canada
[2] Independent Consultant, Wales, UK

Introduction to adverse childhood experiences

The concept of childhood adversity and the long-term psychological and physiological effects associated with it has been written about for centuries in many diverse cultures. The fact that adverse events in childhood and adolescence can cause profound problems throughout life has been a core part of clinical approaches and psychological theories as well as self-help books and family lore. Yet it was not until relatively recently, with the development of appropriate statistical and computing techniques, that early adverse experiences and their effects throughout life became systematically identified, measured and discussed in a manner that could be studied objectively. This research promised to complement research on what is often referred to as the social determinants of health, listed in the Ottawa Charter of 1986. As will be seen, however, the extent to which research on childhood adversity has been integrated with that on social determinants has been limited and inadequate to date. This has been to the detriment of both fields as well as to our understanding of how to deal with the problems raised by such adversity.

Adverse childhood experiences (ACEs) are negative events experienced during childhood which can affect people well into their adult lives. Many of these events are those which children may experience in their own families or in their surrounding environment, such as school. They may also be the product of traumatic experiences due to war, severe social upheaval or natural disasters. There is considerable evidence that ACEs are a common experience in most parts of the world. This book will explore adverse experiences from quite diverse backgrounds and examine their impact on people's lives by including testimony of lived experiences from several countries. Some potential solutions to the problems related to childhood adversity are discussed,

The Intergenerational Effects of Adverse Childhood Experiences: Ripples on a Pond, First Edition. Edited by Richard Pates and Diane Riley.

Published 2026 by John Wiley & Sons Ltd.

ranging from more traditional therapies such as cognitive-behavioural to new, experimental approaches, such as the use of psychoactive substances.

The phrase 'adverse childhood experiences (ACEs)' is a relatively new one, first specifically described in detail by Felitti and colleagues (1998) in their research into the underlying causes of health-related adult problems such as obesity. We know, of course, that these experiences have always existed and had an impact on children, although the extent of this impact was often not recognised or acknowledged. In a book by a distinguished doctor (Lauzun-Brown 1916), the preface states that 'the proper management of the child is a vital subject, though it is one that has hitherto been grievously neglected. Mothers often undertake the responsibility of the rearing of children, without knowledge and without thought' (p. 9). In a section about playing with a baby, he writes, 'Playing with the baby, making it laugh and crow to show off its intelligence may delight the mother, but if repeated with any frequency, it is simply paving the way for a normal baby to grow up into a nervous child. The best treatment for a baby during his first year is to attend carefully to its physical wants and to absolutely neglect the fact that it has a mind at all' (p. 113). We would now suggest the absolute opposite of this, knowing that children respond from a very early age, as well as in the womb, to positive care and stimulation. It is also true that 50 years ago, physical chastisement of children was thought to be important, and there was a saying, 'Spare the rod and spoil the child'. In the United Kingdom, this is now illegal. Corporal (physical) punishment was banned in UK State schools in 1986 and extended to private schools in England and Wales in 1998, in Scotland in 2000 and in Northern Ireland in 2003.

Felitti noted the critical role that childhood experiences can play in later life while running an obesity clinic in San Diego in 1995; he was puzzled as to why two of his female patients who had lost significant amounts of weight, then regained that weight and were resistant to sustained weight loss. On further questioning, it transpired that both women had been sexually abused as children, one from the age of 4 by her father, the other by her grandfather from the age of 10. These findings led Felitti and a colleague, the epidemiologist Robert Anda, to survey 17,421 of Kaiser Permanente patients. They were sent a questionnaire asking about childhood abuse and exposure to household dysfunction and about exposure to current health risk factors such as smoking, drug use and sexually transmitted diseases.

Based on the adverse experiences noted in patients in the obesity clinic, they asked the patients whether they had experienced any of the following:

1. Emotional abuse (recurrent)
2. Physical abuse (recurrent)
3. Sexual abuse (by contact)
4. Physical neglect
5. Emotional neglect
6. Drug or alcohol abuse in the household
7. Mental illness in the household

8. Domestic violence
9. Divorce or parental separation
10. Criminal behaviour in the household (e.g. someone going to prison)

They then correlated the number of ACEs with health outcomes and health risk behaviours. They found two surprising things: firstly, that most patients had experienced at least one ACE, and secondly, that an increase in the number of ACEs increased the risk of adult health problems. For example, people with 4 or more ACEs were twice as likely as someone with no ACEs to develop heart disease and 3.5 times as likely to develop chronic obstructive pulmonary disease (COPD).

The Felitti et al. study has several limitations because it is a cross-sectional study and was carried out on mainly white, middle-class North Americans, and because of a limited number of questions, with no specification of intensity or duration of an experience. Later work by other researchers has tried to address some of these limitations. An exhaustive 2020 overview of research into ACEs suggested that five additional forms of adversity that 'increase children's exposure to trauma' should be added to the list (Asmussen et al. 2020). These are economic disadvantage, discrimination, peer victimisation, low birth weight and child disability. In their excellent report, Asmussen and her colleagues note the limitations of current estimates of prevalence of ACEs and methods used, and caution against the unethical use and overuse of ACE screening practices.

A number of organisations, such as the World Health Organization, the Centers for Disease Control and Prevention in the United States and Public Health Wales, Scotland and Northern Ireland and many parts of England have introduced training and/or screening for ACEs in vulnerable populations. Related research has shown that, in addition to health issues, there can be an increase in many other problems in adulthood for people who have experienced four or more ACEs. In a study for Public Health Wales, Bellis and colleagues found that people who had suffered 4 or more ACEs were 4 times more likely to be high risk drinkers, 6 times more likely to smoke, 14 times more likely to be the victims of violence over the previous 12 months, 15 times more likely to have committed violence on another person in the previous 12 months, 16 times more likely to have used cocaine or heroin and 20 times more likely to have been incarcerated at some point in their lives (Bellis et al. 2016). These studies show the major impact that the conditions in which a child is raised can have on adult behaviour. For example, in a Secure Children's Home in Wales (a residential home for children aged 12–18 who were thought to be at risk to themselves or others), none of these very troubled children had no ACEs compared to 53% of the Welsh population, 10% had experienced 1 ACE compared to 20% of the Welsh population, 26% had experienced 2–3 ACEs compared to 13% of the Welsh population and 64% of them had experienced 4 or more ACEs compared to 14% of the Welsh population (Pates et al. 2019, p. 149).

Since the original work of Felitti and colleagues in the 1990s, there has been a considerable amount of research in the area. A number of these studies will be examined below in the review of the effects of ACEs on adult health and behaviour. Much of this research has been retrospective in nature and suffers from the problems inherent in such studies, but a few studies have been prospective and have therefore resulted in higher-quality data. Some of this research has attempted to move the discussion from the well-established area of correlation to that of causation, but support for the latter remains weak. The correlational relationship between ACEs and later psychological and physical effects renders a person at increased risk of developing a later problem. As noted by Asmussen and colleagues in their research, however, while it is clear that high levels of ACEs significantly increase the risk of physical and mental health problems in adulthood, the absolute size of many of these risks is relatively small and certainly not deterministic. The strongest correlational relationships are between ACEs and mental health issues, especially substance use and PTSD. It is on the mental health effects of ACEs, why some people do develop later problems and others do not, and the pressing need to address these problems appropriately that this book is focused. What is abundantly clear is that ACEs and the circumstances surrounding them can have a major effect on children and these effects can continue into adulthood, hence the need to try to ameliorate them and to find solutions to help those who have experienced problems resulting from them.

ACEs can include a large-scale environmental event, such as war, threat, or man-made or natural disaster, or smaller-scale events in an individual's life, such as abuse, bullying or neglect. Abuse may be physical, emotional or verbal and gestural, and can be short-term but very intense or long-term. Some of these events may be so severe, or the individual so sensitive, that they result in psychological trauma. The effects of ACEs on mental and physical health depend on many factors, including vulnerability, the developmental age of the person, their personal and family history and the protections around the person in the form of family, friends and community. The ACE score doesn't have much predictive power on an individual basis or as a clinical tool; it doesn't convey timing, pattern or intensity of stressors or presence of healing or buffering factors. ACEs are of consequence but as will be illustrated in this book, so is a person's history in relationships and a caring and supportive community; people are resilient or malleable, or, at the very least, with support, they can rebuild themselves.

Stress and PTSD: consequences of ACEs

Stress is a condition of psychological and/or physiological strain caused by demands placed on a person. Hans Selye defined it as the 'non-specific response of the body to any demand'. It gives rise to several diverse psychological, physiological and neurochemical responses. The pioneering work of Walter Canon in 1915 detailed the vital role of acute stress and the autonomic nervous system (ANS) in the fight-or-flight response, demonstrating the need to better understand the sympathetic and the parasympathetic systems, which are not under direct control of the central nervous system.

Canon's work also highlighted the role of Classical or Pavlovian conditioning and contiguity rather than contingency in changes to the ANS and the role of these in emotional behaviours such as fears and phobias.

From the 1940s to the early 1980s, Hans Selye of McGill University investigated the effects of prolonged or chronic stress (general adaptation syndrome) on the organism, dividing the response into three phases: the alarm reaction, the stage of resistance and the stage of exhaustion. Selye found that a wide range of quite different stressors produced similar effects on the hypothalamic–pituitary–adrenal axis (HPA), including adrenal hyperactivity. He was the first researcher to demonstrate that stress is a state of events and a cause of non-specific signs and symptoms of illness, and his work has had a significant effect on many diverse fields, from psychology to endocrinology.

It is not quite clear at what point the term 'toxic stress' entered the literature and it may have been an error when meaning to write about oxidative stress. It is a term that has become widely used in a manner that suggests that it has a firm basis in some scientific fact. The term, however, has no real meaning, although it seems to have acquired a great deal of erroneous explanatory power and emotional impact. In reality, there are acute stress and chronic stress; chronic stress can give rise to problems at many levels of function, from neurochemical to psychological, but there is no need to append 'toxic' to it. Along with 'toxic' stress, high cortisol levels have become the subject of considerable review and criticism, but this is a misunderstanding of the complex roles that cortisol plays, many of which are by no means fully understood. Similarly, 'polyvagal theory' gained popularity and explanatory power for some years, but it has been demonstrated to have no scientific basis. The area of trauma and adversity is rife with such pseudo-neuroscientific terms and overly broad usage of so-called causes. Such misuse defeats the purpose, as a term that is too widely used loses its explanatory power as well as its scientific and clinical value.

PTSD refers to post-traumatic stress disorder, one of the potential effects of severe stress or trauma. Over the past few decades, the definitions of PTSD have changed and expanded in both the DSM-5 (Diagnostic and Statistical Manual of Mental Disorders), used in North America, and the international systems, the ICD-11 (International Classification of Diseases, 11th Revision, WHO 2022).

The two classification systems treat trauma in quite different ways. The DSM-5 focuses on the details and complexity of PTSD, while the ICD-11 takes a less complex but clinically practical approach and introduces CPTSD (complex PTSD) as a formal diagnosis.

DSM-5 Symptom Clusters:

1. Intrusion Symptoms: Flashbacks, nightmares and involuntary memories.
2. Avoidance: Efforts to avoid thoughts, feelings or reminders of the trauma.
3. Negative Cognitions and Mood: Persistent negative thoughts, distorted blame, detachment and emotional numbness.

4. Arousal and Reactivity: Hypervigilance, irritability, sleep disturbances and exaggerated startle responses.

ICD-11 Symptom Clusters:

1. Re-experiencing the Trauma: Flashbacks, intrusive memories, or nightmares.
2. Avoidance: Avoiding memories, feelings or external reminders of the trauma.
3. Heightened Perception of Threat: Hypervigilance and an exaggerated startle response.

The main difference between the two systems is that the DSM-5 does not recognise CPTSD as a distinct diagnosis but uses PTSD in a broad way, mainly for trauma-related disorders. Other diagnoses, such as Borderline Personality Disorder (BPD) or Major Depressive Disorder (MDD), are used in some cases. The ICD-11 includes CPTSD as a separate condition for people with prolonged and repeated trauma (such as childhood abuse or domestic violence). In addition to the core PTSD symptoms, CPTSD has three core changes in self-organisation:

1. Affective Dysregulation: Difficulty managing emotions, with extreme highs or lows, numbness or outbursts.
2. Negative Self-Concept: Persistent feelings of worthlessness, guilt or failure.
3. Relationship Disturbances: Difficulty building trust or maintaining close relationships due to emotional detachment or mistrust.

Globally, PTSD affects about 4% of the population, with rates varying a good deal between countries (Koenen et al. 2017; WHO 2024a). Rates are higher in Canada and the United States, ranging between 6% and 10%, which may be due to greater awareness and reporting or to overdiagnosis from the use of the DSM with its broad, symptom-based approach, rather than the narrower ICD system.

Trauma

Trauma is an ancient Greek word for a bodily wound. The effects of trauma have been recorded throughout history, from the trials of Ajax in Homer's Iliad, the accounts of soldiers from the US Civil War to the descriptions of 'shellshock' in World War 1. Formal definitions, such as Cambridge, Oxford and Merriam-Webster dictionaries, include the common themes of a severe emotional shock, pain caused by an emotionally harmful experience, and a disordered state caused by a severe mental, emotional or physical injury. The dictionary definitions of trauma are quite broad, reflecting the way in which the use of the term has expanded in scope over the years.

Definitions of trauma tend to be very subjective and, at times, controversial. Workers in the area seem to be divided between what can be called narrow and broad definitions of trauma. The narrow definition restricts the term to those events which are life-threatening or close to it, such as war, accident and sexual assault. The broad definition has come to encompass a wide array of psychological and behavioural effects of stressful or painful events. In our discussions, we will restrict our usage to the narrow definitions, although some of the authors in the following chapters may adopt a broader definition. Like Gabor Maté and many other writers, we consider trauma to be what happens inside the person as the result of an event, not the event itself. Unlike Maté, Levine and others, we do not consider the term trauma to be appropriate for describing the effects of hurtful events unless these are extremely serious and/or sustained over a very considerable length of time. We would consider such events to be painful, hurtful or stressful, and regard the term 'trauma' as being too widely used, preferring to reserve it to refer only to the consequence of the most serious of stressful events.

Stress and the nervous systems

To understand the effects of ACEs and the stress response, we need first to review the way in which the human brain is organised and the way in which it processes incoming stimuli. This organisation reflects the development of the human nervous system from the womb onwards.

Sensory input goes first to the brainstem, which is responsible for basic functions such as cardiovascular, respiration and temperature. The brainstem reacts to incoming stimuli in the most basic ways, based on contiguity (not contingency) and past reactions. The diencephalon is involved with appetite, arousal, movement and sleep. The limbic system is involved in bonding, emotion, memory and reward. At the highest level, the cortex, there is involvement in cognition, language, creativity, planning, narrative memory and processing based on contingency rather than simple contiguity. As our brain develops over childhood and adolescence (provided there is no brain damage), the higher levels begin to exert more control and thinking and planning can moderate feeling and acting. Yet it remains the case that input goes first to the brainstem. If that input evokes the stress response, whether directly or due to past association, then the control by higher brain levels can be slowed or modified.

Brain development and the storing of experiences start in the womb, and infants and young children are particularly sensitive to incoming stimuli. Even though they cannot label them, children are sensitive to non-verbal and verbal communication and their associations and responses to stressors shape their nervous systems. Many of these associations are stored at the level of the limbic system and lower levels and are not subject to cognitive control. As a result, early events that provoke fear and the stress response, such as abuse, may in some people continue to do so for years or for an entire lifetime unless they are addressed in a sensitive and effective manner.

The timing of ACEs in the child's development is important. The first 5–6 years of life appear to be key in terms of development of parts of the brain and nervous systems (Lussier et al. 2024). If key neural networks are not exposed to the right sorts of experiences or stimulation at the right times, some parts do not develop in the normal manner. Again, in adolescence, there appear to be key phases of brain development that can have a lasting impact on the individual, as the work of Sara-Jane Blakemore has demonstrated (Blakemore 2019).

Input from any of our senses can evoke a memory that may be linked to trauma. Some senses are particularly evocative, such as smell and taste. A meaningful childhood event can lead to profound memories and reactions decades later, just as the madeleine evoked Proust's remembrance of things past. *And suddenly the memory returns. The taste was that of the little crumb of madeleine which on Sunday mornings at Combray (because on those mornings I did not go out before church-time), when I used to say good day to her in her bedroom, my aunt Leonie used to give me, dipping it first in her own cup of real or of lime-flower tea. The sight of the madeleine had recalled nothing to my mind before I tasted it. And once I had recognised the taste of the crumb of madeleine soaked in her decoction of lime-flowers which my aunt used to give me (although I did not yet know and must long postpone the discovery of why this memory made me so happy) immediately the old grey house upon the street where her room was, rose up like the scenery of a theatre* (Proust 1992, p. 61).

And smell: 'Smell is a potent wizard that transports you across thousands of miles and all the years you have lived. The odours of fruits waft me to my southern home, to my childhood frolics in the peach orchard. Other odours, instantaneous and fleeting, cause my heart to dilate joyously or contract with remembered grief. Even as I think of smells, my nose is full of scents that start awaking sweet memories of summers gone and ripening fields far away', wrote Helen Keller, who was deaf and blind from the age of 19 months.

And of the memories stirred by music, as in the D.H. Lawrence poem *Piano*:

> *Softly, in the dusk, a woman is singing to me;*
> *Taking me back down the vista of years, till I see*
> *A child sitting under the piano, in the boom of the tingling strings*
> *And pressing the small, poised feet of a mother who smiles as she sings.*
> *In spite of myself, the insidious mastery of song*
> *Betrays me back, till the heart of me weeps to belong*
> *To the old Sunday evenings at home, with winter outside*
> *And hymns in the cosy parlour, the tinkling piano our guide.*
> *So now it is vain for the singer to burst into clamour*
> *With the great black piano appassionato. The glamour*
> *Of childish days is upon me, my manhood is cast*
> *Down in the flood of remembrance, I weep like a child for the past.*

Child maltreatment and effects

According to Article 19 of the United Nations Convention on the Rights of the Child: *Parties shall take all legislative, administrative, social and educational measures to protect a child from all forms of physical or mental violence, injury or abuse, neglect or negligent treatment, maltreatment or exploitation.* Child maltreatment refers to the abuse and neglect of children and it is seen in all parts of the world and at all social and economic levels. There are five main types of child maltreatment: sexual abuse (the involvement of a child in sexual activity that he or she does not understand, is unable to give consent to or is not developmentally prepared for), physical abuse (the use of physical force that harms the child's health, survival, development, or dignity), emotional abuse (the failure to provide a supportive environment by, for example, verbally threatening the child), neglect (the failure to provide for all aspects of the child's well-being), and witnessing or experiencing domestic abuse (intimate partner violence, IPV). Verbal abuse is also harmful to children. A clinical psychologist, Prof. Eamon McCrory, said recently, 'As children, we believe what we are told, deeply folding the words into our understanding of ourselves and the world around us. When those words are hostile, demeaning or humiliating, they can have lifelong consequences' (McCrory et al. 2017). He goes on, 'The critical words received in childhood underpin so much of adults' later pain and distress, even if they have spent decades trying to prove those words wrong'. Andrea Danese, a psychiatrist, states that words can harm a child's well-being and development and leave lifelong psychological scars (Danese 2025).

Child maltreatment rates are difficult to determine because of the wide variation in measurement methods. Massullo and colleagues conducted an umbrella review of the epidemiology of child maltreatment and found that differences in age groups, methods and instruments used to collect the data make it difficult to compare the results. Although definitions were quite homogeneous, categorisation of child maltreatment varied widely across studies (Massullo et al. 2023), while there is considerable uncertainty about the frequency and severity of child maltreatment, according to the most recent data from the World Health Organization (WHO 2024b):

- Six in 10 children – or 400 million children – under 5 years of age regularly suffer physical punishment and/or psychological violence at the hands of parents and caregivers.
- One in five women and one in seven men report having been sexually abused as a child.
- Consequences of child maltreatment include impaired lifelong physical and mental health, and the social and occupational outcomes can ultimately slow down a country's economic and social development.
- Child maltreatment is often hidden. Only a fraction of child victims of maltreatment ever get support from health professionals.
- A child who is abused is more likely to abuse others as an adult so that violence is passed down from one generation to the next.
- Preventing child maltreatment before it starts is possible. Effective prevention approaches include supporting parents, teaching positive parenting skills and enhancing laws to prohibit violent punishment.

All forms of maltreatment have been linked with subsequent physical and mental health effects, including trauma (e.g. Asmundson and Afifi 2019; Asmussen et al. 2020; Bellis et al. 2016; Radford et al. 2011). Several additional types of child abuse have been identified in recent years; examples include online child maltreatment, including live streaming of abuse, unaccompanied refugee minors and female genital mutilation and labiaplasty and arranged marriages for teenage girls.

We will review the effects on mental health of some of the main forms of abuse, and a number of chapters also address these issues. Clearly, a child can be subject to more than one form of abuse and so it is often difficult to attribute observed or reported effects to any one cause.

The first graphic description of battered child syndrome and of the physical findings in a large number of child sexual abuse cases was reported in a paper by Ambroise Tardieu in 1860, but his research and child protection recommendations were almost entirely ignored by both professionals and the general public (Vizard et al. 2021). In 1962, Henry Kempe and colleagues observed that the battered child syndrome, a result of serious physical abuse, is a frequent cause of permanent injury or death (Kempe et al. 1984). Due to the weight of the evidence, professionals accepted the fact that physical damage was being done to children, but consideration of abuse of a child by a parent was seen as unacceptable and damaging to the doctor–patient relationship. Following this report, research into the prevalence of child maltreatment was undertaken internationally, but professional and public resistance to accepting the findings remained. Professional denial of the existence of various forms of child abuse is still prevalent in many cultures despite the increasing number of enquiries and high-profile cases, including those in various religious institutions and schools. Indeed, it is still all too often the case that the child is not believed and the perpetrator goes on to abuse other children.

Maltreatment of children varies by country and definition and as a result, rates by country may not be comparable. Most are victims of neglect, with physical abuse, sexual abuse and other types of maltreatment making up 18, 9 and 11% of cases, respectively. Females are especially vulnerable to sexual violence, exploitation and abuse. Most maltreated children referred to child protection services have suffered more than one type of abuse.

Most child maltreatment is perpetrated by parents or parental guardians, or by teachers, many of whom were maltreated themselves as children. A review of meta-analyses published between 2014 and 2018 on antecedents for child abuse and the effectiveness of preventive interventions found the main risk factors for child maltreatment were: parental experience of childhood abuse; low family socioeconomic status; dependent and aggressive parental personality; IPV; and higher baseline ANS activity (van IJzendoorn et al. 2020a,b). Parental use of alcohol and other drugs is also related to levels of abuse.

Physical abuse

Exposure to violence during childhood can have lifelong health consequences, including poor physical, emotional and mental health. It is generally reported that child physical abuse is under-detected and under-reported by medical providers. Abusive head trauma (AHT) is the leading cause of death from physical abuse in children younger than age two. A third of AHT cases have a history of a sentinel injury, 85% have retinal haemorrhages and 30–70% have other injuries like rib fractures, bruising, among others (Biswas and Shroff 2021). Some forms of physical abuse also involve emotional and sexual abuse, as is the case with medical abuse in cases such as Munchausen by Proxy, where a parent or caregiver makes up or exaggerates symptoms of an illness in a child in order to get attention.

Sexual abuse

Childhood sexual abuse (CSA) is a severe public health concern, affecting roughly 1 in 4 girls and 1 in 13 boys worldwide (WHO 2024b). CSA includes sexually connotative physical contact or non-contact activities. The former includes intercourse, attempted intercourse, or oral-genital contact with the penis, fingers or any object; masturbation; and fondling the genitals or other erogenous areas through the clothing or directly. The latter entails forcing a child to participate in adult sexual activity (such as sexual harassment and prostitution) or exposing a child to adult sexual activities, such as pornography, voyeurism and exhibitionism. Since definitions of different forms of sexual abuse vary so widely across studies and countries, it is very difficult to be specific about rates and effects.

Once abuse has happened, the victim may also face threats to end the relationship if they refuse to perform sex or threats to publicly share their sexual images (UNICEF 2020). Many victims report sexual abuse later in their lives, and revictimisation is one of the most common outcomes of child sexual abuse (MacIntosh and Ménard 2021; Papalia et al. 2021).

In the United Kingdom, Ofsted was asked by the government to carry out a rapid review of sexual abuse in schools and colleges (2021). The review included visits to 32 schools and colleges, and interviews with over 900 children and young people about the prevalence of peer-on-peer sexual harassment and sexual violence, including online, in their lives and the lives of their peers. They also spoke to leaders, teachers, governors, parents and stakeholders. This review revealed how prevalent sexual harassment and online sexual abuse are for children and young people. Girls reported that sexual harassment and online sexual abuse, such as being sent unsolicited explicit sexual material and being pressured to send nude pictures, are prevalent. Children and young people reported that sexual harassment occurs so frequently that it has become 'commonplace'. For example, 2% of girls, and 74% of boys, said sexist name-calling happens a lot or sometimes to them or their peers.

Children and young people, especially girls, mentioned that they do not want to talk about sexual abuse for several reasons, such as the risk of being ostracised by peers or that getting peers into trouble is not worth it for something perceived to be commonplace. They think they will not be believed, or that they will be blamed and that the process will be out of their control.

Respondents thought that the curriculum was not equipping them with the advice needed for the reality of their lives, and so they relied on social media or their peers to educate each other; one girl stated, 'It shouldn't be our responsibility to educate boys'. Professionals interviewed underestimated the prevalence of online sexual abuse.

Emotional or psychological abuse

Emotional or psychological abuse is a pattern of behavior perpetuated by a parent that causes a child to experience emotional distress, harms their sense of self-worth, and affects their emotional development. Emotional abuse can happen in all families, but is more likely to occur in families suffering from financial issues, single parents, families going through separation or divorce or families where there is a high level of substance use. There are a number of different types of emotional abuse of children, including rejecting, ignoring, isolating or shunning, threatening, exploiting and corrupting.

Emotional abuse and emotional neglect are among the most prevalent types of childhood maltreatment and are associated with a range of poor mental health outcomes. The nature of the relationships discussed to date has been correlational rather than causal. There has been relatively less societal and research attention to emotional abuse compared with physical and sexual abuse and physical neglect. This might be explained, at least in part, by their less visible immediate impact (i.e. no physical injury or outward signs of abuse) and considerable regional and cultural variations in the definition of what constitutes emotional abuse or (emotional) neglect (Kumari 2020). Certain facets of emotional abuse, such as constant swearing, criticism or humiliation of a child, are easily noted, but others, such as unrealistic expectations or unfair treatment, are not always detected. Emotional neglect, or a failure to attend to the child's emotional needs, is also difficult to detect or may be a culturally accepted practice: hard to detect and very resistant to change.

Meta-analyses of the global prevalence of maltreatment show that childhood emotional abuse is self-reported by a much larger proportion of the adult population (about 36%) compared with physical (about 18%) or sexual abuse (8–18%), or physical neglect (about 16%); childhood emotional neglect is reported by about 18% of the adult population (Hailes et al. 2019; Massullo et al. 2023).

Neglect

Direct forms of abuse are not the only ways in which the behaviours and emotions of caregivers can affect the child. For example, the effects of stress and pressure on the caregiver can be manifested as frequent distraction; even though physically present, the caregiver may be focused elsewhere. This is made worse by financial hardship; even in some wealthy countries such as the United States, many mothers don't get paid leave. If the caregiver is isolated physically or socially, then there will be few supports to ensure sufficient attention to the infant.

If there is inadequate attention from caregivers, children will seek to meet the need for attachment elsewhere. Such attachment is often in the form of peer groups, either physically or via social media. Quite apart from the potential problems with social media attachments and abuse, there is the unreliable nature of peers and the possibility of bullying. A reliable caregiver ensures a sense of safety for an infant. A frightened, insecure or hungry child may well be in a state where several systems are out of balance or 'dysregulated', and in a state of chronic stress, sometimes for prolonged periods. As well established by the work of Canon, acute stress can lead to the fight-or-flight response in humans just as it can in other mammals. In some cases, when the individual cannot flee, there will be dissociation, a retreat into the self. Alcohol and other drugs can help with this retreat and self-protection in a very functional manner. The relief of distress is rewarding and so such self-medication comes to be vital for survival. If the stress becomes chronic, then this response is increased.

Developmental adversity can occur in the womb (e.g. exposure to alcohol and other drugs, nutrition deficit and physical damage), in early relationships with people, or in ongoing or extremely intense periods of stress (e.g. various forms of abuse, war, natural disaster, famine, loss of community and culture). The results of such adversity depend on many factors related to do with the individual person as well as their social and physical environment following the adversity. One result can be hypervigilance, as in PTSD, which can be mistaken for attention deficit hyperactivity disorder (ADHD), just as resistance and defiance due to fear can be labelled as oppositional disorder. 'The pervasive misunderstanding of trauma-related behaviour has a profound effect on our educational, mental health and juvenile justice systems' (Perry and Winfrey 2021, p. 92).

Rapid changeover of caregivers and foster homes is very confusing to a child; people disappear, are not predictable and not comforting. This is not uncommon in children taken into care in the United Kingdom and it is noticeable that the more changes of carer and place, the more unsettled and distressed the child is. If crying makes a caregiver angry or the caregiver is habitually angry, then the child's response might be to disengage and dissociate.

Neglect and lack of consistency can also result in problems, sometimes of a profound nature, as seen with Romanian orphans. More than 500,000 children spent their early lives in state-run orphanages during the Ceausescu regime (after Ceausescu banned abortion and contraception to increase the size of the population), which ended in 1989. The institutions housed 40–60 babies or toddlers in their own cribs in a single large room with 1 or 2 caregivers on 12-hour shifts. The children suffered deprivation, malnutrition and abuse and grew up with a range of deficits, including low IQs, inability to walk and major problems with relationships. In general, the longer they were in an orphanage, the more serious the problems that they showed. The problems persisted into adulthood in the form of unemployment, mental and physical health problems and difficulties with relationships.

The work of Jaak Panksepp on the development of the primary affective systems of the child, corresponding to major life priorities, indicates that in the absence of secure attachment, the Panic-Grief system is more likely to be activated (Panksepp 1998). The impact of neglect and emotional maltreatment on the developing child is less recognised than the impact of other types of abuse, despite neglect being the most challenging and prevalent form of abuse (Brassard et al. 2020; Hibbard et al. 2012). Although there is significant evidence base about the harms caused by neglect, there is persisting professional resistance to intervening in cases that are seen as 'acts of omission'.

The increasing role of online interaction and virtual reality in the lives of children is also contributing to changes in behaviour. On the admission of the software designers themselves, much of this is a deliberate attempt to capture the attention of children as well as adults. For example, the aptly named company Dopamine Labs in the United States was started by neuroscience and software developers who consult with companies to help them design products that engage attention and release dopamine. Tellingly, Steve Jobs forbade his own young children from playing with the iPad that he had designed.

A JAMA Pediatrics 2019 study of effects of screen watching on neurobiology found language delay, poor sleep, impaired executive function, general cognition and decreased parent–child engagement (Bethell et al. 2019). The study also reported autistic-like characteristics in children without autism: lack of smile response, delay of verbal skills, less ability to focus on the normal and deregulation. In contrast, research shows that play with others helps increase mental abilities (Neufeld and Mate 2013). For example, until recently in Finland, children remained in day care and learnt through play, songs, games and conversation. The country has been near the top of educational test scores internationally and is said to be one of the most literate nations in the world.

Domestic abuse

Also known as domestic violence or family abuse, domestic abuse refers to behaviour that is used to hurt, manipulate or gain control over a household member. This may include IPV, or abuse of children, parents, siblings, other relatives and roommates. Financial or economic abuse involves a person attempting to control another's ability to acquire, use and maintain economic resources. People from marginalised groups are at greater risk of experiencing abuse, but anyone can be a victim of such abuse. It is regarded as a global health problem, with those living in countries with poor human rights records being most likely to be victims. An increasingly prevalent and serious form of domestic abuse involves digital or online abuse. This includes excessive monitoring, online harassment and the distribution of explicit photos or videos without consent ('revenge porn').

Children of parents with substance use disorders may face a greater risk of experiencing abuse or neglect. Abuse, in turn, can increase their risk of turning to various substances as coping mechanisms when they grow older.

Online abuse

At the time that Felitti and colleagues compiled their list of ACEs, the notion of abuse through the internet or social media was a minor concern. It is likely that most people would not have imagined the extent and the horrific nature of some of this abuse. Online abuse is a rapidly increasing problem that clearly needs attention, but what should be done, by whom and how remains a very thorny issue. It is an issue that has begun to be addressed by educational bodies, such as Ofsted in the United Kingdom, by countries such as Australia in raising the age of access to social media, and in television programmes such as the shocking and thought-provoking British drama series of 2025, *Adolescence*, which gave a whole new meaning to the question: 'Do you know where your children are?' We may know where they are physically, but of the virtual realm in which they live, we may know very little indeed.

Internet technology facilitates ease of access and ease of use by both abuser and abused. Online abuse against children and young people can be by individuals or they can be by organised groups, and in many cases, the abuser/s cannot be identified. In a 2021 systematic review of the area, Ali and Pasha noted the statistical reports from the UK government showed more than 80,000 suspicious activities in cyberspace against children. Reports from the UK National Crime Agency estimated 2.88 million globally registered online accounts on dark websites. Online sexual abuse of children can involve conversations, sexual images, making sexual content, solicitation, sharing abusive material, blackmail (and sextortion) and other activities. The majority of online pornographic images are of children below 12 years old (Ali and Pasha 2021; Ali et al. 2024).

The effects of online abuse include depression, hostility, panic attacks, disgust, shame, self-harming and suicide, as in some of the cases that involve the Meta social-media company (Ali and Pasha 2021; Ali et al. 2024; Joleby et al. 2021). In 2025, law enforcement bodies in the United Kingdom and the United States called attention to the huge increase in cases of sextortion (online extortion for obtaining explicit images) in children.

Institutional abuse

Institutional or organisational abuse refers to mistreatment by a system which has power over that person. It refers to abuse, neglect and poor care practices within an institution, organisation or care setting. It can take the form of institutional elder abuse, financial exploitation or child abuse. The abuse can be in the form of a single incident or it can be an ongoing process. It can be in the form of inappropriate use of power or control, restraint or restriction; lack of choice or flexibility; financial abuse; physical or verbal abuse or discriminatory abuse based on race, ethnicity, gender, sexual orientation, age or religion. It can be overt abuse as in physical, sexual or emotional abuse, program abuse where a program operates at an unacceptable level or misuses power or system abuse where the entire system is stretched beyond capacity. It is a complex and very powerful form of abuse and it is often very difficult to deal with.

Throughout history, religious institutions, cults, educational facilities, correctional institutions, military establishments, sports associations, hospitals and care homes, large corporations and many more have committed abuse. We seem to be particularly familiar with it in our current times because of the prevalence of media outlets and because it is no longer taboo to speak out in or about many (but by no means all) settings.

Institutions or organisations can exacerbate the abuse by covering it up and silencing or punishing the person harmed. This is often apparent in cases of abuse within religious, educational and military organisations. Such abuse is particularly harmful and difficult to deal with because institutions and organisations are thought to have authority and integrity and to be professional. The result can be depression, despair and PTSD. The fear of shame and damage to career can lead people to sign non-disclosure agreements with the perpetrator.

To mention just a few cases involving abuse of children and young people:

Magdalene Laundries existed in many countries in the 19th and early 20th century. By the 1960s, they had all closed, except those in Ireland. These were run by the Catholic church and seen as places for 'fallen women', women who had become pregnant outside marriage and were seen as prostitutes, even though they may have been sexually assaulted and made pregnant by a family member. Irish Magdalene laundries often admitted girls who were orphaned or abandoned by their families or whose families were financially unable to take care of them. Laundries also admitted girls and women who were considered too flirtatious, who had been physically or sexually abused, who had a physical or developmental disability and who had committed petty crimes as well as serious offences such as infanticide. They were not paid for their work in the laundries. In some of them, the girls gave birth, nursed their child for 2 years and then their child was taken away from them. During births, girls weren't given any painkillers and air or they weren't stitched up after birth because the nuns wouldn't allow it. In 1993, the unmarked graves of 155 women were uncovered in the convent grounds of just one of the laundries. Joni Mitchell wrote a powerful song about the laundries, calling them heartless places, with nuns who wanted to send the girls down the drain or bury them.

Abuse by clergy has occurred in both Catholic and Protestant churches. In November 2024, the Archbishop of Canterbury, Justin Welby, resigned his post as the most senior person in the Church of England because of a cover-up of the abuse by John Smyth, about which he had failed to act. Smyth sadistically abused private schoolboys who attended evangelical Christian holiday camps in the late 1970s and early 1980s. Across 5 decades, he is said to have subjected as many as 130 boys and young men in the United Kingdom and Africa to traumatic physical, sexual, psychological and spiritual attacks, permanently marking their lives. Apparently, at least 11 bishops knew about Smyth's abuse but failed to stop him. In addition, there were literally scores of rank-and-file church leaders and members who stood by, thinking that it was someone else's job to act (Sinmaz et al. 2024).

Yehudis Fletcher grew up in an ultra-orthodox Jewish home in the United Kingdom. In her very moving memoir (Fletcher 2025), she describes being sexually abused by the man in whose house she was staying when she was a teenager. The consequences of this in the very orthodox culture in which she was living were that she was discouraged from complaining and when the case eventually went to court, men of the faith community tried to stop it from being heard in court. She now campaigns against the arranged, forced marriages at a young age.

Richard Burrows, a man who was a scout leader and school housemaster, was charged in April 2025 with 54 offences, including indecent assault of boys, serious sexual assault, attempted serious sexual assault and indecency with a child. At an earlier hearing, he had pleaded guilty to another 43 offences, including indecent assault, making indecent images of children and possessing indecent images of children. He had originally been charged in 1997 but was brought back from Thailand, to where he had escaped, and was jailed for 46 years at the age of 81.

Jimmy Saville was a disc jockey who worked for many years for the BBC and was extremely popular, with programmes such as 'Jim'll fix it'. He also worked as a volunteer in hospitals and in Broadmoor prison. He was a serial paedophile and abuser in hospitals and other places, with at least 450 complaints about his behaviour. Although questions were raised about him, he was never charged with sexual abuse and used his connections in society to shield himself against investigation.

Lawrence Gerard Nassar (born August 16th, 1963) is an American former family medicine osteopathic physician and convicted sex offender. From 1996 to 2014, he was the team doctor of the United States women's national gymnastics team, where he used his position to exploit and sexually assault hundreds of young athletes as part of the largest sexual abuse scandal in sports history. In 2016, Nassar was arrested and charged with sexually assaulting at least 265 young women and girls under the guise of medical treatment. His victims included numerous Olympic and United States women's national gymnastics team gymnasts (Wikipedia).

British Boarding Schools are a good example of the hypocrisy regarding abuse in educational institutions, which was widespread in the United Kingdom. Boarding schools are where the privileged classes send their children for a 'superior' education, but where abuse also sometimes occurs. In his memoir, Earl Spencer, brother of the late Princess Diana, describes sexual abuse at a private boarding school from the age of 7, when the headmaster was habitually physically punishing boys, which included sexual abuse (Spencer 2024).

Another example of abuse in Britain's 'privileged' schools was James Rhodes, a renowned concert pianist who, at the age of 5, was frequently sodomised by a gym teacher at his preparatory school. James once went back into school with blood running down his leg from his shorts as a result of the abuse. This was not taken to be a sign of a serious problem, and nothing was done, so it continued for years. The consequences have inevitably lasted all his life. As Rhodes says in his autobiography, 'It isn't abuse when a 40 year old man forces his cock in a six-year old's arse, it is aggressive rape'. (Rhodes 2015, p. 9). The impact on him was multiple surgeries, spinal damage, scars (inside and out), tics, OCD, depression, suicidal ideation, vigorous self-harm, alcoholism, drug addiction, sexual hang-ups, gender confusion, sexuality confusion, paranoia, mistrust, compulsive lying, eating disorders, PTSD and more.

Abuse also occurs in other residential spaces for children. One notable example of this was the Principal at Brookside school for Maladjusted Children, United Kingdom, Jack Mount, who was repeatedly found not guilty of multiple cases of physical and sexual abuse, with the children, some as young as 8, being labelled as liars and seducers 'obsessed with sex' by the defence.

Lee Anderson, a very right-wing Member of Parliament in the United Kingdom, who supports the smacking of children, said that 'He looks back fondly' on the corporal punishment he was subjected to as a youngster, arguing it gave him a grounding in life. Anderson was quoted in the UK newspaper The Telegraph in 2011, stating that the rod has been spared too long, and that we need physical force for discipline. 'Spare the rod and spoil the child' was a mantra left over from Victorian days.

There are, of course, numerous other examples that could be given, including in the fairly recent area of abuse, the realm of social media, as in the Meta case and demonstration in New York City in 2025.

Some of the most appalling examples of institutional abuse were to be found in residential schools for Indigenous children, such as those in Canada and the United States. One chapter in this book covers some of the issues raised by the school system and other institutional and governmental measures imposed on Indigenous children in Canada.

Mental health effects of ACEs

Adverse events during development have been found to be related to a number of health problems, especially mental ones, in later life and consequently their roles need to be understood for the purposes of determining appropriate responses. The physical symptoms that may be related to stress are often dismissed by the medical profession as functional, non-organic or psychosomatic – 'all in the mind'. Clearly, this is misguided and unhelpful since much is to be gained in terms of understanding and intervention once the role of past stressors is better documented and analysed.

For centuries, health problems that have been linked to stressful events, as with William Osler in 1892, writing of the link between rheumatoid arthritis and shock, worry and grief and Charcot in 1872 speculated about a relationship between multiple sclerosis and long-continued grief and vexation. While there has been much speculation over the centuries, it is only recently with new analytical techniques that there have been scientific studies of such possible links. The work of Hans Selye on stress was a key factor in promoting this research and new areas such as psychoneuroimmunology, which examines the interactions of body and mind. There is now increased acceptance that to understand the health of the whole organism, we need to understand the complex interactions of many different systems throughout the life course. There is also an emerging view that environment and stress can change both an organism and its offspring through epigenetic mechanisms.

Felitti and colleagues' original study of ACEs found 'a strong graded relationship between the breadth of exposure to abuse or household dysfunction during childhood and multiple risk factors for several of the leading causes of death in adults' (Felitti et al. 1998). These findings were supported by evidence from a number of studies, including the US LONGSCAN study, suggesting a causal relationship between child maltreatment and a range of mental disorders, drug use, suicide attempts, inflammatory disease, sexually transmitted infections and risky sexual behaviour (e.g. Danese et al. 2007; Madigan et al. 2023; Norman et al. 2012; Thompson et al. 2012). These results need to be interpreted carefully because children who have been abused may share other, unrecognised factors that are actually the cause of their later mental health problems. More recently, academics and practitioners using ACE instruments in screening programmes have noted that there are unacceptably high levels of both false positives and false negatives (Finklehor 2018). This concern has been emphasised by a comprehensive review by the Early Intervention Foundation into ACE research, which concludes that conceptual and measurement issues point to a need for a new conceptual framework (Asmussen et al. 2020).

In this review, we will focus on the mental health effects and some of the underlying biopsychosocial and neurobiological changes associated with childhood adversity. The lists of effects are in no way meant to be exhaustive, as the literature in this area is expanding rapidly and there are thousands of research papers, but simply to be indicative of the extent and variety of issues involved. For more exhaustive recent reviews, the reader is referred to reviews such as those by Asmussen et al. (2020) and Rokach and Clayton (2023).

ACEs, neurobiology and mental health

As noted above, research has found that adverse events in childhood can be related to later mental health problems. Childhood abuse, neglect and other ACEs can put individuals at risk of a long list of subsequent psychosocial disorders These include behavioural problems, ADHD diagnosis in middle childhood, bipolar disorder, childhood autobiographical memory disturbance, chronic mental health problems, eating disorders, personality disorders, PTSD, psychosis, self-harm, suicide attempts and uncontrollable anger (e.g. Asmundson and Afifi 2019; Asmussen et al. 2020; Madigan et al. 2023; Petruccelli et al. 2019). Felitti and colleagues thought that the link between ACEs and adult ill health could be explained by the behaviours that they learned in order to cope with high levels of stress. This was borne out by the fact that the number of unhealthy behaviours, such as smoking, increased with the number of ACEs experienced. This finding was supported by later prospective studies, but these behaviours still only explained half of the relationship observed between ACEs and later health status. As a result, a number of other factors have been examined as possible mediators, including the effects of stress on neurobiology, conditions which lead to a latent vulnerability of the individual and epigenetic transmission.

Since it is extremely difficult to disentangle the effects of one form of abuse from another, any comments on abuse need to be understood in that context. Although there have been some studies of neurophysiological correlates of childhood maltreatment, they typically have not distinguished between different types of abuse and neglect. For example, they have not specifically focused on emotional abuse or neglect, which can occur independently of physical or sexual abuse, nor examined neurophysiological changes related to specific disorders (e.g. depression versus psychosis). There is also a need for longitudinal studies examining the long-term impact of specific abuse and neglect, along with associated psychobiological changes, on prevalence of psychiatric disorders that usually emerge later in life. In the following discussion, reference to effects of abuse covers all forms of abuse unless otherwise stated.

Some of the most obvious effects of child abuse are the result of physical abuse, which causes damage directly to the brain. For decades, associations have been noted between the maltreatment of children and various forms of traumatic brain injury (TBI) as, for example, 'the battered child' (Kempe et al. 1984). These effects in and of themselves clearly lead to profound effects to physical and mental health throughout life (Biswas et al. 2023). Physical abuse may cause enduring effects on the physical structure and function of neural stress-regulatory circuits in the brain, including the hippocampus and the amygdala (Calem et al. 2017; Farrer et al. 2012).

Many people who suffered emotional abuse as children show feelings of hopelessness, poor self-esteem, reduced sense of social support, poor satisfaction with life, neurobiological changes in stress response systems and structural and functional brain deficits, with the most significant changes in regions associated with emotional regulation (Asmussen et al. 2020; Rokach and Clayton 2023). Those who have suffered emotional abuse also have a heightened risk of developing mental health problems such as depression, anxiety, eating disorders, suicidal symptomatology, psychosis, personality disorder and substance misuse (Asmussen et al. 2020; Mandelli et al. 2015; Taillieu et al. 2016; Teicher et al. 2014). Mandelli et al. (2015) found that emotional abuse showed the strongest association with depression (OR = 2.78), followed by neglect (OR = 2.75) and sexual abuse (OR = 2.42). Significant associations were also found for domestic violence (OR = 2.06) and physical abuse (OR = 1.98). Children who grow up in emotionally abusive environments often have trouble forming healthy relationships later in life, and there is potential for an intergenerational cycle of abuse. Those who experienced emotional abuse as children might themselves behave in the same way with their own children.

Studies have reported associations between CSA and many psychosocial and health-related outcomes. Children may show confusion, lack of self-confidence, conduct disorder, oppositional defiant disorder, overly sexualised behaviour and aggression. With age, they may develop other problems, such as depression, self-harming, chronic pain, sleep problems, drug addiction and relationship issues (Asmussen et al. 2020; Ford and Delker 2018; Goodman et al. 2020; Gupta and Garg 2020; Halpern et al. 2018; Iacono et al. 2021; MacIntosh and Ménard 2021; Sigurdardottir and Halldorsdottir 2018).

The quality of some of these studies and the data resulting from them has been called into question because of concerns over such issues as the definition of sexual abuse, study design and the possible over-reporting of symptoms in individuals with psychiatric disorders (Hailes et al. 2019). Most meta-analytical reviews have examined only mental health outcomes or a single outcome, such as depression, anxiety disorders or substance misuse. Hailes and colleagues aimed to address these limitations and examine the associations of CSA with a range of long-term psychosocial, psychiatric and physical health outcomes (Hailes et al. 2019). They summarised the evidence from 19 meta-analyses, including more than 4 million participants from more than 500 primary studies. CSA was associated with a wide range of psychosocial, psychiatric and physical health outcomes. Among the 26 outcomes that were significantly associated with CSA. Only two were based on systematic reviews with high-quality assessment scores: substance misuse and PTSD. This review found that CSA was associated with elevated risks of long-term psychosocial, psychiatric and physical health outcomes. There was strong evidence for associations between CSA and two psychiatric disorders (schizophrenia and PTSD) and one psychosocial outcome (substance misuse). Notable gaps include the need for further meta-analyses assessing outcomes for which the current review literature is poor or low quality, and reviews on outcomes (bipolar disorder, obsessive-compulsive disorder and homelessness) that currently lack systematic reviews.

The HPA axis can mediate vulnerability to stress-related psychiatric disorders through greater pituitary, adrenal and autonomic responses to stress (Calem et al. 2017; Cross et al. 2017). With the HPA axis, the immune system is likely to be a critical mediator of the greater risk for physical and mental illness associated with ACEs. Many studies have reported an increase in inflammatory activity in those who have suffered abuse, but these alterations may be secondary to other variables, such as higher BMI, drug use, mental health problems and so forth (Baumeister et al. 2016). Bertone-Johnson et al.

(2012) and Calem et al. (2017) conducted a meta-analysis of 1,781 participants examined by imaging of the hippocampus and amygdala. They found no difference in amygdala volume and the small differences in the hippocampus were only found in those with significant mental health difficulties.

In an extension of Selye's research on chronic stress, prolonged, severe abuse has been shown to cause activation of the HPA axis, with neurobiological responses becoming damaging rather than protective, causing an increase in cortisol and inflammatory markers (Danese et al. 2007; Danese and McEwan 2012; Danese 2025). Exposure to ACEs also appears to increase levels of various pro-inflammatory cytokines in the brain, with increased risk of psychological problems (Steel et al. 2021). Child sexual abuse has been associated with several changes in physiological functions including dysregulation of the HPA axis, effects on the endocrine and immune systems and possible changes to DNA through altered methylation and other mechanisms (Asmussen et al. 2020; Iacono et al. 2021; Sigurdardottir and Halldorsdottir 2018).

Disentangling the long-term effects of child abuse on immune system functions is very difficult. One systematic review aimed to describe the association between child sexual abuse and indicators of immune activity, but the diversity in studies that were collected, and the heterogeneity of abuse and trauma assessments prevented a meta-analysis from being performed (D'Elia et al. 2018). Several other factors are commonly associated with child sexual abuse as well as with alterations in immune activity and are potential confounds. In addition, the immune system functions are sensitive to a wide range of factors, including stress, hormones and disease.

There is a growing body of evidence that serious adverse events in childhood can have lasting effects on the brain and the nervous and endocrine systems. Much of this work has been done on rodents and neurobiological changes are small (e.g. Cooke et al. 2023; Johnson and Kaffman 2017). Hence, it is too early to extend implications to humans (Asmussen et al. 2020). There is an increasing amount of evidence in humans that ACEs can lead to chronic activation of the stress response and changes in the HPA axis, which can affect behaviour and cognition and increase risk of various mental health problems (Asmussen et al. 2020; Griffiths and Hunter 2014; Johnson et al. 2013; Oral et al. 2016). McCrory and colleagues have conducted a number of studies on the effects of several kinds of maltreatment on the amygdala, striatum and the anterior cingulate cortex (2017, 2025). They have concluded that their work and that of others indicates altered neurocognitive functioning following maltreatment that leads to a latent vulnerability in the individual.

A number of researchers have reported that there are structural physical changes in the brains of children exposed to maltreatment, including a smaller volume of the prefrontal cortex and hippocampus than in non-abused children (Danese and McEwan 2012). Since in many studies there are no pre- and post-measures in the same subject, it is not possible to assess the validity of such claims (Tiwari and Gonzalez 2018). More recently, however, McCrory, Gonzalez and colleagues have conducted prospective studies involving brain scans and not just comparisons between different subjects. In these studies, reduced volume of the amygdala has been posited to mediate the association between developmental trauma and mental health problems in adulthood (Gonzalez et al. 2019). This line of research is clearly well worth following.

ACEs and genetic mechanisms

It has been proposed that ACEs accelerate cell division and ageing. Research in this area has focused on determining quantitative indicators of these mechanisms in peripheral blood mononuclear cells. The most common indicators include the length of telomeres, the level of mitochondrial DNA, which, when altered, indicates greater oxidative stress and inflammation, and the frequency of micronuclei, indicating chromosomal instability and altered cell division. Findings with respect to child sexual abuse are often inconsistent (Asmussen et al. 2020; Etzel et al. 2020; Flaherty et al. 2013; Iacono et al. 2021; Mason et al. 2015; Shalev et al. 2013; Sigurdardottir and Halldorsdottir 2018; Zarse et al. 2019). Telomere length depends on several factors, including age, parental age at birth and life experiences, and so any effects of ACEs could be easily masked. This area is obviously in its infancy and any suggested mechanisms or relationships are purely speculative in nature.

Childhood neglect and mental health

John Bowlby, one of the major developers of attachment theory along with Mary Ainsworth, wrote the book 'A Secure Base' (Bowlby 1988), a summation of much of his work on attachment. He says in his introduction, 'because successful parenting is a principal key to the mental health of the next generation, we need to know all we can, both about its nature and about the manifold social and psychological conditions that influence its development'. He adds that 'healthy, happy and self-reliant adolescents and young adults are the products of stable homes in which both parents give a great deal of time and attention to the children', and Bowlby goes on to insist it is the role of both parents to provide this.

When a child is born, the behaviour becomes affected by certain conditions. A child's 'attachment behaviour' will be activated by, for example, pain, fatigue and fear, and by the caregiver being or appearing to be available and accessible. This behaviour may be controlled by the intensity of the arousal; at a low level, the mere presence of the caregiver, especially when she or he has signalled their presence, will resolve this anxiety; at higher levels, it will require touch and, in extreme cases, a cuddle. This attachment behaviour also applies to adolescents and even adults when they are anxious or under stress. Bowlby reports, quoting a finding of Ainsworth, that children who develop a secure attachment to their mother are those who in early infancy are held longest in a tender and loving way.

There is clear evidence of the enormous part childhood experience plays in determining, in later years, how a parent treats a child, gathered from studies of parents known to have abused their children physically. A typical pattern emerges of such a childhood, where parental care was erratic or absent, in which criticism and blame were frequent and bitter and where parents behaved violently towards each other. These contribute to the child being abused physically.

Attachment behaviour is any form of behaviour that results in a person attaining or maintaining proximity to some other person who is perceived as being better able to cope with the world (Bowlby 1988). While this is most obvious in early childhood, it may be observed throughout one's life, especially in emergencies. Knowing that an attachment figure is available and responsive gives one a strong sense of security and encouragement to continue the relationship. Bowlby, writing at least 10 years before the conceptualisation of ACEs as specifiable events that can be linked to mental health issues in later life, wrote about associations observed in his own work. For example, a mother who experienced adverse events during her own childhood may be 'anxiously attached' and seek care from her own child, thereby leading the child to become anxious, guilty and maybe phobic. Or that a mother who has experienced neglect and frequent severe threats of abandonment or being beaten is more likely to abuse her child physically, resulting in adverse effects on the child's developing personality and mental health.

Separation anxiety (anxiety about losing or becoming separated from a loved person) is one of the common features of attachment to a loved one. It is a basic human feature, and it explains why threats to abandon a child as a method of control are so frightening. Sometimes, when a child has such a close relationship with his/her caregiver that he/she has difficulty in developing a social life outside the family, the origins may be traced to the caregiver having great anxiety about attachment, having themselves grown up with a difficult childhood and seeking to make their own child their attachment figure. The child, rather than being 'overindulged', is carrying the burden of having to care for his/her own caregiver.

As well as the forms of abuse that are commonly described, Bowlby (1988) also describes a number of scenarios where attachment may be dysfunctional because of the family history, such as:

A child being unwanted by one or both parents, perhaps because of an unwanted pregnancy.

A child being born of the opposite sex to that which was wanted by the parents.

A child being made the scapegoat for an event which may have led to tragedy in the family, which may have been rightly or wrongly attributed to him or her.

Parents using guilt-inducing techniques to control a child, e.g. by suggesting the child's behaviour makes the mother ill.

A parent may have tried to make the child their attachment figure by discouraging him or her from exploring the world away from the parent and then believing that the child will be able to make him or her way on their own.

A child who is the product of a mother having an extramarital affair during the marriage, so the child is not a biological child of the putative father.

In a longitudinal 'natural experiment' after the fall of the Ceauşescu regime in Romania, Rutter and colleagues compared the health and developmental outcomes of 144 orphaned, profoundly institutionally deprived and neglected children with 52 non-institutionally deprived and non-neglected UK children (Rutter, 2007). The serious developmental and emotional problems noted by the research team were tracked at ages 4, 6 and 11 years. For those children subsequently adopted in the United Kingdom, the developmental catch-up of the children from Romania following entry into UK homes was called 'spectacular'.

A review of the evidence on institutionalisation of children examined development before and after institutionalisation and compared these data with the findings from a 2014 randomised controlled trial on the Romanian orphans (van IJzendoorn et al. 2020a,b; Nelson et al. 2014). Findings of the review include:

- attachment difficulties: in the sample of 471 children in 11 studies, a significantly lower proportion of securely attached children (24%) was found in the institution-based children compared with the normative proportion (62%); in addition, there was a much higher rate (57%) of the two most dysregulated types of attachment (insecure-disorganised and unclassifiable) compared with the normative proportion (15%);
- delayed physical growth, brain development, cognitive development and attention: within the institutionalised group of children, at least 80% were below the mean for the comparisons;
- a dose–response association: larger developmental delays and atypical development were predicted by longer stays in the institution.

Reviewing the effects of institutionalisation on child development, researchers proposed a new category of child maltreatment within institutions called 'structural neglect' (Juffer et al. 2023). The importance of secure attachment is emphasised by a study showing how the resilience of the most abused and vulnerable individuals can improve when they are linked to an 'always available adult' with whom a secure attachment is established (Bellis et al. 2017).

ACEs and criminality

People with a history of multiple ACEs are more likely to show antisocial behaviour and be involved with the criminal justice system; studies of male and female prisoners suggest that ACEs may be a risk factor for criminal offences and, in some cases, violence (Messina and Grella 2006; Messina et al. 2007; Rieffe et al. 2007; Vizard et al. 2021; Walsh et al. 2019). Walsh and colleagues found that young people with 4 or more ACEs were 7 times more likely to have been involved in violence in the previous year and 10 times more likely to have felt suicidal or to have self-harmed. Those with 6 ACEs were 46 times more likely to become injection drug users and 35 times more at risk of suicide (Walsh et al. 2019). A study of prisoners in Wales found that at least 80% had 1 ACE, with 46% reporting 4 or more, and these were 4 times more likely to have been in a young offender institution than those with no ACEs and 3.5 times more likely to be prolific offenders (Ford et al. 2020). Hughes found that adults with 4 or more ACEs are 8 times more likely to become perpetrators of violence compared to those who had suffered none and also 8 times more likely to become victims, and over 30 times more likely to attempt suicide (Hughes et al. 2017). Not surprisingly, perhaps, the strongest historical risk factor for committing interpersonal violence is witnessing or being a victim of violence in childhood (Fazel et al. 2018).

The chapter on violence and childhood adversity in this book examines these issues in more detail.

Misuse of psychoactive substances: a cause and a result of ACEs

> *Edgar Alan Poe: 'I have absolutely no pleasure in the stimulants in which I sometimes so madly indulge. It has not been in the pursuit of pleasure that I have perilled life and reputation and reason. It has been the desperate attempt to escape from torturing memories'.*

The use of drugs and alcohol has been prevalent in many cultures throughout history. The ancient Greeks knew about the power of the opium poppy in relieving pain and of psychoactive substances in dealing with fear and trauma, as evidenced by such ceremonies as the Eleusinian Mysteries. Such rituals had been passed down from earlier cultures, including Egyptian, indicating the long history of psychoactive use. In many cultures throughout the world, the use of psychoactive substances, especially hallucinogens, has been part of life through religious ceremonies, often translated into art. These substances would most likely have come from alcohol and locally growing fungi and plants like ergot, opium, lotus blossom, incense, mushrooms, betel and ayahuasca.

Alcohol has been widely used in the United Kingdom for centuries as part of dealing with the quality, or lack thereof, of life. Mild beer was used instead of water (known as small beer) because of the contamination of water supplies, including those in schools. At the beginning of the Industrial Revolution in the United Kingdom, when people moved to slums in the cities to take up work, a problem developed with gin drinking in the face of appalling living conditions. Gin was the 'Mother's little helper' of the day and became known as 'Mother's ruin'; there ran a saying 'drunk for a penny, dead drunk for twopence'. The problem was seen as so severe that the Gin Laws were introduced in 1751 to try to control sales. Similarly, in the 19th century in the United Kingdom, opium was on sale without controls from market stalls and similar places. It was often used to calm children and as an effective cure for diarrhoea, but the problem was so serious for children that the age group with the greatest number of deaths from opium was 0–5 years. In 1868, the Pharmacy Act was introduced to control the sale of these products.

We now know that the misuse of alcohol and other drugs can trigger violence, abuse of children and/or the other parent or caregiver, mental health problems, financial difficulties, inappropriate disinhibited behaviour and neglect. In almost all countries in the world, there are now strict laws controlling the availability of alcohol and other drugs, but these have not stopped the widespread and inappropriate use of these substances. Iran, a country where alcohol is banned, has the highest levels of heroin use in the world. The United States, a country with very strict drug controls, has seen an epidemic of opioid deaths in the early part of the 21st century caused by so-called 'safe' prescription opioid drugs, such as OxyContin.

Clearly, most people who try alcohol or other drugs don't become addicted. These substances provide short-term relief of pain or the experience of pleasure, followed by the absence of these rewards. As a result of this absence, physical and/or psychological withdrawal and craving can occur, which, in turn, may lead to an inability to stop the use of the substance.

The sense of warmth and well-being associated with a number of substances, especially opioids, is both direct and indirect. Direct in the sense that they relieve pain and provide pleasure and can even induce a sense of warmth, indirect in that they mimic the release of the body's own endorphins and oxytocin, which may be unavailable through other means. We will discuss this latter point and its implications in the Interventions section of this book.

Alcohol and other drugs, especially opioids, can provide relief for people living with distressing mental or physical problems or in difficult circumstances. For the politician Winston Churchill, alcohol was a way to try to banish the Black Dog. For the musician, Keith Richards, opiates were a search for oblivion. For the singer Marianne Faithfull, they were a way to turn nightmares into dreams. For the philosopher Sartre, they were a prompt to thought, stimulant or depressant, according to the topic. For those living on the streets or in very poor housing, drugs can remove some of the sense of reality of the situation. On a visit to Merseyside in the 1980s (Merseyside had high levels of opioid use then), editor RP, on asking a man who was unemployed, in poor housing, and using heroin, 'what is the problem with heroin?' the man replied, 'It is not a problem, it is a solution!' Clearly, heroin can be very problematic because of its addictive nature and illegality, causing problems in to do with finance, health (especially when injecting), criminal behaviour and distancing from loved ones, but it helps some people keep on living.

Is it little wonder that those in psychological or physical pain, cold, on the street and otherwise in distress turn to the use of opioids? Who can deny them such relief? In this sense, heroin and similar substances are indeed not a problem but a solution. We need to ask what is right about an addiction for that person in those circumstances, and consider what we would do if we were where they are.

Many addictions are a form of coping mechanism. This can be seen, for example, in Vancouver's Downtown East Side, North America's most concentrated area of drug use, where the editor DR worked for a number of years in the 1990s. Gabor Maté wrote about this area in his book 'In the Realm of Hungry Ghosts'. 'Addictions represent, in their onset, the defences of an organism against suffering it does not know how to endure. In other words, we are looking at a natural response to unnatural circumstances, an attempt to soothe the pain of injuries incurred in childhood and stresses sustained in childhood' (Maté 2007, p. 216). Vancouver resident Bud Osborne, poet and early exponent of harm reduction, said that heroin gave him a warmth in his gut where he had always been cold. Bud's father had killed himself in gaol at three and at the age of five, he saw his mother raped and beaten. Bud became dependent on various drugs, especially heroin, and became very active in the harm reduction movement in Vancouver, where DR worked with him and others in setting up the first safe injection site, Insite, amongst other things. Bud died in 2014 and is greatly missed.

This poem was written by Bud about Insite:

the fight for Insite
began in a political/rhetorical atmosphere
of depraved indifference
regarding overdose deaths and pandemic emergency
..a flame burst inside me
fuelled by grief and rage...
no more! no more! no more!
of this heart-breaking family-shattering community-diminishing
pain of overdose deaths
..... because everyone suffers
when compassion is undone.

Over several decades, DR has talked to and worked with girls and women around the world who have suffered all forms of abuse, and watched their loved ones abused in war, occupation and migration. For them, alcohol and drugs provide, at least for a while, some relief from the torture in their bodies and minds that they can never escape. Similarly, self-harm is self-soothing, a short-term relief provided by the bodies' own opioids. A manageable crisis, unlike the one in your head; it is not about wanting to die but about trying to put up with living. Who can deny them the right to try to end the agony in their minds and bodies in whatever ways they can? In all of this, pain is the central theme and so as therapists and researchers, we need to ask, why the pain? We need to really listen to, and understand, the lived experience.

Psychoactive substances can help stop the incessant voices in the head and make a person feel normal. They can provide a sense of warmth and belonging that cannot be found anywhere else, and certainly not on the streets in minus 10 °C. Repeated use of some substances can lead to long-lasting changes in the brain that undermine voluntary control, and hence the addiction cycle begins. Does anyone choose to be addicted?

Dependence on any substance can be problematic, but when it is an illegal substance, problems are much worse because of the restrictions on obtaining the substance of choice and the consequences for pursuing it. As can be seen from the examples above, addiction to substances can be an answer to some problems, but as dependence continues, it can limit life choices for the individual and those around them. We can see this in relation to children brought up in an environment where one or both parents (or carers) are dependent on drugs or alcohol. This can lead to aggression and disinhibition, which can lead to abuse of children or the witnessing of abuse between parents. It can lead to the absence of parents, maybe when they are most needed, as around bedtime, and a lessening of the parents' ability to behave responsibly. It can lead to temporary loss of memory, missed appointments or not being available when needed.

Prolonged and heavy substance use can lead to major physical and mental health problems in parents or carers, severe financial problems and real problems of neglect. Injecting drug use can lead to major health problems like HIV or hepatitis and heavy use of stimulant drugs may lead to major mental health problems such as psychosis. All these issues, when present, will affect families and the children in those families. It will affect their safety and their attachments to significant adults, frequently leading to neglect. Substance use can be a major issue in relation to ACEs. For example, Lambert and Gill-Emerson (2017) reported the following ACEs among Cork Simon service users: 75.5% verbal, 67% physical, 35% sexual, 26.5% physical neglect, 71.4% substance misuse in family, 30.6% family member in prison, 59% mental illness in family, 67% emotional neglect, 43% mother a victim of domestic violence and 49% loss of a parent.

Children of parents with substance use disorders may face a greater risk of experiencing abuse or neglect. Abuse, in turn, can increase the child's risk of turning to various substances as coping mechanisms when they grow older.

Transfer of problems through the generations: ripples on a pond

All too often, emotional and behavioural problems are passed from caregiver to child. An individual's own problems can affect the way in which they act as a parent (see, for example, Wolwynn 2017). As in other forms of maltreatment, children who are abused may become abusive parents with the intergenerational transmission of abuse.

The multigenerational effects of adversity are nowhere more evident than in Indigenous and First Nations' peoples, such as those of Australia and North America. Peoples were removed from their land, spiritual linkages and culture, killed by disease and slaughter, incarcerated in prisons and institutions and suffered all forms of abuse. This resulted in what has been called intergenerational, multigenerational or transgenerational trauma, also known as historic trauma (Danieli and Figley 1985; Danieli et al. 2016; Herman 1997; Wesley-Esquimaux and Smolewski 2004; Yellow Horse Brave Heart 1998, 1999).

Judith Herman developed a theory of individual responses to psychogenic trauma she termed *complex post-traumatic stress disorder* (1997). Maria Yellow Horse Brave Heart used the term historic trauma to refer to cumulative emotional and psychological wounds over the lifespan and across generations related to massive group trauma (1998, 1999). She explained that this definition is different from what we typically think of as PTSD because the concept of PTSD doesn't capture chronic trauma in one's lifetime or trauma across generations or massive group trauma.

One of the first detailed examinations of historic trauma and Indigenous peoples was prepared by Wesley-Esquimaux and Smolewski for Mike Degagne and the Aboriginal Healing Foundation (AHF) in Canada, one of the authors in this book. Following Herman and Brave Heart, they propose a theory that examines the role of PTSD in what is termed *historic trauma transmission*. In historic trauma, while not every individual shows overt PTSD symptoms in their lifetime, there are latent symptoms as seen in the high incidence of violence, family breakdown and community dysfunction. According to these authors, historic trauma became a part of Aboriginal people's common experience, shaping individual lives and devastating entire communities and regions (Wesley-Esquimaux and Smolewski 2004). This is seen in a legacy of addiction, mental and physical illness, suicide and the ongoing transmission of many serious psychological, physical and spiritual problems. One chapter in this book examines some of these issues in further detail and the work of the AHF is referred to extensively in this.

The term 'genocide' is used throughout the AHF report in referring to the Indigenous people's experiences in Canada and the United States. This is a controversial issue, but it is quite clear that around the world, Indigenous peoples have suffered not only ethnocide, or the elimination of their culture but also what can only be referred to as genocides, even though these may have been said to be 'unknown'. It is worth noting the use of code to record murders of Indigenous people in countries such as Australia. In some cases, these genocides led to extinction, as in the case of the Aboriginal population of Tasmania.

Over the past few decades, research has identified how certain characteristics of an individual can be passed to offspring through what is called 'epigenetic' (or 'above-genetic') modifications. Every cell in a person's body has the same genes, but these genes are not active in all cells; genes are deactivated as specialisation of cells takes place. In some situations, such as during an extreme shortage of nutrition, the genes can receive chemical signals to become activated again. While the genes themselves do not change, the mechanisms within the cell do change. Telomeres (DNA markers at the end of chromosomes) are thought to be markers of events or circumstances in our lives (Aristizabal et al. 2020). Through the working of epigenetics, genes are activated, accented or suppressed and experience determines how genetic potential expresses itself. Epigenetic processes act on chromosomes, delivering messages from the environment that tell the genes what to do without altering the genes themselves. For example, a severe ice storm in Quebec, Canada, in 1998 caused prolonged hardships and severe stress for some pregnant women. Studies of these women by King and her colleagues on Project

Ice Storm have found that the stress on mothers is marked in the children's physiology, in BMI, obesity, insulin, immune system, asthma, increased inflammatory genes and immune genes related to autoimmunity (Aristizabal et al. 2020; King et al. 2012).

Growing evidence shows that some effects of adversity can be transmitted to offspring (Asmussen et al. 2020). Children of individuals who went through ACEs are at higher risks of developmental and mental health and physical health problems, including lower birthweight and asthma (Lê-Scherban et al. 2018) and are more likely to experience ACEs themselves (Schickedanz et al. 2021). Several studies have analysed the transgenerational transmission of telomere length. Estevez and colleagues (2020) found that a higher level of maternal ACEs predicted shorter telomere length in the next generation that was not attributable to demographic factors, prenatal maternal stress score, or postnatal maternal depression. Many factors at different levels contribute to the intergenerational transmission of ACEs. These include ACEs leading to parental poor physical and mental health, social problems and poverty (Russotti 2021a,b). They also include stress-induced changes to the inflammatory system and cellular changes which are passed on to the foetus (Berens and Jensen 2017).

Research in this area has progressed in recent years due to advances in studying central nervous system pathophysiology in peripheral markers such as blood, saliva, urine and tissues. Compared with central markers, peripheral markers are easily and cheaply acquired and can be stored. At the cellular level, high levels of oxidative stress and altered DNA telomerase activity indicate dysregulation, which may be passed on through epigenetic mechanisms. Clearly, this research is only in its very early stages and it is far too early to go beyond the most basic level of speculation. The nature versus nurture debate has a new area to enter.

Other ACEs and risk factors

As noted by Asmussen and colleagues in their overview of research into ACEs, economic disadvantage, discrimination, peer victimisation, low birth weight and child disability have power equal to or greater than many of the traditional ACEs in predicting poor physical and mental health in adulthood (Asmussen et al. 2020). Socioeconomic status is clearly related to the likelihood that a child will experience some form of adversity. Studies reviewed by Asmussen and colleagues showed that family income may be more strongly related to some physical health outcomes than many of the 10 ACEs specified in the original questionnaires (Asmussen et al. 2020). Socioeconomic status also overlaps with other risk factors for ACEs in many ways. What is surprising about the literature on ACEs, however, is the relative lack of discussion of socioeconomic and political factors in the risk for adversity. This seems to be a major shortcoming in the area and one that needs to be addressed if it is provides a meaningful contribution to our understanding of the determinants of health.

Marginalised populations are more at risk for exposure to ACEs than others and also more likely to have problems related to them later in life (Bellis et al. 2016, 2017, 2023; Halfon et al. 2017; Marryat and Frank 2019). There are racial differences in exposure to ACEs, with the highest levels in Black and Hispanic populations in the United Kingdom and the United States and in those communities exposed to racism and violence (Hall et al. 2021; Slopen et al. 2016). Sexual minorities report more ACEs than do others of the same age (Brown et al. 2015). Asmussen and colleagues reported that childhood experiences of social discrimination have been found to increase the risk of adult mental health problems by over 200%. Their review also found that peer victimisation or bullying during the teenage years increases the risk of an adult mental health problem by more than 50% (Asmussen et al. 2020).

Children with disabilities are at greater risk of experiencing abuse and maltreatment compared with non-disabled children (Jones et al. 2012). Childhood disability has been found to increase the risk of problematic drinking in adults by over 80% (Asmussen et al. 2020). Asmussen and colleagues also found that low birth weight has been found to increase the risk of having a stroke before the age of 50 by 200%.

As noted above, it is also known that ACEs can become intergenerational; that is, if a parent suffered ACEs, it is more likely that they will be passed on to the child through learning or possibly through epigenetic mechanisms.

The timing of adversity makes a big difference in determining the risk of consequences. Most ACE surveys, however, if you do not allow for a timing distinction to be made and ask only if any of the 10 ACEs on the standard questionnaire were present in the first 18 years of the individual's life.

Protective factors

Resilience and plasticity

Resilience is the ability to adapt to circumstances, the ability to recover from damage. *Plasticity* is the ability to be moulded or changed; in the case of the brain and nervous system, the term refers to the continuous alteration of the neural pathways and synapses in response to experience or injury.

Whether it be through resilience or plasticity, there are protective factors which can help modify the effects of ACEs (Fritz et al. 2018; Goldenson et al. 2021; Haczkewicz et al. 2024; Perry and Szalavitz 2017; Perry and Winfrey 2021; Zimmerman 2013). This can occur at the individual, family or community level (Farrington et al. 2009; Masten 2019). Longitudinal studies suggest that early damage to a child's developing brain is not necessarily irreversible. There is plasticity in the brain and nervous system, and if the child has had support from a relationship with an 'always available adult', recovery from early ACEs may be possible, at least in part (Bellis et al. 2017).

Perry notes that in the same way as in the plasticity of the brain, people appear to be able to recover, or seem to recover, emotionally and behaviourally from serious stressful events. Being with people who are attentive, supportive and nurturing can help ensure this malleability. Perry and colleagues examined developmental data from over 70 thousand individuals in twenty-five countries – children, youth and adults – with detailed histories of trauma and adversity and histories of relational health. They defined connectedness as the nature, quality and quantity of connection to family, community and culture. History of relational health was found to be more predictive of mental health than history of adversity. This is similar to findings of other researchers looking at the power of positive relationships on health. 'The most powerful predictor of your functioning in the present is your current relational connectedness and then the second most powerful component that we see is your history of connectedness' (Perry and Winfrey 2021, p. 249).

The presence of at least one readily available and supportive adult has been found to be one of the most important factors, especially where there have been several ACEs (Bellis et al. 2016, 2017, 2023; Danielson and Saxena 2019; Hall et al. 2021). Safe schools and communities have also been shown to be important for resilience, although data on community factors are mixed (Masten 2019; Moore et al. 2016). Perhaps not surprisingly, there is an area focusing on the role of positive childhood experiences (PCEs) in reducing the effects of ACEs (e.g. Han et al. 2023).

Some overall considerations on ACEs

Clearly, there is a considerable amount of data and literature on ACEs and their effects and this is growing rapidly. The issues that concern us in this book are the mental health consequences of childhood adversity, how best to deal with these consequences, and, perhaps most importantly of all, how to ensure that evidence-based good practice is conveyed to, and adopted by, the frontline workers in the field. This is happening on a very limited scale at the moment and we need to understand why this is so limited and how to remedy the situation.

In summary, ACEs are widespread, have lasting effects, especially on mental health and substance use, and there are interventions which can be effective in dealing with the resultant problems. The most effective and promising interventions are summarised in the following section of this book.

The research on childhood adversity also shows that ACEs, as originally specified by Felitti and colleagues, are far from alone in determining mental and physical ill-health in adulthood. Other factors such as financial status and discrimination are key determinants of later health and well-being (Asmussen et al. 2020; Bellis et al. 2016, 2017; Waite and Ryan 2017). In addition, prospective studies are needed with large, representative samples to better understand the prevalence and nature of childhood adversity.

While the precise role of ACEs may be in need of considerable clarification, there is clear evidence for the role of a number of other social factors in the determination of adult health and well-being. These include learning abusive and aggressive behaviours in the family and peer environment, exposure to multiple forms of abuse outside of the home, and a lack of positive social interactions with trusted individuals that increase self-worth (Asmussen et al. 2020; Bellis et al. 2017, 2023; Perry 2009; Perry and Winfrey 2021).

In the following chapters, there are a number of very diverse accounts of the childhood adversity faced by individuals in their unique contexts and sociodemographic settings. These accounts show the enormous range of childhood adversity as well as its effects. They are also accounts of what happened to people to either increase or lessen these effects, and it is from these that we can gain so much insight into what can be done to help others.

References

Ali, S. and Pasha, A.S. (2021). A systematic review of the technology enabled child sexual abuse (OCSA) & it's impacts. *Journal of Legal, Ethical and Regulatory Issues* 25 (S5): 1–18.

Ali, S., Pasha, S., Cox, A., Youssef E. (2024). Examining the short and long-term impacts of child sexual abuse: a review study. SN Social Sciences 4. https://doi.org/10.1007/s43545-024-00852-6

Aristizabal, M.J., Anreiter, I., Halldorsdottir, T. et al. (2020). Biological embedding of experience: a primer on epigenetics. *Proceedings of the National Academy of Sciences of the United States of America* 117 (38): 23261–23269.

Asmundson, G.J. and Afifi, T.O. (2019). *Adverse Childhood Experiences: Using Evidence to Advance Research, Practice, Policy, and Prevention*. New York: Academic Press.

Asmussen, K., Fischer, F., Drayton, E. et al. (2020). Adverse childhood experiences: what we know, what we don't know, and what should happen next. Early Intervention Foundation. www.eif.org.uk (accessed 31 March 2025).

Baumeister, D., Akhtar, R., Ciufolini, S. et al. (2016). Childhood trauma and adulthood inflammation: a meta-analysis of peripheral C-reactive protein, interleukin-6 and tumour necrosis factor-α. *Molecular Psychiatry* 21 (5): 642–649.

Bellis, M., Ashton, K., Hughes, K.E. et al. (2016). Adverse Childhood Experiences and Their Impact on Health-Harming Behaviours in the Welsh Adult Population. Technical Report. ISBN 978-1-910768-23-5.

Bellis, M.A., Hardcastle, K., Ford, K. et al. (2017). Does continuous trusted adult support in childhood impart life-course resilience against adverse childhood experiences – a retrospective study on adult health-harming behaviours and mental well-being. *BMC Psychiatry* 17 (1): 110.

Bellis, M.A., Wood, S., Hughes, K. et al. (2023). Tackling adverse childhood experiences – state of the art and options for action. Public Health Wales NHS Trust.https://www.ljmu.ac.uk/-/media/phi-reports/pdf/2023-01-state-of-the-art-report-eng.pdf (accessed 3 April 2025).

Berens, A.E., Jensen, S.K.G., and Nelson, C.A. III (2017). Biological embedding of childhood adversity: from physiological mechanisms to clinical implications. *BMC Medicine* 15 (135): https://doi.org/10.1186/s12916-017-0895-4.

Bertone-Johnson, E.R., Whitcomb, B.W., Missmer, S.A. et al. (2012). Early life emotional, physical, and sexual abuse and the development of premenstrual syndrome: a longitudinal study. *J Womens Health (Larchmt)*. 23 (9): 729–739. https://doi.org/10.1089/jwh.2013.4674.

Bethell, C., Jones, J., Gombojav, N. et al. (2019). Positive childhood experiences and adult mental and relational health in a statewide sample: associations across adverse childhood experiences levels. *JAMA Pediatrics* 173 (11): e193007. https://doi.org/10.1001/jamapediatrics.2019.3007.

Biswas, A. and Shroff, M.M. (2021). Abusive head trauma: Canadian and global perspectives. *Pediatric Radiology* 51 (6): 876–882.

Biswas, A., Krishnan, P., Albalkhi, I., Mankad, K., Shroff, M. (2023) Imaging of abusive head trauma in children. Neuroimaging Clinics of North America 33(2):357–373. doi: https://doi.org/10.1016/j.nic.2023.01.010.

Blakemore, S.J. (2019). Adolescence and mental health. *The Lancet* 393 (10185): 2030–2031.

Bowlby, J. (1988). *A Secure Base: Parent-Child Attachment and Healthy Human Development*. New York: Basic Books.

Brassard, M.R., Hart, S.N., and Glaser, D. (2020). Psychological maltreatment: an international challenge to children's safety and well being. *Child Abuse & Neglect* 110 (1): 104611.

Brown, M.J., Masho, S.W., Perera, R.A. et al. (2015). Sex and sexual orientation disparities in adverse childhood experiences and early age at sexual debut in the United States: results from a nationally representative sample. *Child Abuse & Neglect* 46: 89–102.

Calem, M., Bromis, K., McGuire, P. et al. (2017). Meta-analysis of associations between childhood adversity and hippocampus and amygdala volume in non-clinical and general population samples. *NeuroImage Clinical* 14: 471–479.

Cooke, E.M., Connolly, E.J., Boisvert, D.L., and Hayes, B.E. (2023). A Systematic Review of the Biological Correlates and Consequences of Childhood Maltreatment and Adverse Childhood Experiences. *Trauma, Violence & Abuse* 24 (1): 156–173.

Cross, D., Fani, N., Powers, A., and Bradley, B. (2017). Neurobiological development in the context of childhood trauma. *Clinical Psychologist* 24 (2): 111–124.

Danese, A. (2025) Words Matter: Impact and Prevention of Childhood Verbal Abuse – House of Commons 28 April 2025. Expert-led discussion sponsored by Sharon Hodgson MP.

Danese, A. and McEwen, B.S. (2012). Adverse childhood experiences, allostasis, allostatic load, and age-related disease. *Physiology & Behavior* 106 (1): 29–39.

Danese, A., Pariante, C.M., Caspi, A. et al. (2007). Childhood maltreatment predicts adult inflammation in a life-course study. *Proceedings of the National Academy of Sciences of the United States of America* 104 (4): 1319–1324.

Danieli, Y. and Figley, C.R. (1985). The treatment and prevention of long-term effects and Intergenerational transmission of victimization: a lesson from Holocaust Survivors and their children. In: *Trauma and Its Wake: The Study and Treatment of Post-Traumatic Stress Disorder*, vol. 1 (ed. C.R. Figley), 295–313. New York: Brunner/Mazel.

Danieli, Y., Norris, F.H., and Engdahl, B. (2016). Multigenerational legacies of trauma: modeling the what and how of transmission. *American Journal of Orthopsychiatry* 86 (6): 639–651.

Danielson, R. and Saxena, D. (2019). Connecting adverse childhood experiences and community health to promote health equity. *Social and Personality Psychology Compass 13* (7): e12486.

D'Elia, A.T.D., Matsuzaka, C.T., Neto, J.B.B. et al. (2018). Childhood sexual abuse and indicators of immune activity: a systematic review. *Frontiers in Psychiatry* 9: 354.

Estévez, A., Jauregui, P., Macía, L., and López-González, H. (2020). Gambling and attachment: the mediating role of alexithymia in adolescents and young adults. *Journal of Gambling Studies* https://doi.org/10.1007/s10899-020-09965.

Etzel, L., Hastings, W., Matterna, B. et al. (2020). Intergenerational transmission of childhood trauma? Testing cellular aging in mothers exposed to sexual abuse and their children. *Psychoneuroendocrinology* 120: 104781.

Farrer, T.J., Frost, R.B., and Hedges, D.W. (2012). Prevalence of traumatic brain injury in intimate partner violence offenders compared to the general population: a meta-analysis. *Trauma, violence, & Abuse* 13 (2): 77–82.

Farrington, D.P., Coid, J.W., and Murray, J. (2009). Family factors in the intergenerational transmission of offending. *Criminal Behaviour and Mental Health* 19 (2): 109–124.

Fazel, S., Smith, E.N., Chang, Z., and Geddes, J.R. (2018). Risk factors for interpersonal violence: an umbrella review of meta-analyses. *The British Journal of Psychiatry* 213 (4): 609–614.

Felitti, V.J., Anda, R.F., Nordenberg, D. et al. (1998). Relationship of childhood abuse and household dysfunction to many of the leading causes of death in adults: the adverse childhood experiences (ACE) study. *American Journal of Preventive Medicine* 14 (4): 245–258.

Finkelhor, D. (2018). Screening for adverse childhood experiences (ACEs): cautions and suggestions. *Child Abuse & Neglect* 285: 174–179.

Flaherty, E.G., Thompson, R., Dubowitz, H. et al. (2013). Adverse childhood experiences and child health in early adolescence. *JAMA Pediatrics* 167 (7): 622–629.

Fletcher, Y. (2025). *Chutzpah: A memoir of faith, sexuality and daring to stay.* Doubleday.

Ford, J.D. and Delker, B.C. (2018). Polyvictimization in childhood and its adverse impacts across the lifespan: introduction to the special issue. *Journal of Trauma & Dissociation* 19 (3): 275–288.

Ford, K., Bellis, M.A., Hughes, K. et al. (2020). Adverse childhood experiences: a retrospective study to understand their associations with lifetime mental health diagnosis, self-harm or suicide attempt, and current low mental wellbeing in a male Welsh prison population. *Health Justice* 8: 13. https://doi.org/10.1186/s40352-020-00115-5.

Fritz, J., de Graaff, A.M, Caisley, H., et al. (2018). A systematic review of amenable resilience factors that moderate and/or mediate the relationship between childhood adversity and mental health in young people. Frontiers in Psychiatry 9:230.

Goldenson, J., Kitollari, I., and Lehman, F. (2021). The relationship between ACEs, trauma-related psychopathology and resilience in vulnerable youth: implications for screening and treatment. *Journal of Child & Adolescent Trauma* 14 (1): 151–160.

González, R.A., Vélez-Pastrana, M.C., McCrory, E. et al. (2019). Evidence of concurrent and prospective associations between early maltreatment and ADHD through childhood and adolescence. *Social Psychiatry and Psychiatric Epidemiology* 54 (6): 671–682. https://doi.org/10.1007/s00127-019-01659-0.

Goodman, A., Diggs, M., Balachandran, N. et al. (2020). Repeatability of neural and autonomic responses to acute psychosocial stress. *Frontiers in Neuroscience* 14: https://doi.org/10.3389/fnins.2020.585509.

Griffiths, B.B. and Hunter, R.G. (2014). Neuroepigenetics of stress. *Neuroscience* 275: 420–435.

Gupta, S. and Garg, S. (2020). Causes and effects of child sexual abuse. *International Journal of Innovative Science and Research Technology* 5 (5): 1867–1870.

Haczkewicz, K.M., Shahid, S., Finnegan, H.A. et al. (2024). Adverse childhood experiences (ACEs), resilience, and outcomes in older adulthood: a scoping review. *Child Abuse & Neglect* 168: 106864.

Hailes, H.P., Yu, R., Danese, A., and Fazel, S. (2019). Long-term outcomes of childhood sexual abuse: an umbrella review. *Lancet Psychiatry* 6 (10): 830–839.

Halfon, N., Larson, K., Son, J. et al. (2017). Income inequality and the differential effect of adverse childhood experiences in US children. *Academic Pediatrics* 17 (7S): S70–S78.

Hall, A., Perez, A., West, X. et al. (2021). The Association of Adverse Childhood Experiences and Resilience with Health Outcomes in Adolescents: an observational study. *Global Pediatric Health* 8: 2333794X20982433.

Halpern, S.C., Schuch, F.B., Scherer, J.N. et al. (2018). Child maltreatment and illicit substance abuse: a systematic review and meta-analysis of longitudinal studies. *Child Abuse Review* 27 (5): 344–360.

Han, D., Dieujuste, N., Doom, J.R., and Narayan, A.J. (2023). A systematic review of positive childhood experiences and adult outcomes: promotive and protective processes for resilience in the context of childhood adversity. *Child Abuse & Neglect* 144: 106346.

Herman, J. (1997). *Trauma and Recovery: The Aftermath of Violence, from Domestic Abuse to Political Terror*. New York: Basic Books.

Hibbard, R,. Barlow, J,. Macmillan, H. (2012) Child maltreatment and violence. Psychological maltreatment. Pediatrics. 130(2):372–8. doi: https://doi.org/10.1542/peds.2012-1552.

Hughes, K., Bellis, M., Hardcastle, K. et al. (2017). The effect of multiple adverse childhood experiences on health: a systematic review and meta-analysis. *The Lancet* 2 (8): e356–e366. https://doi.org/10.1016/S2468-2667(17)30118-4.

Iacono, L., Trentini, C., and Carola, V. (2021). Psychobiological consequences of childhood sexual abuse: current knowledge and clinical implications. *Frontiers in Neuroscience* 2 (15): 771511.

van IJzendoorn, M.H., Bakermans-Kranenburg, M.J., Duschinsky, R. et al. (2020a). Institutionalisation and deinstitutionalisation of children 1: a systematic and integrative review of evidence regarding effects on development. *Lancet Psychiatry* 7 (8): 703–720.

van IJzendoorn, M.H., Bakermans-Kranenburg, M.J., Coughlan, B. et al. (2020b). Annual research review: umbrella synthesis of meta-analyses on child maltreatment antecedents and interventions: differential susceptibility perspective on risk and resilience. *Journal of Child Psychology and Psychiatry* 61 (3): 272–290.

Johnson, F., Kaffman, A. (2017). Early life stress perturbs the function of microglia in the developing rodent brain: New insights and future challenge. Brain, Behavior, and Immunity 69. https://doi.org/10.1016/j.bbi.2017.06.008, 18, 27.

Johnson, S.B., Riley, A.W., Granger, D.A., and Riis, J. (2013). The science of early life toxic stress for pediatric practice and advocacy. *Pediatrics* 131: 319–327.

Joleby, M., Lunde, C., Landström, S., and Jonsson, L.S. (2021). Offender strategies for engaging children in online sexual activity. *Child Abuse & Neglect* 120: 105214.

Jones, L., Bellis, M.A., Wood, S. et al. (2012). Prevalence and risk of violence against children with disabilities: a systematic review and meta-analysis of observational studies. *Lancet* 380 (9845): 899–907.

Juffer, F., Bakermans-Kranenberg, M.J., and van IJzendoorn, M.H. (ed.) (2023). *Promoting Positive Parenting: An Attachment-Based Intervention*. New York: Routledge.

Kempe, C.H., Silverman, F.N., Steele, B. et al. (1984). Landmark article July 7, 1962: the battered-child syndrome by C. Henry Kempe, Frederic N. Silverman, Brandt F. Steele et al. *JAMA* 251 (24): 3288–3294. https://doi.org/10.1001/jama.251.24.3288.

King, S., Dancause, K., Turcotte-Tremblay, A.M. et al. (2012). Using natural disasters to study the effects of prenatal maternal stress on child health and development. *Birth Defects Research Part C Embryo Today* 96 (4): 273–288. https://doi.org/10.1002/bdrc.21026.

Koenen, K.C., Ratanatharathorn, A., Ng, L. et al (2017) Posttraumatic stress disorder in the World Mental Health Surveys. Psychological Medicine. 47(13): 2260–2274. https://doi.org/10.1017/S0033291717000708.

Kumari, V. (2020). Emotional abuse and neglect: time to focus on prevention and mental health consequences. *British Journal of Psychiatry* 217 (5): 597–599. https://doi.org/10.1192/bjp.2020.154.

Lambert, S., and Gill-Emerson, G. (2017). Moving-Towards-Trauma-Informed-Care. Cork Simon Community. https://www.drugsandalcohol.ie/28377/1/

Lauzun-Brown, W. (1916). *Useful Information for the Home*. London: Trenner and Son.

Lê-Scherban, F., Wang, X., Boyle-Steed, K.H., and Pachter, L.M. (2018). Intergenerational Associations of Parent Adverse Childhood Experiences and Child Health Outcomes. *Pediatrics* 141 (6): e20174274.

Lussier, P., McCuish, E., Chouinard Thivierge, S,. Frechette J. (2024) A meta-analysis of trends in general, sexual, and violent recidivism among youth with histories of sex offending. Trauma Violence Abuse. 25(1):54–72. doi: https://doi.org/10.1177/15248380221137653

MacIntosh, H.B. and Ménard, A.D. (2021). Where are we now? A consolidation of the research on long-term impact of child sexual abuse. *Journal of Child Sexual Abuse* 30 (3): 253–257.

Madigan, S., Deneault, A., Racine, R. et al. (2023). Adverse childhood experiences: a meta-analysis of prevalence and moderators among half a million adults in 206 studies. *World Psychiatry* 22 (3): 463–471. https://doi.org/10.1002/wps.21122.

Mandelli, L., Petrelli, C., and Serretti, A. (2015). The role of specific early trauma in adult depression: a meta-analysis of published literature. *European Psychiatry* 30. https://doi.org/10.1016/j.eurpsy.2015.04.007: 665–680.

Marryat, L. and Frank, J. (2019). Factors associated with adverse childhood experiences in Scottish children: a prospective cohort study. *BMJ Paediatrics Open* 3 (1): e000340. https://doi.org/10.1136/bmjpo-2018-000340.

Mason, M., Light, J., Campbell, L. et al. (2015). Peer network counseling with urban adolescents: a randomized controlled trial with moderate substance users. *Journal of Substance Abuse Treatment* 58: 16–24.

Massullo, C., De Rossi, E., Carbone, G.A. et al. (2023). Child maltreatment, abuse, and neglect: an umbrella review of their prevalence and definitions. *Clinical Neuropsychiatry* 20 (2): 72–99.

Masten, A.S. (2019). Resilience from a developmental systems perspective. *World Psychiatry: Official Journal of the World Psychiatric Association (WPA)* 18 (1): 101–102.

Maté, G. (2007). *In the Realm of Hungry Ghosts: Close Encounters with Addiction.* Toronto: Knopf Canada.

McCrory, E. (2025). Words Matter: Impact and Prevention of Childhood Verbal Abuse – House of Commons 28 April 2025. Expert-led discussion sponsored by Sharon Hodgson MP. House of commons

McCrory, E.J., Gerin, M.I., and Viding, E. (2017). Childhood maltreatment, latent vulnerability and the shift to preventative psychiatry– the contribution of functional brain imaging. *Journal of Child Psychology and Psychiatry* 58 (4): 338–357.

Messina, N. and Grella, C. (2006). Childhood trauma and women's health outcomes in a California prison population. *American Journal of Public Health* 96 (10): 1842–1848.

Messina, N., Grella, C., Burdon, W. et al. (2007). Childhood adverse events and current traumatic distress: a comparison of men and women drug-dependent prisoners. *Criminal Justice and Behavior* 34 (11): 385–1401.

Moore, K.A., Ramirez, N., and A. (2016). Adverse childhood experience and adolescent well-being: do protective factors matter? *Child Indicators Research* 9: 299–316.

Nelson, C.A., Fox, N.A., and Zeanah, C.H. (2014). *Romania's Abandoned Children: Deprivation, Brain Development, and the Struggle for Recovery.* Harvard University Press.

Neufeld, G. and Maté, G. (2013). *Hold on to Your Kids: Why Parents Need to Matter More Than Peers.* Toronto: Knopf Canada.

Norman, R.E., Byambaa, M., De, R. et al. (2012). The long-term health consequences of child physical abuse, emotional abuse, and neglect: a systematic review and meta-analysis. *PLoS Medicine* 9 (11): e1001349.

Ofsted (2021). Review of sexual abuse in schools and colleges. Gov.UK

Oral, R., Ramirez, M., Coohey, C. et al. (2016). Adverse childhood experiences and trauma informed care: the future of health care. *Pediatric Research* 79: 227–233.

Panksepp, J. (1998). *Affective Neuroscience: The Foundations of Human and Animal Emotions.* Oxford: Oxford University Press.

Papalia, N., Mann, E., Ogloff, J.R. (2021) Child sexual abuse and risk of revictimization: impact of child demographics, sexual abuse characteristics, and psychiatric disorders. Child Maltreatment 26, 1. https://doi.org/10.1177/107755952093266

Pates, R., Davies, A., and Tiddy, D. (2019). A secure children's home in Wales. In: *Children and Their Education in Secure Accommodation* (ed. D. Gallard, K. Evans, and J. Millington). London: Routledge.

Perry, B. (2009). Examining child maltreatment through a neurodevelopmental lens: clinical applications of the neurosequential model of therapeutics. *Journal of Loss & Trauma* 14 (4): 240–255.

Perry, B. D., Szalavitz, M. (2017). The boy who was raised as a dog: and other stories from a child psychiatrist's notebook: What traumatized children can teach us about loss, love, and healing (3rd ed.). New York: Basic Books.

Perry, B. and Winfrey, O. (2021). *What Happened to You? Conversations on Trauma, Resilience, and Healing.* New York: Flat Iron Books.

Petruccelli, K, Davis, J., Berman, T. (2019) Adverse childhood experiences and associated health outcomes: a systematic review and meta-analysis. Child Abuse & Neglect 97:104127. https://doi.org/10.1016/j.chiabu.2019.104127.

Proust, M. (1992). *Remembrance of Things Past.* UK: Random House.

Radford, L., Corral, S., Bradley, C. et al. (2011). *Child Abuse and Neglect in the United Kingdom Today*. London: National Society for the Prevention of Cruelty to Children.

Rhodes, J. (2015). *Instrumental*. Edinburgh: Canongate Books.

Rieffe, C., Terwogt, M.M., Petrides, K.V. et al. (2007). Psychometric properties of the Emotion Awareness Questionnaire for children. *Personality and Individual Differences* 43 (1): 95–105.

Rokach, A. and Clayton, S. (2023). *Adverse Childhood Experiences and their Life-Long Impact*. Cambridge, MA: Academic Press.

Russotti, J., Warmingham, J.M., Handley, E.D. et al. (2021a). Child maltreatment: an intergenerational cascades model of risk processes potentiating child psychopathology. *Child Abuse & Neglect* 112: 104829.

Russotti, J., Warmingham, J.M., Duprey, E.B. et al. (2021b). Child maltreatment and the development of psychopathology: the role of developmental timing and chronicity. *Child Abuse & Neglect* 120: 105215.

Rutter, M. (2007). Resilience, competence, and coping. *Child Abuse & Neglect* 31 (3): 205–209. https://doi.org/10.1016/j.chiabu.2007.02.001.

Schickedanz, A., Escarce, J.J., Halfon, N. et al. (2021). Intergenerational Associations between Parents' and Children's Adverse Childhood Experience Scores. *Children* 8 (9): 747.

Shalev, I., Moffitt, T.E., Sugden, K. et al. (2013). Exposure to violence during childhood is associated with telomere erosion from 5 to 10 years of age: a longitudinal study. *Molecular Psychiatry* 18 (5): 576–581.

Sigurdardottir, S. and Halldorsdottir, S. (2018). Screaming body and silent healthcare providers: a case study with a childhood sexual abuse survivor. *International Journal of Environmental Research and Public Health* 15 (1): 94.

Sinmaz, E., Sherwood, H., and Weale, S. (2024). Justin Welby to quit as archbishop of Canterbury over handling of abuse scandal. The Guardian (11 December 2024).

Slopen, N., Shonkoff, J.P., Albert, M.A. et al. (2016). Racial disparities in child adversity in the U.S.: interactions with family immigration history and income. *American Journal of Preventive Medicine* 50 (1): 47–56.

Spencer, C. (2024). *A Very Private School*. London: William Collins.

Steel, C., Newman, E., O'Rourke, S., and Quayle, E. (2021). Self perceptions and cognitions of child sexual exploitation material offenders. *International Journal of Offender Therapy and Comparative Criminology* 1–20.

Taillieu, T.L., Brownridge, D.A., Sareen, J., and Afifi, T.O. (2016). Childhood emotional maltreatment and mental disorders: results from a nationally representative adult sample from the United States. *Child Abuse & Neglect* 59: 1–12.

Teicher, M.H., Anderson, C.M., Ohashi, K., and Polcari, A. (2014). Childhood maltreatment: altered network centrality of cingulate, precuneus, temporal pole and insula. *Biological Psychiatry* 76 (4): 297–305.

Thompson, R., Litrownik, A.J., Isbell, P. et al. (2012). Adverse experiences and suicidal ideation in adolescence: exploring the link using the LONGSCAN samples. *Psychology of Violence* 2 (2) https://doi.org/10.1037/a0027107: 211–225.

Tiwari, A. and Gonzalez, A. (2018). Biological alterations affecting risk of adult psychopathology following childhood trauma: a review of sex differences. *Clinical Psychology Review* 66: 69–79.

UNICEF (2020). Action to end child sexual abuse and exploitation: a review of the evidence. unicef.org.

Vizard, E., Gray, J., and Bentovim, A. (2021). The impact of child maltreatment on the mental and physical health of child victims: a review of the evidence. *British Journal of Psychiatric Advances* 28 (11): https://doi.org/10.1192/bja.2021.10.

Waite, R. and Ryan, R. (2017). Adverse Childhood Experiences: What Students and Health Professional Need to Know. In:. London: Routledge.

Walsh, D., McCartney, G., Smith, M., and Armour, G. (2019). Relationship between childhood socioeconomic position and adverse childhood experiences (ACEs): a systematic review. *Journal of Epidemiology and Community Health* 73 (12): 1087–1093.

Wesley-Esquimaux, C.C. and Smolewski, M. (2004). *Historic Trauma and Aboriginal Healing*. Ottawa: Aboriginal Healing Foundation.

Wolwynn, M. (2017). *It Didn't Start with You: How Inherited Family Trauma Shapes Who We Are and How to End the Cycle*. New York: Penguin.

World Health Organisation (2022). *International Statistical Classification of Diseases and Related Health Problems, 11th revision (2022)*. Geneva: World Health Organisation.

World Health Organisation (2024a). PTSD. https://www.who.int/news-room/fact-sheets/detail/post-traumatic-stress-disorder.

World Health Organisation (2024b). Child maltreatment. https://www.who.int.news-room/fact-sheets/detail/child maltreatment (accessed 24 May 2025).

Yellow Horse Brave Heart, M. (1998). The return to the sacred path: healing the historical trauma response among the Lakota. *Smith College Studies In Social Work* 68 (3): 287–305.

Yellow Horse Brave Heart, M. (1999). Oyate Ptayela: rebuilding the Lakota Nation through addressing historical trauma among Lakota parents. *Journal of Human Behavior in the Social Environment* 2 (1/2): 109–126.

Zarse, E.M., Neff, M.R., Yoser, R., and Hulvershorn, L. (2019). The adverse childhood experiences questionnaire: two decades of research on childhood trauma as a primary cause of adult mental illness, addiction, and medical diseases. *Cogent Medicine* 6 (1): https://doi.org/10.1080/2331205X.2019.1581447.

Zimmerman, M.A. (2013). Resiliency theory: a strengths-based approach to research and practice for adolescent health. *Health Education & Behavior* 40 (4): 381–383.

Chapter 2

INHERITING TRAUMA: DOMESTIC ABUSE THROUGH THE LENS OF ACEs

Amy Johnson

Department of Community, Social Justice and Health School of Health and Wellbeing, University of Worcester, Worcester, UK

Childhood is often remembered as a time of joy, freedom and possibility, a period filled with happy memories, a supportive family and dreams for the future. For some, it includes the presence of caring parents, few worries and the space to grow and explore without fear. However, this is not the reality for all children. Many are forced to grow up quickly in households marked by volatility, instability and exposure to domestic abuse (Francis-Devine 2025). These children are denied the safety and security that should define childhood. At a time when development is at its peak and when children are learning about the world, forming their sense of self, and understanding right from wrong, experiences such as domestic abuse can profoundly disrupt emotional, cognitive and social growth (CADDA 2014). Such experiences can prevent children from exploring the world with curiosity and confidence, and rather, instil a sense of need for survival, navigating their childhoods through fear, uncertainty and trauma, leading to potential risks for perpetration and victimisation of domestic abuse; the cycle can continue. This chapter examines domestic abuse as an Adverse Childhood Experience (ACE) and its long-term impact on adulthood. It explores the psychological, emotional and social challenges faced by individuals exposed to domestic abuse in childhood, while analysing the systemic barriers that hinder effective intervention and support. Additionally, it considers societal influences, including structural inequalities and economic factors, that shape the experiences of affected children. The chapter concludes by considering how best to support children, particularly around trauma-informed interventions and changes that are required in policies.

The Intergenerational Effects of Adverse Childhood Experiences: Ripples on a Pond, First Edition. Edited by Richard Pates and Diane Riley.

Published 2026 by John Wiley & Sons Ltd.

Domestic abuse is broadly defined as 'any incident of threatening behaviour, violence, or abuse, whether physical, psychological, sexual, financial or emotional between individuals in an intimate relationship or within a family setting' (Robinson 2017). It is a pervasive global issue with far-reaching consequences for victims, children and perpetrators, and is highlighted as a public health concern (Stöckl and Sorenson 2024). While this definition is widely used by professionals, academics and organisations, it only formally recognises individuals aged 16 and over, excluding countless children who experience domestic abuse within their homes.

Throughout the years, I have spoken to male perpetrators of intimate partner abuse and listened to their journeys into relationships and their use of abuse. These conversations have revealed complex and often painful histories that shaped their behaviours. Many of the men I've listened to described backgrounds marked by trauma, instability and social deprivation. For example, Toby spoke of a 'normal' upbringing with two parents, yet recalled his father using a truncheon to calm him down due to his size. He dropped out of university and turned to crime, where he met his ex-partner, someone with her own history of trauma. Toby insisted he was protecting her, but his behaviours, such as constant check-ins and controlling her whereabouts, reflected coercive control masked as care. He often positioned himself as the victim, claiming she 'victimised' him despite his own controlling actions.

Similarly, Sam shared that he was raised in care after his mother couldn't look after him and described being physically and sexually abused throughout his time in the system. He was passed between care homes and spoke of his trauma with detachment, only later recognising its impact. Sam believed no one would ever care for him, which led to emotional isolation and difficulty forming close relationships. He admitted to violent abuse towards his partner, expressing guilt but also describing moments of losing control and 'seeing red', often triggered by sexual jealousy and issues involving his children. The journeys of men like Toby and Sam often intersect with addiction, homelessness and broader offending behaviours, highlighting the need to understand how childhood experiences that include trauma, deprivation and insecure attachments contribute to cycles of abuse.

Under the United Kingdom's Domestic Abuse Act, 2021, domestic abuse involving individuals under 16 is classified as child abuse and addressed under child protection laws such as the Children Act, 1989 (Bekaert et al. 2022). This distinction presents challenges, particularly in cases of abuse within adolescent relationships or family dynamics affecting younger children, which has been identified as a critical period for intervention to prevent future victimisation and perpetration (Lepistö et al. 2011). However, a significant shift in the Domestic Abuse Act (2021) recognises children who 'witness' domestic abuse as victims in their own right, with the hope of strengthening legal protections and access to support services. The Act mandates improved responses from local authorities, ensuring affected children receive trauma-informed care and interventions designed to mitigate long-term harm. However, while this legislative change represents progress, it assumes children will come forward and disclose abuse. In reality, reporting rates remain low due to fear of family separation and distrust in authorities (Callaghan et al. 2017). Furthermore, the term 'witnessing' fails to capture the full sensory and emotional experience of children exposed to domestic abuse. While recent policy changes acknowledge children as victims in domestic abuse cases, there remains a significant gap in fully understanding their distinct needs and lived experiences. Recognition alone is not enough, and effective interventions must consider the complex reality of children growing up in domestic violent environments.

The Crime Survey for England and Wales reports that in 32.4% of cases of domestic abuse, there was at least one child under the age of 16 living in the household (Office for National Statistics 2023) and an estimated 62% of children living in these households are directly harmed by the perpetrator (Cleaver and Rose 2022). Recent media coverage has highlighted cases in the United Kingdom, where children have died due to neglect in the home, some of which have been linked to domestic abuse (Olszowy et al. 2021). In situations where both parents have been charged, it is often the perpetrator who has inflicted fatal harm, while the other caregiver, frequently the mother, faces charges of neglect for failing to prevent the abuse. This presents a complex ethical and legal dilemma. The non-abusive caregiver is often a victim, navigating coercion, fear and systemic barriers that make leaving the abusive environment extraordinarily difficult (Arnull and Stewart 2021). Many believe they are protecting their children by staying, yet the unpredictable nature of domestic abuse means that risk remains ever-present. There has also been an increase in filicide-suicide cases in the United Kingdom, where coercive control and obsession with punishing the victim takes a darker meaning (Moen and Bezuidenhout 2023). In addition, children can be at risk from the victim of domestic abuse too, as a way of 'protecting' them from further harm (Vileisis and Laufer 2024), and it is recognised that suicides linked with domestic abuse have increased over the last few years (McManus et al. 2022), further heightening risk of harm to children.

Further, as family structures continue to evolve, the traditional concept of the nuclear family is becoming increasingly outdated. Contemporary families may include same-sex parents, stepfamilies, blended households and other diverse caregiving arrangements (Bengtson 2001). These shifts necessitate a broader understanding of how domestic abuse manifests within varied family dynamics and raising the need for professionals to identify ways to effectively work with perpetrators without increasing the risk to children, beyond the heterosexual lens (Devaney 2015).

Children growing up in households affected by domestic abuse are often already facing systemic disadvantages (McCoy and Hanno 2023). Poverty and socioeconomic disadvantage strongly increase the likelihood of exposure to ACEs (Lacey et al. 2022; Page et al. 2014). Those from minority ethnic backgrounds and lower socioeconomic households are statistically more likely to witness domestic abuse, highlighting the intersection between structural inequality and family violence. The ongoing cost-of-living crisis in the

United Kingdom has exacerbated these vulnerabilities, with more families experiencing financial hardship than ever before. Economic instability increases stress within households, heightening the risk of domestic abuse and limiting access to essential support services (Hughes et al. 2024). It is well-established that children raised in socially and economically deprived areas face significant barriers to opportunity, including limited access to quality education, healthcare and supportive community resources. When domestic abuse is present in these environments, it introduces an additional layer of complexity and adversity and compounds the negative impacts on emotional, cognitive and social development. This reality highlights the urgent need for government intervention, not only in addressing domestic abuse but also in tackling the broader structural conditions that contribute to its prevalence.

When considering the impact of domestic abuse on children, it is critical to think beyond the immediate and visible effects. While immediate responses such as fear, bedwetting and visible emotional distress, particularly when witnessing a parent in pain, are alarming, the deeper psychological impact is often more complex and enduring (Noble-Carr et al. 2020). Children typically view their parents as protectors and figures of strength. Witnessing these same caregivers in vulnerable or victimised states can be deeply confusing and destabilising, challenging a child's sense of safety and reshaping their understanding of relationships and trust. It also raises questions about the child's identity and their role within the family home. Children growing up in a household affected by domestic abuse often develop complex and fragmented identities as they navigate survival in a volatile environment. Some take on the nurturer role, feeling a deep responsibility to care for younger siblings or even the abusive caregiver, trying to maintain peace and stability (Chester and Joscelyne 2021). Others become the protector, attempting to shield family members from harm, whether emotionally or physically, often internalising a heightened sense of vigilance. Some children struggle with anger, expressing their pain through rebellion, defiance or emotional withdrawal (DeBoard-Lucas and Grych 2011). In extreme cases, they may adopt the role of the bully, modelling aggressive behaviours they have witnessed, either as a means of asserting control over an unpredictable world or as a learned response to conflict (Lee et al. 2022). Some children may 'externalise' their feelings and confusion through aggressive or anti-social behaviour, whilst others may 'internalise' the behaviours, resulting in higher levels of depression, anxiety and trauma symptoms. Research indicates the impact of domestic abuse on both boys and girls is similar with regard to internalising behaviours, but that boys are more likely to display externalising behaviours.

These identities are fluid, shaped by fear, coping mechanisms and survival instincts, leaving lasting effects on a child's self-perception and relationships. Without intervention, these roles may persist into adulthood, influencing behavioural patterns, attachment styles and mental health outcomes. A trauma-informed approach to care and intervention is crucial in helping children rebuild a sense of self outside of these survival-driven roles, particularly when entering adult intimate relationships or becoming parents themselves.

Whilst research has focused on the primary perpetrator inflicting abuse on the children, little has been discussed around the parent who is experiencing intimate partner abuse. As a result of sustained trauma, psychological distress and the pressure of an unsafe environment, some victims engage in harmful behaviours towards their children (Castro et al. 2017). These responses, while often rooted in survival mechanisms, can have profound consequences for children's well-being. This complexity challenges traditional binaries of victim and perpetrator. For example, when mothers are subjected to coercive control or domestic abuse, the impact often extends beyond the immediate abuse, influencing their parenting and the overall family dynamic. Research indicates that mothers who experience such control may, in response to their trauma, exhibit controlling or authoritarian behaviours towards their children as a means of coping or attempting to reassert autonomy. This can contribute to a cycle wherein children not only witness abuse but also experience it directly, reinforcing patterns of control, fear and emotional instability within the household (Pu and Rodriguez 2021). Addressing these complex and often hidden dynamics is essential to breaking intergenerational cycles of abuse and ensuring the safety and well-being of all family members. These points raise the importance of trauma-informed, whole-family approaches to understanding and addressing domestic abuse. It also reinforces the need for services that are sensitive to the diverse ways in which abuse can manifest and the broad spectrum of those affected within the household.

In addition to the roles within the household, children also have a role to play outside in the community. Living in a household where domestic abuse is present often brings with it feelings of shame, embarrassment and secrecy (Summer 2009). Children may avoid inviting friends over or become hypervigilant in school settings, anxious that a teacher might ask about home life. For some, frequent relocations to refuges or temporary accommodations result in instability, social disruption and a fragmented sense of identity. Constantly having to adjust to new environments, friendship groups and expectations can be overwhelming and also creates a space for children to create 'new identities' and mask emotion even further, disassociation with the reality and for others, it will raise concerns about how much they share: 'Why have we moved here again?', 'How much of my story can I share?' What this can also bring is a higher risk of further victimisation from other situations, particularly in refuges and temporary accommodation, where other children have also been victimised and are presenting with their own challenges. Mixed-gender settings and the presence of other children experiencing trauma can lead to further exposure to harmful behaviour, compounding a child's vulnerability (Hock et al. 2024). As refuges may lack adequate facilities or specialised support for children's needs, the absence of wraparound services such as counselling, education support and trauma-informed care can hinder recovery for both survivors and their children (Arnell and Thunberg 2025). Meanwhile, as caregivers navigate their own loss of stability, home and identity, children can feel overlooked or even used as pawns in family court disputes or as leverage in controlling dynamics (Sowter 2021). This is, of course, if the child stays with one of their parents;

in some cases, children will be removed from the household and taken into care or rely on a family member to take them in. Domestic abuse is a key factor in many child protection cases, with research showing that it is present in over 50% of referrals to children's social care (Mayrhofer et al. 2025). In England alone, nearly 50,000 babies are referred to social care each year with domestic abuse as a contributing factor, and approximately 1,924 babies aged 0–2 enter care annually for this reason. Additionally, a number of children experience three or more placements within a single year, increasing their vulnerability. Children who experience multiple placements often struggle with feelings of rejection, instability and difficulty forming trusting relationships (Maguire et al. 2024).

The pathway from childhood to adulthood is a complicated one for those who have experienced so much trauma from a young age. The ACEs framework highlights the lasting impact of childhood trauma on a person's well-being in adulthood, which is why it is crucial to understand such experiences when working with children who may be at risk of future risks. Studies show that the more ACEs a child experiences (e.g. parental substance use, witnessing DV, children neglect/abuse), the greater their risk of developing mental health issues, addictions and other challenges (Morton et al. 2022). These factors have been strongly linked to increased likelihood of both victimisation and perpetration of domestic abuse later in life. Recognising the effects of ACEs is crucial when intervening in adulthood, as understanding past trauma can help shape effective strategies to minimise future risks of domestic abuse, with many questioning whether domestic abuse should be taught at schools and embedded within the mandatory curriculum (Stanley et al. 2015).

Earlier in the chapter, we identified different roles and identities children may adopt, and it would seem that such roles have an impact on their adulthood. For instance, those who adopt the role of protector may develop a heightened need for control, which can lead to relationship difficulties later in life (Forke et al. 2018). Conversely, individuals who take on caregiving or people-pleasing roles may struggle with self-worth and become more vulnerable to victimisation due to an ingrained need for approval (Goodman et al. 2020). These behavioural patterns may remain dormant until adulthood, often surfacing in intimate relationships or parenting dynamics.

To address these intergenerational effects, early, sustained and trauma-informed interventions are crucial. Such approaches should not only support the non-abusing parent but also foster safe, nurturing environments and promote healthy parenting practices. Effective interventions must be responsive to ACEs, considering the child's developmental stage, identity and unique lived experiences to break the cycle of abuse and foster resilience.

This chapter has explored the complex and far-reaching impact of domestic abuse on children, emphasising that harm extends beyond the immediate moment of violence. Children living in abusive households often face emotional turmoil, disrupted development and identity confusion, particularly when those who are meant to protect them become sources of harm. These experiences are not limited to witnessing abuse between caregivers; many children are direct victims themselves, sometimes at the hands of the non-abusing parent, who may be coping with trauma and stress. The chapter considered broader social issues, such as poverty, housing instability and the rising cost of living, and how this can contribute to the prevalence and complexity of domestic abuse. These intersecting challenges point to the need for a shift in how we approach prevention and intervention. Rather than focusing solely on crisis response, the emphasis must be on trauma-informed, long-term strategies embedded across key systems, particularly education. Schools often have the most consistent contact with children and are uniquely placed to provide early support, build trust and promote resilience.

Furthermore, it questions whether current protective measures, such as temporary accommodation and refuges, always serve children's best interests, especially when these settings expose them to additional harm or instability. The chapter argues for a more child-centred approach that prioritises stability, addresses perpetrator behaviour and strengthens wider support networks beyond the immediate family.

Ultimately, the chapter calls for systemic change that not only protects children but also gives them a voice, supports struggling parents and acknowledges the societal conditions that perpetuate cycles of abuse. Breaking this cycle requires collective responsibility, cross-sector collaboration and a compassionate, preventative approach rooted in the realities children face every day and maybe then we can start to reduce domestic violence in adulthood and intervene in the intergenerational cycle of domestic abuse.

References

Arnell, L. and Thunberg, S. (2025). Young children's lives at domestic violence shelters: mothers' perspectives on their children's experiences. *Child & Adolescent Social Work Journal* 42 (1): 123–134.

Arnull, E. and Stewart, S. (2021). Developing a theoretical framework to discuss mothers experiencing domestic violence and being subject to interventions: a cross-national perspective. *International Journal for Crime, Justice and Social Democracy* 10 (2): 113–126.

Bekaert, S., Seemungal, F., and Nott, E. (2022). The Domestic Abuse Act 2021 England and Wales: implications for nurses. *British Journal of Nursing (Mark Allen Publishing)* 31 (20): 1046–1050.

Bengtson, V.L. (2001). Beyond the nuclear family: the increasing importance of multi-generational bonds. *Journal of Marriage and Family* 63 (1): 1–16.

CAADA (2014). In plain sight: effective help for children exposed to domestic abuse. https://safelives.org.uk/node/450 (accessed 25 April 2025).

Callaghan, J.E.M., Fellin, L.C., Mavrou, S. et al. (2017). The management of disclosure in children's accounts of domestic violence: practices of telling and not telling. *Journal of Child and Family Studies* 26 (12): 3370–3387. https://doi.org/10.1007/s10826-017-0832-3.

Castro, M., Alcántara-López, M., Martínez, A. et al. (2017). Mother's IPV, child maltreatment type and the presence of PTSD in children and adolescents. *International Journal of Environmental Research and Public Health* 14 (9): 1077.

Chester, J. and Joscelyne, T. (2021). "I thought it was normal": adolescents' attempts to make sense of their experiences of domestic violence in their families. *Journal of Interpersonal Violence* 36 (11–12): 5250–5276.

Cleaver, H. and Rose, W. (2022). *Caring for Children Who Have Experienced Domestic Abuse*. London: CoramBAAF.

DeBoard-Lucas, R.L. and Grych, J.H. (2011). Children's perceptions of intimate partner violence: causes, consequences, and coping. *Journal of Family Violence* 26 (5): 343–354.

Devaney, J. (2015). Research review: the impact of domestic violence on children. *Irish Probation Journal* 12: 79–94.

Forke, C.M., Myers, R.K., Fein, J.A. et al. (2018). Witnessing intimate partner violence as a child: how boys and girls model their parents' behaviors in adolescence. *Child Abuse & Neglect* 84: 241–252.

Francis-Devine, B. (2025, April 4). House of Commons Library. https://commons library.parliament.uk (accessed 25 April 2025).

Goodman, M.L., Hindman, A., Keiser, P.H. et al. (2020). Neglect, sexual abuse, and witnessing intimate partner violence during childhood predicts later life violent attitudes against children among Kenyan women: evidence of intergenerational risk transmission from cross-sectional data. *Journal of Interpersonal Violence* 35 (3–4): 623–645.

Hock, E.S., Blank, L., Fairbrother, H. et al. (2024). Exploring the impact of housing insecurity on the health and wellbeing of children and young people in the United Kingdom: a qualitative systematic review. *BMC Public Health* 24 (1): 2453. https://doi.org/10.1186/s12889-024-19735-9.

Hughes, K., Bellis, M.A., Cresswell, K. et al. (2024). Examining relationships between adverse childhood experiences and coping during the cost-of-living crisis using a national cross-sectional survey in Wales, UK. *BMJ Open* 14 (5): e081924.

Lacey, R.E., Howe, L.D., Kelly-Irving, M. et al. (2022). The clustering of adverse childhood experiences in the Avon longitudinal study of parents and children: are gender and poverty important? *Journal of Interpersonal Violence* 2022 (37): 2218–2241.

Lee, H., Russell, K.N., O'Donnell, K.A. et al. (2022). The effect of childhood intimate partner violence (IPV) exposure on bullying: a systematic review. *Journal of Family Violence* 37 (8): 1283–1300.

Lepistö, S., Luukkaala, T., and Paavilainen, E. (2011). Witnessing and experiencing domestic violence: a descriptive study of adolescents. *Scandinavian Journal of Caring Sciences* 25 (1): 70–80.

Maguire, D., May, K., McCormack, D., and Fosker, T. (2024). A systematic review of the impact of placement instability on emotional and behavioural outcomes among children in foster care. *Journal of Child & Adolescent Trauma* 17 (2): 641–655. https://doi.org/10.1007/s40653-023-00606-1.

Mayrhofer, A., Mansuri, N., Sarma, K. et al. (2025). Implementing family safeguarding in the context of domestic violence and abuse: a case study of a local authority in England. *The British Journal of Social Work* 55 (2): 763–781.

McCoy, D.C. and Hanno, E.C. (2023). Systemic barriers and opportunities for implementing school-based social-emotional learning interventions in low-income and conflict-affected settings. *Frontiers in Psychology* 14: 1011039. https://doi.org/10.3389/fpsyg.2023.1011039.

McManus, S., Walby, S., Barbosa, E.C. et al. (2022). Intimate partner violence, suicidality, and self-harm: a probability sample survey of the general population in

England. *The Lancet Psychiatry* 9 (7): 574–583. https://doi.org/10.1016/S2215-0366(22)00151-1.

Moen, M. and Bezuidenhout, C. (2023). Killing your children to hurt your partner: a South African perspective on the motivations for revenge filicide. *Journal of Investigative Psychology and Offender Profiling* 20 (1): 33–47.

Morton, S., Curran, M., and Barry O'Gorman, M. (2022). Adverse childhood experiences, domestic violence and substance misuse: an action research study on routine enquiry and practice responses. *Frontiers in Psychiatry* 13: 892849. https://doi.org/10.3389/fpsyt.2022.892849.

Noble-Carr, D., Moore, T., and McArthur, M. (2020). Children's experiences and needs in relation to domestic and family violence: findings from a meta-synthesis. *Child & Family Social Work* 25 (1): 182–191.

Office for National Statistics (2023). Domestic abuse in England and Wales overview (November 2023). www.ons.gov.uk > crimeandjustice > bulletins > november2023.

Olszowy, L., Jaffe, P., and Saxton, M. (2021). Examining the role of child protection services in domestic violence cases: lessons learned from tragedies. *Journal of Family Violence* 36 (8): 927–939.

Page, A., Lewis, G., Kidger, J. et al. (2014). Parental socio-economic position during childhood as a determinant of self-harm in adolescence. *Social Psychiatry and Psychiatric Epidemiology* 49 (2): 193–203. https://doi.org/10.1007/s00127-013-0722-y.

Pu, D.F. and Rodriguez, C.M. (2021). Spillover and crossover effects: mothers' and fathers' intimate partner violence, parent-child aggression risk, and child behavior problems. *Child Maltreatment* 26 (4): 420–430.

Robinson, A.L. (2017). Serial domestic abuse in wales: an exploratory study into its definition, prevalence, correlates, and management. *Victims & Offenders* 12 (5): 643–662.

Sowter, D. (2021). The future harm exception: coercive control as serious psychological harm and the challenge for lawyers' ethics. *Dalhousie Law Journal* 44 (2): COV8.

Stanley, N., Ellis, J., Farrelly, N. et al. (2015). Preventing domestic abuse for children and young people: a review of school-based interventions. *Children and Youth Services Review* 59: 120–131. https://doi.org/10.1016/j.childyouth.2015.10.018.

Stöckl, H. and Sorenson, S.B. (2024). Violence against women as a global public health issue. *Annual Review of Public Health* 45 (1): 277–294.

Summer, B. (2009). 'Keep it in the family': casting sociological lights on the secrets of my life. *Human Architecture* 7 (3): 105–116.

Vileisis, J. and Laufer, B. (2024). *Domestic Violence as a Risk Factor of Maternal Filicide*. Archives of Women's Mental Health.

Part 2
Experiences of ACEs

Chapter 3

YES, IT HAPPENED TO ME!: THE LIVED EXPERIENCE OF ACEs, A NUMBER OF STORIES

Richard Pates[1] *and Diane Riley*[2]

[1] Independent Consultant, Wales, UK
[2] Independent Consultant, Ontario, Canada

These are the true stories of a number of adults, which describe different sorts of ACEs and their effects on the individuals. They describe a wide range of experiences, all of which have affected people throughout their lives. These are mostly people known to the authors or contacts of the authors, although names have been changed for all but one of them to protect the individuals.

Alf

Alf is 58 years old and has recently retired from a stressful job working with troubled children. He was very good at his job, despite being a very large man, a former rugby player. Alf was the second of four children, in a working-class family with a brother 3 years older than him and a younger sister 7 and a younger brother.

Alf's adverse childhood experiences started when he was about 4 years old. On Friday and Saturday nights, his parents would go out drinking in the local public houses. When they came home, they would start arguing and this would develop from arguing to violence. Alf would hear them until the early hours of the morning. In the morning, when the family came down to breakfast, nothing would be said, but father might have a scratch across his cheek and mother a pair of black eyes. This violence was extreme and was a contrast with the rest of the week, when they weren't drinking there would be no violence. After a while, they would go out separately and when they came home, they would accuse each other of what they might have been doing when they were out drinking with other people, triggering more violence. Alf's older brother would

The Intergenerational Effects of Adverse Childhood Experiences: Ripples on a Pond, First Edition. Edited by Richard Pates and Diane Riley.

Published 2026 by John Wiley & Sons Ltd.

put on a pair of headphones over his ears to block out the noise and when the young ones were born, they would be asleep in bed.

Alf experienced this every weekend, and it terrified him. As previously stated, the rest of the week they would be a normal family without violence. On holiday, they would go away with relatives, so the violence did not happen. The violence stopped when Alf was 17 years old, very tall and strong, and one night when the violence started, he hit his father. The effect of this violence has lasted all his life, developing into complex post-traumatic stress syndrome (CPTSD) after severe stress at his place of work.

He eventually went to work in the local steelworks in a tough manual job. In his mid-forties, he started working in a secure children's home. There are 15 of these across the United Kingdom and they are there to serve the most troubled children, often from very difficult backgrounds. They are called 'secure' because the children, aged from 12 to 17, are locked in because they are deemed to be potentially dangerous to others or at risk to themselves because of their behaviour. These are children who have experienced a lot of neglect, and physical and sexual abuse and because of their previous experiences, can be very violent or self-harming. Alf worked very well with these children, could be calming when needed and could stop violence when necessary and despite being a large, well-built man, was very gentle and caring. He was very good at this job and much appreciated by colleagues and management, but latterly, as the management changed did not receive the support that people working in this field require, good supervision.

The effects on Alf

Alf states that as a child, he had feelings of helplessness and loneliness as there was no one to tell about the terror of witnessing what was happening, shame because of the neighbours being able to hear what was going on, fear and trepidation because of the levels of verbal and physical violence. Up to the age of 9, he would stay upstairs with his head under the pillow, then he started to go downstairs to try to reason with his parents. At the age of 12–13, he would try physically to stop the violence and then would not sleep until 3 or 4 in the morning.

When he was a young man, he would drink with friends and play rugby, but he could lose his temper and be more aggressive than he should have been. He started to catastrophize because of not knowing what would happen, and this continued into adult life. He also became overprotective of his girlfriends and other friends.

He now has Complex PTSD, which has been exacerbated by the traumatic effects of working in a secure children's home and then not getting proper supervision when he experienced traumatic events at the home. These events included a child he was close to and supported, dying following an undiagnosed heart condition, removing 13 ligatures in a short space of time from a child, and pulling a girl from her burning bedroom when she wanted to stay there. Alf eventually went on sick leave and then retired because what had once been a rewarding job had become a nightmare for him.

In terms of symptoms related to his Complex PTSD/PTSD, he has suffered the following:

- Anxiety and depression
- Hyperarousal
- Mistrust of others and fear of others (he keeps an iron bar in his outside toilet for his own protection)
- An impact on his relationship despite the fact that his wife is extremely supportive
- Self-harm including cutting his own arms
- Poor sleep and nightmares

The impact of his parent's behaviour has lasted all his life and although he has now left working at the children's home, the effects of both his childhood experiences and what he had to deal with at the children's home have had a lasting and difficult effect on him.

Maria

In truth, I can't recall ever feeling truly normal. Throughout my life, I've carried the heavy sense that something was fundamentally wrong with me. It felt as though I was living two lives: one outwardly presented to society and those around me, and another – a much darker, lonelier existence, filled with sadness and guilt – hidden from view. It wasn't until my thirties that therapists and doctors gave me the language to articulate my struggles: complex trauma, hypersensitivity, pharmacoresistant depression, somatisation and insomnia. While these words weren't easy to hear, they offered a strange relief. For the first time, my feelings and experiences began to make sense.

I was fortunate to eventually find empathetic and understanding professionals (after many difficult encounters). But even with their help, the biggest work lies within me, and I know I have a long road to recovery ahead. One of the hardest aspects of this journey has been confronting my past – acknowledging what I endured as a child – and replacing shame, guilt and embarrassment with understanding and compassion for myself. It has been a slow and painful process, and one I am still navigating.

Growing up in my family felt like living on a battlefield. My parents' arguments were relentless, spanning money, extended family relationships and often, me. They frequently claimed I was the cause of their fights, though I never understood why. I began to feel like my very existence was a problem. I was often thrust into the role of mediator, standing between them as they yelled, tasked with deciding who was 'right' this time. At its worst, their fights escalated into threats of self-harm. I vividly remember pulling my mother back from a window she threatened to jump out of and wrestling knives out of her hands.

There were times when my parents disappeared – sometimes for hours, sometimes days. My sister and I were left to search for them. My mother's health deteriorated over time, and after particularly intense arguments, she would have seizures, leading to multiple hospitalisations. My parents' passionate reconciliations were just as intense as their battles, creating a chaotic and unstable environment.

Adding to this was the fact that we were migrants coming from Ukraine, living in a foreign country (Czechoslovakia) where my parents didn't speak the language and struggled financially. My younger sister's severe autoimmune disease had prompted our move, as treatment options in our home country were limited. This added another layer of stress, which only intensified the volatility between my parents. My mother, perpetually anxious and angry, was often aggressive towards me. She treated my sister differently – most likely due to her illness – but I bore the brunt of physical and psychological violence. My mother leaned on me as her ally against my father, as her confidant, therapist and emotional crutch.

I also experienced inappropriate behaviour from a family member, but even after years of therapy, I struggle to confront or articulate those memories. I doubt myself, questioning the reliability of childhood recollections and the fear of falsely accusing someone feels unbearable.

Therapy has revealed how much of my childhood I spent in dissociation, retreating into a dream world to escape reality. I've never dreamed about the *big things* – just a quiet, peaceful home where I felt safe and a job I like (and do not hate as my dad hated his). It's only recently that I've been able to create such a space for myself. But before that, I fell into patterns of choosing partners who mirrored the chaos of my upbringing, leading to depression and further struggles.

Seeking professional help has been a turning point. I am now undergoing ketamine-assisted depression therapy and trauma-focused psychotherapy. It's a difficult path, but I believe in the process.

My relationship with my parents remains complicated. With my father, I've reduced contact to a minimum. He still blames me for my mother leaving him. My mother, on the other hand, has mellowed over time but struggles to acknowledge my mental health struggles. She denies my depression and insists she is the one who suffers, often accusing me of 'abusing' her by not calling frequently enough. The further I progress in therapy, the harder it is to be around her. Therapy has given me distance and clarity, but it's painful to see my childhood with open eyes.

I also feel a strong calling to speak openly about depression. It's important to me that people understand it isn't a one-size-fits-all experience. While there were days when I couldn't leave my bed, I also managed to maintain my studies and work. But that effort came at a cost. I was drained, disconnected from my hobbies, my relationships, and most importantly, myself. I hope one day to feel fully integrated – to look at life without the heavy filter of depression and to feel at home in my own existence. It's a journey, and while it's far from easy, I am learning to believe that I deserve peace.

Anthony

Anthony's story was told by his foster parents and not by him. Anthony lives in Germany, and his life began under difficult circumstances. From an early age, he was confronted with violence, neglect and his parents' drug addiction. These experiences had a deep impact on him and often left him feeling alone.

Anthony was born at the beginning of 2008. He was born prematurely and suffered from foetal alcohol syndrome due to both parents' alcohol and drug addiction. His rectum was connected to his bladder, and after a lateral outlet was placed, two heart defects were operated on. He spent more than half his first year in hospital. After the successful heart operation, the lateral outlet was moved to the anus. However, Anthony's sphincter muscle was not fully attached, so he was incontinent for longer than normal.

Anthony was then able to return home to his mother. His mother then met another man, married him and had a healthy daughter. The stepfather denied Anthony the right to live and treated him very badly, including abusing him. For example, he would put him under a cold shower with his clothes on as punishment. At the age of four, Anthony suffered a severe stroke, which was only diagnosed sometime later, and which had a lasting impact on his life. This caused his condition to deteriorate severely. His right side is affected, especially his head, and through weakening of his tongue, this has had an extreme impact on speech development. The arm and hand are also severely restricted and not recognised by the body structure. The right leg, which is often severely affected in childhood strokes, is only slightly restricted.

At the end of 2012, the situation in the family escalated such that his mother turned to the youth welfare office for help. The youth welfare office immediately removed Anthony from the family and was then faced with the task of finding a placement. In the end, a retirement and care home took him in at short notice, not the ideal option for a 4-year-old child in need of care. His guardian finally managed to place him in the intensive care group of a children's home. This group has a better staffing ratio and looks after children who are due to return to their families. Anthony blossomed here and quickly made up for lost time.

After a while, Anthony realised that the other children sometimes went to their families at the weekends. He was then often left alone with a carer in the group. He didn't receive any visits, neither from his mother nor from his grandmother, who lived in the same neighbourhood. His development began to stagnate and some of what he had already learnt was lost. Anthony's guardian tried to place him in a foster family. Through an acquaintance, she asked his future foster parents whether they could imagine providing a disabled child from the home with outside contact in a kind of sponsorship by taking him on weekend outings and sometimes taking him home with them. After an initial meeting, during which the couple were amazed to see a fit little boy whom they had imagined to be more disabled, Anthony was picked up the following Sunday. The first weekend was followed by others, and after some time, Anthony began to stay overnight from Saturday to Sunday.

The student's son's room was converted into his room. The couple also took over incontinence care at weekends. Anthony still had to wear a nappy because his sphincter was not fully attached. He then came for a few days during the holidays, and finally, the youth welfare office and youth home asked whether the couple could imagine taking him in as a foster son. He now referred to them as his parents to third parties. After a period of consideration and discussions with their own three grown-up children, the couple decided to go ahead and agreed on the summer after their youngest daughter had finished school. The youth welfare office stipulated that one parent must not work full-time. In the summer of 2016, his foster parents took him on holiday to the seaside to get him started. When the couple explained to Anthony that he would now be staying with them full-time, he said to his little cuddly toy tiger, 'now the little tiger has a home'. He has had many appointments, has received occupational therapy, physiotherapy and speech therapy and has developed well. Longer stays in rehabilitation clinics have also brought progress.

The start in the foster family was not easy. Anthony brought with him the knowledge of his difficult past: He knew that drugs and alcohol played a central role in his parents' behaviour. He initially found it difficult to trust and feel safe. However, with the support of the foster family, he slowly learnt to come to terms with his history and build new relationships.

Over time, Anthony's determination to carry on despite his experiences became apparent. He was diligent, learned new behavioural patterns and developed the goal of taking responsibility for his own life. Today, he feels part of a large family, which gives him strength and support.

Despite all the setbacks, Anthony has managed to move on. His experiences have shaped him, but they have also made him stronger. He says of himself: 'You have to admit that you are disadvantaged, but you can still achieve a lot in life.'

Anthony has already achieved a lot in his life: he has flown to America, appeared on television and won the European Championship title for a Fitness without Limits organisation. But there are still unanswered questions that keep Anthony busy. One day, he wants to meet his biological sister and his mother to ask them: 'What exactly happened? Why was I abused? Why did you take drugs?' These questions accompany him as he continues his journey. Anthony also has plans for the future: one day, he would like to write a song lyric or a poem about his life to express and share his experiences.

Today, Anthony lives with a life motto that reflects his development: 'I am who I am, and everybody is okay the way they are'. His story shows that with support from others, determination and a willingness to work on yourself, you can overcome many hurdles.

Julie

Julie had a very troubled childhood, coming from a family with a history of difficulty. She had very strict grandparents, with both of them serving in the army. They were very strict with her mother, causing a lot of unhappiness. Her mother became pregnant in her teens and had a baby (Julie) when the father was in prison. She married the father the day he came out of prison; she was 18 years old.

They were living in social housing. She had another baby the following year and another baby the year after that. Julie was then 3 and the 3rd baby was given up for adoption. They went to live in a caravan. When her mother went out, her father left her alone in the caravan as a young child, left for hours and hours. Juie said that her father behaved in many bad ways, including being a 'peeping Tom'! He had autism and attention deficit hyperactivity disorder (ADHD), was kicked out of the parental home and lived a life of petty crime.

In the first year of life in the caravan, a younger sister was born but the council would not house them. They went to live in a hotel in Cardiff until Julie was 6. Father got involved in guns and robbery and he wasn't allowed in the hotel and went to prison again. Her mother finished with him.

The family went on to a BBC TV programme of current affairs called Nationwide to discuss their homelessness situation and as a result of this, they were contacted by many people to offer housing and so they went to live in a house in Chippenham, Wiltshire in England. Julie stayed in Wiltshire until 2014, for about 40 years! The mother moved into the house with the barman from the hotel in which they had been living. She started being sexually abused at the age of 6 by her mother's partner and this continued until she was 16. After the abuse started, she started going missing from home at the age of 9.

At the age of 9, her mother told her to pack her case and took her to Social Services and gave her up. Julie spent the rest of her childhood in the care system. She was very confused because of the abuse, angry and had feelings of helplessness. She became very aggressive in adolescence and at the age of 12, she would leave the home where she was living and hitchhike to the nearby city of Bath. She was in a school but was expelled for fighting, had a home tutor for a while and was then sent to live in a boarding school. During the school holidays, all the other children went back to their parents, but Julie had to stay on her own at the school. She would run away from the boarding school and when she was 14, her father took her away from the school for 6 months. She then went missing again and the police were looking for her and she went back to the school. All the progress she had made at the school was lost as the school downgraded her privileges. So she gave up and behaved badly. She had run away from school during the exam times and so left school without any qualifications.

She left school at 15 and the social worker took her to live in a bedsit in Swindon. She met a boyfriend and lived with him for 2 years, became pregnant at 16 and had her first baby at 17. The father did not want the child and so moved out of the bedsit. He did not come back on the scene until the baby was 5 years old. She then got into another relationship, which lasted for 10 years and during this time, she had 3 more children. She then had another relationship and another baby.

She had two more children from a following relationship, another relationship which gave her another child, had a relationship with a very abusive man, with whom she had another child and left him for another, who it turned out had mental health problems. Julie has had 8 children, and she has proved to be a very good mother.

One of her sons, who is now aged 24, has been in prison since he was 15. He stabbed someone and was sent to prison for 8 years. This son has had problems with some developmental delay and possibly autism and when he was in primary school, he would regularly escape. It came to the point that Julie had to go to school with him and stay with him until he was 9 years old. This young man had spent time with two of his older brothers, who were persistent young offenders and often in trouble with the police who had observed their criminal behaviours.

When she was in her teens, she worked in a charity and started a club for teenage mothers. When she was 17, she got funding for this club and it became an international charity.

She met someone who she had known at the children's home, who said to her, 'I thought that you would be inside for murder or dead'.

As can be seen, she has had a very difficult childhood and life, relationships with some difficult men and has had many children. She has worked with others in difficult situations and is now looking to go to college to undertake studies she could not do when she was younger. She is very settled now and is a grandmother and a really caring, intelligent woman. She has overcome such a great series of adversities, but says that she has learned from them and they have helped her become the woman she is.

Martha

I was born in 1944, during the war, in a large town in the South of England. My parents moved out of the town 2 years later to a more rural area. We lived in a new bungalow near a small village on an unmade road where the houses were built mostly after the Second World War. In 1947 and subsequently in 1949, I gained two brothers. I was their big sister and we were a happy family. Our parents, who were Christians, regarded church attendance as an important part of their lives. A village about three miles away was larger and this was where I went to school and where we attended a nonconformist chapel. It was a welcoming chapel with some pleasant people we got to know well. There was no Pastor at that time, so the chapel relied on visiting preachers, many of whom were lay preachers. Although I knew no other way of life and I had a pleasant childhood, including involvement in this church, it was a part of my life which I have sometimes struggled with and which caused me some distress over a number of years when I was quite young.

I was brought up to go to Sunday School, which was on a Sunday afternoon and also Sunday morning services, and from the age of seven onwards, even evening services as well. We didn't have a car, so we would cycle or go by bus to church, which meant that Sundays were completely taken up with this involvement.

The difficult memory I have of this period was the Billy Graham Crusade. For those unfamiliar with such an event, a little explanation may be required. Billy Graham held evangelistic crusades in America, whereby he preached about Jesus and attracted many converts with his method of asking people to 'come to the front' to accept Jesus as their Saviour. A team of locally recruited people would be on hand to help out at these events by being there to lead the new converts into churches they could attend and to give them more information about Christianity. He came over to the United Kingdom on a number of occasions to repeat the process here. When I was young, a Crusade was to be held in the nearby town and there were a number of converts who decided they should follow the same procedure as Billy Graham by using similar tactics to acquire new recruits, even if they were campaigning at a church where people attended regularly anyway.

Some of these new Christians came to preach at the chapel we attended and usually in these evening services, which my father thought, at the age of seven or eight, I was old enough to attend. They all followed the same aggressive methods as Billy Graham, standing at the front waiting for any converts to come up. I would feel very embarrassed and uncomfortable and it had a really devastating effect on me. I would go to bed every night and be afraid I would die in my sleep. I would keep getting up and going to see my parents and say, 'I'm afraid I'm going to die'. As this went on for a few years, my parents began to get rather fed up with me. I remember being called a 'silly goose' at some point. My mother arranged for me to see a doctor who tested my heart and told me I was fine. I suppose this may have made me feel a bit better, but I think I knew I was fine. This problem lasted for at least 2 years – possibly longer. Looking back, I think it was mainly relating to the fact that we kept being told, 'This may be your last chance'. In other words, unless you accept Jesus now as your Saviour, you might not get to heaven if you die soon. What a threat! No wonder so many people walked up to the front to be 'saved'. In my church, as far as I remember, nobody ever went up to the front and I sat there tense and sweating, not knowing quite what to do because I certainly didn't feel the call. After all, I was only a child.

Also, a little girl I knew of died suddenly and later, after reading Louisa May Alcott's 'Little Women', I found the death of Beth very upsetting. These two factors added to the anxiety.

A few years later, I would spend Saturday mornings crying without knowing why. I had a friend in the road who had moved away and my two brothers had plenty of friends to play with. I'll never know whether or not it was linked to the previous problem, but my parents saw the need for us to move, as it would also make my father's journey to work much easier. After selling the house and moving to an area nearer a small town, I was much happier, joined various organisations and a new school, and I recovered from these fears. But since this experience, I have always been sceptical of such a coercive evangelical approach to religion of any kind.

To exonerate my father, I should mention something else which happened when I was a teenager and which perhaps gave me a different perspective.

Our new church, which was Baptist but not too evangelical, was liked very much by our parents. I remember my father, with my mother's help, running a Sunday Youth Fellowship. He had this idea that we should get to know how other people worshipped in other churches. So we went to a number of other churches as a group and discussed it afterwards. It was very revealing and started me on the road to realising that everyone is different and that to stay in your own tight little group all your life gives you a very narrow view of the world. From then on, I began to feel that it didn't matter where you worshipped and later on, whether you went anywhere to worship before I did eventually take it up again as a way of living my life, perhaps because it was in me from the start.

Recently, I spoke to my two brothers about my experience. They were surprised, having never heard about it before. I asked them about their earlier experiences and found that although they understood some of the things I was referring to, it hadn't affected them in quite the same way as me. Perhaps our parents had learnt that certain things their eldest child had experienced should not be repeated with the younger children. We'll never know. However, the memory of this still does impact me some 70 years later, although I have come to terms with it.

Gwyneth Lewis

This is the story of the abuse Gwyneth Lewis suffered and as will be seen, it affected her throughout her life. This is recounted in her book 'Nightshade Mother' (2024). It is significant in that there was little physical or sexual abuse, but it had an enormous effect on her and was again intergenerational in that her mother had suffered similar experiences.

Gwyneth Lewis is a significant figure in Welsh cultural life, being the inaugural National Poet of Wales. A highly intelligent and artistic woman, she arrived at this despite a very difficult childhood. This was a childhood where she experienced a great deal of verbal and emotional abuse from one parent, her mother. For Gwyneth, the impact of her mother's emotional abuse lasted a lifetime. Despite a lot of verbal abuse, Gwyneth's parents were financially generous to her and her sister all their lives, especially during the long years of their education. Her mother was also scrupulously even-handed between the sisters, both getting the same, toys, dolls and clothes and so forth, and being a teacher herself (and a good one, according to past pupils), supported them in their education.

The impact of emotional abuse is perhaps underestimated compared to physical and sexual abuse, but when it happens throughout a person's childhood, indeed lasting into adulthood, it has severe consequences. Our parents are the most important influence on our early lives, helping develop our own perceptions of ourselves, our self-belief and self-confidence and, hopefully, a model of how we will then treat other people. We know that a careless or thoughtless remark made when we are young can have an impact far greater than the person issuing that remark realises, but it can have an impact that lasts a lifetime. In therapy, one hears the stories of remarks made, or of negative events that are trivialised that have had a lifetime's impact. Consideration of this needs to be used not only by parents but also teachers and carers. But in Gwyneth's case, it was not just a casual remark but an early lifetime of criticism and rejection.

Gwyneth came from a Welsh-speaking family from Ceredigion in west Wales. Her grandmother, Sarah Ann, whom she describes as 'ferocious', was born in 1894 and lost her first daughter. Sarah Ann then gave birth to another daughter (Megan), a year later and Gwyneth's mother, Eryl, was born 10 years after Megan. Sarah Ann was in poor health for much of her life and Gwyneth was not used to seeing her grandmother fully dressed and without a walking stick. Gwyneth commented that by the time she knew her grandparents, Sarah Ann was bedridden and mean-tempered. Megan, the elder daughter and aunt of Gwyneth, was living in America so that Gwyneth's mother suffered the consequences of her own mother's behaviour alone. One of the interesting things about this is the coincidence of losing siblings as did both Gwyneth's grandmother (Sarah Ann) and her mother (Eryl) and then treating a daughter in such an unpleasant way; such repetition is not unusual.

When Eryl's father, Ben, who had been the carer of Sarah Ann, died, Gwyneth's parents suggested that Sarah Ann come to live with them. Five-year-old Gwyneth was excited to pass on this good news to her grandmother, but received the admonition 'What's all this about?', to which Eryl screamed at the young Gwyneth 'Why on earth did you tell her?', which has stuck in her memory for more than 50 years. The last few years of Sarah Ann's life were spent with Gwyneth's family, and the grandmother did not make things easy for her daughter, with frequent screaming, which affected Gwyneth and her sibling.

From the time she was a young child until she left home, Gwyneth had to suffer her mother's negative and belittling comments. She states that when they were alive, she never addressed her parents by their first names and was not allowed to address them as 'ti' (in Welsh, this is the equivalent of 'tu' in French, i.e. what we call those close to us) but had to address them as 'chi' (vous in French). So, there was a barrier to familiarity established by her mother.

As an adult, her mother would call her a fool for things which were quite everyday, such as feeling disappointed about a commission on which she had worked very hard but for which she did not feel she had appropriate recognition. And when she was a child, her mother mocked her for saying that she loved a new best friend that she had made in school. She feels that she has been 'gaslit' since childhood. Gaslit is a term that describes 'a form of psychological abuse or manipulation in which the abuser attempts to sow self-doubt and confusion in their victim's mind'. This is such an insidious form of abuse, especially to a child, which can lead to a complete lack of self-confidence and self-belief.

Gwyneth describes the sort of language her mother used with her, 'You are totally impractical', 'Oh, what's the use?', 'Get out of my sight'. To have this constant level of abuse is so damaging. Gwyneth admits to having learned this behaviour herself – 'It is catching' – and when riled, she uses it, another example of the intergenerational nature of this form of abuse. But as with her own experience, where Eryl was verbally abused by her own mother and her sister Megan to a lesser degree, Gwyneth describes a moment when she went to Eryl's house when she was not expected. Her sister Marian was expected and Eryl, mistaking Gwyneth for Marian, greeted her in an intimate tone of voice she had not heard before. A tender and confiding conversation continues until Eryl realises her mistake and immediately reverts to her confrontational style. Gwyneth realised how differently her mother treats her from Marian, which must have been devastating for her.

At the age of 5 or 6, she accidentally drops a glass milk bottle which shatters and spreads milk onto her and over the step. Gwyneth attempts to clear it up and asks others for help. Her mother's reaction is wildly inappropriate. Criticising her for dropping the bottle, asking for help from others (what would the neighbours think), she magnifies every aspect of it before she screams, 'Get out of my sight!' Eryl then continues to shout at Gwyneth for this inconsequential accident. As she got older, it became no easier. At the age of 12, when she wanted to go out with her friends at weekends, her mother would make her stay at home and work on schoolwork, despite the fact that she was very successful at school. Eryl's constant chivvying to do more, do better, showed a total lack of trust. She drove her very hard at school, expecting her to always be the best in class, and sometimes taking over her homework. When she wrote poetry for an Eisteddfod (a traditional Welsh festival celebrating language and poetry, including competitions), Eryl pushed her to compete and edited Gwyneth's work.

Eryl also had difficulty with any boyfriend Gwyneth took home. She actively tried to interfere in her relationship with a man with whom Gwyneth had formed a serious relationship and she also interfered with her first boyfriend from college, sometimes putting the phone down on him when he phoned to speak to Gwyneth.

The impact of this early abuse has had a huge impact on Gwyneth. She has had serious migraines for all her adult life, sometimes for most days of the month, and these are crippling, making it very difficult to do anything. She also had a nervous breakdown in her second year at university. When she returned to university after the Christmas break, she ended up in the sick bay, skeletally thin and having serious panic attacks. She also developed a problem with alcohol, becoming an alcoholic, from which she recovered in later life. This again is a not-untypical reaction to continual abuse.

During a conversation near the end of Eryl's life, when she said to Gwyneth, 'I've always treated you and your sister exactly the same', which clearly was not true. Gwyneth challenged it and eventually Eryl said, 'You were always so bright!' suggesting that her mother was maybe intimidated by Gwyneth's intelligence. When Eryl was dying and clearly suffering, she called out for her own mother but commented to a nurse, 'I don't know why I want her, we didn't even get on'. But the last thing she said to Gwyneth on her deathbed was, 'Shut up'. Gwyneth asks the question towards the end of her book, 'What did Eryl want from me?' and her conclusion was that it was herself, she wanted to be Gwyneth.

Despite a childhood of verbal and emotional abuse, Gwyneth has made great success of her life, gaining a first-class degree from the University of Cambridge, teaching at Harvard University in America, becoming a well-renowned poet and being the first National poet of Wales. In her personal life, she has had a happy and successful marriage to Leighton, her very supportive husband. She has achieved extraordinary success given her appalling childhood.

Vivienne

Vivienne is a mixed-race woman now in her 60s. Her father came from Sierra Leone in the 1950s by stowing away on a ship and then joined the Merchant Navy. His ship eventually docked in Butetown in Cardiff, an area of Cardiff that used to support Cardiff docks, once a very busy port. Her grandmother was a white Welsh woman from Gelligaer in the South Wales Valleys, who had married a man from Barbados, and her mother was therefore mixed race.

She was a bright child, always in the A or B stream and early in her life had what she describes as a happy childhood. This began to change because of a lot of domestic violence from her father to her mother, and she remembers at the age of 8 trying to drag her father from her mother, who he was trying to strangle. She frequently had a black eye on a Sunday morning after a night out and had 6 miscarriages as a result of his violence.

At the age of 10, the family moved from Cardiff to Newport, a neighbouring town, some ten miles from Cardiff. Her mother had family in Cardiff, so there was always a safe place for her mother to go, but this was removed when she moved to Newport. Once in Newport, the beatings got worse until, on one occasion, he held a knife to her throat. Her father had been out drinking with friends while her mother was working, and when she got in, she asked him for some money for food for the family. Her father started hitting her mother, then got a knife. Vivienne then ran up the hill to the police station shouting, 'My dad is going to kill my mother, please come'. The policeman told her to go home, eventually turning up at the house. Her mother's eye was swollen and there was blood everywhere, but the father answered the door and said everything was alright, that it was over. The policeman did not ask to see her mother and treated it as a 'domestic' incident. When he had gone, the father started again; her mother managed to get into her car, but the father dragged her out by grabbing her throat and pushing her head into a thorn bush. Her mother got away and went to live with her family in Cardiff.

This was not an uncommon treatment of domestic violence in the 1960s, with little concern for the women involved. Vivienne and her two brothers were then left living with her father. She says she loved him, but he was very strict: you only spoke when you were spoken to. They didn't have much money and although her dad could buy boxing boots for his sons (he was a former boxer and encouraged them), but no money to buy gym shoes for Vivienne for her gymnastics. So she had to withdraw from a competition as she had no appropriate shoes.

When Vivienne was 12 years old, her father's uncle told him he needed a woman to look after the kids. So one day he came back from Manchester with a woman and child, and her father told Vivienne, 'This is your new mother'. Vivienne thought, 'Nobody takes the place of my mother!' The new woman hated Vivienne from the start as she was very jealous of her. She told lies about Vivienne to her father, which resulted in Vivienne being battered by him. She could no longer concentrate at school, and she couldn't take her homework home, so she fell behind academically.

By the age of 13, Vivienne was in care and getting rebellious, missing school and running away. She used to hitch-hike to London, hanging about the streets and shoplifting. The police had picked her up several times and returned her home, only for her to run away again. She was eventually placed in a children's home. At first, she enjoyed the home because staff paid attention to her, which she had not had at home, but she eventually got bored and ran away. She was then placed in a remand home, a secure children's home, met some like-minded girls and ran away again, back to London. This became a pattern for her. When she came to leave the children's home, her social worker found a residential post in an old people's home in Newport. In 1973, while in the care of Social Services and 17 years old, she became pregnant, the job at the old people's home finished and things started going downhill.

She left the home and found herself a bedsit. Here, she started hanging out with people using drugs. She felt at home with these new friends, but didn't use drugs initially; but, after a while, she started experimenting. Before she used drugs, she says that life was an endless cycle of being picked up by social services or the police and nobody cared about how she was. Once she started using drugs, there was something she could control and friends who did not control her. She vowed she would never inject.

Before her pregnancy, she had tried Mandrax (a pharmaceutical synthetic hypnotic drug), and she had also tried 'uppers' (stimulants). She then met a partner who was injecting barbiturates. When the baby was born, Social Services found a place for her at a mother and child home and wanted her to have her son adopted, but she moved back to live with her mother and the baby.

She hadn't used drugs while she was pregnant, but once her son was born, she went back to using drugs and started injecting and subsequently breaking into chemists to get drugs. When her son was 1 year old, she got caught and was sent to a youth detention centre. Interestingly, the two people who broke into the chemists' with her were not sent to prison; they are white, and she is black. While she was in prison, her son was looked after by her family. She was sentenced to 2 years, but because of good behaviour, she only served for 6 months. While she was in detention, she studied and got O levels in English literature and language. When she came out, she went back on drugs for relief of her psychological pain and went back to live with her mother. Drugs were an important part of her life, and she lived by shoplifting and breaking into chemists until her son was 3. Her mother was very controlling and, after years of domestic abuse, became a bully herself. Her son, however, was well looked after and went to school on time. They eventually moved out into their own flat near her mother, where she was heavily into heroin, overdosed a couple of times and was often in court for drug possession and shoplifting.

In 1978, she moved to Manchester and got a job in a burger bar. She loved the job and within 2 months, she had been promoted to supervisor. For 2–3 years, she stopped using drugs, was promoted to manager and sent to Amsterdam to open new burger bars there. Her son had moved with her to Manchester, but couldn't settle, started school and hated it. So he went back to Cardiff to live with his grandmother between the ages of 6 and 10. She took a job as manager of a burger bar in Wales in the early 1980s, which she says was the worst decision she ever made, as the town was 'the drugs capital of Wales!' Vivienne started using heroin again and was arrested for drug use and sacked from her job.

She returned to Cardiff and started being prescribed methadone (a treatment substitute for heroin). For a while, she was using methadone on top of the heroin. In Cardiff, she was using heavily and eventually got arrested again, with the police bursting into the house when her son had just come home from school. Vivienne decided that enough was enough, so she stopped using street drugs, stopped criminal activity and started using her methadone properly. She got referred to a drug treatment clinic, picked up her methadone weekly and followed her reduction programme properly. She was on methadone between 1986 and 1990. She also started volunteering at a youth club.

She was also doing some cleaning work when she was recognised by a manager of a burger bar with whom she had worked before and was offered a job managing a burger bar in Cardiff. While working in this job, she saw an advertisement for trainee black housing officers working for Cardiff County Council. She got the job, another significant moment in her life. She later bought herself a house with a mortgage, also very significant, having been on welfare benefits for most of her life.

Since becoming free from drugs, she has had a number of jobs in the care sector, working with the Children's Society with children who had run away from home or care, who had frequently been sexually abused and turned to drugs or alcohol to cope. She also worked helping disadvantaged people with alcohol problems, with homeless people and helping others recover from addiction problems and has been a very successful and renowned person in this sector in South Wales.

In the course of the work she has done, and because she was recognised as being so effective in what she was doing, she won the prestigious St. David award for citizenship from the Welsh government for her recovery work. Vivienne also designed and delivered drug/alcohol recovery workshops in Sierra Leone, Somaliland and India.

She has met well-known people, including Desmond Tutu, Barack Obama and Prince Charles. She has made an amazing and successful recovery despite an appalling childhood and youth. She had many ACEs, witnessing domestic violence, suffering violence herself, rejection by parents, the effects of racism and a long history of drug use. She was in and out of children's homes from a young age due to domestic violence and her mother escaping to a safe place. Despite an abusive childhood, Vivienne became a success and an inspiration to others.

Ronnie

This was written when Ronnie was in prison.

Ronnie is the older brother of Vivienne.

My childhood was good, growing up with my mother, father and two siblings who were both younger than me. We were looked after, well fed and basically happy with our lot. Around 1965–66, we moved from Cardiff to Newport, settled in a new house and changed schools. I had won a scholarship to a Cardiff grammar school, but the family's move to Newport meant that couldn't happen.

I started a new school, and this is where my first sexual experience with a man took place. This was my art teacher who took an interest in me from the word go. I was aged 12. He made me tuck shop monitor, which meant I would run the shop at break times and while I was putting the stock away, he would come into the stockroom and lock the door. Things went from kissing to anal penetration.

I started missing school and that is where my criminal record started, hanging around with people I shouldn't have. The police came and questioned me over allegations made about the teacher and I told them everything. I had to go to court and give evidence, which ended in him getting a jail sentence. I kept getting into trouble, mainly stealing cars and I got sentences in Approved School and Borstal.

After coming out of Borstal, I met my first wife, Sue, whom I married in March 1974 and went on to have five children, four boys and a girl. My offending against my daughter (sexual abuse) started in 1994, with oral sex taking place in my home in Newport. My first marriage ended, I married again and had three more children, two girls and a boy. I began abusing a 2nd daughter. This was later disclosed by my daughters to my sister Vivienne, who immediately notified the authorities and police. I was sentenced to 12 years.

I am sorry for all the wrong I have done in the past and I hope to lead an offence-free life on my release. Ronnie was released in December 2024.

Caitlin

Caitlin was a First Nations girl, born and raised in a large city in the Prairie provinces. Two of her grandparents attended residential school and another attended an Indian day school. Cailtin's mother had a very disrupted childhood and adolescence, suffering from emotional and physical abuse, as well as sexual abuse from one male relative. She was only 16 when Caitlin was born, and three other children were born in a 10-year period following. When Cailin was 3, her father left the family for good, having been away periodically before that on drinking bouts. When he was at home, there was a great deal of verbal and physical abuse of both mother and children, and at times, the grandparents would become involved in verbal fights.

Once Caitlin's father had left, her mother turned increasingly to the use of drugs, including opioids, for relief from depression and to help deal with her own traumatic memories of abuse. When Caitlin was 9, she was taken into the foster care system, like many other Indigenous children. She stayed briefly with three different foster families, leaving one because of physical abuse by the foster-father and another because of racism towards her (as in many cases, all three of Caitlin's placements were with non-Indigenous families). During this time, Caitlin's self-harm increased and she began to increasingly use razor blades to cut herself.

At the age of 13, she entered a foster home that she liked and where she was clearly liked and, eventually, loved. She had three other female foster children living with her, and she got on reasonably well with them, although there were the usual sorts of fights over hairbrushes and 'stolen' clothes. During this time, she continued to self-harm, to steal from local stores and to run away from home.

She then entered into regular psychotherapy with a therapist whom she came to trust and to like, and to confide some of her experiences of abuse and resulting self-hatred. Her self-harming behaviour decreased markedly. Along with her stabilisation of lifestyle, Caitlin's behaviour in the small school she attended improved. She was given schooling that allowed her to start each subject at her level of ability and was able to work towards catching up to her age level in each.

As Caitlin became more secure in the home and with regular therapy, she expressed much more about herself; her desire for a job doing something creative, for a family of her own, and a house with a garden in the countryside. She started to have dreams of a happy future.

At the age of 15, Caitlin's foster parents were advised that Caitlin would be moved to another home. The rationale for this was that Caitlin was becoming too 'attached' to her foster parents. This reasoning, so common in fostering, is contrary to all that we know about the problems that abused children face with attachment disorder and their need to be able to become attached to safe and loving caregivers. On learning of this imminent move, Caitlin reverted to many of her troubled behaviours: arguing, self-harming, running away, stealing from shops, using a variety of street drugs and giving sexual 'favours' to boys in the local town. On several occasions, her behaviour led to police involvement. On one of the very few visits with her birth mother, now on methadone, Caitlin used some of the opioid and was hospitalised. From this time on, her mood and behaviour began to deteriorate seriously, returning to the level that she had been at when she entered her current foster home.

Caitlin's therapist and foster parents were able to persuade the managers of the foster homes to allow her to remain at her current home until the age of 18 (when all foster children are required to leave that system) and to receive more frequent therapy sessions. Slowly over the following long period, she stabilised, but in this time, she disclosed much more of the childhood events, which had traumatised her as well as her conflicted feelings about her mother. These disclosures were often short in nature, but extremely emotional and draining, and after them, she needed to be reassured that she was safe in the home and cared for.

Before leaving the home, she graduated from her special schooling with a high school certificate and began to look for work to help support her once she was released from the home. At 18, she moved into a shared housing arrangement and worked in a local restaurant. She was given some supportive therapy until the age of 19, in which it was clear she was struggling terribly with fear of being alone and that her anxiety and depression were increasing to the point that she resumed self-harming behaviour and use of street drugs, and involvement with short-term sexual partners and unprotected sex. When she was 19, she experienced her first overdose with the drug fentanyl and lost her job. She experienced racism and harassment by police and the law enforcement system that so many Indigenous people suffer.

Local harm reduction services provided a way for her to stabilise, but her access to the level of therapy that she still needed was limited because of her lack of financial resources or insurance. Over the next few years, her life revolved around her access to harm reduction services and a number of shortlived jobs. At this time, she had a number of overdoses and continued to self-harm. She was fortunate to be able to see a therapist who helped her deal with her childhood and family issues and became stabilised on methadone. Today, she has a regular job and a steady partner but still suffers from mood swings, anxiety and a pervasive sense of insecurity. She struggles with mixed feelings of anger and pity for her mother and her family. Recent short-sighted cutbacks by the government to harm reduction services threaten to undermine some of her current stability.

Sadly, Caitlin's story is rather typical of many young First Nations people raised in a family where there is and has been abuse over generations, but no access to adequate therapy or support. While many of her issues relate to personal abuse and adversity, much of what she and her family and community have undergone and continue to face are the result of socioeconomic issues and discrimination and a failure of society to provide a safety net.

Reference

Lewis, G. (2024). *Nightshade Mother, A Disentangling*. Calon.

Chapter 4

LETTER TO BRESLAU

Maya Lasker-Wallfisch

Independent Therapist, London, UK

Language

There were two languages spoken in our house, one was music and the other was German. I didn't speak either of them. That was the start of the problem.

My parents were both professional musicians. Every day, my father went upstairs in our tiny flat to the attic room to practise the piano. It was forbidden to interrupt him. He would sit playing his piano for at least 8 hours every day. With iron self-discipline, his routine did not falter. Throughout the flat, you could hear him playing. My mother too spent hours every day playing her cello, although not at home. She was always out rehearsing or performing with the English Chamber Orchestra, of which she was a founder member. When she was at home, her cello sat in the corner of the living room, like a briefcase. She picked it up and went out to work with it on most days. When *they* were not playing, it was the turn of my older brother, Raphael. He picked up the ability to play the cello beautifully. He was lucky and extremely talented. He spoke my parents' language.

One of my earliest memories is of hearing my mother talking on our big (or so it seemed to me), black, Bakelite telephone. Though nearly 55 years have passed, that phone number remains lodged in my memory. 'Can Maya come too?' my mother was asking of whoever she was taking to – probably the Conductor of that day's rehearsal for the English Chamber Orchestra. I was taken along, sat on a chair and told to be quiet. The room was filled with music with which I felt I had no connection. On more than one occasion, I was responsible for ruining a Barenboim recording session with the sound of ripping a piece of paper because I had ignored the all-important red light. Not surprisingly, I never felt welcome. I desperately wanted my Mum to be like other mummies, at home and playing with my brother and me. And when I grew a little older, I had to invent an explanation to friends

The Intergenerational Effects of Adverse Childhood Experiences: Ripples on a Pond, First Edition. Edited by Richard Pates and Diane Riley.

Published 2026 by John Wiley & Sons Ltd.

who wanted to know why she seemed to have her telephone number written on her arm.

Being different is most definitely a disadvantage for a child.

I also soon absorbed that everything German was bad. For instance, I was told that German cars were bad. Hearing German unexpectedly being spoken on a bus or a tube train would quickly worsen my mother's mood, making her uneasy and suspicious. But my parents spoke to each other in German. It was the language in which they were intimate. How on earth do you figure that out? I was not able to participate in their conversations. I could not understand what was going on and so I grew up in a state of bewilderment and confusion. Nothing felt safe in my life.

My mother, Anita Lasker-Wallfisch, grew up in Breslau, the youngest of three sisters. She was the cellist in the famous Girls' Orchestra of Auschwitz (*Mädchenorchester von Auschwitz*) who played at the camp gate every morning when the emaciated slave labourers headed off to work in nearby factories. The Orchestra played again when the exhausted work gangs returned in the evenings and they also performed at times for the SS. It was music that kept her alive. Otherwise, she would probably have perished in the death camp along with more than a million others. As a cellist in the orchestra, she was part of a group whose membership ensured her survival…as long as the SS required music.

The Nazis abandoned Auschwitz when the Red Army approached, and my mother was transferred to Bergen-Belsen concentration camp in October 1944. From there, starving and desperately ill, she was liberated by British troops in the last weeks of the war. She soon recovered and when she was eventually able to get out of Germany, the logical place to go was Britain, as she had relatives there.

She arrived in London in March 1946 and began to build a new life. After a few years, she remet my father, Peter Wallfisch. Remarkably, they were not only from Breslau, but they had known each other at school. He had spent the war in Palestine. They married in 1952. Life was not easy for a couple of impoverished classical musicians. My father was an artist and played across Europe and around the world. My mother was the breadwinner, the musician who went out to work every day.

They moved into a small flat off the Portobello Road, then a poor and run-down part of London. Today, it has been gentrified and is super smart. But in the 1950s, we lived above a black family on the ground floor and other immigrants on the first floor. There was no political correctness in those days.

In some rented apartment blocks, there were signs up that said 'No Blacks. No Dogs. No Irish'. Our landlords clearly weren't like that, and we occupied the two floors at the top of the building. My brother Raphael was born in 1953, and I came along 5 years later.

We had a 'char' lady in those days who used to come in regularly to do some cleaning in the flat. We called her 'Icky'. Sometimes she doubled as a babysitter, and I always looked forward with relish to the supper she gave me. Fish fingers and baked beans. This was the sort of English plain fare that

I longed for as a child. Icky was probably the most uncomplicated person I encountered in the first decade of my life. She was a rare species. She lived in even more reduced circumstances than we did, yet I found my occasional visits to her council flat, rather exotic. She was a real cockney, which was becoming increasingly unusual in London in the 1960s.

I soon developed strategies at primary school to make myself liked by the other children. They were vital to my survival. I would buy sweets and share them out. That always made me popular. But it cost money. So I would steal money to buy sweets, in order to buy friends. Usually, I stole money from my mother's purse. Just a few pennies to start with. But I grew bolder and bolder and ended up stealing larger sums. I knew I would be found out, but I went on with it. And, of course, I was found out when I stole a Ten-Shilling note (50p today). My mother said, 'If you admit that you stole the money and tell me the truth, then we can spend the ten shillings together'. I can't now remember if I confessed or not.

By the time I went to secondary school at age 11, we had moved to another part of London, to Willesden. This was supposed to be moving up in the world. It certainly meant that for the first time, I had my own bedroom, which didn't double as the dining room. However, there was a problem within the local Education Authority in that there were not enough places in the local schools, on top of which my school papers got mislaid. As a result, I ended up in a school that I hated. I was bullied and then beaten up as the only white Jewish girl in the school. Things were going from bad to worse.

But throughout all these years, I never knew anything about what my mother had been through. There was never any talk about the camps, about Auschwitz or Belsen, or about what had happened to my grandparents. I had vaguely heard about the Holocaust but had no clear idea about how the Nazis had carried out what they called the Final Solution to the European Jewish 'problem'. In the late 1960s, this was rarely taught in schools in Britain and stories about the Holocaust almost never appeared in television programmes. And at home, there was a code of silence. My mother wrote much later that when she and her sister had gone to Britain in 1946, they wanted to talk about what they had been through. But no one asked them any questions. It was too painful to listen to and as the horror of it defied imagination, people just didn't want to know. She knew that her experiences in the Auschwitz death camp and at Belsen had never really left her. Those experiences had become an integral part of her character. But she closed up and never talked about them.

I must have been about 12 or 13 when I tried to find some cigarettes in the house. Rummaging was by then a common activity of mine and I thought my mother might have some hidden away in a particular cupboard she used in a sideboard in the hall. I knew the sideboard was private, but nevertheless I was desperate for a fag. So I opened the sliding doors and rummaged through them. I couldn't find any cigarettes, but there was a folder in there. I knew it was something personal of my mother's, but I opened it anyway. What I found there was a set of photographs of corpses piled high. Bulldozers were pushing them into a giant grave. There were huge numbers of mostly naked bodies outside wooden huts. I had no idea what they were or what they related to. I knew nothing of the liberation of Belsen by British troops and the discovery of hundreds or thousands of dead and dying inmates … and there was an image that resembled my very own mother. The pictures were awful. At 13, none of these made any sense to me. Why would my mother want to keep such photos and hide them away?

What on earth did it mean? I knew that I wasn't supposed to be looking in the cupboard. I put the photos back in the folder and shut the doors. I never asked her what they were or what they meant. And I was confused about the guilt that I felt – was I wrong in looking for cigarettes or wrong for looking into the hidden folder? My mother never knew that I had discovered the photographs. The silence continued.

My mother has more recently said that she wanted to bring up Raphael and me in a 'normal' atmosphere at home. In fact, 'normal' is one of her favourite words. But how can a home be normal when one parent has been through the trauma that my mother had? She didn't want to tell us about our grandparents, for example. Did we ask about them? Strangely, I don't think we did. There were lovely pictures of them around the house, and they looked beautiful. But my mother didn't want to alarm us or give us nightmares by telling us that they were lying in a mass grave somewhere in Poland, having died a tortured death. As I knew nothing about her earlier life or about how the Nazis had rounded up her parents and taken them away, I didn't have the questions to ask. The silence went on and on throughout my childhood. It was to be nearly 40 years before my mother very bravely began to scribble down memories of what she had been through. That was in the 1980s. The result after many years was a typed manuscript called *My Story* that she gave to Raphael and me 1 year ago for Christmas. It was a strange present. Not one that was on my Christmas list. It became the basis for her book *Inherit the Truth*.

Primary school had been, on the whole, a safe place for me. I performed reasonably well and seemed to get away with only minor misdemeanours. Most significant was that it was the first place I felt secure. The end of this period, when I went on to secondary school, served as the catalyst for my life to spiral out of control.

I went from one secondary school to another. The breakdown in my education not only impacted my capacity to learn but also meant that I had no peer group with whom I could socialise. I was asked to leave Holland Park Comprehensive, where I played truant and was advised by the headmistress that a smaller school would be appropriate. At the time, Holland Park was considered the most progressive school in London, but not progressive enough to tolerate a non-attender. I resisted everything and having exhausted all of the school's efforts to contain me, they expelled me. Eventually, aged 14, a crammer was found in Kensington. It could hardly be described as a school. It consisted of four or five dusty rooms at the top of a four-storey townhouse.

This time, I was in my element. My fellow classmates, of which there were only four, consisted of two titled aristocrats and one French girl. I began to dress wildly, outrageously. I got heavily into rock music. It was the early '70s. Wishbone Ash, Emerson Lake and Palmer, Led Zeppelin and the Doors were my favourites. I played the music loudly from my bedroom. My parents most certainly did not approve. I was also stoned most of the time. My parents were mortified. My voyage into substance abuse had begun. Firstly, it was over-the-counter stimulants. Then I progressed to smoking dope. Then I went on to hallucinogenic drugs like LSD. I didn't particularly like 'acid' or the effect it had, of not being in control. But I persevered anyway. Drugs gave me a sense of identity. I started dealing drugs with my friends. I had missed a lot of schooling and left at age 16 with just one O-Level, about as poor a performance as was possible in Britain at the time.

My father had two great passions. The piano and cats. Cats were to be our only connection; they were conduits to expressing his emotional life. His music students were the envy of my eye. It was in this domain that he demonstrated generosity. Often giving 3-hour lessons rather than the expected 1 hour. Frequently, I was in the adjacent room when a lesson finally came to an end and I would watch my father with the student, smiling, approving and congratulating them. I so longed for that sort of approval. But when they left, he would quickly disappear back into his music room, shut the double doors and continue practising.

My father performed at the Wigmore Hall, a concert hall in central London, annually. I was often tasked with distributing the programmes in the foyer. It was at these occasions that I felt I genuinely was his daughter and could successfully do what was expected of me. He had a ritual before a concert or a recording session, where he would ask me intensely, 'How will I play?' as if I had some influence. Mostly, I responded with what he wanted to hear, but on one occasion, I did not, and I felt horribly responsible and anxious that if he played a wrong note, it would be my fault. I pretty much always felt to blame and soon enough, my behaviour became such that I at least knew, I knew why my father didn't like me.

My father was not equipped with many life skills, which made him very reliant on my mother. I think he found the world both alienating and frightening and I don't think he ever adjusted to British culture. He hated any of the schmoozing that is incumbent upon having a successful musical career and suffered because of it. I think he deeply feared rejection. Contempt and criticism were his defences. Fundamentally, he was not a happy man.

His life was centred around being a concert pianist and so he chose to engage with the world as little as possible. He enjoyed his uncomplicated rituals of posting a letter or going to the local delicatessen. The rest was left to my mother. Whenever he would return from one of his outings, he would proudly show his purchases to my mother and ask her and later me to guess the cost. This guessing game became emblematic of a deep disapproval of anyone else's spending. There could be no pleasure in finding a bargain because it was never cheap enough for him. I don't think my father allowed himself many pleasures in life and because of this, his capacity to understand the needs of others was non-existent.

Whatever was wrong with him, it somehow got absorbed by me and whilst he silently disliked me, I noisily rebelled. This always met with disapproval. Punishment was delivered in various ways.

Shouting, glowering and as I had no room to be sent to, I would on occasion be sent to my father's music room in the attic. This meant I had to pass a curtained-off area at the top of the stairs, which led to his room. My brother had teased me that there were monsters lurking behind the curtain and I believed him. I knew there were monsters somewhere.

On one occasion that I can recall, I found myself being sent up there and whilst in 'time out', I proceeded to scribble angrily all over several sheets of music. This was not well received. 'You're impossible, Maya, a shrew!' My brother commented recently that his memory of me as a child was that I was in a permanent state of bewilderment. He was right. Being 5 years older than me, we didn't have many points of connection. He seemed to manage his world with far greater ease than I could, not unusual among survivor families in the dynamic that one child absorbs the trauma whilst the other seems well integrated.

There are many factors at play here. My mother found it a lot easier to parent a son, and his personality, which was far more stable than mine, seemed to make life easier for him. He was not given the name of a dead or murdered family member and, unconsciously, I think this gave him the freedom to be who he is, rather than a replacement person. I was envious of him for a long time.

Home was not a place I associated with cosy, happy, contented feelings. The atmosphere was predominantly tense and unpredictable. I recall feeling anxious much of the time. I also knew that I had to find ways of dealing with this. The main source of my fears was my mother's absence. On reflection, I must have absorbed a great deal of my father's unhappiness about this too. I felt on the edge of life all the time. Nothing seemed ordinary in our house. There was always talk about music. But I was never part of this. I didn't understand it and couldn't relate to it. Food was not ordinary. Mealtimes were always tense for me and could become traumatic. Silence and glaring looks seemed to be the permanent atmosphere around the dining table. Everything that happened to me seemed to happen in crises. Why was I always so frightened? I knew my mother loved me. But she didn't show it in an ordinary way. She didn't 'do' affection. Now I understand much more about how the brain works and have a language to describe my early experiences. I can see that I was 'hard-wired' as it were from an early age. There were certain parts of my brain, the parts of the brain that today we know deal with depression and anxiety, that were on red alert and very active. Other parts of my brain were slow and sluggish.

For many years, I felt powerless, unable to create a life for myself, always stuck with being known as 'a problem'. I was desperately unhappy. It was very difficult to be in the world. I felt as though I had no skin, nothing to protect me, nothing which enabled me to cope with the usual ups and downs of everyday life. The daily challenges which everyone else seemed to manage perfectly well always hit me hard. How I felt was not compatible with life, yet if not sufficiently brave to take my own life, I had to find ways to exist. This quest for survival manifested at a very young age and could be seen from when I was 2 years old. Throughout the years, my escape routes were varied and extreme and nearly always illicit. I became addicted not just to drugs but to all sorts of things, like shopping. Addictions are all about fixing things from the outside in and so require excessive repetition. But victim mentality is destructive.

Finally, after many years, decades even, I realised what I had to do. I had to build a new relationship with myself and in order to get out of this sense of victimhood, I needed to make a bridge between myself and the past I came out of. I started to think more and more about my grandparents, who they were, what their lives were like in Breslau and what dreadful challenges they faced. Their lives were so different to mine, yet I felt a strong connection. A couple of years ago, on a visit to Germany, I found myself thinking intently about them. I went for a walk by myself in beautiful countryside. As I contemplated their lives, I suddenly realised that I was not just thinking about them, but I was talking out loud to them. I felt that I had established a form of communication with them. I wanted to tell them about their family and what had happened after their deaths, about the remarkable fortitude of their daughters and the lives they had led after the war was over and fascism was defeated. But also, I wanted to tell them about the world today and the new threats we face.

I decided to write to my grandparents even though they had died in 1942. By trying to relate to the past, I felt I could better cope with the present. I started writing that evening, after I got back from my country walk. Here is my first Letter to Breslau.

My Dearest Grandparents

I am your granddaughter, Marianne (Maya), born to Anita Lasker your youngest daughter in 1958.

I arrived 16 years after you were both murdered in Nazi Germany. Your grandson Raphael was born 5 years earlier.

We were both born in London, the city that eventually in 1946 offered your daughters, Anita and Renate, a place to call home.

For too many years, Germany and all that happened there was not spoken of. The silence that sat alongside the 'normal' life that my dear mother tried so hard to create, was despite her best intentions, both impenetrable and confusing ... but more of this later.

I want first to tell you more about your three remarkable daughters, of whom you would be so proud.

I cannot imagine the last days you spent together, although they are well documented, but what I can tell you is that Anita and Renate were both astoundingly dignified and resourceful. These qualities, which I think quite literally 'saved' them, is a tribute to you both.

There are many ways to survive and several ways to no longer exist; but living, and living well, is I think a different matter altogether. To remain optimistic and with desire, speaks to the people your daughters were as you knew them.

The letters that follow are a tribute to you both and a conduit to conversations that we never had; a way for me to have a relationship with you.

All my love
Maya

Chapter 5

THE FORGOTTEN GENERATION, THE WAR CHILDREN IN GERMANY

Sabine Bode

Köln (Cologne), Germany

I consider them as the key generation. These people are now aged from 70 to 85. My work with them started 25 years ago. I asked, 'How are the German war children doing today?', 'How did they cope with their early experiences of violence, bombs, escape, hunger and the death of family members?' and 'To what degree were their later lives affected by these experiences?'

The new issue of the 'war children' is not the horror of war, as research has long established that children particularly suffer under collective violence. What is new, however, is that we are seeing a large group of people who experienced horrendous things in their childhood, most of whom continued for many decades without realising they had experienced something terrible. Until they got older, they didn't have an emotional connection to these experiences and thus failed to recognise the most significant characteristics. When life conditions are continuously unbearable, children survive by strategies of self-pacification to reach emotional numbing. The dictum *An Indian's heart does not know any pain* was helpful as were other convictions of invulnerability gained by Nazi children's groups.

Until a short time ago, the war children in Germany had rarely contemplated that they shared a special fate. Hardly anyone would have said, '*I am a war child*': It was not part of identity. They did not realise their own suffering. Typical quotes: *It did not do us any harm. Our parents suffered a lot. But we? No! We were children! It was normal for us.*

That is the way children think of collective catastrophe. For the large majority, this was never questioned in their later life. They could not *feel* that something really bad had happened to them.

Very little research was done on the late repercussions of the war on the German population. The term 'trauma' was used in reference to victims of National Socialism, mainly Holocaust survivors. Public interest in the subject of 'German war children' simply did not exist. The topic finally gained

The Intergenerational Effects of Adverse Childhood Experiences: Ripples on a Pond, First Edition. Edited by Richard Pates and Diane Riley.

Published 2026 by John Wiley & Sons Ltd.

attention when the first major war children congress took place in Frankfurt in 2005. The public media's concentration on National Socialism in the past was suddenly supplemented by a thematic complex of German history – the terrifying experience of the bombing attacks and displacement from the children's point of view.

There was no lack of contemporary witnesses. For decades, war children had suppressed or distanced themselves from their early traumatisation, but now the time had come to put these experiences into words – memories they had long been unable to communicate. It soon became evident that these encounters with war, violence and the loss of one's home had long-term repercussions, even if they hadn't consciously perceived how they were influenced by them. But now, older or old, many of them have been noticing it and are starting to ask questions. They often deal with these emotions by writing down their childhood memories. Countless numbers of older people are busy writing their memoirs as we speak. Many of their generation have the feeling that they *have to* do it because they find it's becoming more difficult with age to suppress their memories. It is no exaggeration, therefore, to say we are witnessing a 'memory explosion'.

Today, things have changed. Research was done. Several studies have produced similar results: eight to ten percent of those who experienced war and displacement as children now suffer from psychological ailments, in particular, post-traumatic stress disorder (PTSD). In contrast to similar data collected in Switzerland, a country without war, only 0.7 percent of senior citizens suffer from PTSD. Another 25% of older Germans are influenced by the late repercussions to a lesser, but clearly recognisable extent. Many older citizens are full of mistrust, deeply insecure and easily stressed, and consequently, do not wish to be swayed by new experiences or new ideas. This, of course, encumbers contact with the younger generation, and their relationships tend to be less emotional. Changes in living conditions cause them enormous stress. They also tend to think in 'black and white' and have a very strong need for material security.

Research findings have shown that people who have not recovered from their traumas have abnormal cortisol levels, which makes them more prone to stress. Air raids, strafers, the loss of family members, displacement and hunger – all of this causes physical and mental aftereffects.

What we have to consider: Germany, especially West Germany, was extremely busy in the process of coming to terms with the past for 30 years. But it was done academically – mainly the work of historians and publicists. In most families, a voiceless past still reigned. Guilt and shame hindered even the perception of feelings and the dealing with traumatic experiences.

Only a few years ago, the *emotional* process of coming to terms with the past started. And where else should it begin if not in the own family. Which leads me now to the legacy of the children of war children. In Germany, a cultural movement in the age group from 40 to 60 is growing considerably: They call themselves 'war grandchildren' and have begun to challenge family myths by asking parents and grandparents uncomfortable questions and searching in archives. It appears like a late awakening. Due to the silence about family past and the lack of emotions, how memories were passed over to the next generation, the children of war children had been far away from measuring their parents' childhood drama. But 70 years after the end of World War II, quite a number of media presentations focused on the group of 'war grandchildren' and pushed the issue of the aftermath of war in contemporary family relationships.

Mainly, the search starts with a personal crisis that one finds hard to overcome. War grandchildren see their problems in a lack of self-confidence and confidence in life. Problems with making decisions and therefore far away from a self-sufficient life. Problems of fear – until recently not recognised as a heritage from their parents. Strongly dependent on their parents' comments and moods – even when they disagree. Most of war grandchildren say they had a somewhat good childhood, but grew up in a rather cool climate, a family of low temperature relationships. Many war grandchildren today see – as they told me – their life energy blocked, they suffer depression.

Let me quote Merle Hilbk,. born in 1968, a journalist and activist in – what we can call – war grandchildren movement:

They call themselves 'war grandchildren': the children of war children who ask themselves how war experiences shaped their own lives. They have established networks, organised scholarly conferences, discovered Eastern Europe – and changed the perception of the war and post-war history. The war grandchildren follow a long-repressed need; a need that was under a taboo, a taboo on talking about one's suffering, sorrow, feelings of guilt and shame. Their parents and grandparents repressed their pain and sorrow, guilt, shame and fear, and yet these remained present in the form of a latent mood, like a fog lying over everyday life. A fog in which the grandchildren, the children of the 1960s and 1970s affluence grew up, harried by the thought that something was wrong with them. How else can they explain that they were haunted by feelings for which there seemed to be no occasion in their own lives: feelings of homelessness and restlessness, chronic mistrust, fear of commitment and lack of self-esteem?

Time to look closely at one of those families. While I was working on my book 'The Forgotten Generation', (Bode 2005) I always kept thinking back to the Schneiders[1]. In the neighbourhood where I used to live, there were two older people who lived two floors below me and whose children visited them almost daily. The eldest children, in particular, didn't merely look in, but stayed for coffee and talked about their days. They kept talking even while they were saying goodbye in the stairwell. What an unusually close family, I thought. When I mentioned this to Mrs. Schneider once, she replied, beaming, 'Thank God we are an intact family!' She was a small, stout woman with grey curly hair and quick movements. Though our encounters were brief, they were quite informative, so that I eventually learned a great deal about the

[1] All names have been changed.

Schneider clan. Their conversations primarily dealt with matters of everyday life. Willingness to help was the largest common denominator. Nobody was left in the cold – if someone's car broke down, if someone was laid off or their spouse left them.

The father was an administrative officer now in early retirement – heart problems and a heart attack patient. I learned later that the family tried to keep bad news away from him if possible. The children didn't regard their mother, a housewife, as especially hardy either. Whenever they broached a difficult topic in her presence, tears would well up in her eyes. I even witnessed this myself on occasion, for example, when I told her that the flower shop on the corner was going to close. Apparently, she couldn't be confronted with anything negative. Not even 'problematic films' on television. She could find relaxation in quiet music, crossword puzzles and novel collections by Reader's Digest. She was a sweet, warm-hearted person. No one wanted to hurt her. And so things were kept from her.

I suppose the Schneiders' tragedy was that the mother kept everyone in check. She was the one who decided which topics were allowed and which ones weren't. It was definitely not allowed to openly discuss – although all the children knew about it – the fact that the daughter was scraping by because she was always lending her lover considerable amounts of money to keep him afloat. For her parents, 'their Doris' was someone who simply couldn't manage money, and they willingly balanced her bank account.

And no one ever dared to say aloud what the father might have surmised and what the three siblings knew for sure, namely that the younger son was taking drugs on a regular basis. One night, when I met him at the corner pub, Klaus told me why: 'I can only bear the atmosphere at the family table when I'm high'. Which is why he was the only child who occasionally didn't participate in the ritual. But only with a lame excuse, never in terms of clarifying distance. Looking at him, you wouldn't know he had a drug addiction. An inconspicuous, conventionally dressed man in his mid-thirties, an insurance agent, married, no kids.

The other siblings had no children either and were all divorced. They all seemed to have bad luck when it came to relationships. Each of their former spouses had been affectionately welcomed into the family. They were practically showered with attention and willingness to help. But when the marriages failed, the daughters- and sons-in-law were cut out of the family at once. They received the blame that the relationships didn't hold. And anyone who didn't toe the Schneiders' line one hundred percent quickly fell into disfavour.

As Klaus, the younger son, revealed during our chats at the pub, the Schneiders always saw the causes of failure outside of the family. And this provided plenty of topics for conversation at the dinner table when everyone would get riled up about how rudely someone had behaved, how unfair the son's boss was, how their daughter's department head put her down, how the world was bad and why a Leftist-Green government would be a catastrophe for Germany. Suddenly, all of these friendly, upstanding people revealed their hostile, resentful characters. A family fortress, arrows flying from every battlement.

One day, I helped the older son tow his car to a garage. They told us they would repair the car immediately; we could wait there. Peter came across as rather shy. When I asked him what he did for a living, he sidestepped the question and mumbled something about import-export. I had learned from Klaus that their parents had never quite understood why not one of their children had become an academic. After all, the mother and father graduated with an *Abitur*, but their three children only achieved the intermediate levels. 'Tears immediately well up in mother's eyes when she talks about the difficulties we used to have in school', Klaus had told me. He was with her when an acquaintance asked her what the reason might be for her children's failure at school. She replied, 'They were probably late bloomers ...' All three of them? How could that be possible?

Mrs. Schneider came from the Sudetenland (today part of Czechia). She was forced to flee with her family when she was 5 years old. Her husband, 3 years older than her, had been a child refugee from Silesia and had survived the destruction of Dresden. As one can easily imagine, the parents' wartime childhood was also a taboo subject in the family. The two sons and daughter would never have imagined that they might be burdened by their parents' past. When I dropped a comment to Klaus to this effect, he immediately changed the subject. Obviously, all of the Schneiders played 'Blind Man's Buff' – with serious consequences.

None of the three adult children ended up leading a self-sufficient life of their own. The younger son took drugs, the daughter deceived her parents, the older son lost his job twice in 1 year, the mother was always on the verge of tears and the father would die soon. And everyone firmly clung to the belief: 'Thank God we are an intact family!'

A stressed family as it appears to me. A castle family, a very common pattern found in families with expulsion and other trauma experiences: Belonging to a castle family may cause extreme difficulties when trying to become independent from the parents. Those who long for individual ways tend to suffer from strong feelings of guilt. Once they dare to cross the border, they may be kicked out of the castle.

What I prefer are harbour families. They say: 'Our harbour is safe – but gives us a chance to meet foreigners. That is what we need for personal growth and good business. Daughters and sons being raised in harbour families continue appreciating their parents' opinions. As adults, they like to confer with them. They want to communicate details before making high-level decisions. Thus, they enjoy coming back home to make – what I call – a harbour tour'.

Only a short time ago, I got to know a woman, maybe 40 years old. She talked to the audience with a Polish accent. Her family was of German descent and left Poland only a couple of years ago. She said she always thought she was a person of 'disorder'; and had a number of health problems, for example, deafness in one ear. After having read 'The Forgotten Generation', her understanding of problems and talking about her family's past started.

All members began feeling better and experienced a healing of relationships. For the first time in his life, the father talked about his own childhood. Being a little boy, he only spoke German, no Polish – thus he was forced to visit a school for deaf-mute children. The daughter told us: 'Being able to communicate and reflect made a break free for all of us in the family. I myself have fewer health problems, my ear healed, today I can hear well'. And she added: 'I am so happy I am living in Germany, otherwise I would not have learned that I am a war grandchild'. I told her that in the meantime, the term 'war grandchild' has crossed the border and is now existing in the Polish language.

They call themselves 'war grandchildren' and ask not-yet-been-answered questions about their own identity. How did I become the person I am today? Where are my roots? Which fears have I taken on from my parents and grandparents; and which talents? As a result of this process, it is not unusual for the children of war children to know more about their parents than the parents know about themselves.

Reference

Bode, S. (2005). *The Forgotten Generation, Children of war beak their silence, (Die Vergessene generation, Die Kriegskinder brechen ihr schweigen)*. Piper Verlag.

Chapter 6

WRITING AS THERAPY FOR MY DEEP PERSONAL TRAUMA

Alison Knight

Fiction author, Somerset, UK

On Monday, September 15th, 1969, my father, unable to cope with the fact that my mother had left him for her married boss, confronted them in the offices where they worked. Minutes later, my mother was dead, her lover was injured, and my father followed my mother into the next world by throwing himself from a fifth-floor window. I was in another room in the same building and heard my father's fall, although I didn't realise that's what it was at the time.

It was just 3 weeks after my 10th birthday in an era when children weren't privy to what went on in grown-ups' lives. The first I knew of anything being wrong was a few days before, when my mother had packed my things and taken me with her to be with this man, whom I didn't know, leaving my beloved Daddy behind.

What followed was a confusion of fear, disbelief and heartbreak. I had loved both of my parents equally and had been devastated to be separated from my father. On being told of their deaths, the thought that I would never see either of them again was more than I could comprehend.

The extended family around me were drowning in their own grief and would stop speaking as soon as I entered the room. None of them wanted to upset me and so began many years in which they were reluctant to talk about my parents in my presence. For me, it seemed as though, with their deaths, all trace of them had been wiped from the earth. At the same time, seeing my grandparents weeping left me distraught, so I tried to act as though I was alright so that I didn't upset them further. I would lock myself in the toilet to cry.

When it was decided that I couldn't go to their joint funeral, I began to wonder whether they had really died or not. Maybe, I thought, they were really alive and just needed some time together away from me and my 18-year-old sister in order to work out their problems. I began to look for them everywhere I went, expecting to see them open their arms to me the moment we were reunited. But, of course, it never happened, and in the meantime, no one would talk to me about what had happened. I finally managed

The Intergenerational Effects of Adverse Childhood Experiences: Ripples on a Pond, First Edition. Edited by Richard Pates and Diane Riley.

Published 2026 by John Wiley & Sons Ltd.

to get my sister to tell me that Dad had stabbed Mum and her lover before he jumped to his death and I realised that I had heard his final moments. To this day, I can't watch a scene where someone falls from a building. It immediately takes me back to that moment and terrible sound. None of us realised that was the first sign of post-traumatic stress disorder (PTSD).

We stayed with our maternal grandparents for a while, fussed over by our grieving aunts. But it wasn't practical for us to stay there permanently and for a while, I was convinced that I was going to be sent to an orphanage and lose the whole of my extended family. I couldn't voice that fear because I was afraid they would confirm it. But thankfully, it never happened. I wasn't aware at the time, but the grown-ups were actually arguing over who was going to look after me. Apparently, it was decided by the Family Court because my parents hadn't made wills or named guardians. I knew nothing of the proceedings because in the 1960s, children weren't consulted when life-changing decisions were being made on their behalf. I'm thankful that today children have a say in their destiny.

In later life, I campaigned on behalf of a charity called Will Aid to encourage parents to make wills and appoint guardians for their young children and I used my experience of uncertainty and fear in the middle of the terrible grief of being orphaned to persuade people that they really should do something to safeguard their children. It was tough to do, but worth it. I was interviewed on various radio shows, including BBC Radio 4's *You and Yours* programme, and Will Aid reported that they got 20,000 enquiries as a result.

Eventually – it was probably a matter of days, but I honestly can't remember much about that time – we went to live with one of our father's brothers. It was decided on the basis that my uncle had been very close to my parents and was married to Mum's lifelong best friend. They already had six children of their own in a four-bedroomed house, so we were squeezed in with our cousins. My sister, being legally an adult, left within a year. She and I had never been particularly close because of the 8-year age gap, but her leaving felt like another abandonment. I was absorbed into my cousins' family and told to tell people I was their sister. If anyone who knew I wasn't their sister asked about my parents, I was to tell them they died in an accident.

I remember just one visit from a social worker. She never spoke to me, and I don't think she even looked at me. If she had, I'm not sure what I would have said. I was unhappy, of course I was. I loved my cousins, but I wanted to have my old life back. But I still had that fear that, if I wasn't good, I'd be sent to an orphanage, so I was on my best behaviour at all times. There was no such thing as counselling in those days. You just got on with it. I locked what had happened away in a virtual box, never talking about it for many years.

We muddled along like that for 8 years. Once my sister left, I shared a room with the two youngest girls, who were several years younger than me. One of them, who had been three when I moved in, resented me, but it wasn't until decades later that we realised why. While the rest of us were at school, she and her baby sister had gone with their parents to my old family home to clear it. She hadn't known what was happening, but was aware that her mum and dad were crying as they sorted through my parents' things. In her infant mind, she associated their distress with me, whose house they were in, and from then on, she hated me. Thirty years later, she made the link while receiving counselling for an unrelated matter and explained this to me.

So, how did I cope?

- As already mentioned, **I was on my best behaviour**, never daring to rebel or cause trouble in case I was sent away.
- **I learned not to ask anything about my parents** – something I regret now, but having seen grown-ups crying around me just after my parents died, I was reluctant to upset them again.
- **I didn't give up looking for my parents** in crowded streets for a long time, but eventually accepted that I was never going to see them again.
- **I decided to count my blessings.** I was fortunate that, despite the nature of their deaths, both sides of my family kept in touch with me. I realised that I had become someone extra special amongst my relatives. I had 26 first cousins in my extended family. After what happened, I stood out from the crowd, and I knew that everyone cared about what happened to me. It wasn't the same as having my parents, but I clung to the fact that I was important to people.
- **I wanted to make my parents proud.** I had to believe that they were watching over me somewhere in the universe, so I tried to fulfil the dreams my mother, in particular, had had for me – do well at school, get a good job, travel the world, etc.
- **I decided to be a survivor, not a victim.** This was in contrast to my sister, who chose the path of a victim. She turned her back on the family, entered an abusive marriage (she eventually married three times), and once said to me, 'With my background I can get away with anything'. She was talking about how, if she was arrested for handling the stolen goods her then husband had brought into their home, she could use the my-dad-killed-my-mum-and-left-me-an-orphan card to garner sympathy. At that moment, I vowed I would live my life well, in spite of what happened, and I would never, ever use it as an excuse for anything that went wrong in my life.

Those strategies kept me going through my teens and twenties. I had a few blips. My mother had wanted me to go to grammar school, but my aunt and uncle couldn't afford to send me – and anyway, my uncle, like many men at that time, thought that too much education wasn't good for a girl. I was sent to the local girls' comprehensive school, where I did alright anyway. I was also reunited with an old friend – someone outside of the family who had known my mum and dad. At school, we could talk about them, keeping them alive in my mind, although she had no more understanding than I of why it had happened. We agreed that my parents had seemed perfectly happy, there had been no clues that they were drifting apart or that my mother would fall in love with another man and my father wouldn't be able to live without her. We remembered how beautiful and elegant Mum was and what fun we had with Dad, who was, until the very end, a happy-go-lucky chap that everyone loved.

I had a few boyfriends while I was at secondary school. I told one about what had happened to my parents. He didn't say anything at the time, but I later learned that he hadn't believed me, and he dumped me because of it. I became a bit more cautious about who I told after that. Years later, another boyfriend went so far as to visit the newspaper archives to check out my story because he hadn't believed me. When he confessed and apologised, I dumped him because I would never lie about something like that and if he didn't know that, then we weren't right for each other.

After O levels, I wanted to do A levels and go to university and my teachers encouraged me. But my uncle put his foot down. I must find a job in a shop or a bank that didn't need any more book learning. He expected me to be married and have a family, so staying at school would all be a waste of time. I was devastated, desperate to fulfil my mother's wish that I get a good education and have a career, but he wouldn't be swayed – in fact, he said it was getting a 'fancy job' that had 'ruined' my mother and caused his brother's death. Without A levels, I hadn't a hope. I was scared I'd never be able to support myself – something that was becoming increasingly important to me as I approached adulthood. My uncle's veto over my plans left me feeling isolated and helpless.

But my uncle hadn't reckoned on my teachers. They persuaded him to let me take a secretarial course at a local college. What he didn't realise was that it was a 2-year intensive course which, as well as secretarial qualifications, led to an OND in Business Studies and an A Level in Law. This, I was quietly assured, would be enough to get into university once I was eighteen and able to make decisions for myself. I left college armed with qualifications and choices and an offer of a place at Oxford Polytechnic to study Business.

But my underlying insecurity and feelings of vulnerability got the better of me. I was all set to go to Oxford and arranged to spend the summer before my course started living with another aunt – my mother's youngest sister – and her family in Swindon. It was close enough that I could get a bus to Oxford and prepare to start my course. Using my secretarial skills, I got some temp work in a solicitor's office in Swindon to earn some money before the beginning of term. When they offered me a job as a trainee legal executive, I had a hard choice to make.

I had no formal means of support once I had turned 18, and I had to weigh up whether it was sensible to be a student, living on a grant with no guarantee of a job at the end of a 4-year course, or accept the job offer so that I would be earning a living while learning a profession. The fact that my mother had been a legal cashier in a law firm in the City persuaded me that my mother would be proud of me following in her footsteps. I stayed in Swindon and worked in the legal profession for 13 years. But in the back of my mind, I started to wonder whether I was trying to live Mum's life for her. I didn't want to be her. I just wanted to feel secure and able to support myself.

At 19, I got engaged to a teacher. I took him to meet the family in London. To my surprise, my aunt took me aside and referenced my mother for the first time in years. 'I know your mum would say this', she said, 'so I'm going to say it for her. If you change your mind about marrying this man – even if it's at the church door – you only have to say so and it will be alright. You don't have to do anything you don't want to'.

I was stunned. I'd been sure that my mum would have been thrilled that I was getting married to a teacher – someone with a degree and good prospects. I laughed it off, until 6 weeks before the wedding, I realised that this man was controlling and wanted to restrict my life in ways I didn't feel comfortable with. I realised that my life had been controlled and restricted ever since my parents had died and I needed to take control myself. I called the wedding off and went to London to tell the family. I was afraid they'd be angry, but actually they were relieved. For the first time, I felt supported and able to make my own decisions.

Changing my path in such a drastic way was hard for me and I was afraid of what the future held. I felt very isolated and vulnerable. I was desperate for the security of a family of my own, but I needed to know that my life partner loved and respected me for who I was, not who they wanted me to be.

Fate is a strange thing. Three weeks after calling the wedding off, I met the man who is now my husband. The relationship was completely different to the one I'd ended and within 6 weeks, we were living together. He was the son of an East End couple, his father was a career soldier – an officer, and his mum was a former seamstress like my own mother. He was a petrol-head, like my chauffeur father, and was working in the motor trade. My whole family loved him and more than one of them said how my parents would have approved of him (something they never said about my former fiancé). Even a decade after losing my parents, I still wanted to please them. Thankfully, though, this time I'd chosen a good man, and we're still married after 44 years together.

Life was good. We married in 1982, had a son in 1985 and a daughter in 1992. It was the year before the birth of our daughter that things started to go wrong for me. I had what I refer to as my *annus horribilis*. As I later wrote, you don't have to be royal to have a crap year. (Knight 2012). In fact, that particular piece of writing was the first time I had gone public about the effects of my parents' deaths on me. It won a prize in a competition. Apparently, it made the judges cry.

In the space of a few weeks in 1991, I lost a friend to cancer, was made redundant, my husband's grandmother died, and I suffered a miscarriage. My life began to spiral. I ate for comfort and put on a huge amount of weight. I became anxious, didn't sleep well, my old feelings of isolation and vulnerability returned, and I suffered badly with IBS. I went back to my GP time and again, but nothing helped. For the next few years, with a new baby and a school-age child, I worked at home as a registered childminder – my ever-present need to earn my own money keeping me going. It was hard. My symptoms didn't ease, but I had to carry on; I didn't dare give in to the overwhelming feelings that were threatening to take over my life.

It was years before we got to the bottom of it all, and even then, I missed an opportunity to get help.

The psychiatrist Dr Dora Black was interviewed on Radio 4 on the morning radio. She described her work at the Traumatic Stress Clinic in London, dealing with children who had lost a parent at the hands of the other parent. She mentioned that the work was so new that they had no idea what the future held for these children in terms of their mental health. I contacted her clinic and said, 'It happened to me twenty years ago. Can I help with your research?'

One of her researchers interviewed me. After a couple of hours' conversation, she asked me if I'd like some help from the clinic. I was shocked. I'd spent the afternoon telling her how well I'd done with my life after the trauma of my parents' deaths, and she was offering me psychiatric help? I laughed it off, saying thank you, but I don't need it.

I struggled on for another few years. By now, my daughter was at school, and I was working for a children's charity as a legacy officer. I didn't talk about my background until one day at an event, a social worker mentioned two children whose father was in prison for the murder of their mother. Their maternal grandmother was trying to ensure that they couldn't have any contact with him, while the charity was trying to find a way to ensure they maintained a relationship with him. Some of the audience were incensed, demanding that the children be kept away from this monster. I couldn't stay silent. I stood and explained that I had lost my mother in the same way these children had. If my father had lived, even if he'd been sent to prison, I would have been desperate to see him. Because he wasn't a monster. He was my daddy, a good father whom I loved. But he was also a man who'd found himself in a situation he couldn't cope with and he'd done something terrible that I know he would have regretted because he'd adored my mother (which is, I'm sure, why he immediately committed suicide). I asked these people to imagine how those children felt. If their father, like mine, had never shown any violence towards the family prior to this, was it really fair to deprive them of contact with their surviving parent after losing their mother?

That incident made me realise that everyone who heard the bare bones of my story would assume my father was a violent monster. I hated that. It planted a seed within me to tell their story properly in one day. But I wasn't in the right place then, so I struggled on a bit longer until I discovered Dora Black's book (Black et al. 1993) and her documentary.

I watched it on my own, seeing her working with young children who were, I could see, being torn between their love of their father in prison and their grandmother, who was now their guardian. I could read their expressions and their body language and recognised myself in them. It made my heart ache for them all. The next subject was a woman in her late twenties who had witnessed her mother's death when she was 4 years old. Like me, she had got on with life within her extended family, never referencing the trauma, until one day she began suffering from worrying symptoms – all of which mirrored my own. I heard Dora Black say that the young woman was suffering from Delayed Post-Traumatic Stress Disorder and would need a course of counselling to help her deal with her childhood trauma.

The next day, I walked into my GP's office and told him about my parents and the TV documentary. He reached for his phone and called the Traumatic Stress Clinic, relieved, I think, to at last have a diagnosis for me.

I travelled to London, not knowing what to expect. My counsellor simply asked me what had happened on the day my parents died. It was the equivalent of Aladdin saying 'open sesame'. No one had ever asked me that question before. Suddenly, all those long-buried memories emerged, playing out in my mind like a movie. I talked for 2 or 3 hours straight, pouring out of me. It had been 27 years since that awful day, but it came back to me as though I was living it all over again.

Thus began years of counselling, first at the Traumatic Stress Clinic, and later with more local psychologists. It was hard. After years of keeping silent, years of denying that I was any different from anyone else, I had to bring it out and examine it in detail, learn to accept it, to allow myself to grieve, to learn to live with the reality of what had happened and its aftermath. It was hard. So hard, not only for me but for my husband and children.

I naively thought that having counselling would make it all better, but of course, it's not a miracle cure. It doesn't change what happened. However, it changed my perception of myself. I learned about the things that trigger me (e.g. falling men, feeling helpless, fear of being unable to support myself financially), and my coping mechanisms (avoidance, comfort eating, always having a means of earning a living). I recognised my feelings of abandonment and the need to be loved and respected. I learned that I'm stronger than I thought I was. I counted my blessings.

Is that the end of my story? No! Remember that I mentioned I won a writing prize and how I spoke up at the charity event? Both of those things led me to the best and hardest therapy of all.

I'd always regretted choosing not to go to university, even though I've done alright for myself without a degree. So, in my mid-forties, with my daughter talking about going to university, I decided that I wanted to do it, too. But this time round, I didn't need a degree to lead to a career, so I decided to study creative writing – something I'd always been interested in. We still had a mortgage, and I couldn't give up my job, so I enrolled as a part-time student. I had been trying to write romance – something uplifting and with a happy ending. But I also started to work out how to best tell my parents' story so that my children and future generations could see them as real people, not monsters and victims, or simply statistics.

It took me nearly a decade to earn a first-class degree and then a master's in creative writing and in that time, I began to write their story. A year later, I got my first publishing contract for two romances and a time-travel adventure. But my family story was rejected time and time again. It was finally published as a novel by a small press in 2020 (Knight 2020) on what would have been my mother's 90th birthday. Following the closure of that press, it was reissued under my new pen name in October 2024 (Ellis 2024) by my current publisher.

Having lived with this story since 1969, I learned some valuable lessons by writing it as a novel.

- First, I chose to write the story of the last year of their lives, ending it with their deaths, rather than continuing into the aftermath. I did this because, first, to attempt to understand what happened, and secondly, I wanted it to be *their* story, not mine. I had seen the 1980s trend for 'misery-lit' and did not want it to end up categorised as a writer of *My Tragic Life Story*. Something tragic happened, but that doesn't make my whole life a tragedy.
- I wrote it as a novel, mainly because I wasn't able to find out for sure about certain aspects of the story – how the affair started, how long it continued, how my father found out about it, etc. I knew I had to fill in those gaps and chose to do it with fiction based on what I knew of the people involved and the culture of the time, including the post-war class system, sexual politics and life in general in the late 1960s.
- I realised that, when thinking about it, my reactions were always those of the 10-year-old child I had been then – confusion, fear, lack of understanding. By making those involved fictional characters based on the real people (including myself as a child), I had to do what I do with all of the fictional characters I write about – to put myself in their shoes, in their minds, and learn what made them tick. This made me step back and look at them and the situation with an adult's perspective for the first time in my life. I was finally able to put aside my inner child's emotions and focus on the motivations and desires of the adults involved. And I began to understand why it happened the way it did. They were victims of their time, when society was changing rapidly. They embraced those changes in different ways and were taken in different directions.
- I will never know the real truth, other than those parts of the story that I witnessed personally or are a matter of public record. I studied newspaper reports, many of which contradicted each other or were simply wrong. I was given access to the inquest files at the City of London Coroner's Office. Again, contradictions in witness statements highlight that different people recorded different things at the time – some of which differ from my own memories of that day. This has shown me that writing this as a novel – as my imagining of what might have happened – was the right thing to do and I have made my peace with that.

Has it 'cured' me? Of course not. I will live with PTSD for the rest of my life, but that's part of who I am. I recognise it and accept it. I recognise my triggers and know when I need to take care of myself. I can still function successfully and few people who don't know my story would guess that I have lived with this trauma for so long. But these days I feel a stronger sense of peace, albeit tinged with sadness that my parents' lives were cut short and they never got to see me grow up, marry, have children and now grandchildren.

But at least my writing means that their story has been told and generations to come will have the opportunity to get to know the real people behind the awful tragedy.

References

Black, D., Harris Hendrik, J., and Kaplan, T. (1993). *When Father Kills Mother.* London: Routledge.

Ellis, M. (2024). *Lily's Choice.* London: Boldwood Books.

Knight, A. (2012). *A Flawed Reflection, pp174–176 in the Body Gossip anthology compiled by Ruth Rogers and Natasha Devon.* London: Rickshaw Publishing.

Knight, A. (2020). *Mine – What's Mine I Keep.* Darkstroke: Crooked Cat Books.

Chapter 7

THE ABERFAN DISASTER

Gaynor Madgwick

Merthyr Tydfil, UK

A catastrophic collapse of coal waste, the Aberfan mining disaster remains one of the darkest chapters in British history, one of unimaginable loss and profound sorrow but also of resilience and the enduring strength of a community united in grief.

Merthyr Vale Colliery was the largest pit in the South Wales Coalfield, generating vast amounts of waste. The waste was dumped in spoil tips directly above Pantglas Junior School and the neighbouring County Secondary School, houses, farms and the village. There were seven spoil tips on the hills above Aberfan; Tip 7 – the one that slipped onto the village at the time of the disaster – was 111 ft (34 m) high. The tip had been created on a mountain slope and overlaid a natural spring. After 3 weeks of heavy rain, the tip was saturated and approximately 140,000 cubic yards (110,000 m^3) of spoil debris began to move rapidly, sliding 700 yards, and avalanching down the mountain as liquefied material, destroying two farm buildings and killing the occupants. Hitting the disused canal, the flow destroyed and fractured two water mains buried in the embankment, and the additional water further saturated the spoil. It then leapt over the old railway embankment onto the village.

The landslide destroyed Pantglas Junior School, 18 houses, nearby roads, a farm and part of the neighbouring County Secondary School, before finally coming to rest on Aberfan Road at 09:15 am. After the disaster, a tribunal concluded that the accident 'could and should have been prevented'. The tribunal also blamed the National Coal Board (NCB) for the catastrophe, as it had failed to heed warnings about the coal waste tip. To date, neither the NCB nor any of its employees have been prosecuted, nor has the organisation received any fines. A local doctor later wrote, 'By every statistic, patients seen, prescriptions written increased, deaths, I can prove that this is a village of excessive sickness'.

I am a survivor of the Aberfan disaster of what would have been the last day of the school term. My only brother, Carl and my sister Marylyn both lives

The Intergenerational Effects of Adverse Childhood Experiences: Ripples on a Pond, First Edition. Edited by Richard Pates and Diane Riley.

Published 2026 by John Wiley & Sons Ltd.

were traumatically taken that dreadful day when 116 children and 28 adults lost their lives. I was just 8 years old, 'a survivor', some would say a 'victim', some would say, 'I am lucky I survived'. Many survivors of tragedies would celebrate their lives, living them to the full (being given a second chance?) The death of my two siblings and my friends, myself seriously injured, I was handed a life sentence that, from day one, has been filled with trauma. Left with a wounded heart, manifested in a kaleidoscope of physical and mental behaviours that have echoed long after the trauma I experienced. Like ripples in a pond, the effects of my childhood suffering have spread, touching every aspect of my young life and persisting well into adulthood, and will remain until I die.

Life before the Aberfan disaster

I was born Gaynor Minett, my parents Iris and Cliff, and five siblings. I was 8 years old, Carl (the only boy) was 7 years, Marylyn 10 years, Belinda 12 years, Michele 5 years and our baby sister Sian 6 months, one perfect family. We were the happiest, loving family any child could ever wish for, money was very tight, clothes were handed down to the next sibling, one pair of best shoes, the other school shoes, many times mam would take us to the local cobblers in Aberfan Road to mend our shoes when a hole appeared or to renew the sole.

We lived in a terraced three-storey house called Bryntaf, in Aberfan, with a full view of the huge seven tips that stood high, separated by the cemetery wall. Growing up in a mining village, the tips were part of our heritage, as children, we took for granted what horror they would pose. My family lived in the middle and front room; we all lived mainly in a small 12 × 12 square living room, where mam cooked and a table was placed under the window, with chairs on each side. We could sit and look at the view of the Taff Trail and Merthyr Vale colliery, where the mining tipping gangs would carry all the coal slag waste (spoil) from the mines onto trams and take the black waste several times a day up to the tips. The sofa was in the middle of the room facing the coal fire, having no central heating, we used to huddle together to keep warm. Baby Sian was in her pram or cwtched (hugged), wrapped in the Welsh shawl by mam.

The tall pull-down cupboard where mam kept all her food (considered retro now) stood beside the bosh (sink), there was no room to play, our play area was the passage, (snakes and ladders, dicky stones, fuzzy felt). We had no television, our treat was going into our neighbours to watch *Twizzle*, *The Wooden Tops* and *Bill and Ben*. Our childhood was fun. We slept 3 to a bed, I slept with Belinda and Marylyn, our beds were tight up against each other (looking back now, how lucky was I to have the closeness, affection and love of my family during Carl's and Marylyn's short lives).

Our toilet was outside in our garden, an old wooden bench toilet dad had made. We were always scared of the spiders and cobwebs, mam would shine a torch to take us to the toilet and wait outside, toilet paper was 'newspapers' cut up in squares and hung by a rope (I cannot imagine children using these now).

Dad and mam had dreams of building their own bungalow. Dad bought a plot of land, opposite the cemetery, mam, dad, and us siblings all helping to build the foundations, all excited to move to our new home. After the disaster struck, dad didn't have any strength to finish building, leaving the foundations idle for many years. The bungalow was later built in memory of Carl and Marylyn, 'Carlyn Bungalow', where our teenage years and new family life began.

Mam washed all our clothes in the basement, many hours squeezing the water with a mangle, but they were soaking wet when she tried to hang them on the line. Mam was a stay-at-home housewife. Dad had his own quarry business where he made breeze blocks, contracting out for demolition work. With his small yellow truck picking up coal chippings from the gulleys of Aberfan and recycling, dad was an entrepreneur who worked hard. We had horses and bred chickens, often the chicks would hatch beside our fireplace, and we had several breeds of rabbits on the quarry tump. Dad would kill some rabbits and chickens for our Sunday lunch; I would help dad skin the rabbits and pluck the chickens. Food was always fresh, stews and home-cooked dinners.

Carl, the only boy, was wicked, handsome with a cheeky smile and was blond like dad. I remember the woolen tank top he always wore, and his balaclava. He would be up to all kinds of mischief, never once did he get told off. Dad recalls he took each of us five daughters around the neighbours when we were born, and he was so proud. When Carl was born, he was elated, going around the neighbours as proud as a peacock, with Carl wrapped in a blanket, delighted to have a son. Dad painted the name HCM Minett & Son on his machinery, a statement of how much Carl meant to him.

All our school friends lived in houses either side of ours; we were all 7 years to 11 years, and due to large families, we would play in the streets all day. My dad held events in his quarry, building a huge shed which we used for street parties and carnivals, and games with cups for the winners. We loved our community, one big happy family. Our yearly street trips to seaside Barry were so special, flags aligned the street, all the community came together, all the children cheered as the buses arrived. Our village was vibrant with many shops, a local fish shop where friends congregated to play the pinball machine; the sweet shop was always my favourite, and we had our own Saturday Cinema. The village was a joyous place to grow up.

Christmas was magical for our family, 6 piles of toys around the living room, we would stand on the top stairs trying to peep, calling to mam and dad 'has Santa been', several times throughout the night. We fought each other for who was to run downstairs first, the excitement, laughter echoed, dad's woolen stockings filled with fruit and sweets hung on the fireplace. We opened our presents, a doll, a train set, a post office set. Lots of hugs a joyous moment, mam and dad never gave more attention to one than the other. We had a perfect life, full of happiness, love. We were blessed with mam and dad's looks, mam with her striking black hair, dad with his blond hair. We were all special in our own way, each with our own personalities, mam and dad idolised us, we were their life.

Mam would get up early to light the fire before we woke for school. Marylyn, Carl and I attended Pantglas Junior School, a short walk along the Taff trail. I loved school, a very sociable child, always had plenty of friends, always a caring nature towards others. My eldest sister Belinda passed her eleven plus (an exam for entry to grammar school) in the September of 1966, moving to Quakers Yard School. This was a blessing, otherwise, she would have remained in Pantglas! Michele 5 years attended the nursery school near our home.

We all went to Sunday school, full of village children, our friends; there we played games, sang and had fun. We were Christians, we always said our prayers. Our grandparents would visit us every Sunday, from Troedyrhiw, and Sunday lunch we always had together; we siblings would fight for whose turn it was to pull the wishbone on the chicken. I loved my family life, so simple, so happy, but how life was about to change!

Disaster 1966

In the days leading to 21st October 1966, it rained for days; dark, damp, dreary, misty, foggy days, this was the norm living in the Valleys. We were all excited for Half Term, with thanksgiving at school only days before, mam gave us veg and fruit for our school harvest festival. Twenty First October, Friday, half day! With a week off school, we were all excited to have a holiday.

Getting dressed for school that morning was exciting. Carl, I wrote in my childhood diary, didn't want to go to school, trying to persuade mam to have the half day off, but mam encouraged Carl to go to school! Marylyn, me, Carl and our friends walked in the foggy, wet, rain across the Taff trail across the embankment near the tips down into school. Nothing was out of the ordinary. We had walked this way so many times before. Entering Pantglas Junior School, we all parted and looked forward to seeing each other later, 'Long, see you later', we all went to our separate classrooms, which were facing the tip. Carl was on the left side of my classroom, Marylyn to the right and I sat in my usual seat next to my friend Paul. Mr Davies, the teacher, was preparing our lesson standing near the tip side window but within seconds, a monstrous roar of thunder clap noises began, rumblings got louder and louder and the pounding noise was so loud and profound. I felt the thuds in my chest, louder and louder. I was frozen in fear. You could hear a pin drop in the class and school, time stood still, no child moved. I sensed danger, but from what? I knew something was coming, but from where? I started to get up, one foot in front, to run for the door, but I never made it. I glanced up and a black mass of slurry smashed through the huge window. Within seconds, I was hurdled in the mass of debris, swept up in the river of slurry to the back of the classroom. I woke up in a scene of horror. The roof had caved in on top of my class. I was buried up to my waist and chest in a thick mass of slurry, rubble and desks. Blood trickled down my face; a large, heavy school radiator wrenched from the wall had landed on my legs (later I was to find out a rescuer witnessed roof beams lying across me). My hand, sealed tight, stuck through the wall, which had been forced open with the slurry pressure. A child's lifeless arm hung from the wall. I held the child's hand. My classmates were around me, trapped and injured. One boy, with his head cut open, blood trickling down his face, was alive. Another boy lay under me. I was shouting, 'My legs have gone'. I couldn't see them or feel them. Beside me lay another boy, with fluid running from his mouth. Even as a child, I knew he was dead.

I recall in my school diary, picking up a book, *Through the Garden Gate*, from the slurry, and there was blood on the book, I just opened the book to read, why I don't know. Another class friend Janett was climbing onto the caved in roof, trying to go for help. I can still see that picture in my mind as I lay there witnessing the horror: all my class friends and teacher had been buried under the sea of slurry.

A man's voice called out from the hallway, breaking the glass, there my grandfather stood, his eyes in despair as I started crying. Time stood still, Grandad Stan, Jack, and Ken waded through the debris to rescue me, and were carrying children through the window. My leg was swinging and broken, my shoes had gone, in agony, I was passed along a chain of men through the window, hall, outside to a scene of carnage and devastation. The sound of sirens filled the air, parents were wading through the mountain of slurry, toxic debris, to find their children. Dad carried me to the ambulance, mam came and cuddled me, I wanted to go back to find my shoes (mam recalls telling me she would buy me hundreds of shoes), I was rushed to hospital while mam and dad searched for Carl and Marylyn in the rubble.

At St Tydfil's hospital, children were brought in and laid on beds either side of mine. I was made comfortable, my leg put into an iron cast, bewildered, in shock, I was given pain relief, I was alone. I was taken to a third floor ward in a small, enclosed lift shaft and little did I know that the fear of enclosure was to become a lifelong burden. Later that day mam and dad came to visit me came to visit me, not knowing what had happened, I asked 'were Carl and Marylyn ok?' mam told me 'They have gone to heaven' with all my best friends that lived either side of my home. In that moment of profound hurt and grief my life changed forever. I was a different child, living in a different family household, with no Carl, no Marylyn and all my best friends gone. I just stayed silent.

Mam and dad came to visit daily, but never sleeping with me. Mam was heavily sedated for her grief, weighing 5 stone (70lbs), dad was grieving, trying to keep us all together, they had to look after my other 3 siblings. Mam would visit with baby Sian; she would sit at the bottom of my bed. My sisters visited, but not once did they ask what had happened. I didn't know how they felt either, they were grieving too, they didn't want to upset me, so the silence continued for the rest of my life (my childhood diary entries are in a book called *Struggling out of the Darkness*).

My hospital bed was aligned with a window, outside stood a tall chimney stack and this traumatised me, mam recalls me crying to her during her visits as I was fearful that the chimney would fall on me. I was then moved to the back of the ward near the wall. The ward was chaotic and overwhelming; here I would remain for months, laying on my back unable to move. Important visitors came, charities showering me with gifts, I was given a huge doll by Princess Margaret. The TV in the ward was never on, I was protected from the outside world. What had happened? My rehabilitation was focused on my physical health only; my mental health was ignored.

I was in the hospital for 3 months with head and hand injuries, a broken femur, strapped up in weight tractions in bed, unable to move, lying on my back. No bathing, unable to walk, left alone in the hospital to grieve on my own in complete silence. Having to use a large steel bedpan (I was humiliated), being bed bathed, unable to wear underwear, mam had to cut and sew poppers on the sides of my panties, as my leg was raised high on weights. I felt embarrassed, I lost all my independence, I had no choice, I was vulnerable. No-one stayed with me over night; in those days, you didn't, and mam was too ill, I was left alone, the days were long, nights were lonely.

I was the last survivor to leave the hospital, returning home from the hospital after 3 months on Christmas Eve, in a wheelchair, for 1 week. I had to return to the hospital after Christmas for a further week to learn to walk. I still have vivid memories of the day I left the ward on the third floor and the anxiety of being put in the small, enclosed lift; it still disrupts my life today at 67. My siblings and best friends had all gone, my generation didn't exist, I returned to a different home and family. I remember the journey well, there was silence when I passed my school, gazing out of the car window to the mass of black destruction, no school, no houses, a mass of black dirt, there was an eerie silence. Nothing was said. I was silent. Neighbours greeted me, I was carried into my home by dad, overwhelmed, scared how to react. Carl, Marylyn and my friends gone, they had been buried without me. I was told in 2016, 50 years after the disaster, the burial day was 27th October, the only day mam and dad didn't visit me in hospital. This broke my heart.

Leaving hospital – short-term effects

Life would never be the same. Short-term effects and physical traumas would heal; the lasting psychological trauma would never end. Just some of the emotional factors included feelings of numbness, being unable to eat, panic, outbursts of temper, acute anxiety, bitterness, tension, anger, restlessness, being overcome with grief, guilt, severe withdrawal from family and friends and many more listed below.

Mam was gaunt, sedated on Valium, in a dazed state. I was still not told, or I was too afraid to ask, what had happened. Mam became very protective of us, recalling that she didn't want us out of her sight, with our grandparents supporting our welfare; mam was in shock. I had lots of visitors to my home, I still couldn't walk, and dad carried me around. No one asked me what had happened, I was too afraid to ask my eldest sister and survivors what had happened! I was isolated from the disaster, protected from the outside world, no counselling, no psychiatrist support, nothing. I was now left to survive, to grieve for my siblings and friends, alone, the horror and the aftereffects have been lifelong.

The three-weekly visits to hospital, the general practitioner, GP, and the physiotherapist took a toll on my mother, my shoes were built up, my leg was now an inch shorter, I had a prominent limp, which I hated. I became withdrawn, I had home tuition from school for many months. Traumatised, I didn't want to return to the prefab temporary school in the park at Aberfan.

Marylyn and Carl had gone, I now slept in between mam and dad, baby Sian in the cot, refusing to sleep alone and with the lights off, afraid of being on my own, the darkness scared me, bedwetting now became the norm. Afraid of loud noises, thunder, darkness, my mood had changed, becoming withdrawn, refusing to talk about siblings or friends who had died, an abnormal quietness. (I was told by the nurse who cared for me in hospital, 'I just stared into space', vacant with dazed expressions, I became very tearful over nothing). My generation had been wiped out, the huge void left me and my other siblings playing with other children who were much older than us. I was still a young child; our childhood had vanished.

On returning to the newly built school, Ynysowen, I would scream, hands over my ears in a panic state, when the locomotive trains passed by, reminding me of the Aberfan disaster rumbling noise. I was moved to three schools, one school in another village, away from my friends, which too was near the railway having the same effect. My mam recalls me behaving erratically in panic when a train passed over a bridge on the way to a GP appointment. Thunder still provokes anxiety on hearing it today. Mam would hide us under the table on hearing thunder; the effects were instilled in her too.

I was pitied in both Junior and Secondary School, as my identity changed, I was now 'the survivor', teachers, and others were not equipped to deal with my emotions and trauma, feeling sorry for me. My education was dysfunctional. Secondary School I bunked, I was left to my own devices, rebellious, playing tricks on teachers. My concentration was limited. It was when I started at Afon Taf school aged 12 years that I had a profound, overwhelming urge to write what had happened to me and my family. Like a voice within me that kept pouring out, I wrote on a blue exercise book 'My story', calling it 'a sad story'. No lesson mattered, I just wanted to keep writing down the words continually pouring out from my head.

I left secondary school with no aspirations other than to have children. It took decades for me and other surviving children to bear their children for Aberfan's generation to replace the 116 children that were lost. There was a strange bitterness between families who lost children and those who hadn't, people just could not help it. Guilty men who blamed themselves for tipping, parents who had sent their children to school when they didn't want to go; my mother lived with the guilt for sending Carl that day.

Our family faith was tested to the core, mam and dad became atheists. Mam explained 'why couldn't God, if there was one, part the sea of Slurry'?

Theoretically she was right. Nuns, reverends, Mormons, people from the Church regularly knocked on our door, mam would take time to chat, but never regained her faith, and many times mam and dad would get angry and shout. Grief amongst parents were profound and intense. I and other survivors carried the guilt, parents would scold us if we played near their home, or in sight (we would remind them of their child, 'seeing us play was too painful', their child had gone). Some were hostile to us, asking us to play elsewhere, so we isolated ourselves and moved out of sight to neighbouring fields. Graveside lamps were lit day and night, alongside all the graves, parents would sit for hours by their children's graves to give them comfort. Many lost a brother, sister, cousin, aunt, uncle; grief was shared and everyone knew how the other was feeling, each supporting the other. We still have the lamps in our family today.

Mam yearned to have another baby after the disaster, but the GP advised her that having another child wouldn't bring back Carl or Marylyn, as they had their own unique personalities; no child could replace them. Mam and dad contemplated moving away, some families did, later returning to Aberfan.

In my early teens I was too afraid to show my emotions to anyone, I couldn't cry in front of them, I didn't know how too. I would sob my heart out in bed, I couldn't breathe, putting the pillow over my head to conceal my whining, the guilt was unbearable, I had survived, (thinking to myself, my mother and father would only be grieving for one child, not two, if they had only lost me). I wanted to die, and have Carl and Marylyn come back alive. I had no one to help me, I was too ashamed to ask and say I was suffering. Mam and dad and my sisters were all suffering too, so we all just got on with it in our own way, every second of the day, with no help in sight we all suffered in silence. I used to talk to Sam the farm horse, when I was sad, I felt safe, Sam couldn't judge me, laugh at me. I believed Sam understood my despair, I felt better after talking to Sam, I could off load my feelings would hug Sam, he was my saviour.

Psychiatrist visits

To my shock and horror, my parents took me to the psychiatrist without my consent, pretending I was going shopping. The most vivid, traumatic memories that I endured during these sessions live with me today. The drive up the hill to the Church Village Mental hospital, my hands being prised from the car handles, by mam and dad and staff dragged into the hospital screaming and kicking. I was humiliated, scared I would be admitted to the mental hospital, (as talk among the survivors said you wouldn't come out in those days) mental health was a stigma, you would be sectioned. I was subjected to 'Frankenstein' tests (ECT), left alone in a white room, laid on a bed, with an electrode head cap fixed to my head, gel would be placed all over my skull, the round space-like modules were wired to my head and the electric board above me, told to open my mouth, close my eyes, several times. As a young girl I felt degraded, embarrassed, whole sessions were traumatic. Patients were wandering around, in a confused state. (This was recalled in my childhood diary). This went on for many weeks (I was later to find out these tests were to determine my mental state to determine the amount of grant from the Disaster fund; people had given their money to support us). Still today I am sickened by the way were treated, a Secondary Trauma!

Sheila Lewis, the nurse who cared for me, was my neighbour. Sheila carried on working in St Tydfil's hospital as a nurse despite losing her own daughter in the disaster and dealing with her own trauma. Sheila recalls 'I nursed you, in hospital and I know how hard it was for you to lie in bed for 3 months, your father and mother coming to see you, and then you thinking that you should have died with the other two, your brother and sister. I told Sheila I would have done anything to die and the others live. Sheila recalls she remembered the 8-year-old girl, me, I was grieving in a strange place, unable to go home, Sheila recognised my wounds were deeper than broken bones', you were suffering apart from that, I remember you in bed your eyes wide open, because you were in trauma. You never spoke much, you were quiet, I never saw you crying in hospital. 'I thought to myself, if only she would cry'.

Long-term effects

My sister Sian, 6 months old at the time of the disaster, was robbed of knowing her brother and sister. Becoming a teacher who is so passionate about her work has helped her deal with her own personal loss.

Mam always said, 'I was the vulnerable sibling', protecting me all my life. I went running back to mam and dad when I couldn't deal with any issues or my emotions. I struggled and still struggle to make decisions, constantly needing reassurance. With difficulty in concentrating, I was robbed of an education and qualifications. To this day, I have never again read a book, not even my own, right through. I lose interest very quickly. Like a switch I can just turn off, losing focus and concentration.

I displayed risky and destructive behaviours in my teens. I would bait flocks of birds in the farmyard and see how many birds I could shoot and kill with a 12-bore shotgun, with no emotion or upset at seeing the horror which I had caused. (I was later told, many years later, by my High-Intensity Psychotherapist, that this was traumatic play).

For many years, I was unable to enter the memorial garden, feeling it was a sacred place; it didn't feel 'right'. I didn't have the courage and was afraid of how I would react. This caused more anxiety and guilt as I couldn't pay my respects. I visited the graves regularly. For many years, I was unable to attend the memorial services on the 21 October, again fearful of how I would feel and leaving myself wide open, leaving my guard down; it was easier if I didn't go, but then I felt guilty, which was worse. For many years now, I have attended all anniversaries in the cemetery, the laying of wreaths takes you back to the silent moment the disaster struck; I try and detach myself of that thought so as not to break down, but many times fail, the feelings are too powerful to conceal.

Mam, since the disaster, has never been able to attend school concerts. It is too painful for her to listen to the children singing. Mam never attended the anniversary services, as I wrote in my earlier writings: 'Mam stated, every day is an anniversary for her'. 'Damn flowers', she would say, 'I can only give you damn flowers now, no gifts, presents, no hugs, just flowers'. Her words are heartbreaking.

This guilt of survival has been lifelong since the loss of my brother and sister. Believing I was only spared to help others, dedicating my life to others, in exchange for my own life, and the children, teachers and others who died. It has taken a mental and physical toll on my life, where I have worked relentlessly, setting high standards of work, supporting disadvantaged families, individuals and offenders, even though I felt physically ill with anxiety, exhausted from little sleep from nightmares, fluctuating moods and failed relationships (my marriage at 19 didn't have any chance of survival). I was drinking, with anxiety states, excessive jealousy, low self-esteem and still with no counselling; the trauma was unbearable.

Traumatic nightmares have been part of my life, often involving being trapped, faces in the dark looking down at me, but it's not me, it's my family. In a panicked dream state, I am running away, trying to fly to get away, never getting to my destination, I wake up in heightened anxiety, my heart racing and breathless. After one dream in my thirties, very vivid till this day, I woke up in a distressed state, wide awake, frozen to the bed, I wanted to run, I couldn't move, with dark faces surrounding my face, heart bounding, it was horrific, it felt so real. I attended the GP the following day. I was so scared of the feeling of being frozen but awake (it was later diagnosed as psychosis).

Throughout my life, I have tried to avoid a feeling of enclosure, a fear which has increased the older I have become, in lifts, trains, planes, even in my house, I can feel claustrophobic and compelled to escape. I have tried to overcome this, but the feelings are too overwhelming. I have caused distress for my three children, as I have moved several times when the feelings of everything coming towards me get overwhelming. One time, a few years ago, the feelings were overwhelming just opening my front door, so I ran to my mam's house, sobbing, but feeling embarrassed. Mam was upset, shouting and pointing to the disaster tip site from the kitchen window, 'THE TIPS HAVE DONE THIS!'. I stayed there for 6 months before returning to my home. Constantly rearranging my furniture, uprooting my children from one home to another, moments where I am overwhelmed and cutting up my furniture have caused great instability in my children's lives. I am blessed that my three children, now adults, have made me proud both in their work and as a grandmother to six beautiful grandchildren.

Throughout my teenage years and into adulthood, I have used alcohol as a coping mechanism for my anxiety. This behaviour leaves the deepest marks, one which I have always regretted as a parent with three children. Along with surviving friends and others in my early teens, I hid away from our parents, drinking flagons of cider in the gulleys around Aberfan. Binge drinking, continued into adulthood, became the norm. Unable to have meaningful relationships and finding it hard to trust. As my anxieties increased, the consumption of alcohol increased, so I would drink before I went out, intoxicated, to give me more confidence in myself. The consequences were many serious falls and accidents, needing hospital treatments. Since a serious injury occurred from drinking, I have now been abstinent from drink for ten years. Stopping has had an impact on having meaningful relationships with friends and has increased isolation, with me losing the confidence that drink once gave me.

Since the disaster, I have learned to avoid my own emotions about what happened. While knowing I am one of the survivors, but not feeling I am – it's hard to explain – I dissociate from myself when I do public speaking. Dissociating from the event and the rest of my emotions has helped me cope since a child. I picture 'another little girl' trapped under the mountain; actually, it is me, I am speaking, but cut off from myself, emotionally dissociated from the event. This has led to failed relationships and social isolation. If I allow my emotions to dominate that detachment, I hate to think of the horrors that would creep back into my head, the story would become reality, 'IT IS ME'; so, I try not to leave my guard down

Dad was instrumental in the politics and the fight for justice against the NCB, as their neglect caused the disaster to happen. Sadly, today, there is still no justice for the horror we all endured and the lifelong trauma 1966 inflicted. I have childhood memories of dad always shouting and angry, attending committee meetings, campaigning to raise funds from the public to upkeep the graveside and memorial; mam always trying to calm dad down became the norm. Having two siblings lying in the cemetery – that fire within him kept dad, mam and us all going. Fighting for justice kept dad going until he passed away in 2015, aged 83.

Dad's death caused all the years of despair our family had experienced to reappear on the surface; a ripple of emotions hit us all hard, grieving not just for our dad, but grieving for the man who fought so hard, sacrificing his life for justice, tirelessly, keeping us all together. In 2022, mam died suddenly at 86. Having to bury them both with Carl and Marylyn, their graves being opened, unleashed all the emotions again. There was also comfort knowing that mam and dad had waited a long time to be united with their children. Mam's death left an emptiness, and the profound grief evoked a memory for my eldest sister, breaking down for the first time and describing her own memories of the 21st of October. She recalls mam and dad returning home time after time that day while searching for Carl and Marylyn, and that she was told they had died; the trauma of the memory was clearly devastating. My eldest sister Belinda has dedicated many years as Trustee of the Aberfan memorial charity, working tirelessly to ensure the graves, memorial and families of the victims are supported with the utmost respect.

I display hypervigilance of situations, places around me, fearful, paranoid of situations I am unable to control and afraid that situations or activities could provoke danger. I avoid any activity that could theoretically suffocate me, such as water above my shoulders and wearing a face mask (COVID-19).

These fears and behaviours have transferred onto my children and grandchildren where I find my anxiety state escalates when they go on holiday to the seaside or to a fair where my catastrophic thinking dissolves into a panic state, worry, where I have made them anxious too and then they panic as a result of my behaviour.

On the 30th anniversary, I was hospitalised for a week due to severe panic attacks. Persistent anxieties starting immediately after the disaster have taken on a physical form – specifically jaw pain, avoidance of emotions, fast heart rate, feelings of panic, insomnia, chronic body pain, terror, trembling caused by the traumas I have faced, and my symptoms have continued to escalate. This is particularly evident since up-dating and writing my book about the disaster, taking two years to complete. I needed answers and closure, which involved me speaking to my parents, survivors, teachers, reverends, GPs, royalty, anyone who came into my life's journey since the disaster. And especially my parents' perceptions of me, how I had changed, a different child, and about what happened to them that day and how they had the will to go on, I needed to know!

In 2016, the 50th anniversary, 'A Story of Survival, Love and Community' was published. Since then, I have experienced a loss of interest in activities, no motivation to socialise and feeling more isolated, yet unable to do anything about it, as socialising means going out. Living solely on my own for 38 years, since my divorce, I have had to work continually to support myself and my three children, with feelings of being emotionally and physically burnt out. Since 2016, I have not been driven in the way I am used to and feel guilty for this; taking time off work, but taking annual leave instead of sick leave, as I felt guilty for letting people down. I was always afraid of letting anyone down, so I overcompensated in everything I did in work and personal life. I survived, always feeling that I was meant to live for a reason, and that reason was to save others, support others in life. This guilt has been everlasting.

Describing myself today in 2026, I am often angry, irritable, being pessimistic of my future, my physical health has deteriorated, anxieties have continued to disrupt my life and I rarely, if ever, feel happy or content. Life has been extremely difficult and challenging. Mam and dad's house has been sold, evoking feelings of emptiness and despair. From my early adulthood through to now, pension age, I have suffered ongoing anxieties, depression, psychosis, palpitations, insomnia, nightmares, chronic pain and instability, unable to settle in my homes, jobs and drinking, with failed relationships. With many visits to the GP and hospital to deal with these issues, in 2020, a consultant linked my symptoms to post-traumatic stress disorder (PTSD). From 2020 to December 2025, I continued to receive counselling to unravel the traumas from my past, to make sense of why I displayed these behaviours, which were truly justified. Reading a report and seeing and processing the content about me made me cry – the child I tried to detach from and spoke about, pretending it is not me. It so hard to imagine or comprehend how anyone can survive what's written. But the report is Me!

I am 67 and recently retired from over 50 years of working in Welfare to Work, Youth Justice, Barnardo's and family support, supporting others to overcome their own life issues. My childhood diary is on display at St Fagan's Museum, a folk museum in Cardiff, my book has become a book of world interest, it has helped others, as part of history, schools, and even part of exams. I have attended many public speaking events within schools, museums, churches, memorial garden, live links to Hampstead USA Primary School, documentaries, podcasts, radio, and TV.

In 2026, it will be the 60th anniversary of the Aberfan disaster. These events and the emotional journey just never end. Until my dying day, I will endeavour at all costs to my health, and continue my father's legacy to ensure all generations never forget Aberfan. Many people still don't know and are shocked by the revelations. Never feeling free of the disaster, I am destined to be alone for the rest of my life, not being able to truly feel unconditional love from a partner saddens me. The after-effects have been debilitating and lifelong. I can only imagine what life would have been like if I had not been a victim of this trauma. My life has been challenging and traumatic, taking a toll on my mental and physical health. I was only given a small amount of money from the compensation fund and I have become angry and feel bitter that I have been burdened with this life, all because of the disaster. The torrent of that day never leaves, the emotional traumas are never-ending and they continue to tear apart the lives of our families. It is a life sentence.

My legacy after death

The story of my life experiences and the impact the disaster has inflicted. I have been able to document and share with others all over the world and generations to come. My legacy, and that of my mam, dad and family, will be remembered when I am gone.

Chapter 8

ADVERSE CHILDHOOD EXPERIENCES AND INTERNATIONAL ADOPTIONS: EXPERIENCES FROM THE VOICES OF ADOPTED INDIVIDUALS[1]

Diana S. Lesme Romero

Departamento de Psicología, Universidad Católica "Nuestra Señora de la Asunción", Asunción, Paraguay

> Three seconds are enough for a man to become a parent; parenting is something very different… in truth, only adoptive parents exist; every true parent must adopt their child ... *Françoise Dolto*

Background

Adoption has long been a relevant topic in psychology. Several studies reveal that adoptions not properly processed by all parties involved can negatively impact the socio-emotional well-being of the adoptee and the bonds within this unique family configuration, leaving subjective marks of suffering, pain, abandonment, frustration and guilt. Adoptions can become an Adverse Childhood Experience (ACE) and trigger trauma, stress and psychological suffering in the adoptee, as well as in the adoptive and biological parents. Alongside theoretical reflections, assessments are added from interactions with Paraguayan individuals adopted in the United States, contacted at two points in time: in 2008, the experience was systematised with children and adolescents who were assisted in searching for their biological roots in Paraguay and in organising reconnection meetings among them. On August 1st, 2024, a focus group was conducted with a group of adults

[1] Based on a Dissertation at: 3rd Multidisciplinary Congress on Community Health of MERCOSUR. Powers and Limitations in Community Health – a Challenge for the Region. October, 2008. Paraguay.

The Intergenerational Effects of Adverse Childhood Experiences: Ripples on a Pond,
First Edition. Edited by Richard Pates and Diane Riley.

Published 2026 by John Wiley & Sons Ltd.

adopted in the United States, mostly around 30 years old. Informed consent was obtained in all cases. Qualitative assessments record a significant relationship between international adoptions, ACEs and the development of psychological disorders in adulthood.

Introduction

Early childhood is a vital stage in which the foundations of human subjectivity are established. The journey through various developmental spaces must be supported by others, as the child's physical, psychological, physiological and social immaturity does not yet allow them to navigate these spaces effectively towards their overall well-being. Winnicott, the renowned English psychoanalyst, expresses it this way: '*... a baby cannot exist alone; it is essentially part of a relationship*'. (Winnicott, 1987, p. 88) That baby needs a family, the first space for socialisation, integration into culture and the writing of his own history.

The International Convention on the Rights of the Child (1990) states that every child has the right to a family, whether or not it is bound by formal blood ties. Disciplinary literature indicates that this is the space where favourable conditions for a person's development and growth can be fostered, as well as unfavourable ones that may impact their later life development.

There are different ways of 'creating' families, by various relational configurations, all of which are inherently complex and challenging in life. One of these is the development of motherhood and fatherhood through non-biological means, such as adoption. This paper aims to examine adoption experiences and how, depending on how these processes are 'managed', they can become an adverse factor in childhood, potentially triggering trauma, stress and psychological suffering in the adoptee, as well as in adoptive and biological parents, leaving subjective marks of suffering, pain, abandonment, frustration and guilt.

It is within such families that a higher prevalence and the consequences of **Adverse Childhood Experiences (ACEs)** have been identified. A study conducted by the CDC-Kaiser ACEs Study indicated that adverse experiences during childhood impact physical and mental health, as well as behaviour, opportunities and economic stability throughout the life cycle (Boullier and Blair, 2017). The study, conducted in the United States in the late 1990s, focused on the relationships between adverse experiences (such as abuse, neglect and family problems) and health outcomes in adults.

In addition to a brief review and theoretical reflections on the topic, qualitative assessments from interactions with two groups of individuals born in Paraguay and adopted in the United States are presented. These interactions occurred during private clinical practice at two different times: in 2008, the experience was systematised with Paraguayan children and adolescents who were assisted in searching for their biological roots and in organising reconnection meetings among adopted children, their adoptive parents and their biological families. A second intervention took place in July 2024, when a group of Paraguayan adults, mostly around 30 years old, visited the country and a focus group was conducted with five of them. The visits of both groups were coordinated by TIES, an Adoptive Family Travel Agency, founded in 1994, which organises trips for adopting families to their country of origin. Some references are included in this material to illustrate the hypothesis that international adoptions that have not been sufficiently supported and processed by all members of the process can become risk factors for the development of ACEs and psychological disorders in adulthood.

The story of origin

Questions about origin are an important part of identity and the construction of human subjectivity. **Who am I? Where do I come from?** These are crucial questions in people's lives. In adopted children, these questions are more intense and diverse, as seen in the questions and comments from participants in the experience, questions addressed to their biological mothers (BMs):

- Why was I given up for adoption?
- Have you thought about me since giving me up for adoption?
- Was it hard for you to give me up for adoption?
- Do I have brothers and sisters? Why did you give me up for adoption but not them?

Paraguay is a country with a Judeo-Christian tradition, where motherhood is highly valued, making the issue of adoption controversial. To analyse this situation, some elements identified by Ortiz (2006) will be used:

1. The adopted person
2. The BM (*I would also include the father and extended family*)[2]
3. The adoptive parents
4. The context

For brevity, this work will focus on the adopted person and the context.

The history of humanity records various ways in which families have organised, both formally and informally, to raise their descendants. In Paraguay, there is a culturally established tradition known as 'criadazgo' (Informal fosterage with labour exploitation), which, according to Montes (2001), cited by Ortiz, has its roots in the colonial era. In the late 1990s, there was an increase in adoptions carried out through the Adoption Centre, established in 1997. Before this date, it was common for families to 'give' (hand over) their children to another person or family, who would then register

[2] The italics are my addition.

them as if they were their biological children (direct registrations), thereby losing traces of the child's origin and violating one of their fundamental rights: their identity.

Psychological literature recognises the importance of identity in the formation of subjectivity. It is imperative to inform the adoptee about their origin, which is addressed in most international adoption legislations. Knowing their origin helps the child **construct their personal history**[3]. As Rotenberg (2007) states, '*identity is linked to our history and prehistory (the mystery of their origin, the real and phantasmatic history of their conception, everything that precedes their conception...), both of which are constitutive of oneself*'.

It is essential for an adopted child to be informed at a time when the parents are able to do so because **they have accepted it themselves.** Adoptive parents constitute a primary source for the representations the child will build about their origin. Adoption exposes individuals who have accessed motherhood or fatherhood through a path different from the biological one, which implies accepting a **grief process** for themselves, that of infertility or the inability to conceive for other reasons. A **narcissistic wound**[4] that must be processed. Alvarez (2018) states that 'adoptive parents may have aggressive responses toward their child, especially if they are expecting the 'ideal' child, the one who, in their fantasy, will fulfill them and repair their damaged narcissism due to their inability to procreate ...'

On the other hand, it is acknowledged that the adopted child has the task of connecting with at least two sets of parental figures: biological parents and adoptive parents. This situation requires greater effort and presents challenges regarding primary attachment to that voice, that smell, that body that is recognised as familiar, a subjective mark that then disappears, implying a new effort to connect with a voice, smell and body different from the first one. In the case studied, involving international adoptions, another element is added: a language different from that of the biological parents.

The bond between the adopted child and his biological mother/father

The children in the group studied in 2008 were informed about their adoption by their adoptive families. A significant number of participants referred to the figure of the BM as 'the other mother', with whom there was either no early bond, a deficient bond, or neglect. In some cases, situations of family violence against the child's mother and against the child were described, as well as instances of hospital violence towards the pregnant mother, also referred to as

[3] Bold text is my addition.

[4] Idem.

obstetric violence[5], as defined in Law 5777/16 on Comprehensive Protection for Women against all forms of violence.

According to *Oxford Learner´s Dictionary*, the etymological reference of 'bond' refers to: '*something that forms a connection between people or groups*' (Oxford Learner's Dictionaries, n.d.). That connection or tie between mother and child is always a subjective, unique investment from each mother with each child. According to the mothers' testimonies, different 'ties' can be distinguished: **When the initial contact between the biological mother and child was insufficient (in quantity and/or quality)**, mothers remembered little of that moment and have not kept symbols or rituals that preserve the memory of the child (photos, clothes and birthday celebrations). When the **contact was greater**, mothers had vivid memories and had kept items that reminded them of their child.

Attachment or attachments?

Several questions arose during the interventions: **What was the attachment like that these children had with their mothers and/or primary caregivers? How did they transition from attachment to their biological mothers to attachment to their adoptive mothers?**

John Bowlby and Mary Ainsworth's Attachment Theory provides some references regarding the emotional bond established between mother and child. The comments from the BMs in the study show that although they formed the first attachments with these children, there were other attachments formed later, which Bowlby referred to as **multiple attachments.** (Bowlby & Ainsworth, 1978) Many babies were 'detached' from their mothers before their first year of life. In many cases, they went through several caregivers, who also subsequently disappeared from their lives. That seems to reveal that their primary attachments were difficult. Bowlby and Ainsworth suggest that separation between a young child and an attachment figure (primary caregiver) is inherently disturbing and makes the child vulnerable to experiencing intense fear easily. When the child perceives further prospects of separation, a certain degree of anxiety arises within them.

> **Cinthia**, adopted at 18 months, refers: "*......basically it just made me very quick to attach myself to people, especially as a child and also just like I had a very unstable attachment style with my parents were like I ...* ***I didn't want them ever to leave my sight,*** *like I was very, very attached, and I know that that's normal for babies, but like I remember feeling very stressed, even as a young child about like my parents not being or like me not knowing where they are or ... even if they were*

[5] Obstetric violence. It refers to the practice of healthcare personnel or traditional midwives over the bodies of women and the physiological or pathological processes present during pregnancy, as well as the stages related to gestation and childbirth.

> *just going to the store or something …*" (D. Lesme, personal communication, August 1, 2024)[6].

An interesting aspect is how the bond between the child and their BM is perceived from the social imagination. In the focus group, **Cinthia** refers:

> …." *I remember getting very upset because, I don't have a connection to anyone else, like any other family, like, that's my family and although I do feel like a black sheep in that family, is still mine, so …. I've had a few experiences in my life, like at, mostly when I was much younger, about other people putting their opinion of adoption on me and making it feel like, "Ok, well, your family unit isn't legitimate" or "Isn't valid because you're not actually with your family. You're not actually with your birth family"*. (D. Lesme, personal communication, August 1, 2024).

The type of bond that a child can establish with their biological parents is also influenced by the social imagination. This is evident in Jessica's words, who was adopted at 5 months:

> *…. I remember a time with …. my science teacher in 4th grade where I guess I was pulled out of class for some reason, I don't know why, I was probably sad or something and I had told her. She was like "What's wrong?" and I had told her: "I miss my birth mother" and she said "You can't miss someone you don't know", …. so, I think that was another kind of painful memory, but I still remember until today ….* (D. Lesme, personal communication, August 1, 2024).

This bond, in some cases, resulted in the development of psychological distress, as **Cinthia** reveals:

> *I've never been formally diagnosed with* ***reactive attachment disorder****, but that's kind of what me and my mom think I … you know, was one of the consequences of me being adopted, because I was taken from, like, my primary caregiver at a very crucial age, at about one and a half (1½) and that's kind of one of the triggers of reactive attachment disorder and basically it just made me very quick to attach myself to people, especially as a child and also just like had a* ***very unstable attachment style with my parents were like I … I didn't want them ever to leave my sight, like I was very, very attached …*** (D. Lesme, personal communication, August 1, 2024).

Adverse childhood experiences

ACEs are stressful situations that occur before the age of 18 and were conceptualised by Vincent Felitti and Robert Anda in the 1990s. According to Priego-Parra et al. (2022), they '*are associated with an increased risk of adverse*

[6] Private recording of focus group facilitated by D. Lesme.

outcomes in physical health, life opportunities, education, social behavior, and mental health in the short, medium, and long term'. In the ACEs Study conducted by Felitti and Anda at the Centers for Disease Control and Prevention (CDC) and Kaiser Permanente in the United States, the results demonstrated that ACEs, such as abuse, neglect and family dysfunction, can have a profound and lasting impact on individuals' physical and mental health throughout their life cycle. Children exposed to ACEs may suffer from toxic stress and its consequences, related to the immaturity of various physiological systems, and this could even be transmitted transgenerationally through epigenetic mechanisms that have yet to be sufficiently studied.

ACEs include abuse (physical, sexual and emotional/verbal); neglect (physical and emotional/psychological); and household dysfunction (parental mental illness, domestic violence, divorce or separation, incarceration, and alcohol or substance abuse) (Felitti et al. 1998).

International adoptions and ACEs

The field of ACEs and its relationship with international adoptions has not yet been widely studied. So, it cannot be asserted that there is a direct and unequivocal relationship between adoptions and ACEs; it is only a working hypothesis at this point. Some studies suggest that internationally adopted children may present a higher potential risk for developing various pathological conditions, including early separation from their biological parents, lack of early emotional attachment and neglect in primary care within institutions operating on a mass-care basis – at a time when the first rudiments of the child's subjectivity are being formed.

Therefore, if attachments in adoptions are inadequate or negligent, this could lead to emotional suffering and distress, impacting the adopted child's development and producing long-lasting effects on their socio-emotional development that, in many cases, ultimately manifest as psychological disorders.

Many people adopted by families from a different cultural context experience ACEs before and during the adoption process. In Paraguay, adoption processes have been complex and lengthy and lack support systems for any of the parties involved: neither for adoptees nor their families. Some ACEs that may come upon in the process include physical, emotional or sexual abuse or trauma experienced by the mother. Certain ACE-generating processes in this context include: institutionalisation often occurring before the formalisation of adoption, frequently associated with neglect in early, individualised care; inappropriate birth conditions, such as a lack of infrastructure or trained personnel to support childbirth (the stories of BMs from the studied cases revealed that some did not have access to a hospital and gave birth at home with an 'empirical' midwife[7]).

[7] A common term used to refer to women who assist in childbirth without any formal technical training, usually relying on practical experience.

These experiences contribute to the development of adverse neurodevelopmental and behavioural conditions, such as attachment disorders, anxiety and emotional dysregulation. Dinkler et al. (2017) explored the relationship between neurodevelopmental disorders and maltreatment, finding that adoptees who have experienced maltreatment – common among institutionalised children or those with negligent care prior to adoption – are more likely to develop attachment disorders and other mental health conditions, such as neurodevelopmental disorders, attention deficit hyperactivity disorder (ADHD) and autism spectrum disorders.

Tovar's words, shared below, show that **ACEs can disrupt expected developmental trajectories and cause long-lasting impacts** on the physical, psychological and social health of adopted individuals throughout their lives.

> *.... I had a lot of negative experiences, emotional, neglected I would say .... I had struggled with addictions, hardcore, which none of my parents knew about.* (D. Lesme, personal communication, August 1, 2024)

And in Katie's words:

> *.... So I struggled a lot with like, drinking and like... finding affection from anybody, well, not anybody, I really liked male affection, so I would do risky behaviours. I was ... I was always just trying to feel something because I knew ... I had trouble, feeling things. I had trouble identifying who I was ...* (D. Lesme, personal communication, August 1, 2024)

Support systems

One aspect highlighted in the interventions is that, although the presence of ACEs in families and individuals increases the risk of mental health conditions and developmental disorders, support systems that promote resilience and address these experiences – such as therapeutic spaces and family, social and community support – can help mitigate adverse effects. Protocols and tools exist for evaluating ACEs and measuring their levels. One essential strategy for addressing these experiences is 'trauma-informed practices'. This concept is based on methods that recognise the impact of trauma on individuals and adapt interventions and services to respond sensitively to these experiences in a safe environment, minimising the possibility of revictimisation and retraumatisation.

In the cases reviewed, there was no support system in place for adoptive families, biological families, or the adopted individual to process these experiences. Although local regulations have since changed and now include mechanisms to provide support to adoptive families and the adoptee, there are no published studies to date demonstrating their effective implementation. This lack of a support system is highlighted in **Tovar**'s words:

> *I did not have a good support system from my adopted family. They... my mother should have never been allowed to adopt children.* (D. Lesme, personal communication, August 1, 2024).

However, in cases where there was a family support system, the process of adoption, along with its challenges related to identity, was smoother and could evolve towards an acceptance of their origin story as part of their identity. This is reflected in **Cinthia**'s words:

> *My mom has always been very, very supportive of me returning to Paraguay and finding out more about, ... where I come from, and my dad's not unsupportive, he's just uninvolved, he's kind of indifferent about it, but my mom has always been, like, whenever you wanna find out more about where you come from, you just tell me and ... and we'll do it .... I had a very ... my childhood wasn't without its difficulties, but I did have a very supportive home life* (D. Lesme, personal communication, August 1, 2024).

In the 2008 study, many BMs became emotional upon learning about their children. They expressed feelings of fear, guilt and anguish regarding the fate of the child placed for adoption.

> ***Juana** said she had been waiting for this moment of reunion. In her bedroom, she had a framed photo of **María** at the head of her bed. She remembers that after placing María for adoption, she felt very sad and worried for a long time because there were rumors that adopted children were destined for organ trafficking. She prayed to God and requested him to let her know that her daughter was okay.* (G. Escobar, personal communication: interviews with biological mothers 2004–2008.)

Although many mothers felt the need to reconnect with their children or know about them, they did not ask anyone. They indicated that they believed they would be rejected by the child for 'abandoning' them, or because of their physical appearance and/or their precarious living conditions; for thinking they had no right to see them and participate in their lives 'after what they did'; and for fear of involving the 'agents' of the adoption (nurses, midwives, doctors, lawyers and judges) and exposing corrupt practices that in some cases implicated them as well. This highlights the deficiencies of the state system towards these women who decided to give their children up for adoption, stripped of any type of support and follow-up.

International adoptions in Paraguay

There are different approaches to the issue of how international adoptions are regulated in various parts of the world. International adoptions in Paraguay between 1989 and 1995 were carried out under Law 903/81, which dedicates several chapters to regulating adoptions, but does not mention international adoptions in any of them. It can be inferred that this regulation did not have a protective vision for the child or the parties involved in the international adoption. In 1995, the national government suspended the procedures for international adoptions to address systematic abuse and irregular practices in this area.

According to data from the US Department of State, Paraguay has carried out 2,440 international adoptions from 1989 to 1996, when they were temporarily suspended by Law 678/95. However, Ortiz (2006) claims that estimates suggest between 4,000 and 5,000 children have been sent abroad, 98% of whom went to the United States.

In Paraguay, Law 900/96 approved the Convention on the Protection of Children and Cooperation in Respect of Intercountry Adoption, signed in The Hague in 1993. This convention emphasises the need to prioritise the best interests of the adopted child in international adoptions and that states promote the development of counselling services related to adoption and follow-up of such adoptions. In our country, the law that regulates adoptions is 1136/97 (1997), which established the Adoption Center, a state institution that serves as the central administrative authority for adoptions. It is important to note that this law was enacted after the period when the majority of international adoptions took place. It defines, in its article 25°, international adoptions as: '*... those carried out by persons residing abroad in favor of children and adolescents domiciled in Paraguay*'.

Law 6486/19 'on the Promotion and Protection of the Right of Children and Adolescents to Live in a Family, which regulates alternative care measures and adoption' reintroduces the figure of international adoptions as permitted, as stated in Article 64: Regarding adoption by persons residing abroad: '*International adoption shall be granted exceptionally and on a subsidiary basis to national adoption for persons residing in States that have ratified the United Nations Convention on the Rights of the Child and the Hague Convention on the Protection of Children and Cooperation in Respect of International Adoption, within the framework of which agreements have been established between countries of origin and receiving countries*'.

Law 1680/01, the Code of Childhood and Adolescence, establishes in Article 3 that '*any measure adopted regarding the child or adolescent shall be based on their best interests. ... To determine the prevailing best interest, their family ties, education, and ethnic, religious, cultural, and linguistic origin shall be respected...*'

Methodology of interventions with adopted individuals

In both interventions, with children and adolescents in 2008 and later with adults in 2024, the interventions were organised at the request of TIES, a civil organisation that arranges cultural reconnection trips for families who have adopted internationally. In all cases, informed consent was obtained from the children, adolescents and their families, as well as from the adults in the second group. A pseudonym selected by them was used in the focus group. The case systematisation of the children included data from reports by the social worker and the author of this communication regarding the searches and reconnection meetings between the adopted individuals and their families: adoptive and biological. For the group of adopted adults, a recorded focus group was conducted with five voluntary participants, all female, around 30 years old.

Between 2004 and 2008, 54 searches for biological families of children aged 11 to 20 years were conducted, with the majority of searches registered for individuals between 13 and 16 years old. The studied group consisted of 27 males and 27 females.

The BMs reported upon being contacted during the search that they were unaware that their children were living abroad; in all cases, they had no way to reach their biological children. All of them were asked about their willingness and availability for a meeting. Ninety-four percent accepted with excitement, even though many had kept the adoption a secret, which could potentially cause issues with their current families.

> ***Juana***[8] *remembers very well the day she gave her daughter up for adoption. When the person arrived, she was breastfeeding, and the person told her to kiss the baby a lot as a farewell. Juana saw that the baby had milk at the corners of her lips and kissed her until she dried the rest of the milk. She states that it was very hard for her to give up her daughter, and she never imagined that she would go to the United States; she was unaware of her daughter's whereabouts.* (G. Escobar, personal communication: Social Worker Report 2007).

Conclusions and recommendations

- The topic of adoptions continues to be little discussed openly, resulting in a scarcity of scientific production, especially in the area of mental health. It would be advisable to continue researching this topic.
- Children, adolescents and adopted adults express an imperative need to explore questions about their origins and to find answers that serve as support for the formation and/or consolidation of their identity, aiming at overall health and ensuring the fulfillment of their rights.
- The better prepared the adopted child or adult is at the time of meeting his/her roots, the more enriching the encounters are for everyone. Adequate preparation includes having information of their history, photos, narratives and memories, but above all, having a space to discuss the topic with a trusted and relevant person, which can be a family member or a professional who offers psychological assistance.
- International adoptions impact the development of ACEs by involving weak attachment to their biological roots and/or multiple attachments,

[8]To maintain confidentiality, adopted girls will be referred to as María, the biological mothers as Juana. The initials FA will refer to adoptive families, and FB to biological families. MB will refer to biological mother.

which affect the subjectivity of the adopted child and increase their socio-emotional vulnerability.

- The experiences of the five adopted women reveal an important relationship between their adoption stories and the development of psychological distress, including traumas, particularly attachment disorder, generalised anxiety disorder, selective mutism, self-destructive ideation and behaviours, substance and alcohol use disorders and depression.
- The reconnection of internationally adopted individuals with their biological roots is timely only if it occurs under appropriate conditions, with a deep understanding and respect for both cultures (the culture of origin and the adoption one), without bias and discrimination against any of the parties involved, and with human resources trained both personally and professionally to act as cultural and emotional 'bridges'.
- The reconnection stories studied show that the experience of reconnection can serve as an opportunity for growth and acceptance of the life history of both the adopted children and their adoptive and biological families.
- Satisfactory experiences, as recounted by adopted individuals aged 15–20 and their families, have been observed during reunions. For children aged 11–14, this is a particularly challenging period for connecting with this aspect of their lives and the associated challenges, possibly linked to typical adolescent crises.
- One of the challenges of the reconnection experience was to create a non-invasive meeting for the BMs, respecting their privacy, their right to remain silent and not to expose themselves to others with their choices and decisions. In all cases, the mothers were consulted about their willingness and availability for the meeting. This consideration recognises that they, as part of the system, may also have experienced ACEs due to the separation from their children, which in some cases was non-consensual.
- As mental health professionals working with internationally adopted individuals, we are called to raise awareness in communities and governments about the responsibilities that each party has in preventing ACEs in the adoption processes and promoting resilient behaviours, as well as support systems for adopted individuals, their social context and its imagery, and for both adoptive and biological families.

In closing this chapter, I would like to quote Rosa Ortiz (2006) with words that reflect the complexity of the issue and challenge us to continue thinking about it from the dignity that every human being deserves:

> **In the concert of affections, desires, problems, and opportunities, the respectful treatment of each of the parties involved is important for everyone ...**[9]

[9] Bold text is my addition.

References

Álvarez, A. K. (2018, [mes no especificado]). *De adopción y psicoanálisis*. Sociedad Psicoanalítica de México. https://spm.mx/2018/de-adopcion-y-psicoanalisis

Boullier, M. and Blair, M. (2017). Adverse childhood experiences. *Pediatrics and Child Health* 28 (3): 132–137. ISSN 1751-7222. https://www.sciencedirect.com/science/article/pii/S1751722217302913, https://doi.org/10.1016/j.paed.2017.12.008.

Bowlby, J. and Ainsworth, M. (1978). The Bowlby-Ainsworth attachment theory. *Behavioral and Brain Sciences* 1 (3): 417–464. https://doi.org/10.1017/S0140525X000757726.

Código del Menor (Ley N° 903), Pub. L. No. 903, 20 de agosto de 1981 (Paraguay). https://www.bacn.gov.py/leyes-paraguayas/903/codigo-del-menor (accessed January 20, 2026).

Dinkler, L., Lundström, S., Gajwani, R. et al. (2017). Maltreatment-associated neurodevelopmental disorders: a co-twin control analysis. *Journal of Child Psychology and Psychiatry* 58 (6): 691–701. https://doi.org/10.1111/jcpp.12682. PMID: 28094432.

Escobar de, G. (2004–2008). *Informes de Archivo de la Trabajadora Social (inéditos)*. Paraguay: Asunción.

Felitti, V.J., Anda, R.F., Nordenberg, D. et al. (1998). Relationship of childhood abuse and household dysfunction to many of the leading causes of death in adults. The Adverse Childhood Experiences (ACE) Study. *Am J Prev Med* 14 (4): 245–258. https://doi.org/10.1016/s0749-3797(98)00017-8.

Ley de adopciones. Ley 1136/97 (1997). Paraguay.

Ley de promoción y protección del derecho de niños, niñas y adolescentes a vivir en familia, que regula las medidas de cuidados alternativos y la adopción. 6486/19 (2019) Paraguay

Ley N° 5777, 27 de diciembre de 2016 (Paraguay). https://www.bacn.gov.py/leyes-paraguayas/5777/ley-n-5777-de-proteccion-integral-a-las-mujeres-contra-toda-forma-de-violencia

Ortíz, R., Palau, M., and Cálcena, S. (2006). *La adopción. Un acto de amor y de derechos. Los beneficios del cumplimiento de la ley*, 1e. Asunción: Edit. Global Infancia.

Oxford Learner's Dictionaries. (n.d.). Bond. In Oxford Learner's Dictionaries. Retrieved January 20, 2026, from https://www.oxfordlearnersdictionaries.com/definition/english/bond

Rotenberg, E.Y. and Wainer, A.B. (compiladoras)(2007). *Homoparentalidades. Nuevas Familias*. Buenos Aires: Ed. Lugar.

U.S. Department of State – Bureau of Consular Affairs (2008). Travel.State.Gov. https://travel.state.gov/content/travel/en/Intercountry-Adoption.html (accessed 2008).

Winnicott, D.W. (1987). The theory of the parent-infant relationship. In: *The Collected Works of D. W. Winnicott: Home is where we start from*, vol. 6, 88–95. Tavistock/Routledge.

Chapter 9

GREEK ADOLESCENTS

Anna Tsiboukli

Department of Pedagogy and Primary Education, School of Education, National and Kapodistrian University of Athens, Athens, Greece

Introduction

Greece has experienced economic turmoil for over 10 years, followed by the COVID-19 pandemic. Austerity measures introduced then had a significant socioeconomic impact on the population, increased unemployment rates and a higher risk for poverty and social exclusion (Melidis and Tzagkarakis 2022). At the same time, major cuts to health and mental healthcare services left the population in need without adequate support, with all the consequences of major cuts to healthcare (McKee and Stuckler 2016, p. 41). Patterns of drug and alcohol misuse in youth also changed during the fiscal crisis, with an increase in the illegal trade of alcohol (Pomini et al. 2014). Together with the fiscal crisis, a new drug, the 'cocaine of the poor', also called 'the crisis drug' (Triantos et al. 2014), appeared in the streets of Athens in the year 2010. This cheap and contaminated drug is produced in small labs, and it is mainly used by young drug users. International media life, The Guardian, VICE, CNN, BBC Radio 4, etc. (Miller 2013), have covered the issue extensively with reportage at that time, linking fiscal crisis and austerity measures with the new Athenian drug scene. Furthermore, UN Annual Report claimed that Greece was developing into a cannabis hub and one of the main trafficking routes for heroin (International Narcotics Control Board, 2015). However, all data from EMCDDA and ESPAD Report 2019 (2020) research, which addresses high school students (17.733) aged 16–18 years old, continue to demonstrate that 16-year-olds in Greece exhibit lower drug use rates than their counterparts in other European countries (ESPAD, 2020).

The socioeconomic crisis was followed by service reduction (Tsiboukli 2017) as staff numbers in drug treatment, prevention and parole services who retired were not replaced or they were replaced by temporary staff. Thus, services experience a staff shortage with a one-fifth turnover rate.

The Intergenerational Effects of Adverse Childhood Experiences: Ripples on a Pond, First Edition. Edited by Richard Pates and Diane Riley.

Published 2026 by John Wiley & Sons Ltd.

The socioeconomic crisis was also followed by hard confinement measures during COVID-19 that contributed to the increase of mental health issues, especially amongst the youth, that are not yet well researched or documented. The economic crisis was also linked with depression, anxiety, suicidal attempts and an increase in drug and alcohol use in adolescence (Basta et al. 2021, 2022). Also, social solidarity health and mental health services developed at that time in Greece to serve vulnerable groups, made similar anecdotal reports. Public Health services addressing adolescents who use illicit drugs, also show an increase in their numbers, even though they are not enough to cover the treatment demands of the country's entire population. Therefore, existing services strive to respond to the increasing treatment demands with limited resources.

Adolescents' engagement with illicit drug use in Greece

Data available for adolescents' engagement with illicit drug use in Greece derives mainly from publicly funded facilities that provide counselling and intervention programmes. Therefore, data is limited to a certain population and fails to capture the extent of the problem. Other information coming from the ESPAD research, which is carried out mainly with self-administered questionnaires addressed to high school students, measures tendencies and experimentation with alcohol and other drugs. The European School Survey Project on Alcohol and Other Drugs for the year 2024 is still not available. Hence, all relevant data is derived from the last ESPAD study carried out in Greece in the year 2019. According to these findings, cannabis use in the high school population reaches 8%, inhalants 4.8%, painkillers without prescription (5%), all other illicit drugs (cocaine, heroin, etc.) less than 2% and alcohol misuse 11.7% (5+ drinks in a row in the last 30 days) (ESPAD, 2020). According to ESPAD Report 2019 (2020), approximately 32.3% report that someone important to them consumes alcohol excessively. Nonetheless, most of the 16-year-old students (84%) have never experimented with drugs in their lifetime. However, there are three issues concerning with ESPAD data. First, the research is addressed to high school students only, therefore, missing the population of school dropouts and more at greater risk. Second, the study concerns experimentation with drug and alcohol use and not necessarily excessive use and third, the next ESPAD research is currently running. Hence, the effects of confinement due to the pandemic on the adolescent population experimentation with drugs and alcohol are not yet available. Nonetheless, an interesting finding of the ESPAD study in Greece is that most high school students who are experimenting with drugs come from either a high-class economic background or a low-class socioeconomic background.

A significant source of data comes from KETHEA STROFI, a facility that has operated for more than 30 years in Greece to offer services to adolescents who use illicit drugs and their families. KETHEA STROFI, in more than 30 years of its operation, offered counselling and treatment services to

5.236 adolescents and approximately 8,000 family members. In the current year 2024, counselling was offered to 114 adolescents and 160 significant others (parents, siblings). Most adolescents are 17.5 years old and of Greek origin (only 4.3% of other nationalities), men (68.1%) who live with their parents (83.6%). Most are primary (13.8%) and middle school (25.4%) graduates, or they are still registered, not necessarily attending high school. When they report transgenerational use of drugs, excessive use of alcohol or mental health challenges, 28.3% of them suggest that their father faced such issues in their family of origin, some (17.4%) suggest that this was an issue of their mother's side and 15.2% of their siblings. In half of the cases (50.5%), parents are divorced. Most adolescents report initiation to drugs at the mean age of 14.8, with cannabis being the main substance of use (96.6%), accompanied by 35.3% with cocaine and for 15.7% with sedatives. Some (7.5%) report use of cocaine and others (3.7%), heroin as their preferred substance of use. In addition, 39.1% of adolescents report experiencing mental health issues, 29.8% legal issues and 2.6% convictions for criminal offenses. Most adolescents report that this is their first attempt to seek help for reducing or abstaining from illicit drug use (87.1%), mainly due to family pressure (55.2%). (Source: KETHEA, 2023). The above data suggests that adversities are present in the lives of adolescents who misuse drugs and concern not just familial patterns of use but also other contributing socio-economic conditions.

Lived experiences of adolescents who use illicit drugs in Greece

Adverse childhood experiences amongst adolescents who seek treatment for illicit drug use in Greece include illicit drug and alcohol use and/or child abuse in the familial environment. However, these findings derive from the narratives of adolescents who attend treatment programmes in Greece (Cullen and Tsiboukli 2019) rather than from systematic research studies. There are not many studies focusing on transgenerational nature of ACEs in Greece that pay particular attention to the adolescent period. One of the few studies available (Sakkopoulou and Tsiboukli 2024) concerns mainly the recollection of memories of adult women who had at least one guardian misusing alcohol and/or drugs in their underage years within their family context. The study concluded that in the dynamics of these families, there was abuse, neglect, emotional difficulties, financial problems and mental health issues in at least one of the two guardians. Additionally, in almost all of the above families, the children experienced divorce and/or the death of one of their parents, which in most cases was due to drug or alcohol misuse. Greek society, at the time these women were brought up, was characterised as a patriarchal society when compared to other and, especially Northern European countries. This had a result that some of the study participants perceived family adversities (violence, abuse, neglect, addiction, etc.) during childhood as normal, even though familial roles were reversed and children were often taking up adult parental roles. Some participants took care of themselves both practically (e.g. waking up on their own, preparing their school meals, household chores, etc.) and emotionally. Others had to mature early in life to help their parents face their own issues with drugs and alcohol (Sakkopoulou and Tsiboukli 2024; Smyrnaki et al. 2021, 2024).

Another significant set of adversities concerns the socioeconomic factors and structural inequalities that adolescents who seek treatment for illicit drug use at the Greek treatment facilities experience. In Greece, the number of children at risk for poverty and social exclusion is among the highest in the European Community, exceeding 30% (Eurostat 2024). A relatively new law (4375/2016) in the country extended vulnerability to also include unaccompanied minors who are asylum seekers. Unaccompanied minors are exposed to traumatic events and adverse experiences, as some might have lost their families, others might be victims of trafficking and others were child soldiers in war zones. These adverse experiences are often related to mental health disorders, post-traumatic stress, depression, anxiety and increased risk for drug and alcohol use (Björkenstam et al. 2021). The same law (4375/2016) also made specific reference to the fiscal crisis-stricken socially vulnerable groups, recognising socioeconomic conditions as significant adversities, especially for minors. Adverse childhood experiences place adolescents at risk for social exclusion by minimising their access to education, training, health and social care facilities (Downes 2014). Interventions aimed at connecting adolescents with training and education and tackling social exclusion (Toiviainen and Hyytia 2019) do not always succeed.

Therefore, the number of adolescents and young people facing adversities in Greece increased, especially at the peak of the fiscal crisis (Drakaki et al. 2014), leaving 20% of adolescents and young people in general and 30% of young women in particular out of training, education or employment (European Statistical Office, 2024). School dropout is another factor relevant to illicit drug misuse, as Greece is classified as one of the EU countries with a high rate (8.6%) in the number of young people (15–19 years old) who are not in training, education or employment. This population is not, however, well researched. Therefore, it is not clear to what extent adolescents and young people who face socioeconomic adversities are engaged in illicit drug use and other related activities, even though almost all adolescents who reach treatment facilities report a family background where socioeconomic adversities are present. Furthermore, most adolescents facing adversities remain invisible to traditional institutions. Relevant facilities addressing the multiple needs of adolescents who use illicit drugs were established in Greece only in the last 30 years.

To capture their lived experiences, a focus group meeting with eight (8) adolescents at the social re-entry centre of KETHEA STROFI drug-free treatment facility was carried out with the purpose of narrating their own life stories. The themes that emerged include: (i) relationships with others, (ii) the facades of Athens, (iii) involvement in drug-related activities, and (iv) the need for a safe environment. One of the main issues adolescents focused on was the need to build strong relations with significant others, as they often feel disconnected. They introduced their own term 'de-socialisation' to describe their perception of isolation and 'self-absorption' as a condition in which none is interested in communicating with others. Building strong personal relationships seems to be very important as in the urban environment of modern Athens, they perceive others and especially adults, as being absorbed with superficial things. When discussing the lived experiences in the city of Athens, they often refer to an inner city neighbourhood with a long tradition of drug trafficking and gang fighting that often concerns the police and the inhabitants. They also describe post-crisis and post-COVID Athens as a place with two facades, the tourist façade, where the real part of the city is hidden and the façade of misery they perceive in people's sad faces, in the dirty streets, the ruined playgrounds and the air pollution where people's health issues seem to get worse or relationships with old friends broken. Another central theme raised in their narration was that of criminality and drug trafficking and the hidden fear that prevails in the city. Many of them feel that several young people are being involved in drug use and criminal activity and that some adolescents in Athens form groups that act as 'gangs' to protect them from other groups with similar activities. They also give their own explanations in relation to the causes of adolescents' involvement with offensive behaviour. Some raise the issue of power relations and others suggest that it is a matter of principle. They also suggest that drug use has become a more and more acceptable behaviour amongst the youth, and even that parents no longer see it as a behaviour that requires attention and intervention. Discussing the effectiveness of their intervention programme, the ability to form meaningful relations with peers and significant others (parents and counsellors) in a safe environment was revealed as an important factor. However, available interventions for adolescents who use illicit drugs are not many in Greece. Thus, few have the opportunity to be exposed to positive experiences that may be linked with informed decisions.

Interventions for adolescents who misuse drugs in Greece

In Greece, the civil war after WWII and dictatorship (1967–1974) were two major reasons for the late development of social sciences and treatment services for drug and alcohol users. In the early 1980s, social change services and drug-free treatment to people who misused illicit drugs were made possible with the establishment of the first therapeutic community in Greece, ITHACA (1983) and subsequently KETHEA (1987), a not-for-profit organisation where all drug-free treatment facilities were included, later a member of ECOSOC, United Nations. The KETHEA programmes were initially addressed to adults misusing mainly heroin and later treatment facilities for adults misusing alcohol or being engaged in excessive gambling were also included. Up to that time, people who misused alcohol and drugs were either incarcerated or held in psychiatric hospitals against their will. In the early 90s, a governmental organisation

(OKANA) providing low threshold substitution treatment was also established. In addition, three more treatment facilities for illicit drug misuse at the psychiatric hospitals of Athens and Thessaloniki, respectively, and two facilities for excessive alcohol use and/or gambling, one in Athens and one in the psychiatric hospital of Thessaloniki, were also established. Later, in early 2000, AA and NA groups started to operate mainly in big cities. Recently, a new law was passed in autumn 2024 in Greece, merging all of the above organisations into one, possibly for reducing costs, effective from January 1st, 2025. This government decision found strong opposition amongst parents, members in treatment and the workforce.

The first programme for adolescents and young adults aged 13–21 years old was established in 1988 within KETHEA as an open care facility. In order to host adolescents from rural Greece, the facility now offers residence. The programme also provides free counselling to parents and siblings following the peer support approach. Parents whose children have already achieved abstinence act as group leaders, sharing their experiences. KETHEA STROFI also consists of a counselling centre, a residential therapeutic community, a social re-entry centre and a family programme. All services are offered free of charge, as the main source of funding remains the Greek state. The programme supports abstinence, reintegration into education, work and social life. Counselling services are also offered at the Special Detention Centre for Young People in Avlona and in Athens' Juvenile Courts, where KETHEA STROFI can also support adolescents and young adults who are brought before the court for criminal offences or traffic violations. KETHEA STROFI also runs a Recording Studio and a Web Radio to give community members the opportunity for training in music and sound engineering and to broadcast their own radio show every Monday. Other facilities addressed to adolescents who use illicit drugs (Plefsi, Pilotos and Anadisi) operate under KETHEA, the first in Athens, the second in the city of Volos and the third in the city of Thessaloniki, respectively, whilst in Athens, there are two more facilities for adolescents, one (Atrapos) operating under OKANA and one under the psychiatric hospital of Athens (18 Ano Adolescent Unit). In other cities and rural Greece, there are some groups for adolescents under adult services, mainly of KETHEA. Therefore, most families, especially from rural Greece, have limited access to adolescent drug treatment facilities.

KETHEA STROFI provides significant psychological support interventions to adolescents and their parents and siblings. These interventions are very important to restore relations with the familial environment. A meeting was carried out with six adolescents (five men and one woman), who were asked to talk about their lived experience in the therapeutic community and focus mainly on what they have found significant in this process of change. Participants were asked to sit down and write at their own time and pace their experience and share with the author their writings. The quotes are based on their notes sent to the author:

> Well, many things contributed to me being who I am today. I will start with the most important, which is family and relationships in general. Before the

community, with the passage of time, I realised that more and more often my friends pushed me aside and as I was living alone ... So, at some point and since I lost all this and my circle was really very small and not the best, I realised the situation and wanted to change. My parents played a very important role as for a long time, I was using drugs, we didn't talk. So, it was a motivation for me to get my life back and they too. In the community, being 28 months sober, I have received many things which are invaluable, but the most important is that I finally started setting goals which I am achieving. I got motivated to go to a school to study and to do something that I like and love. I saw that I have people around me and that they support me in all this. And they really gave me a lot of strength and a lot of motivation. I am truly grateful because I have my life back and all thanks to the Strofi family... (D.)

I was a cheater, which had led me to use ... I liked to lie to satisfy the other, to say what is, at any cost, the community with me. It helped a lot to change this trait of mine ... I have realized how important it is to have clear relationships ... I found a place where they loved me for who I am ... I always wanted to please others and think about what they will say about me ... they helped me to love me and then others for what they really are without expecting to gain anything from them ... I feel grateful because I found the reasons I did drugs ... these are my supplies ... the feelings of using I have found much stronger in community ... in education the Family Association supported me ... I got a scholarship to a school that deals with tourism ... I am very thirsty ... I managed to set goals, limits, values ... to step on my feet ... to be proud (N.)

The impoverishment, the downfall I experienced in the piazza ... in the therapeutic community, I managed to finish school, get a scholarship to another school ... my motivation to change was my social brother, he was my role model as an only child ... I wanted to look like (G.)

... honesty and honesty ... I were received with great care ... all this kept me going when I felt difficult ... over time I started to feel safe ... (Th.)

...drugs made me lose everything and everyone ... nothing made sense unless I was under the influence ... everything was about drugs ... I would wake up and sleep with the same stress and anxiety about finding drugs and getting high ... there was no B plan for me if I wanted my life back, I would have to fight for it ... I am almost 31 months sober ... the most important thing in this journey is friendship ... without the friends I've made in the therapeutic community, I wouldn't have been able to make it ... being able to communicate, share my feelings, without being criticized ... this is the biggest gift for me ... I feel safe, protected, loved ... I started finding the parts of me that were buried ... loving myself and the people around me ... I don't want to be treated the wrong way (Na).

What helped me to change my behaviour was clearly the structure of the programme ... I started to understand what boundaries are, I was more active and stopped thinking about drugs ... that was at first ... but what kept me going is

> the relationships and my goal to finish school ... today I am enrolled in a cooking school and I am also working ... I feel that without KETHEA STROFI I would still be a society's ghost (Y).

Reading carefully their notes, it becomes clear that four significant elements emerge from their treatment experience: (i) safe structure provided by the treatment programme that allows to set up realistic and tangible goals, (ii) clear boundaries set for the first time not only from others but also from oneself (iii) the ability to form meaningful relationships with significant others, being either peers or counsellors and (iv) setting and achieving a specific goal such as completing education and/or finding a job that helps better integrate in society. These elements make the programme unique, given its intensity (several hours per day), time needed to complete treatment (at least 12 months) and the clear boundary to remain sober while in treatment or else be excluded from the process. These are challenging conditions for several adolescents and their families, but others seem to benefit enormously from such experiences.

Other counselling or treatment efforts in Greece concern piloting programmes to prevent alcohol use in the school environment (Angeli et al. 2024). However, these programmes do not necessarily address the population at risk. In order to increase protective factors (Fazel and Betancourt 2018), psychological support is offered to restore past traumas and restructure family life and increase resilience as a dynamic process dependent on time and space, individual and family characteristics, cultural influences, education and social support networks. Interventions focus on learning new skills and making new friends in the new environment that can help resolve personal issues.

Conclusion

Most adolescents who reach facilities addressing illicit drug use mainly come from backgrounds where illicit drug and/or alcohol misuse was part of their upbringing. Transgenerational behavioural problems, such as use of drugs (Ezard 2012), seem to be part of their lived experience. However, another significant issue and a major adversity for adolescents was early school dropout. Thus, adversities are not only transgenerational but they are also linked with other factors, including socioeconomic ones. Available facilities for adolescents are very few. The one residential facility offers, together with psychological counselling, other creative opportunities. Participating in music groups, radio broadcasting and other creative activities helps adolescents replace dysfunctional behavioural patterns with functional, healthy choices. These adolescents perceive the 'community' not only in terms of space and time but also in terms of interest and identification with certain groups. However, the upcoming merging of all organisations into one and the cost reduction in treatment facilities place a significant organisation at risk. The effects have to be evaluated and addressed at a later stage in relation to quality of services addressed to adolescent drug users, if such programmes will continue to exist in post-fiscal crisis, post-COVID and post-modern Greece.

Acknowledgements

I would like to express my gratitude to KETHEA STROFI programme director, Ms. Kiratso Skodrogianni and the group of adolescents attending the social re-entry facility of the programme for trusting me and sharing with me their valuable experience. Also, many thanks to my excellent colleague Dr. Gerassimos Papanastasatos, Head of KETHEA Department of Education, for his kindness in sharing with me the relevant data.

References

Angeli, M., Hassandra, M., Krommidas, C. et al. (2024). The effectiveness of a TPB Educational Program for Preventing Alcohol Use Among Adolescents. *Alcoholism Treatment Quarterly* 42 (4): 451–469.

Basta, M., Micheli, K., Karakonstantis, S. et al. (2021). Suicidal ideation in adolescents and young adults in Greece: prevalence and association with sociodemographic variables, mental health and substance use. *European Child & Adolescent Psychiatry* 30: 1129–1136.

Basta, M., Micheli, K., Koutra, K. et al. (2022). Depression and anxiety symptoms in adolescents and young adults in Greece: prevalence and associated factors. *Journal of Affective Disorders Reports* 8: 100334.

Björkenstam, E.M., Norredam, M., Helgesson, M. et al. (2021). Common mental disorders among young refugees in Sweden: the role of education and duration of residency. *Journal of Affective Disorders* 266: 563–571. https://doi.org/10.1016/j.jad.2020.02.015.

Cullen, J. and Tsiboukli, A. (2019). Using lifeworld analysis to co-design a new role in youth work. *Exartiseis* 32: 27–45. https://doi.org/10.57160/PKRP1155.

Downes, P. (2014). *Prison Education: Indicators at Micro-Messo Levels. Access to Education in Europe. A Framework and Agenda for System Change.* UK: Springer https://www.dcu.ie/sites/default/files/edc/pdf/eucislllbrusselsdec10th2014.pdf.

Drakaki, M., Papadakis, N., Kyridis, A., and Papargyris, A. (2014). Who's the Greek Neet? Neets' profile in Greece: parameters, trends and common characteristics of a heterogeneous group. *International Journal of Humanities and Social Science* 4 (6): 240–254.

ESPAD Report 2019 (2020). Results from the European School Survey Project on Alcohol and other Drugs. The ESPAD Group-EMCDDA. https://www.espad.org/sites/default/files/2020.3878_EN_04.pdf (accessed 22 November 2025)

European Statistical Office (2024). Children at risk of poverty of social exclusion, 2024. https://ec.europa.eu/eurostat/statistics-explained/images/0/00/Children_AROPE%2C_2024.png (accessed 23 November 2025).

European Statistical Office (2024). Statistics on young people neither in employment nor in education or training. https://ec.europa.eu/eurostat/statistics-explained/index.php?title=Statistics_on_young_people_neither_in_employment_nor_in_education_or_training (May 2025).

Ezard, N. (2012). Substance use among populations displaced by conflict: a literature review. *Disasters* 36: 533–557. https://doi.org/10.1111/j.1467-7717.2011.01261.x.

Fazel, M. and Betancourt, T.S. (2018). Preventive mental health interventions for refugee children and adolescents in high income settings. *The Lancet Child and Adolescent Health* 2 (2): 121–132. https://doi.org/10.1016/S2352-4642(17)30147-5.

International Narcotics Control Board (2015). Report of the International Narcotics Control Board for 2014. UN. ISBN: 978-92-1-148279-9. https://www.incb.org/incb/en/publications/annual-reports/annual-report-2014.html (accessed 23 November 2025).

KETHEA (2023). KETHEA Project Report. htpps://www.kethea.gr/wp-content/uploads/2024/09/KETHEA_APOL_2023_web_CC.pdf (accessed 23 November 2025) (in Greek).

McKee, M. and Stuckler, D. (2016). Health effects of the financial crisis: lessons from Greece. A commentary. *The Lancet* 1: 40–41. http://www.thelancet.com/pdfs/journals/lanpub/PIIS2468-2667(16)30016-0.pdf.

Melidis, M. and Tzagkarakis, S.I. (2022). The evolution of social vulnerability in Greece during the economic crisis (2008–2017). *European Societies* 24 (2): 229–250. https://doi.org/10.1080/14616696.2021.2007973.

Miller, A. (2013). Austerity's drug of choice. VICE. https://www.vice.com/el/article/austeritys-drug-of-choice-000757-v20n5/ (accessed 23 November 2025).

Pomini, V., Mellos, L., Paparrigopoulos, T., and Liappas, J. (2014). Alcohol misuse in Greece: a 15-year experience from a specialized outpatient service. *Psychiatriki* 25 (3): 208–216. PMID: 25367665.

Sakkopoulou, A. & Tsiboukli, A. (2024). Recollection of childhood memories from parental drug and alcohol misuse in a Qualitative Study of Women in Greece, *Alcoholism Treatment Quarterly*, 42 (2), 153–167, https://doi.org/10.1080/07347324.2024.2304193

Smyrnaki, M., Skoulas, M., Liodaki, A., Papadimitriou, D., Papanastasatos, G.& Tsiboukli, A. (2021). Developmental pathways to pathological gambling and reasons for treatment seeking in a Greek rural sample, *Journal of Substance Use*, 1–8. https://doi.org/10.1080/14659891.2023.2231558

Smyrnaki, M., Skoulas, M., Liodaki, A., Papadimitriou, D., Papanastasatos, G. & Tsiboukli, A. 2024 Family history of pathological gambling pathological gambling, related factors, effects and suicidality in rural Greece, *Alcoholism Treatment Quarterly*, 42 (4), 509–525. https://doi.org/10.1080/07347324.2024.2376085

Toiviainen, H. and Hyytia, J. (2019). Understanding vulnerability and encouraging young adults to become active citizens through education: the role of adult education professionals. *Journal of Adult and Continuing Education* 25 (1): 45–64. https://doi.org/10.1177/1477971419826116.

Triantos, P., Papanastasatos, G., Poulopoulos, C., and Zaxaropoulos, Y. (2014). Patterns of use and perceptions of drug addicts in Greece about "shisha" (a new synthetic drug) at economic crisis era. *Drugs and Alcohol Today* 14 (1): 10–18. https://doi.org/10.1108/DAT-10-2013-0041.

Tsiboukli, A. (2017). Greek crisis: impact on drug treatment service. *Nordic Studies on Alcohol and Drugs* 32 (3): 333–337. https://journals.sagepub.com/doi/abs/10.1515/nsad-2015-0031.

Chapter 10

ADVERSE CHILDHOOD EXPERIENCES AND MENTAL HEALTH: MICRO AND MACRO SOCIAL FACTORS IN MEXICO

Liliana Templos-Núñez

Departamento de Investigación Psicosocial y Documental, Centros de Integración Juvenil, Mexico City, Mexico

Adverse Childhood Experiences (ACEs) are 'childhood events, varying in severity and often chronic, occurring in a family or social environment and causing harm or distress' (Kalmakis and Chandler 2014, p. 1490). This concept encompasses the characteristics of being chronic, harmful, cumulative, stressful and with variations in severity. Its presentation is so complex that it encompasses the family and social sphere, including micro and macro social factors (Kalmakis and Chandler 2014).

Worldwide, a 24-country study of 68,894 adults in the general population found that more than 70% reported having experienced a traumatic event; 30.5% were exposed to 4 or more of them. Globally, the five most common types were: witnessing a death or serious injury, the unexpected death of a loved one, being assaulted, suffering a life-threatening traffic accident and suffering a life-threatening illness or injury (Benjet et al. 2016).

Most of the studies conducted to determine the magnitude of the problem and the impact of ACEs have been carried out in developed countries. Paradoxically, in low- and middle-income countries, there are economic, political and social situations that may represent a greater exposure to traumatic or potentially adverse events (Benjet 2010). For example, according to the United Nations Children's Fund, nearly two-thirds of children aged 1–14 in Latin America and the Caribbean experience violent discipline at home and the mortality rate from homicide among children and adolescents is four times higher than the global average (United Nations Children's Fund 2022).

In Mexico, unfavorable economic conditions, geographical characteristics, cultural issues (such as machismo and gender-based violence) and social violence resulting from the war on drugs and organised crime have been shown to be an important source of traumatic events.

The Intergenerational Effects of Adverse Childhood Experiences: Ripples on a Pond,
First Edition. Edited by Richard Pates and Diane Riley.

Published 2026 by John Wiley & Sons Ltd.

The objective of this chapter is to present the reader with an overview of the adverse events that Mexican children and adolescents face as a result of these characteristics.

Mexico and the potentially traumatic events

Mexico is a Latin American country with a population of approximately 129 million people, of which about a quarter are under 15 years old (OECD 2024). After the beginning of independence from Spain, the country of which it was a colony for 300 years, the Mexican population has gone through different social situations and conflicts that have served as potentially traumatic events for the Mexican population. In addition, the country's geographical position, tectonic faults and other factors make Mexico one of the countries with the longest history of natural disasters in the world.

The so-called 'war on drugs' has been linked to a series of social nuances permeated by violence in the form of assassinations, forced disappearances, attacks, extortion and forced migration.

These issues will be discussed in greater detail below.

Natural disasters

According to the World Risk Index (Bündnis Entwicklung Hilft and The Institute for International Law of Peace and Armed Conflict 2023), Mexico has a risk index for natural disasters of 38.17, which places it in fourth place worldwide, after the Philippines, Indonesia and India and before Colombia. This risk is considered very high and is the sum of exposure and vulnerability. The index assumes that risk is composed of the degree of exposure to natural events and the degree of vulnerability of society to that event. Social inequalities, the level of economic development, the weakening of the population due to political instability, violence, disasters, general health conditions, response capacity of the health system, among other factors, come into play (Bündnis Entwicklung Hilft and The Institute for International Law of Peace and Armed Conflict 2023).

Exposure is composed of the frequency and intensity of natural events such as earthquakes, tsunamis, floods, cyclones, droughts, among others, in a given area. Mexico ranks second globally, after China, with a score of 50.08, which is also considered very high.

Potentially dangerous natural events may be due to natural environmental conditions or to climate change, the way in which human beings have used and influenced their environment. Historically, a large number of natural disasters have occurred in Mexican territory; since the period of the Spanish conquest, for the construction of colonial cities, the lakes of Tenochtitlán were drained and large areas of land were deforested (Alcántara-Ayala 2019).

From 1980 to date, there have been numerous natural events such as floods, hurricanes, volcanic eruptions, earthquakes and cyclones that have left an average of 443.2 deaths per year between 1988 and 1999, 190 deaths per year from 2000 to 2018 and 2,357 million dollars of cost between 2000 and 2018 in 2024 (Centro de Prevención Nacional de Desastres n.d.). It is worth noting the case of the earthquakes that occurred on September 19th, 1985 and September 19th, 2017, which left substantial damage and material losses, in addition to marking a date on which two major earthquakes occurred.

Adverse social conditions

Adverse social conditions in Mexico are a reflection of profound social, structural and economic problems. They manifest themselves in poverty, inequality and violence, which are interwoven to result in a panorama where the free development of children and adolescents is hindered.

Poverty

In Mexico in 2022, more than a third of the population (36.3% or 46.8 million people) lived in poverty. Of these, 9.1 million lived in extreme poverty. Almost 65 million people (half of the population) lacked access to social security, 50 million lacked access to health services and 23 million lacked access to nutritious and quality food. In terms of education, in 2022, almost 16% of the population between the ages of 3 and 21 did not attend school and did not have compulsory education. (Consejo Nacional de Evaluación de la Política de Desarrollo Social 2023).

Violence

According to the Global Peace Index, 2024 (The Institute for Economics and Peace 2024), Mexico has a low peace index, ranking 138th out of 163. In Central America and the Caribbean, it ranks second to last, only ahead of Haiti, and in the Americas, it is the third country with the lowest index, only after Colombia and Venezuela.

The manifestations of violence in Mexico are varied and diverse in nature. They cover the public and private spheres in the form of crimes such as murder, kidnapping, extortion, crimes against health or aggressions that occur within the family. The origin of violence in Mexico can be traced to different variables that have to do with the level of poverty, marginalisation, lack of spaces and infrastructure that prevent the construction of values of social and community cohesion, lack of opportunities for development and lack of optimism to improve one's own economic and social conditions, the presence and expansion of organised crime, the availability of weapons, drugs and alcohol, the precarious presence of authorities and the lack of justice, the absence of a culture of legality, the transnational impacts of crime and domestic violence (Herrera-Laso 2013).

Crime

It is estimated that in 2023, 31 million crimes occurred with a rate of 33,267 crimes per 100,000 inhabitants. The most common crimes are fraud, extortion and robbery. Likewise, almost 90 thousand kidnappings of a household member are estimated for the same year. Regarding the perception of public safety, 16.7% of people aged 18 and over felt unsafe at home. For women, this percentage is higher: 18.5% did not feel safe at home (INEGI 2024a).

Between 2015 and 2022, 229,182 homicides occurred, of which more than 110 thousand happened in public spaces: in second place, in Ministry of Health hospitals (23,925) and in third place, at home (22,841). Women are more likely to suffer a violent death at home, regardless of the medium and on public roads, due to physical or chemical mechanisms. Men, on the other hand, are killed by firearms and sharp objects. This is related to a complex mechanism associated with sex, gender and structural elements such as place of residence, marginalisation, poverty and education, and where women are in a state of vulnerability in family environments that make them more likely to experience various types of violence (López-Ortiz et al. 2024).

Violence against women

At the national level, 70.1% of Mexican women over the age of 15 had experienced violence in their lifetime, while 42.8% had experienced violence in the last 12 months. 51.6% had experienced psychological violence; 49.7%, sexual violence; 27.4%, economic violence; and 34.7%, physical violence. The community setting is where most violence against women over 15 years old is exercised, with 45.6% in their lifetime (psychological, physical and sexual). The second place is occupied by intimate partner violence: 39.9% of women have been subjected to violence in their last or current relationship. Regarding violence in childhood, 41.8% of women aged 15 years and older reported having suffered some kind of aggression, the most frequent being physical violence, followed by psychological and sexual, and sexual abuse and rape or attempted rape (INEGI 2022).

War on drugs

The war on drugs in Mexico is a complex and multifaceted conflict that began to intensify in the late 2000s. This struggle involves the authorities and drug cartels that have evolved and diversified their range of action, now also carrying out forced disappearances and trafficking of Mexican nationals and migrants, extortion, money laundering and racketeering. For this reason, more than just cartels, they are now considered organised crime.

Since the beginning of a military offensive against cartels in 2006, violence has increased dramatically. The cartels, which control the production and trafficking of various substances, have responded with brutality, resulting in thousands of deaths, forced displacements and disappearances. The violence not only affects those involved in criminal activities but also impacts entire communities, creating a climate of fear and distrust (Olivera and Fuerte-Celis 2024).

Drug trafficking in Mexico is linked to social and economic problems, such as poverty and lack of opportunities. Many young people, attracted by the promises of wealth and power, become involved in these criminal organisations.

The situation of children and adolescents in Mexico

In 2022, there were 36.3 million children aged 0–17, 28.1% of the country's population. The main caregiver was the mother (83.2%). This was followed by grandmother (6.7%) and another person (father, aunt, uncle, grandfather, etc., with 10.1%) (INEGI 2024b). It is estimated that in 2015, 4.9% of children and adolescents between 0 and 17 years old were orphaned by a father or mother or both (Instituto Nacional de Salud Pública and UNICEF Mexico 2016). Estimates suggest that the COVID-19 pandemic orphaned around 130 thousand Mexican children (Hillis et al. 2021).

Discipline, care and environmental stimulation

In the area of discipline, it was found that 63.1% of children between 1 and 14 years old were subjected to at least one form of physical or psychological punishment by a family member in the previous month. While 53% of the children were subjected to psychological aggression, approximately 44% were subjected to physical punishment. More severe forms of physical punishment (blows to the head, ears or face, repeated hard blows) are generally less common: 6% of children were subjected to severe punishment. Boys were more subject to physical discipline (45%) than girls (42%) (Instituto Nacional de Salud Pública and UNICEF Mexico 2016).

In terms of care, 4% of children aged 0 to 59 months were left in the care of other children (under 10 years old), while 2% were left alone during the week prior to the interview. It is estimated then that a total of 5% of children had inadequate care during the week prior to the survey, either because they were left alone or in the care of another child. Inadequate care in the poorest households (8%) is almost three times more prevalent than in wealthier households (National Institute of Public Health and UNICEF Mexico 2016).

Regarding environmental stimulation through adult participation in activities with children and in the existence of books in the home, it was found that 3% of children aged 36–59 months did not receive participation of an adult in the home in any activity, this percentage rises to 15% among children whose mothers have no formal education, making it clear that poverty, lack of education and inequality are factors that feedback on each other and result in more adverse environments. Another example is that the proportion of children with whom some member of the household participated in learning support activities was 94% in the wealthiest households, in contrast to only 62% in the poorest households (Instituto Nacional de Salud Pública and UNICEF Mexico 2016).

Regarding physical and motor, socio-emotional, cognitive and language development, it was found that 23% of children aged 4 months to 4 years present developmental difficulties in at least one of the three areas. Children from poorer households present much higher prevalences of inadequate development in the cognitive (9%) and motor (10%) domains than children in wealthier households (2 and 4%, respectively) (Instituto Nacional de Salud Pública and UNICEF Mexico 2016).

Child labour

In Mexico, during 2015, 10.4% of the population between 5 and 14 years old was engaged in child labour. 10% of children aged 5–11 years perform some economic activity for at least 1 hour, compared to 15% of children aged 12–14 years, and 26% of children aged 15–17 years who perform some economic activity for less than 14 hours. In addition, 3% of the children aged 12–14 years and 4% of the children aged 15–17 years performed some economic activity for more than 14 hours. It is noteworthy that 8% of children aged 5–17 work in hazardous conditions (Instituto Nacional de Salud Pública and UNICEF Mexico 2016).

Considering socioeconomic level, it was observed that 22% of children and adolescents from the poorest quintile work (16% in hazardous conditions), while only 6% of their counterparts from the richest quintile work (3% in hazardous conditions). It was also observed that the percentage of children and adolescents belonging to indigenous households who work is almost double that of those in non-indigenous households (21 and 12%, respectively).

Marriage and teenage pregnancy

Regarding teenage marriage, 15% of young women aged 15–19 years were married during the survey conducted in 2015 (National Institute of Public Health and UNICEF Mexico 2016). 4.0% of women aged 15–49 were married for the first time before age 15, while 23.6% of women aged 20–49 were married for the first time before age 18. The proportion of women married at an early age is directly related to school level: 31% of women aged 15–19 with primary education are currently married compared to only 2% of women with higher education (Instituto Nacional de Salud Pública and UNICEF Mexico 2016).

Among married women aged 15–19, 8% had a partner who is at least ten years older than them (National Institute of Public Health and UNICEF Mexico 2016).

Mexico ranks first in teenage pregnancy among the countries that make up the Organisation for Economic Co-operation and Development. The average birth rate in young people aged 15–19 years, in the period from 2017 to 2021, was 35.3 per 1,000 adolescents. 2017 was the year with the highest rate: 44.3. In 2023, the birth rate in adolescents aged 15–19 was 26.3 per thousand; in girls, it was 0.2 per thousand under 15 years old (INEGI 2023).

Research on adverse childhood experiences in Mexico

Up to this point, several environmental, social, political, economic and family conditions that put millions of Mexican children at risk have been exposed. ACEs in Mexico are a reality that affects many children, influencing their physical, emotional and social development. These experiences, which include exposure to natural disasters, family violence, abuse, neglect, poverty and violence due to conflicts with organised crime, have a significant impact on children's lives.

Using data from the National Institute of Statistics and Geography, Brown (Brown 2018) found that early gestational exposure to drug war violence is associated with a substantial decrease in newborn birth weight. This association is more marked in children who were born into a family of low socioeconomic status and whose mothers have mental disorders. He argues that the effects on weight may be due to the biological effects of violence and stress (e.g. the secretion of cortisol, norepinephrine and epinephrine or the amount of blood reaching the fetus) or to social and behavioural factors, such as a reduced supply of prenatal care services, the decision to move as a result of violence or to engage in risky behaviours (such as drug use as a coping style in the face of anxiety and depression caused by social conditions).

In one study (Madrigal Gonzaleza et al. 2024) that analysed the relationship between ACEs, stress and chronic diseases in 450 people over the age of 65, it was found that the most prevalent ACEs were emotional abuse (36.7%), household substance abuse (33.1%) and physical abuse (26.4%). The ACEs score showed that 58.7% of the subjects experienced one to three ACEs, while 26% of the participants experienced four or more ACEs. Adults who experienced more than one ACE were more likely to have perceived stress than those without ACE exposure. Participants who reported experiencing domestic violence against their mother and physical and emotional neglect during childhood had an increased risk of stress (by 2.67-, 2.47- and 2.45-fold, respectively) compared with those who did not suffer from these experiences.

Another similar study (Nevárez Mendoza and Ochoa Meza 2022) with the participation of 389 people aged 18–65 years, examined the frequency of ACEs and their relationship with mental disorders and physical health in one of the most violent cities in Mexico (Ciudad Juárez). 71.5% of participants reported at least one type of ACEs, while 31.4% declared three or more. The most frequent were substance abuse at home (31.6%), psychological abuse

(23.4%), parent loss due to abandonment or divorce (22.6%), family member mental illness (21.1%), incarceration of a family member (21.1%), emotional neglect (21.3%) and sexual abuse (17.2%). Three or more ACEs predicted a higher risk of depression, anxiety, psychosomatic severity, obesity and limitations due to physical or emotional discomfort.

Baker et al. (2009) analysed the effect of ACEs on adulthood physical health among a randomly selected sample of 2,177 adults (*N*=) in urban Mexico. They found that traumatic events had a prevalence of 35%. Men reported more childhood trauma than women, but women reported more exposure to childhood sexual violence. They also found that depression mediated the relationship between childhood sexual violence and physical health symptoms for men and women.

Another study conducted in Ciudad Juárez too, Esparza-Del Villar et al. (2022) developed and validated a past child abuse and neglect scale. With the information of 763 adults, they developed a six-factor scale with good internal reliability. Most reported ACEs included being touched sexually by someone, being forced to perform a sexual act and physical and verbal abuse.

Regarding indigenous and non-indigenous populations in Mexico, Casas Muñoz and collaborators (Casas Muñoz et al. 2024) found that there were no statistically significant differences in ACE experimentation, but both groups reported neglect and exposure to collective violence as the most experienced event.

The effects of poverty have also been documented in Mexican population (Torres and Wong 2013). Using national, representative data (8,696 respondents), these authors found that the lack of sanitation facilities in the participants' households before age 10 is significantly associated with past-week depressive symptoms for Mexican adults 50 years and older.

Conclusions

Adverse events in childhood exposure in Mexico represent a critical challenge that requires urgent and multifaceted attention. Natural disasters, violence, poverty, lack of access to basic services, and forced displacement profoundly affect the physical, emotional and social development of millions of children. These factors not only limit their present opportunities but also perpetuate cycles of disadvantage that impact future generations.

To effectively combat these issues, it is crucial to invest in programs that foster community cohesion and resilience. Initiatives that promote social engagement, education and mental health support can help rebuild trust and provide a stable environment for children. Prevention efforts must focus on addressing the root causes of adversity, offering resources and support to families, and creating safe spaces for children to thrive.

Furthermore, timely and accessible treatment for those affected by trauma is essential. Providing mental health services and educational support can empower children and families to overcome their challenges and break the cycle of disadvantage. By prioritising the regeneration of social networks, enhancing prevention strategies and ensuring effective treatment options, we can pave the way for a healthier future where every child has the opportunity to flourish in a nurturing and secure environment.

Currently, Mexico has begun to develop a comprehensive plan to combat the deep inequalities that affect communities. This strategy contemplates cutting government spending to allocate a greater amount of the budget to social supports that promote greater social mobility, that is, that the most disadvantaged sectors have access to food, housing, social security and employment that will allow them to improve their quality of life and thereby reduce vulnerabilities. Mexican government has also created and implemented laws for the protection of children and women to promote families as safe spaces for the healthy development of children.

References

Alcántara-Ayala, I. (2019). Desastres en México: Mapas y apuntes sobre una historia inconclusa. *Investigaciones Geográficas 100*: https://doi.org/10.14350/rig.60025.

Baker, C.K., Norris, F.H., Jones, E.C., and Murphy, A.D. (2009). Childhood trauma and adulthood physical health in Mexico. *Journal of Behavioral Medicine* 32 (3): 255–269. https://doi.org/10.1007/s10865-009-9199-2.

Benjet, C. (2010). Childhood adversities of populations living in low-income countries: prevalence, characteristics, and mental health consequences. *Current Opinion in Psychiatry* 23 (4): 356–362. https://doi.org/10.1097/YCO.0b013e32833ad79b.

Benjet, C., Bromet, E., Karam, E.G. et al. (2016). The epidemiology of traumatic event exposure worldwide: results from the World Mental Health Survey Consortium. *Psychological Medicine* 46 (2): 327–343. https://doi.org/10.1017/S0033291715001981.

Brown, R. (2018). The Mexican Drug War and early-life health: the impact of violent crime on birth outcomes. *Demography* 55 (1): 319–340. https://doi.org/10.1007/s13524-017-0639-2.

Bündnis Entwicklung Hilft, and The Institute for International Law of Peace and Armed Conflic (2023). *World Risk Report 2023*. Ruhr University Bochum.

Casas Muñoz, A., VelascoRojano, Á.E., Rodríguez Caballero, A. et al. (2024). Associations between mental health problems and Adverse Childhood Experiences ACEs in indigenous and non-indigenous Mexican adolescents. *Child Abuse & Neglect* 147: 106595. https://doi.org/10.1016/j.chiabu.2023.106595.

Centro de Prevención Nacional de Desastres (n.d.). *Desastres en México*. CENAPRED. https://www.cenapred.unam.mx/es/Publicaciones/archivos/318 (accessed 10 October 2024).

Consejo Nacional de Evaluación de la Política de Desarrollo Social (2023). *Medición de pobreza 2022*. CONEVAL.

Esparza-Del Villar, O.A., Montañez-Alvarado, P., Gutiérrez-Vega, M. et al. (2022). Past child abuse and neglect in adults from Northern Mexico: development of a scale and prevalence. *Journal of Interpersonal Violence* 37 (5–6): 2851–2876. https://doi.org/10.1177/0886260520943729.

Herrera-Laso, M.L. (2013). *Factores que propician la violencia y la inseguridad: Apuntes para una estrategia integral de seguridad pública en México*. El Colegio de México / Centro de Estudios Internacionales https://cei.colmex.mx/archivos/213/Luis_Herrera-Lasso__Factores_que_propician_la_violencia_y_la_inseguridad.pdf. (accessed 10 October 2024).

Hillis, S.D., Unwin, H.J.T., Chen, Y. et al. (2021). Global minimum estimates of children affected by COVID-19-associated orphanhood and deaths of caregivers: a modelling study. *The Lancet* 398 (10298): 391–402. https://doi.org/10.1016/S0140-6736(21)01253-8.

INEGI (2022). *Encuesta Nacional sobre la Dinámica de las Relaciones en los Hogares 2021. ENDIREH. Nacional.* INEGI https://www.inegi.org.mx/contenidos/programas/endireh/2021/doc/nacional_resultados.pdf (accessed 8 October 2024).

INEGI (2023). *Comunicado de prensa núm. 556/23. Día mundial para la prevención del embarazo no planificado En adolescentes (Datos nacionales)*. INEGI https://www.inegi.org.mx/contenidos/saladeprensa/aproposito/2023/EAP_EmbNoPlanificado23.pdf (accessed 8 October 2024).

INEGI (2024a). *Encuesta Nacional de Victimización y Percepción sobre Seguridad Pública 2024.* INEGI https://www.inegi.org.mx/contenidos/programas/envipe/2024/doc/envipe2024_presentacion_nacional.pdf (accessed 9 October 2024).

INEGI (2024b). *Estadísticas a propósito del Día del Niño y de la Niña. Comunicado de prensa núm. 238/24*. INEGI.

Instituto Nacional de Salud Pública, and UNICEF México (2016). *Encuesta Nacional de Niños, Niñas y Mujeres 2015—Encuesta de Indicadores Múltiples por Conglomerados 2015, Informe Final.* Instituto Nacional de Salud Pública y UNICEF México https://www.unicef.org/mexico/media/1001/file/UNICEF_ENIM2015.pdf (accessed 9 October 2024).

Kalmakis, K.A. and Chandler, G.E. (2014). Adverse childhood experiences: Towards a clear conceptual meaning. *Journal of Advanced Nursing* 70 (7): 1489–1501. https://doi.org/10.1111/jan.12329.

López-Ortiz, E., Altamirano, J.M., Romero-Henríquez, L.F., and López-Ortiz, G. (2024). Characterization of Homicides in Mexico: analysis of 2015–2022. *International Journal of Environmental Research and Public Health* 21 (5): 617. https://doi.org/10.3390/ijerph21050617.

Madrigal Gonzaleza, I.J., González-Castroa, T.B., Tovilla-Zárate, C.A. et al. (2024). Adverse childhood experiences, perceived stress, and chronic diseases among older adults: a cross-sectional study in Mexico. *European Journal of Trauma & Dissociation* 8 (2): 100412. https://doi.org/10.1016/j.ejtd.2024.100412.

Nevárez Mendoza, B. and Ochoa Meza, G. (2022). Adaptación del Cuestionario de Experiencias Adversas en la infancia en muestras mexicanas. *Psicologia y Salud* 32 (2): 203–214. https://doi.org/10.25009/pys.v32i2.2742.

OECD (2024). *OECD Economic Surveys: Mexico 2024*. OECD https://doi.org/10.1787/b8d974db-en.

Olivera, S.M. and Fuerte-Celis, M.D.P. (2024). Enclaves de violencia: El crimen organizado y los territorios estratégicos en México. *Revista Latinoamericana de Población* 18: https://doi.org/10.31406/relap2024.v18e202328.

The Institute for Economics & Peace (2024). *Global Peace Index 2024: Measuring Peace in a Complex World*. Institute for Economics & Peace (11 October 2024). https://www.economicsandpeace.org/wp-content/uploads/2024/06/GPI-2024-web.pdf (accessed 2 October 2024).

Torres, J.M. and Wong, R. (2013). Childhood poverty and depressive symptoms for older adults in Mexico: a life-course analysis. *Journal of Cross-Cultural Gerontology* 28 (3): 317–337. https://doi.org/10.1007/s10823-013-9198-1.

United Nations Children's Fund (2022). *A Statistical Profile of Violence Against Children in Latin Americaaand the Caribbean.* UNICEF https://www.unicef.org/lac/media/38241/file/A-statistical-profile-of-violence-against-children-in-latin-america-and-the-caribbean.pdf (accessed 2 October 2024).

Chapter 11

CHILDHOOD TRAUMA AND ADVERSITY AS RISK FACTORS FOR VIOLENCE

Jiaying Chen[1], Saima Ali[2], and Gwen Adshead[3]

[1] Oxford, UK
[2] London, UK
[3] Broadmoor Hospital, Berks, UK

Introduction

It is part of the human story to assume that experiences in childhood influence later actions and experiences in adulthood. But it was not until the 20th century that technical advances in data collection and statistical analysis made it possible to test the assumption. The most robust studies are prospective studies of cohorts of children into adulthood. However, studies of retrospectively recalled childhood experiences have also provided useful information about how childhood adversity (and its absence) might impact physical and mental health in adulthood.

The best known of these studies were carried out in the late 1990s by Felitti et al. (Felitti et al. 1998; see Hughes et al. 2017 and Madigan et al. 2024 for review) using a convenience sample of 17,000 members of a health insurance programme in the United States. Those studies indicated that people who had been exposed to four or more kinds of adverse childhood experiences (ACEs) were at greatest risk of poor physical and mental health. Since then, major international public health bodies such as the World Health Organization (WHO), Centers for Disease Control in Atlanta, and Public Health Wales have all recommended using screening tools for ACEs in communities to identify this vulnerable group and offer some kind of intervention.

Violence has been identified by WHO and other bodies as a major threat to public health, and so the study of childhood adversity in violent perpetrators seems eminently sensible. This is especially so given that drug addiction and substance misuse are both associated with exposure to ACEs and are also recognised risk factors for crime of all kinds, especially violence. In 1944, Bowlby published the first formal study of the effect of neglect on delinquency,

The Intergenerational Effects of Adverse Childhood Experiences: Ripples on a Pond, First Edition. Edited by Richard Pates and Diane Riley.

Published 2026 by John Wiley & Sons Ltd.

comparing children caught for thieving with a comparison group who had not. Later prospective studies of cohorts of children in the 1970s and 1980s in Dunedin and Cambridge identified the developmental roots of antisocial behaviour and the impact of family adversity on criminological risk (Poulton et al. 2015 for review of the Dunedin study; Farringdon et al. 1998, 2009).

In 1989, Widom published work on the concept of 'the cycle of violence' (Widom 1989), based on prospective studies of children with court-validated maltreatment, which included comparison with a matched cohort of non-maltreated children. She also looked at retrospective studies of self-reported trauma in prisoners (Weeks and Widom 1998) and concluded that childhood maltreatment could be a risk factor for later offending in some individuals. A more recent study using her data suggests that the mediating link between childhood trauma and later violence is disturbance of the human attachment bonds (Papalia and Widom 2024; discussed in more detail below).

The Felitti studies have encouraged researchers to explore childhood adversity more systematically in different populations of offenders. Messina and Grella (2006) and Messina et al. (2007) studied the prevalence of ACES in male and female prisoners and suggested that the cumulative effect of these experiences might be a risk factor that required intervention. In a study comparing prisoners convicted of violent and nonviolent offences, Reiff et al. (2007) argued that exposure to childhood trauma might interact with genetic variants of serotonin metabolism to cause increased risk of violence perpetration.

How ACEs interact with other risk factors of violence

Numerous studies have established that ACEs are common. Approximately half of the English population reports exposure to at least one ACE, and around one in ten individuals have experienced four or more (Bellis et al. 2014). A 2017 study found that adults who have suffered four or more ACEs are 8 times more likely to become a perpetrator of violence compared to those who had suffered none (Hughes et al. 2017), and the prevalence of ACEs is over-represented in prisoner populations compared to the community (Ford et al. 2020). This group also has an 8-fold risk of becoming victims of violence, and over 30-fold risk of attempting suicide, which could be interpreted as an extreme form of violence towards the self (Hughes et al. 2017).

However, rates of violence have been falling over the last 50 years, and only a minority of crime involves violence. Equally, it is becoming clear that only a minority of those exposed to ACEs will go on to commit violence in adulthood. Violence is a *relatively* unusual way for people to break the law in societies with stable governments (which is not to minimise its harmful impact, physically and emotionally). Violence involves a complex interaction between different individual factors across the life course, and it is the interaction of these factors with ACEs that may increase violence risk. These factors include developmental delays in childhood (Font and Berger 2015), reduced self-esteem (AlShawi and Lafta 2014), lower educational attainment (Houtepen et al. 2020), poorer financial well-being (Harter and Harter 2022) and experience of chronic illnesses and pain.

There is substantial overlap between risk factors associated with ACEs and for violence commission. An umbrella review on meta-analyses studying the risk factors of interpersonal violence by Fazel and colleagues in 2018 identified that the strongest *historical* risk factor was witnessing or being a victim of violence in childhood. Among the *dynamic* (i.e. changeable) risk factors, the most influential were neuropsychiatric disorders (including substance use disorders, schizophrenia, personality disorders and traumatic brain injuries), which are also more common in individuals with high ACE scores. Mood disorders, such as depression and PTSD, may be especially influential (Herzog 2018).

Some ACEs may cause enduring effects on the physical structure and function of neural stress-regulatory circuits in the brain, including the hippocampus and the amygdala (Calem et al. 2017). Such damage may cause mental disorders to present earlier and more severely and make them less responsive to standard treatments.

It seems that the same risk factors for exposure to childhood adversity also increase the risk of mental disorders and the risk of later violence, but it is not yet clear if these are separate risk trajectories, interacting trajectories or both.

Intergenerational transmission

Other than horizontal influences via interpersonal violence, ACEs could also have a lasting vertical effect on future generations. Children of individuals exposed to ACEs are at higher risk of developmental, mental health and physical health problems, including lower birthweight and asthma (Lê-Scherban et al. 2018) and are more likely to experience ACEs themselves (Schickedanz et al. 2021).

Multiple factors contribute to the intergenerational transmission of ACEs. The factors can be broadly grouped according to the biopsychosocial model: changes to the inflammatory system and genetic expression in response to the stress caused by ACEs, and this being passed on to the foetus (Berens et al. 2017); ACEs leading to poor parental mental health and health-harming behaviours; and greater social isolation and socioeconomic deprivation due to limited educational attainment, unemployment and early retirement from poor health (Russotti et al. 2021).

Social milieux and environment as risk factors

Through horizontal and vertical impacts, the consequences of childhood adversity extend beyond the individual experiencing them. It forms a ripple effect, affecting the people around them and wider society. The compounding impact of ACEs fuels the vicious cycle of deprivation and poverty, and deprivation in turn exacerbates the impact of ACEs. Madigan et al. (2023), in a large meta-analysis of studies of ACES, found particular harmful effects on people who were unhoused and noted the potential for interactional effects between substance misuse and addiction, which is also associated with high ACE exposure. Other studies report that ACEs disproportionately affect marginalised populations, both in terms of the risk of exposure and the consequences suffered. For example, the likelihood of exposure to ACEs increases in communities characterised by poverty (Marryat and Frank 2019) and in people who have already experienced ACEs. Lower-income households suffer from poorer health outcomes and mental well-being compared to those coming from higher-income households (Bellis et al. 2017; Halfon et al. 2017). Halfon also found that having an 'always available adult' mediated the detrimental effects of ACEs, which suggests a link with other studies that have explored the importance of early attachments (see below).

Social learning theory may also play a role in the propensity to use violence in individuals exposed to ACES. This theory proposes that children learn to mirror actions and behaviours that they are exposed to (Fox et al. 2015). This is supported by Shen and Wu (2024), who linked exposure to ACEs in childhood with future harsh parenting, perpetuating the cycle of violence.

Minority stress: ethnicity and gender

Being 'different' from the population 'norm' in some way may cause minority stress and contribute to the prevalence of ACE exposure and its impact. For example, children with disabilities are at greater risk of experiencing abuse and maltreatment compared with non-disabled children (Jones et al. 2012). Higher levels of ACEs are also reported in people belonging to sexual minorities, and those who have experienced ACEs are more likely to have earlier sexual debuts compared to cisgendered heterosexual counterparts (Brown et al. 2015).

Racial disparities in ACE exposure have been reported in countries characterised by a history of immigration, with the prevalence of ACEs reported in descending order: Black and Hispanic populations, White populations and Asian populations in the United States and the United Kingdom (Slopen et al. 2016). Exposure to racism and community violence has also been linked to poor health outcomes in adolescents with ACE histories (Hall et al. 2021). Ethnicity and cultural practices may influence the sequelae of ACEs in different groups, although research is largely restricted to Anglo-American studies of White, Hispanic and African Americans, and more research is needed in different African and Asian countries and cultures.

Gender role construction and expectations may further influence the prevalence of ACEs and their outcomes. For example, more boys experience physical abuse by parents in their early years, but more girls experience sexual abuse in adolescence (typically by peers; see Finkelhor's 2025 commentary). Differences in brain development between the sexes may be especially prominent during and after the onset of puberty (which may explain the rarity of violence by the under-10s). It is possible that girls and young women are more prone than men to heightened stress responses *after* trauma exposure (Mather et al. 2010) and more vulnerable to developing stress-related psychiatric conditions (Bangasser and Valentino 2014), especially in adolescence. However, these findings may be confounded by the use of self-report measures of subjective distress, which may be subject to gender role bias.

Burke et al. (2023) found that exposure to ACEs in childhood was more strongly linked to violent behaviour in biological women than men, which is counterintuitive, given the prevalence of ACEs in both men and women and the historically low prevalence of violence by women. Such findings highlight the need for research that addresses gender role bias in its methodology, especially in populations where violence commission is relatively rare but psychological hostility is not (Burke et al. 2023; Hein et al. 2020).

Neurobiological and epigenetic influences

Early childhood exposure to trauma has lasting impacts on the brain (Tiwari and Gonzalez 2018). Johnson et al. (2013) reported that exposure to early life stress in rodents altered and impaired multiple developmental processes linked to microglial function, for example, within the hippocampus, a part of the brain involved in memory, learning and emotion. In their recent systematic review, Cooke et al. (2023) found that whilst such neurobiological changes appear to be small, they contribute to behavioural outcomes over time and ultimately may alter the brain's neurochemical landscape, which might contribute in some way to violence commission later. One possibility is the effect of ACE exposure on gene expression (Lang et al. 2020), especially genes affecting synaptogenesis or synthesis and breakdown of neurotransmitters implicated in human stress responses.

It is widely accepted that repeated negative experiences, such as ACEs, can lead to chronic or sustained stress response system activation (Johnson et al. 2013; Oral et al. 2016). For example, long-term dysregulation of the hypothalamic–pituitary–adrenal axis in response to such stressors can affect cognitive function, behaviour and increase vulnerability to developing various mental health conditions (Griffiths and Hunter 2014). Exposure to ACEs also appears to increase levels of various pro-inflammatory cytokines in the brain, further increasing the risk of developing psychological sequelae (Steel et al. 2020). The timing of ACES may be relevant here with one recent study suggesting that adversity in the first 5 years of life may be especially risky in terms of outcomes (Lussier et al. 2023).

Attachment insecurity: disorganised attachment and violence risk

In many countries, homicide rates vary in terms of prevalence and social context. One distinguishing factor is whether or not victims and perpetrators of violence have been emotionally connected in some way, implying that relational distress and disruption of emotional attachments may contribute to the violence risk (Elbogen and Johnson 2009). Understanding the emotional impact of making and breaking attachment bonds may therefore help us understand why only a sub-group of people exposed to high levels of ACES become violent perpetrators.

Attachment theory, as described by Bowlby (1973) and Ainsworth (1978), argues that the extended vulnerability in childhood in humans means that infants must make enduring bonds with their carers for protection when stressed. Those emotional bonds also enable the child to build trust with others and learn about their own mind and the minds of others. If this process of attachment is 'good enough', then the child develops a *secure* attachment, which means that they seek care confidently when stressed and use their memories and cognitive models of attachment as a template for making positive social relationships.

Conversely, if the attachment is *insecure*, then the child may avoid others when distressed or develop preoccupied and disorganised relationships with those on whom they depend. Attachment security can change over the life span, but, in general, insecure infants become insecure children and adolescents who become insecurely attached adults. A recent review suggests that attachment insecurity is common in communities, affecting about 40% of the general community, but this figure is considerably higher in clinical populations and offender populations (Bakermans Kranenburg et al. 2024).

Attachment insecurity has been identified as a risk factor for violence (Afifi et al. 2011; Ogilvie et al. 2014). Although not predictive, it may be the mediating factor between ACE exposure and later violence (Papalia and Widom 2024) because of the implications of attachment insecurity for the development of social trust and mentalising skills. Mentalising is the understanding of thoughts, behaviour and emotions in one's own mind and in the mind of others. An impaired ability to mentalise may contribute to an increased risk of violence in those with insecure attachment (Schwarzer et al. 2021). Lack of trust and impaired mentalising skills are commonly found in people with personality dysfunction, especially in both antisocial and emotionally unstable personality disorders. Adults with insecure attachment may struggle to provide secure parenting to their offspring (Finch et al. 2024).

A specific attachment-related mediating factor may involve disorganised attachment, which is a kind of attachment insecurity, found in children exposed to high levels of fear in their earliest years, typically as a result of living with frightened or frightening parents. Children with disorganised attachment develop a fragmented sense of self, and when stressed, may oscillate between hostile or helpless states of mind (Turgeon et al. 2022). Disorganised attachment is commoner in clinical groups, including those who have been violent to others (Barone and Carone 2021; Giachetti et al. 2023).

Protective factors and resilience

Violence is not an inevitable consequence of ACE exposure. A growing body of research is examining why some individuals appear to be protected from the numerous negative health outcomes associated with traumatic childhoods, including engaging in violent behaviour.

The concept of resilience

In broad terms, resilience could be understood as an ability to positively manage and adapt in difficult circumstances, resulting from the effect of protective factors which can nullify or mitigate the impact of stressful childhood experiences (Zimmerman 2013). These factors may be assets located within an individual or external resources (Fergus and Zimmerman 2005). Rutter (1987) introduced the challenge model of resiliency, suggesting that low levels of adversity may help build resilience to allow the development of coping mechanisms: a kind of 'inoculation'.

Goldenson et al. (2020) noted that resilience buffered against trauma-related symptomology in a sample of adolescents with histories of ACEs. In their scoping review of 27 studies, Haczkewicz et al. (2024) found that resilience 'mitigated or reduced harms associated with ACEs' leading to healthier adult lives.

Protective factors that help build resilience

Resilience may be thought of as a spectrum that develops within systems: the individual, family and the wider community (Masten 2019). At the individual level, intelligence and better attainment at school appear to protect against troubled parenting (Farrington et al. 2009). Self-esteem and an internal locus of control also appear to be protective (Fergus and Zimmerman 2005).

At the family level, the presence of one or more consistent, supportive adult(s) appears to be an important protective factor (Hall et al. 2021). Crouch et al. (2018) found this was particularly true for those exposed to four or more ACEs. For a child exposed to significant stress, a positive relationship with an adult could help them tolerate stress better (Danielson and Saxena 2019), and there is now considerable interest in the protective impact of positive childhood experiences (PCEs), which might mitigate ACE exposure risk (Han et al. 2023).

At the community level, access to safe neighbourhoods and safe school have been shown to be important in building resilience (Moore et al. 2016), as well as participating in sport clubs (Di Lemma et al. 2019). However, in their systematic review and meta-analysis, Masten (2019) noted that available data are heterogeneous and further research is needed to better understand the multifaceted components of resilience in the context of ACE exposure.

Conclusion

Our understanding of how ACE exposure could increase the risk of violence commission remains limited and so inevitably further research is needed. ACE exposure can contribute to violence risk, but this may not apply to all kinds of violence and may occur only if other risk factors for violence are present. Resilience theory and PCEs offer some avenues for study of how and why some who are exposed to adversity appear to fare better than others.

What is clear is that reducing and preventing ACEs in our communities could improve physical and mental health in adulthood, which in turn might help make societies safer, healthier and happier. But until we know more about prevention, violence risk will have to be mediated using interventions with violent perpetrators. At present, violence reduction interventions focus on work with young people and adults who have already offended. These include reducing substance misuse and addiction; improving mental health using medication and evidence-based interventions to improve emotion regulation; and encouraging those who have been violent to study their offending history in detail, understand how they came to cause such harm, and explore their agency to desist from violence in future. Not causing further trauma to already traumatised people may also be salient for violence reduction (Adshead 2025).

Often these kinds of interventions entail people reflecting on their experience of victimisation as children, and how that impacted on their sense of self-worth, inner security and perceptions of others. Offenders need compassionate and clear-eyed support at this time. Group interventions, such as prison therapeutic communities, have been found to be especially effective (Beaudry et al. 2021), perhaps because they offer a way to feel less isolated, to connect to others and become pro-social again.

What we do not yet know is how best to mitigate the effects of extensive childhood trauma in younger children whose minds and brains are still developing. This is partly because children are not distinct entities from their family members (who may be the source of the trauma). It may be that the best way to help children who have endured high levels of childhood adversity is to provide them with attachment figures who can soothe and comfort them and prevent them from suffering more trauma. Or it may be the case that supporting the adults who care for children may be most effective. The question is urgent as children around the world are exposed to a variety of ACEs, including war (Ford 2025), and the financial cost of those ACES becomes unaffordable (Hughes et al. 2021).

References

Adshead, G. (2025). Can we change violent minds? In: *The BBC 2024 Reith Lectures: Four Questions About Violence*. London: Faber.

Afifi, T.O., McMillan, K.A., Asmundson, G.J. et al. (2011). An examination of the relation between conduct disorder, childhood and adulthood traumatic events, and posttraumatic stress disorder in a nationally representative sample. *Journal of Psychiatric Research* 45 (12): 1564–1572. https://doi.org/10.1016/j.jpsychires.2011.08.005.

Ainsworth, M.D.S., Blehar, M., Waters, E., and Wall, S. (1978). *Patterns of Attachment: A Psychological Study of the Strange Situation*. Erlbaum.

AlShawi, A.F. and Lafta, R.K. (2014). Relation between childhood experiences and adults' self-esteem: a sample from Baghdad. *Qatar Medical Journal* 2014 (2): 82–91. https://doi.org/10.5339/qmj.2014.14.

Bakermans-Kranenburg, M.J., Dagan, O., Cárcamo, R.A., and van IJzendoorn, M.H. (2024). Celebrating more than 26,000 adult attachment interviews: mapping the main adult attachment classifications on personal, social, and clinical status. *Attachment & Human Development* 27: 1–38.

Bangasser, D.A. and Valentino, R.J. (2014). Sex differences in stress-related psychiatric disorders: neurobiological perspectives. *Frontiers in Neuroendocrinology* 35: 303–319. https://doi.org/10.1016/j.yfrne.2014.03.008.

Barone, L. and Carone, N. (2021). Childhood abuse and neglect experiences, Hostile-Helpless attachment, and reflective functioning in mentally ill filicidal mothers. *Attachment & Human Development* 23 (6): 771–794.

Beaudry, G., Yu, R., Perry, A.E., and Fazel, S. (2021). Effectiveness of psychological interventions in prison to reduce recidivism: a systematic review and meta-analysis of randomised controlled trials. *The Lancet Psychiatry* 8 (9): 759–773.

Bellis, M.A., Hughes, K., Leckenby, N. et al. (2014). National household survey of adverse childhood experiences and their relationship with resilience to health-harming behaviors in England. *BMC Medicine* 12: 72. https://doi.org/10.1186/1741-7015-12-72.

Bellis, M.A., Hardcastle, K., Ford, K. et al. (2017). Does continuous trusted adult support in childhood impart life-course resilience against adverse childhood experiences – a retrospective study on adult health-harming behaviours and mental well-being. *BMC Psychiatry* 17 (1): 110. https://doi.org/10.1186/s12888-017-1260-z.

Berens, A.E., Jensen, S.K.G., and Nelson, C.A. III (2017). Biological embedding of childhood adversity: from physiological mechanisms to clinical implications. *BMC Medicine* 15 (135): https://doi.org/10.1186/s12916-017-0895-4.

Bowlby, J. (1973). *Attachment and Loss: Separation*, vol. 2. Basic Books.

Brown, M.J., Masho, S.W., Perera, R.A. et al. (2015). Sex and sexual orientation disparities in adverse childhood experiences and early age at sexual debut in the United States: results from a nationally representative sample. *Child Abuse & Neglect* 46: 89–102. https://doi.org/10.1016/j.chiabu.2015.02.019.

Burke, C., Ellis, J.D., Peltier, M.R. et al. (2023). Adverse childhood experiences and pathways to violent behavior for women and men. *Journal of Interpersonal Violence* 38 (3–4): 4034–4060. https://doi.org/10.1177/08862605221113012.

Calem, M., Bromis, K., McGuire, P. et al. (2017). Meta-analysis of associations between childhood adversity and hippocampus and amygdala volume in non-clinical and general population samples. *NeuroImage Clinical* 14: 471–479. https://doi.org/10.1016/j.nicl.2017.02.016.

Cooke, E.M., Connolly, E.J., Boisvert, D.L., and Hayes, B.E. (2023). A systematic review of the biological correlates and consequences of childhood maltreatment and adverse childhood experiences. *Trauma, Violence & Abuse* 24 (1): 156–173. https://doi.org/10.1177/15248380211021613.

Crouch, E., Radcliff, E., Strompolis, M., and Srivastav, A. (2018). Safe, stable, and nurtured: protective factors against poor physical and mental health outcomes following exposure to adverse childhood experiences (ACEs). *Journal of Child & Adolescent Trauma* 12 (2): 165–173. https://doi.org/10.1007/s40653-018-0217-9.

Danielson, R. and Saxena, D. (2019). Connecting adverse childhood experiences and community health to promote health equity. *Social and Personality Psychology Compass* 13 (7): e12486. https://doi.org/10.1111/spc3.12486.

Di Lemma, L., Davies, A.R., Ford, K. et al. (2019). *Responding to Adverse Childhood Experiences: An Evidence Review of Interventions to Prevent and Address Adversity Across the Life Course*. Cardiff and Bangor University Public Health Wales.

Elbogen, E.B. and Johnson, S.C. (2009). The intricate link between violence and mental disorder: results from the National Epidemiologic Survey on Alcohol and Related Conditions. *Archives of General Psychiatry* 66 (2): 152–161.

Farrington, D.P., Lambert, S., and West, D.J. (1998). Criminal careers of two generations of family members in the Cambridge Study in Delinquent Development. *Studies on Crime and Crime Prevention* 7: 85–106.

Farrington, D.P., Coid, J.W., and Murray, J. (2009). Family factors in the intergenerational transmission of offending. *Criminal Behaviour and Mental Health* 19 (2): 109–124.

Fazel, S., Smith, E.N., Chang, Z., and Geddes, J.R. (2018). Risk factors for interpersonal violence: an umbrella review of meta-analyses. *The British Journal of Psychiatry* 213 (4): 609–614. https://doi.org/10.1192/bjp.2018.145.

Felitti, V.J., Anda, R.F., Nordenberg, D. et al. (1998). Relationship of childhood abuse and household dysfunction to many of the leading causes of death in adults: the Adverse Childhood Experiences (ACE) Study. *American Journal of Preventive Medicine* 14 (4): 245–258. https://doi.org/10.1016/S0749-3797(98)00017-8.

Fergus, S. and Zimmerman, M.A. (2005). Adolescent resilience: a framework for understanding healthy development in the face of risk. *Annual Review of Public Health* 26: 399–419. https://doi.org/10.1146/annurev.publhealth.26.021304.144357.

Finch, K., Lawrence, D., Williams, M. et al. (2024). Relationships between adverse childhood experiences, attachment, resilience, psychological distress and trauma among forensic mental health populations. *The Journal of Forensic Psychiatry & Psychology 35* (5): 660–684. https://doi.org/10.1080/14789949.2024.2365149.

Font, S.A. and Berger, L.M. (2015). Child maltreatment and children's developmental trajectories in early to middle childhood. *Child Development* 86 (2): 536–556. https://doi.org/10.1111/cdev.12322.

Ford, J. (2025). Commentary: responding to the need for psychotherapeutic respite by war exposed Ukrainian children. *JAMA Network Open* 8 (3): e253060. https://doi.org/10.1001/jamanetworkopen.2025.3060.

Ford, K., Bellis, M.A., Hughes, K. et al. (2020). Adverse childhood experiences: a retrospective study to understand their associations with lifetime mental health diagnosis, self-harm or suicide attempt, and current low mental wellbeing in a male Welsh prison population. *Health Justice* 8: 13. https://doi.org/10.1186/s40352-020-00115-5.

Fox, B.H., Perez, N., Cass, E. et al. (2015). Trauma changes everything: examining the relationship between adverse childhood experiences and serious, violent and chronic juvenile offenders. *Child Abuse & Neglect* 46: 163–173. https://doi.org/10.1016/j.chiabu.2015.01.011.

Giacchetti, N., Lattanzi, G.M., Aceti, F. et al. (2023). States of mind with respect to attachment: a comparative study between women who killed their children and mothers diagnosed with post-partum depression. *Nordic Journal of Psychiatry* 77 (1): 3–13.

Goldenson, J., Kitollari, I., and Lehman, F. (2020). The relationship between ACEs, trauma-related psychopathology and resilience in vulnerable youth: implications for screening and treatment. *Journal of Child & Adolescent Trauma* 14 (1): 151–160. https://doi.org/10.1007/s40653-020-00308-y.

Griffiths, B.B. and Hunter, R.G. (2014). Neuroepigenetics of stress. *Neuroscience* 275: 420–435. https://doi.org/10.1016/j.neuroscience.2014.06.041.

Haczkewicz, K.M., Shahid, S., Finnegan, H.A. et al. (2024). Adverse childhood experiences (ACEs), resilience, and outcomes in older adulthood: a scoping review. *Child Abuse & Neglect* 106864. Advance online publication. https://doi.org/10.1016/j.chiabu.2024.106864.

Halfon, N., Larson, K., Son, J. et al. (2017). Income inequality and the differential effect of adverse childhood experiences in US children. *Academic Pediatrics* 17 (7S): S70–S78. https://doi.org/10.1016/j.acap.2016.11.007.

Hall, A., Perez, A., West, X. et al. (2021). The Association of Adverse Childhood Experiences and Resilience with Health Outcomes in Adolescents: an observational study. *Global Pediatric Health* 8: 2333794X20982433. https://doi.org/10.1177/2333794X20982433.

Han, D., Dieujuste, N., Doom, J.R., and Narayan, A.J. (2023). A systematic review of positive childhood experiences and adult outcomes: promotive and protective processes for resilience in the context of childhood adversity. *Child Abuse & Neglect* 144: 106346.

Harter, C.L. and Harter, J.F.R. (2022). The link between adverse childhood experiences and financial security in adulthood. *Journal of Family and Economic Issues* 43 (4): 832–842. https://doi.org/10.1007/s10834-021-09796-y.

Hien, D., Kropp, F., Wells, E.A. et al. (2020). The "Women and Trauma" study and its national impact on advancing trauma specific approaches in community substance use treatment and research. *Journal of Substance Abuse Treatment* 112 (Supplement): 12–17. https://doi.org/10.1016/j.jsat.2020.02.003.

Houtepen, L.C., Heron, J., Suderman, M.J. et al. (2020). Associations of adverse childhood experiences with educational attainment and adolescent health and the role of family and socioeconomic factors: a prospective cohort study in the UK. *PLoS Medicine* 17 (3): e1003031. https://doi.org/10.1371/journal.pmed.1003031.

Hughes, K., Bellis, M., Hardcastle, K. et al. (2017). The effect of multiple adverse childhood experiences on health: a systematic review and meta-analysis. *The Lancet* 2 (8): e356–e366. https://doi.org/10.1016/S2468-2667(17)30118-4.

Hughes, K., Ford, K., Bellis, M.A. et al. (2021). Health and financial costs of adverse childhood experiences in 28 European countries: a systematic review and meta-analysis. *The Lancet Public Health* 6 (11): e848–e857.

Johnson, S.B., Riley, A.W., Granger, D.A., and Riis, J. (2013). The science of early life toxic stress for pediatric practice and advocacy. *Pediatrics* 131: 319–327.

Jones, L., Bellis, M.A., Wood, S. et al. (2012). Prevalence and risk of violence against children with disabilities: a systematic review and meta-analysis of observational studies. *Lancet (London, England)* 380 (9845): 899–907. https://doi.org/10.1016/S0140-6736(12)60692-8.

Lang, J., McKie, J., Smith, H. et al. (2020). Adverse childhood experiences, epigenetics and telomere length variation in childhood and beyond: a systematic review of the literature. *European Child & Adolescent Psychiatry* 29 (10): 1329–1338. https://doi.org/10.1007/s00787-019-01329-1.

Lê-Scherban, F., Wang, X., Boyle-Steed, K.H., and Pachter, L.M. (2018). Intergenerational Associations of Parent Adverse Childhood Experiences and Child Health Outcomes. *Pediatrics* 141 (6): e20174274. https://doi.org/10.1542/peds.2017-4274.

Lussier, A.A., Zhu, Y., Smith, B.J. et al. (2023). Association between the timing of childhood adversity and epigenetic patterns across childhood and adolescence: findings from the Avon Longitudinal Study of Parents and Children (ALSPAC) prospective cohort. *The Lancet Child & Adolescent Health* 7 (8): 532–543.

Madigan, S., Deneault, A.A., Racine, N. et al. (2023). Adverse childhood experiences: a meta-analysis of prevalence and moderators among half a million adults in 206 studies. *World Psychiatry* 22 (3): 463–471.

Madigan, S., Thiemann, R., Deneault, A.A. et al. (2024). Prevalence of adverse childhood experiences in child population samples: a systematic review and meta-analysis. *JAMA Pediatrics* 179: 19–33.

Marryat, L. and Frank, J. (2019). Factors associated with adverse childhood experiences in Scottish children: a prospective cohort study. *BMJ Paediatrics Open* 3 (1): e000340. https://doi.org/10.1136/bmjpo-2018-000340.

Masten, A.S. (2019). Resilience from a developmental systems perspective. *World Psychiatry: Official Journal of the World Psychiatric Association (WPA)* 18 (1): 101–102. https://doi.org/10.1002/wps.20591.

Mather, M., Lighthall, N.R., Nga, L., and Gorlick, M.A. (2010). Sex differences in how stress affects brain activity during face viewing. *Neuroreport* 21 (14): 933–937. https://doi.org/10.1097/WNR.0b013e32833ddd92.

Messina, N. and Grella, C. (2006). Childhood trauma and women's health outcomes in a California prison population. *American Journal of Public Health* 96 (10): 1842–1848.

Messina, N., Grella, C., Burdon, W., and Prendergast, M. (2007). Childhood adverse events and current traumatic distress: a comparison of men and women drug-dependent prisoners. *Criminal Justice and Behavior* 34 (11): 1385–1401.

Moore, K.A., Ramirez, N., and A. (2016). Adverse childhood experience and adolescent well-being: do protective factors matter? *Child Indicators Research* 9 (299): 316.

Ogilvie, C.A., Newman, E., Todd, L., and Peck, D. (2014). Attachment & violent offending: a meta-analysis. Aggression and Violent Behavior, 19(4), 322–339. https://doi.org/10.1016/j.avb.2014.04.007

Oral, R., Ramirez, M., Coohey, C. et al. (2016). Adverse childhood experiences and trauma informed care: the future of health care. *Pediatric Research* 79: 227–233. https://doi.org/10.1038/pr.2015.197.

Papalia, N. and Widom, C.S. (2024). Do insecure adult attachment styles mediate the relationship between childhood maltreatment and violent behavior? *Development and Psychopathology* 36 (2): 636–647.

Poulton, R., Moffitt, T.E., and Silva, P.A. (2015). The Dunedin Multidisciplinary Health and Development Study: overview of the first 40 years, with an eye to the future. *Social Psychiatry and Psychiatric Epidemiology* 50: 679–693.

Reiff, A., Rösler, M., Freitag, C.M. et al. (2007). Nature and nurture predispose to violent behavior: serotonergic genes and adverse childhood environment. *Neuropsychopharmacology* 32(11): 2375–2383. https://doi.org/10.1038/sj.npp.1301359.

Russotti, J., Warmingham, J.M., Handley, E.D. et al. (2021). Child maltreatment: an intergenerational cascades model of risk processes potentiating child psychopathology. *Child Abuse & Neglect* 112: 104829. https://doi.org/10.1016/j.chiabu.2020.104829.

Rutter, M. (1987). Psychosocial resilience and protective mechanisms. *American Journal of Orthopsychiatry* 57: 316–331.

Schickedanz, A., Escarce, J.J., Halfon, N. et al. (2021). Intergenerational Associations between Parents' and Children's Adverse Childhood Experience Scores. *Children (Basel, Switzerland)* 8 (9): 747. https://doi.org/10.3390/children8090747.

Schwarzer, N.H., Nolte, T., Fonagy, P., and Gingelmaier, S. (2021). Mentalizing mediates the association between emotional abuse in childhood and potential for aggression in non-clinical adults. *Child Abuse & Neglect 115*: 105018. https://doi.org/10.1016/j.chiabu.2021.105018.

Shen, A.C. and Wu, B.C.Y. (2024). From adverse childhood experiences to harsh parenting: psychological symptoms as a mediator. *Child Abuse & Neglect* 149: 106672. https://doi.org/10.1016/j.chiabu.2024.106672.

Slopen, N., Shonkoff, J.P., Albert, M.A. et al. (2016). Racial disparities in child adversity in the U.S.: interactions with family immigration history and income. *American Journal of Preventive Medicine* 50 (1): 47–56. https://doi.org/10.1016/j.amepre.2015.06.013.

Steel, J.L., Antoni, M., Pathak, R. et al. (2020). Adverse childhood experiences (ACEs), cell-mediated immunity, and survival in the context of cancer. *Brain, Behavior, and Immunity* 88: 566–572. https://doi.org/10.1016/j.bbi.2020.04.050.

Tiwari, A. and Gonzalez, A. (2018). Biological alterations affecting risk of adult psychopathology following childhood trauma: a review of sex differences. *Clinical Psychology Review* 66: 69–79. https://doi.org/10.1016/j.cpr.2018.01.006.

Turgeon, J., Milot, T., St-Laurent, D., and Dubois-Comtois, K. (2022). Hostile-helpless states of mind: a scoping review of risk factors, correlates, and consequences. *Infant Mental Health Journal* 43 (4): 597–623.

Weeks, R. and Widom, C.S. (1998). Self-reports of early childhood victimization among incarcerated adult male felons. *Journal of Interpersonal Violence* 13 (3): 346–361.

Widom, C.S. (1989). The cycle of violence. *Science* 244 (4901): 160–166.

Zimmerman, M.A. (2013). Resiliency theory: a strengths-based approach to research and practice for adolescent health. *Health Education & Behavior* 40 (4): 381–383. https://doi.org/10.1177/1090198113493782.

Chapter 12

INDIGENOUS PEOPLE IN CANADA: THE ROLE OF EDUCATION BOTH IN CREATING PROBLEMS AND IN ALLEVIATING THEM

Diane Riley[1] *and Mike DeGagné*[2]

[1] Independent Consultant, Ontario, Canada
[2] Department of Sociology, University of Toronto, Scarborough, North Bay, Ontario, Canada

This chapter is dedicated to the Late Murray Sinclair, Mizanay Gheezik, 1951–2024.

> Intergenerational or multigenerational trauma happens when the effects of trauma are not resolved in one generation. When trauma is ignored, and there is no support for dealing with it, the trauma will be passed from one generation to the next.
>
> (Aboriginal Health Foundation 1999, A5)

> Without truth, justice is not served, healing cannot happen, and there can be no genuine reconciliation between Aboriginal and non-Aboriginal peoples in Canada.
>
> (Truth and Reconciliation Commission 2015)

The Indigenous population of Canada are also referred to as Native or Aboriginal people and comprises the First Nations, Inuit and Métis. Indigenous people account for approximately five percent of the population of Canada (2021 census by StatsCan), which is one of the highest levels in countries with a similar history of colonisation. About three-quarters of these live in large urban centres and while a large number of First Nations people live on reserves, this number is decreasing.

Indigenous people in all parts of the world have suffered at the hands of colonisers throughout time. They have been killed in conflicts, suffered from numerous diseases, been confined, sterilised, placed in residential schools, had their lands removed from them and had their former lifestyles almost totally erased.

The Intergenerational Effects of Adverse Childhood Experiences: Ripples on a Pond, First Edition. Edited by Richard Pates and Diane Riley.

Published 2026 by John Wiley & Sons Ltd.

The Catholic church issued the doctrine of discovery in 1452. This was to:

> invade, search out, capture, vanquish and subdue all Saracens and pagans whatsoever health and other enemies of Christ whatsoever placed and the kingdoms and dukedoms, principalities, dominions, possessions and all movable and immovable goods whatsoever held and possessed by them and to reduce their persons to perpetual slavery, and to apply and appropriate to himself and his successors the kingdoms, dukedoms, counties, principalities, dominions, possessions and goods, and convert them to his and their use and profit.

This was used by colonisers in conjunction with the principle of *terra nullius*, meaning territory without a master or owner, to take ownership of new lands inhabited by Indigenous peoples.

For 500 years, Indigenous peoples of the Americas suffered from physical, social and spiritual devastation (1). After epidemics ended, Indigenous peoples remained under control by colonial governments, church and government-run residential and day schools and Christian missionaries. The huge loss of life they experienced immediately after contact – 90–95% of the population of the Indigenous people of the Americas – destroyed many leaders, artists, teachers, healers and holy people. As Wesley-Esquimaux and Smolewski note, Indigenous people were incarcerated on reservations and in missions, held in residential schools and prisons, forcibly sterilised and aggressively assimilated and acculturated. Their own ways of life were broken, their culture stripped bare and the needs as human beings completely neglected (Wesley-Esquimaux and Smolewski 2004; see also Barker 2023 for an excellent review of the role of incarceration in controlling Indigenous people).

Many of the changes that colonisers brought can be regarded as forms of ethnocide or the destruction of a culture without physically killing people in order to cause religious conversion (Chalk and Jonassohn 1986). Economic resources were restricted, social structures and cultural norms destroyed and their religion forbidden so that Indigenous people became poor and marginalised. This was followed by an enforced loss of languages and ritual practices, re-education in mission schools, lowering of the status of women in what had been, in many cases, matriarchal societies, breakage in the kinship system and the diminution of the role of traditional spiritual leaders and healers. The Christian tradition of blaming epidemics and destruction on the wrath of God was a useful way for the colonisers to rationalise and excuse the vast number of deaths of Indigenous peoples (Wesley-Esquimaux and Smolewski 2004).

By the early 1790s, Canadian traders routinely took women from their families to ensure debt repayment and sold them; 45% of government officials living in what was then the northwest territories were involved in relationships with young Indigenous girls. In 1886, it was reported to parliament that girls as young as 13 were being sold to white men in the West for as little as $10. Rations were withheld from Indigenous women unless they provided sexual favours to the Indian agents. Member of parliament

Hector Langevin, a father of Confederation, rejected the idea that Indigenous girls and women were being trafficked, claiming that to them, marriage was 'simply a bargain and sale' and that the parents of a young woman were always looking for a buyer for her (Wesley-Esquimaux and Smolewski 2004). Indigenous women are still seen as disposable, as a commodity to be used (Goode 2023, p. 73). It took many years and many voices for there to be an inquiry into the thousands of missing and murdered Indigenous women in Canada; it was claimed that one of the factors leading to the demise of these women was the assumption that they lived high-risk lifestyles by working in the sex trade (Goode 2023, p. 75). When releasing the report handed down by the Royal Canadian Mounted Police (RCMP), an RCMP representative once again voiced the myth that these women had put themselves in harm's way.

To Indigenous people, land was capable of sensing and feeling, and so their separation from it was a profound loss. The loss of land, culture and community changed traditional gender roles, core values and family structures. Alcohol was introduced by the coloniser and traded for fur, and drinking became an escape for many Indigenous people, which led to dependence. In recent decades, this has been replaced by or accompanied by the use of other substances, including opioids such as fentanyl, with high levels of death (see data below). Excessive drinking and other drug use became a way to regain some control over one's own body and destiny, and to provide an escape from the mental and physical anguish that life had brought.

Prior to contact, the community was the main force of social cohesion, providing support and resolving problems together. These communities were broken apart by the settlers, as, for example, Father LeJeune, a Jesuit priest, who aimed to 'civilise' the Montagnais-Naskapi of the Saint Lawrence Valley in the mid-16th century. He advocated the institution of punishment and was distressed that the 'savages' thought physical abuse a terrible crime; he believed that the children should be taken from their families and placed in Jesuit-run institutions located far away. LeJeune, like other missionaries, wanted to replace a peaceful, non-punitive, non-authoritarian social system in which women held power with one based on punishing and frightening children, male dominance and the submission of women (Allen 1986, 1994; Wesley-Esquimaux and Smolewski 2004). 'What he had in mind was more along the lines of torture, imprisonment, battering, neglect, and psychological torment – the educational methods to which Indian children in government and mission schools would be subjected for some time after Conquest was accomplished' (Allen 1986, p. 39).

Before contact, Indigenous people lived in complex, interconnected communities with a high level of cooperation. After contact, Indigenous people faced serious barriers in obtaining resources and having access to social opportunities as the colonisers introduced marked distinctions in status and strict rules of conduct (Wesley-Esquimaux and Smolewski 2004). The effects of these socioeconomic and psychological abuses on individuals included isolation/alienation, shame, anger towards school and parents, self-hatred, internalised racism, fear of authority, low self-esteem, self-destructive behaviours (substance use and alcoholism, gambling and suicidal behaviours) and aggressiveness. Effects on families included unresolved grief, difficulty with parenting, family violence, loss of traditions and loss of identity. Effects on community and culture included loss of connectedness with traditions, languages and cultural history, loss of support from Elders and healers as well as collective support, lack of control over land and resources, increased suicide rate, loss of communal raising of children and communal violence. The effects on women were particularly profound as her traditional role as head of the home and family and community nurturer was taken away. Women were often abused or abandoned and, as a consequence, suffered from depression, turned to substances for help or committed suicide (Bombay et al. 2014; Wesley Esquimaux and Smolewski 2004).

Residential schools: destruction through education

The Indigenous people of Canada consist of the First Nations, Inuit and Métis. In the early 1900s, Catholic nuns and priests received funding from the Federal government to set up schools for Indigenous children, the Indian Residential School (IRS) system. These religious schools were established under the Indian Act to assimilate Indigenous children into Euro-Canadian culture and remove them from the traditional methods of education and child rearing. Some of the rationale went as follows: 'Indian culture is a contradiction in terms. They are uncivilised. The aim of education is to destroy the Indian' (Nicholas Flood Davin Report 1879, in the Canadian Encyclopedia, 2025). 'When the school is on the reserve, the child lives with his parents who are savages; He is surrounded by savages ... he is simply a savage who can read and write' (Sir John A. Macdonald, Prime Minister, address to House of Commons 1883, in the Canadian Encyclopedia 2025). Short of having 'abandon hope all who enter here', there is not much more that can be said about the aims of Indigenous education than is conveyed in the foregoing quotes. The Indigenous Residential School system was one of the main means the government used to try to eliminate the 'Indian problem' (Royal Commission on Aboriginal Peoples (RCAP) 1996).

In total, an estimated 150,000 First Nations, Inuit and Metis children attended residential schools, some as young as three years old. Thousands of children died either at school or because of their experiences in the system or at mental institutions, where experiments were performed on them. They were forbidden to wear traditional clothing, their hair was cut, they were not allowed to participate in ceremonies, they were often referred to by number and not by name and were punished for speaking their own language, some having pins driven through their tongues, and for praying in the way that their elders had taught them (Canadian Encyclopedia, accessed April 9, 2024;

Truth and Reconciliation Commission, Final Report 2015). Abuse was common; children were burnt, beaten, given electric shocks, suffered racism, psychological, emotional and sexual abuse and were forced into labour. Most did not receive enough food to eat, some were starved as part of experiments and since living conditions were poor, many became sick with preventable diseases such as tuberculosis and influenza. Only a few hours a day were spent in the classroom, most teachers were unqualified even for the basic curriculum and students spent long hours working to maintain buildings and grow food. When they left school, most children did not have the skills needed to find well-paying work. There were also Indian Day Schools, which were in use until 2000, and Indian Hospitals, in which students and patients were abused in many different ways, including being part of experiments without their consent (Barker 2023; Canadian Encyclopedia, accessed April 9, 2024; Truth and Reconciliation Commission 2015).

Many people have written moving accounts of their or their relatives' experiences in the Indigenous school system. These are well worth reading as they humanise the otherwise empty data and bring into clear focus the sheer scope of this human-made tragedy. They make us all too aware of the levels of cruelty and abuse that human beings are capable of bestowing on their fellow beings. Above all, these accounts make us aware of the incredible capacity of Indigenous people to find hope and to rebuild after eras of adversity. One searing account can be read and heard in Dennis Saddleman's poem about his experience of residential school, Monster (2013). In this, Saddleman recalls a steel and cement monster, built to devour innocent native children, its veins clotted with cruelty and teeth that chewed the Indian out of him.

The sixties crucible

Residential schools began closing in Canada in the 1960s when there was a mass removal of Indigenous children and youth from their homes, predominantly into non-Indigenous households, often without the knowledge or consent of families and band councils. Termed the Sixties Scoop, for three decades, children were placed in foster care and adopted into non-Indigenous families throughout Canada, the USA and overseas (Bombay et al. 2014; Canadian Encyclopedia, accessed April 10, 2025). The process began in 1951 when amendments to the Indian Act gave the provinces jurisdiction over Indigenous child welfare where none existed federally. By law, social workers did not have to ask permission of parents to take the children away and between 11,000 and 20,000 children were adopted between 1960 and 1990. The last residential school closed in 1996; since then, former students have demanded recognition and restitution, resulting in the IRS settlement agreement in 2007.

The 1960s proved to be a crucible for the causes of Indigenous distress and trauma: the Indian Act, and enfranchisement (in which an Indigenous person had to surrender their Indigenous rights and those of their children in order to access certain rights in Canadian society), residential schools and the Sixties Scoop combined to ensure the erosion and undermining of families, communities and ways of life. The harms that were done continue to have effects in the present and intergenerationally in what has been called historical trauma (Alioff and Schouten Levine 1987; Bombay et al. 2014; Danielli et al. 2015, 2016; Evans-Campbell 2008). 'We don't just carry out our everyday pain we are carrying the pain of our fathers and our mothers our grandfathers and our grandmothers; it's part of the land' (Alioff and Schouten Levine 1987). The government of Canada has repeatedly been in violation of the treaties it has negotiated with Indigenous peoples, and over generations, this has caused marginalisation, dispossession and ill-health (Wesley-Esquimaux and Smolewski 2004). As Talaga has said, people need to understand how the failure and betrayal of the treaties, together with the Indian Act, led to the isolation of Indigenous people on remote reservations and their subservience to Ottawa for over a hundred years (Talaga 2017).

The result has been that Indigenous people in Canada today experience serious psychological, social and cultural challenges and suffer from physical and mental health problems at rates that are much higher than those of the general Canadian population.

The current health status of indigenous canadians

The following data are from Indigenous Services Canada, Medical Services Branch (MSB) of Health Canada, and Statistics Canada and unless otherwise stated, were updated in 2023 and 2024.

The physical and mental health of Indigenous people in Canada is significantly worse than that of non-Indigenous people. There are higher rates of chronic and infectious diseases, particularly tuberculosis and Type II diabetes, inadequate access to healthcare, poor housing conditions, and more poverty and food insecurity (Indigenous Services Canada 2024). Life expectancy is significantly lower than the Canadian average, and in some areas, infant mortality rates are up to three times (Indigenous Services Canada 2023). The suicide rate amongst Indigenous youth is particularly high, at 6 times that of the general population, and even higher among Inuit youth. Overdose deaths are significantly higher than in non-Indigenous Canadians.

On reserves, infant mortality rates vary from three to seven times the national average, and off reserves, from two to four times higher than the non-Indigenous population. Indigenous children are four times more likely to be hungry than non-Indigenous children and have a 40% chance of living below the poverty line. Indigenous children are significantly over-represented in the child welfare system in many provinces of Canada. Housing on reserves and in the north tends to need repair and be seriously overcrowded. Racism, discrimination and marginalisation within the healthcare system remain barriers to healthcare and extensive travel to access healthcare is necessary for some, which can be financially and emotionally stressful.

In many provinces, alcohol and other substance problems are the biggest health and social issues facing Indigenous people living off-reserve. A review of case files for 127 residential school survivors in British Columbia found very high rates of substance use, and only two were without mental issues (AHF 2003). The same study showed that 30.4% of residential school survivors experience a major depressive episode, while 26.1% experience chronic depression and 64.2% experience repercussions from post-traumatic stress disorder.

Incarceration rates of Indigenous people are much higher than those of non-Indigenous Canadians. On an average day, there are 42.6 Indigenous people in provincial custody/10,000 population compared to 4.0 non-Indigenous. Incarceration rates for Indigenous women are almost double those for Indigenous men (see Barker 2023, for an excellent overview of the role of incarceration in the lives of Indigenous people).

Intergenerational issues and historical trauma

There is an increasing body of evidence that the trauma experienced by one generation can be passed on to following generations by a variety of mechanisms at psychological, social, biological and epigenetic levels (Bombay et al. 2014, 2020; Danieli 1982, 1985; Danieli et al. 2015, 2016; Evans-Campbell 2008; Herman 1992). The adverse effects on Indigenous individuals who attended residential and other schools in Canada, as in other colonised countries, include depression, substance use, family dysfunction, suicide and post-traumatic stress disorder. Reports prepared for the Aboriginal Healing Foundation set out the ways in which schools for Indigenous children were one of the main factors in bringing about these effects. These, in conjunction with the 'Sixties Scoop', have resulted in serious social and mental health issues for Indigenous people of this and recent generations, but there have been many other instances of injustice and ill-treatment since colonisation began.

Combined over generations, the effects on individuals, family and community can be profound and constitute historical trauma. There is evidence from a number of health surveys and studies on the effects of familial residential school attendance on the response to stressors and general well-being, with the adverse effects on individuals being higher when several generations of their family had attended the schools rather than just one. The residential schools had intergenerational effects throughout the whole community, with the result being changes to traditional social norms and weakened social structures (Yellow Horse Brave Heart 1998). Evans-Campbell posited that the lack of traditional parental role models in those who had attended residential schools was a cause of negative parenting practices

(Evans-Campbell 2008). Having a parent who attended a residential school has been associated with a child having greater involvement with the child welfare system on the grounds of sexual abuse. The high level of sexual abuse at residential schools has been proposed as a determinant of high rates of sexual abuse in certain communities as a result of changed social norms, amongst other factors (Bombay et al. 2014).

There is a marked similarity in the experiences of Indigenous peoples around the globe with respect to the intergenerational effects of colonisation. The treatment of Indigenous people in the Americas and elsewhere had all the characteristics of genocide, resulting in psychosocial effects that are seen in survivors of genocide and their descendants (Wesley-Esquimaux and Smolewski 2004). Indeed, some Indigenous writers describe the process of transforming independent, healthy societies into dispossessed peoples on the verge of cultural and physical extinction as a form of genocide (Short 2010).

Truth and reconciliation

Recognition of the legacy of Indigenous trauma has come to the fore in Canada in more recent years through the truth and reconciliation process. In the 1990s, residential school survivors began to speak publicly about the abuse they endured at the schools. They demanded that the federal government and the churches tell the truth about what happened and that the government give support in the form of monetary compensation to the survivors. Churches began apologising in 1986, with an increase two decades later, and since 2008, apologies and compensation have been provided to some but not all survivors. Recent settlements have also occurred with Indian Day School and Indian Hospital groups following class action lawsuits against the Federal Government.

Some of the money from the IRS settlement was used to create the Truth and Reconciliation Commission (TRC) in 2009, where survivors were able to tell their stories, most for the first time. Therapists and support workers were on hand to provide care for these individuals (Truth and Reconciliation Commission of Canada, Final Report 2015).

In 2015, after 6 years of work, the TRC released a report of its findings based on the testimony of seven thousand former school students; the report spanned 6 volumes and contained 94 Calls to Action. These Calls to Action outline the structural changes necessary for Indigenous peoples to move on from the effects of colonialism and live side by side with non-Indigenous Canadians as mutually respectful equals. The enquiry revealed the systematic abuse by the schools against the children, policies that the Chief Commissioner, Anishinaabe judge and professor Murray Sinclair referred to as one of the darkest, most troubling chapters in Canada's collective history and as 'cultural genocide'. This included compulsory sterilisation and at least 3,200 deaths from disease and malnourishment; Sinclair argued the number is closer to 6,000. One of the commissioners, Marie Wilson, commented: 'One quarter of the time the students name was not recorded, for almost half of the students who died the cause of death was not recorded; the indignity of this the utter sadness of this, can you imagine?' (Truth and Reconciliation Report 2015). In recent years, many unmarked graves and areas of uncertain purpose have been uncovered at the schools in Canada and the United States, and more are discovered every year.

The Calls to Action include requests for imploring the Federal Government, in consultation with Indigenous peoples, to bridge the gap in health outcomes between Indigenous and non-Indigenous people and provide funding for Aboriginal healing centres to address the physical, mental, emotional and spiritual harms caused by residential schools. Call to Action 22 asks 'the Canadian health-care system to recognise the value of Aboriginal healing practices and use them in the treatment of Aboriginal patients in collaboration with Aboriginal healers and Elders where requested by Aboriginal patients'. One of the Calls to Action (53) called for the creation of the National Council for Reconciliation and this was incorporated in March of 2025. This Council will promote reconciliation and monitor progress in all sectors of society.

To date, 14 of the 94 Calls to Action of the TRC have been implemented, the rest are being acted upon but are still incomplete, 21 are stalled, and 14 have not been started (Indigenous Watchdog, July 1st, 2025). Over the past decade, there have been a number of other enquiries into Indigenous issues, one of the most important being that into missing and murdered women and girls. Currently, there are demands to form an enquiry into police killings of Indigenous people. Sadly, these enquiries and calls are met with much talk but little or no action.

The Canadian government has committed to implementing the United Nations Declaration on the Rights of Indigenous Peoples and it must do so without further delay.

The path forward: a solution through education

The recently deceased Murray Sinclair (died on November 4th, 2024), Chief Commissioner of the Truth and Reconciliation Commission, wrote of some of the ways that the harms caused by the residential school system have continued to reverberate throughout the Indigenous community and Canada at large. He criticised the country's public education system, which for decades extolled the virtues of colonialism and diminished Indigenous peoples. He spoke powerfully of the generational and emotional trauma felt by Indigenous communities and of the poverty and systemic prejudice that persists. Sinclair stated that a chronic national and systemic erasure of Indigenous peoples has sanitised versions of Canadian colonisation and history and has led to a profound misunderstanding of the contributions that Indigenous cultures and communities have made to Canada. Sinclair believed that education has perpetrated some of the worst harm in our national history, creating damaging public attitudes and facilitating brutal, divisive policies. For example, most Canadians are aware of the dysfunction that exists in many Indigenous communities but have no idea how it came to be that way, or how governments, taxpayers and laws contributed to the situation through such policies as those that established and maintained residential schools.

While Sinclair pointed out the harms done to Indigenous people in the past by educational systems, he also stressed the need to look to education as a solution to problems now and in the future: 'Education is what got us into this mess it will be education this will get us out of it' (2024). He called for inclusive education programs that move beyond a focus on the business world to developing philosophers, artists and writers who can influence societies. For example, a recent report from British Columbia called for healthcare systems and educational institutions to critically examine their hiring practices in order to bring more Indigenous healthcare workers and decision makers into their teams. Medical schools need to include Indigenous topics and engage students with Indigenous people in the learning process (ref report): First Nations Population Health and Wellness Agenda: First Interim Update, 2024, by First Nations Health Authority's Office of the Chief Medical Officer and the BC Office of the Provincial Health Officer. There are also many examples of Indigenous community initiatives addressing mental health issues as well as Indigenous healing practices that need to be incorporated into broader programming.

Though Indigenous people have had a difficult history with formal education, there is a need to rely on education to move forward. The past decades have shown that Indigenous people have a great interest in all levels of education, including at the post-secondary level. Post-secondary education is a vital step in moving forward as well as in the process of reconciliation because the knowledge and skill sets provided by it allow people to live comfortably in two worlds, the Indigenous and the non-Indigenous.

Although Indigenous students continue to be underrepresented in higher education (only 9.8% of Indigenous people in Canada have a university degree, compared to 28% of non-Indigenous people), over the past few decades, there has been a huge increase in university attendance and success by Indigenous students. The impact of education on reconciliation can be illustrated by the guiding work of Universities Canada, which represents 97 universities across the country. Their new Principles on Indigenous Education were developed in close consultation with Indigenous communities and released in 2015 with the aim of closing the education gap and '... creating resources, spaces and approaches that promote dialogue and intercultural engagement between Indigenous and non-Indigenous students. The principles also highlight the need to provide greater exposure and knowledge for non-Indigenous students on the realities, histories, cultures and beliefs of Indigenous people in Canada' (Universities Canada 2015).

The rationale underlying closing the education gap is not only that it will strengthen Indigenous students and their communities but that it will also benefit Canada as a whole. It is anticipated that, as well as the social and cultural advantages brought by higher education, there will be significant economic benefits to both Indigenous and non-Indigenous people.

In Canada, we have begun to parse out reconciliation in many ways and we are currently in an era of economic reconciliation. Indigenous people cannot move forward without inclusion in the economic life of Canada, and for that, there is a need for capital, control over the treaties, and the necessary level of education to participate in, and contribute meaningfully to, this life. As Dennis Sadleman wrote in his poem Monster, this is the time for stories of renewal and stories of tomorrow.

> This is not a time for the timid. It is a time for the daring. I invite you to join in this challenge. I invite you to move forward and write a new book of knowledge for the future. Let's dare to live greatly together.
>
> (Sinclair 2024)

1. We are particularly indebted to Cynthia C. Wesley-Esquimaux and Magdalena Smolewski for their excellent investigation of historic trauma and other research that they did, along with all those who worked with the Aboriginal Healing Foundation.

References

Aboriginal Healing Foundation (1999). *Aboriginal Healing Foundation Program Handbook*, 2e. Ottawa: Aboriginal Healing Foundation.

Aboriginal Healing Foundation (2003). *Aboriginal People, Resilience and the Residential School Legacy*. Ottawa: Aboriginal Healing Foundation.

Alioff, M. and Schouten Levine, S. (1987). *The Long Walk of Alanis Obomsawin*. Cinema Canada.

Allen, P.G. (1986). *The Sacred Hoop: Recovering the Feminine in American Indian Traditions*. Boston: Beacon Press.

Allen, P.G. (1994). *Voice of the Turtle: American Indian Literature, 1900–1970*. New York: Ballantine Publishing Group.

Barker, A.J. (2023). Carcerality and the elimination of indigenous people in Canada. *Canadian Geographies* https://doi.org/10.1111/cag.12962.

Bombay, A., Matheson, K., and Anisman, H. (2014). The intergenerational effect of Indian residential schools: implications for the concept of historical trauma. *Transcultural Psychiatry* 5 (3): 329–338.

Bombay, A., McQuaid, R.J., Youong, J. et al. (2020). Familial attendance at Indian residential school and subsequent involvement in the child welfare system among Indigenous adults born during the sixties scoop era [Record]. *First Peoples Child & Family Review: An Interdisciplinary Journal Honouring the Voices, Perspectives, and Knowledges of First Peoples* 15 (1): 62–79.

Canadian Encyclopaedia (n.d.). https://www.canadianencyclopedia.ca (accessed 15 and 23 May 2025).

Chalk, F. and Jonassohn, K. (1986). Conceptualizations of genocide and Ethnocide. In: *Famine in Ukraine* (ed. R. Serbyn and B. Krawchenko), 1932–1933. Edmonton: Canadian Institute of Ukrainian Studies, University of Alberta.

Danieli, Y. (1982). Families of survivors of the Nazi Holocaust: some short and long-term effects. In: *Stress and Anxiety*, vol. 8 (ed. C.D. Spielberger, I.G. Sarason, and N. Milgram), 405–421. New York: McGraw-Hill.

Danieli, Y. (1985). The treatment and prevention of long-term effects and Intergenerational transmission of victimization: a lesson from Holocaust Survivors and their children. In: *Trauma and Its Wake, Vol. 1: The Study and Treatment of Post-Traumatic Stress Disorder* (ed. C.R. Figley), 295–313. New York: Brunner/Mazel.

Danieli, Y., Norris, F.H., Lindert, J. et al. (2015). The Danieli Inventory of Multigenerational Legacies of Trauma, part I: survivors' posttrauma adaptational styles in their children's eyes. *Journal of Psychiatric Research* 68: 167–175.

Danieli, Y., Norris, F.H., and Engdahl, B. (2016). Multigenerational legacies of trauma: modeling the what and how of transmission. *American Journal of Orthopsychiatry* 86 (6): 639–651.

Davin, N.F. (1879). Nicholas Flood Davin. The Canadian Encyclopedia. https://www.canadianencyclopedia.ca (accessed 15 April 2025).

Evans-Campbell, T. (2008). Historical trauma in American Indian/Native Alaska communities: a multilevel framework for exploring impacts on individuals, families, and communities. *Journal of Interpersonal Violence* 23 (3): 316–338.

Goode, M. (2023). *Truth Telling: Seven Conversations about Indigenous Life in Canada*. Toronto: Harper Perennial.

Herman, J.L. (1992). *Trauma and Recovery*. New York, NY: Basic Books.

Indigenous Watchdog (7 July 2025). https://www.indigenouswatchdog.org (accessed 21 August 2025).

Macdonald, J.A (1883). Indigenous Education, in the Canadian Encyclopedia (accessed 15 April and 23 May 2025.

Royal Commission on Aboriginal Peoples (1996). The Canadian Encyclopedia. https://www.canadianencyclopedia.ca (accessed 15 April and 23 May 2025).

Saddleman, D. (2013). Monster. http://www.cbc.ca/radio/thecurrent/apr-3-2014-1.2908353/monster-by-poet-dennis-saddleman-i-hate-you-residential-school-i-hate-you-1.2908356 (accessed 15 April 2025).

Short, D. (2010). Cultural genocide and indigenous peoples: a sociological approach. *The International Journal of Human Rights* 14 (6): 833–848.

Sinclair, M. (2024). Canda, education holds the key to reconciliation. Globe and Mail September 20, 2024, theglobeandmail.com (accessed 15 April 2025).

Talaga, T. (2017). *Seven Fallen Feathers*. Toronto: House of Ananasi Press.

Truth and Reconciliation Commission of Canada (2015). Final Report. https://www.pm.gc.ca (accessed 15 April, 23 May and 21 August 2025).

Universities Canada (2015). Enhancing indigenous education. https://www.univcan.ca (accessed 23 May 2025).

Wesley-Esquimaux, C.C. and Smolewski, M. (2004). *Historic Trauma and Aboriginal Healing*. Ottawa: AHF.

Yellow Horse Brave Heart, M. (1998). The return to the sacred path: healing the historical trauma response among the Lakota. *Smith College Studies In Social Work* 68 (3): 287–305.

Part 3
Interventions

Chapter 13

INTERVENTIONS AND TREATMENT FOR THE EFFECTS OF ACEs

Diane Riley[1] *and Richard Pates*[2]

[1] Independent Consultant, Ontario, Canada
[2] Independent Consultant, Blaenau Gwent, Wales, UK

While many interventions have been used to deal with psychological and behavioural problems related to childhood adversity, much of the information on them is anecdotal or speculative in nature, and very few have been examined in a controlled manner. Interventions include those for anger, anxiety, depression, post-traumatic stress disorder (PTSD) and substance use and many of the other psychological problems associated with the effects of adverse childhood experiences (ACEs). Some of the most promising interventions are covered in this section and, where appropriate, reference is made to other, more thorough, reviews and books, of which there are many.

There are also interventions at the socioeconomic and political levels, both for preventing and dealing with the effects of ACEs. These will not be dealt with here, although some chapters will touch on these (for example, Andrew Bennett's chapter on training). Reviews of interventions for prevention and at other levels (organisational, societal, etc.) can be found in Asmussen and colleagues' review (2020) and the books by Asmundson and Afifi (2019) and Waite and Ryan (2019).

Psychological and psychosocial interventions

Psychological interventions focus on the cognitive, emotional and motivational processes of the individual. These include psychophysiological interventions such as heart rate variability feedback, exercise and acupuncture.

Psychosocial interventions focus on interpersonal, social and environmental factors that relate to recovery in addition to, or instead of, the individual factors.

The Intergenerational Effects of Adverse Childhood Experiences: Ripples on a Pond, First Edition. Edited by Richard Pates and Diane Riley.

Published 2026 by John Wiley & Sons Ltd.

The following interventions can be used either alone or in combination and in an individual or group format:

Cognitive behavioural therapies (CBTs), including cognitive therapy, cognitive processing therapy (CPT), compassion focused therapy, exposure therapy/prolonged exposure therapy (PET), virtual reality exposure therapy (VRET), imagery rehearsal therapy, mindfulness-based cognitive therapy (MBCT), narrative exposure therapy (NET), stress inoculation training (SIT), CPT, eye movement desensitisation and reprocessing (EMDR), psychodynamic therapies, counseling, solution-focused brief therapy, combined somatic and cognitive therapies, parent training/couple and family interventions, meditation, mindfulness-based stress reduction, psychoeducational interventions, and peer support.

Other non-pharmacological interventions, which may be included either alone or in combination:

Acupuncture, exercise, yoga, relaxation techniques (including heart rate variability biofeedback), art, sound and music, haptic, adventure, nature "bathing", substance use interventions, other psychosocial interventions, Indigenous, and traditional healing.

Pharmacological interventions include prescription drugs and psychoactive and psychedelic substances.

Other interventions include brain stimulation and repetitive transcranial magnetic stimulation.

The nature of interventions

Psychosocial interventions are intended to improve mental health and well-being through focusing on biological, behavioural, cognitive, emotional, interpersonal, social or environmental factors. Although many psychosocial interventions have demonstrated effectiveness, the findings have not been well synthesised, and so it can be difficult to know which treatments are effective (for definitions, see the list of psychological therapies on the Cochrane common mental disorders (CCMD) website (cmd.cochrane.org/psychological-therapies-topics-list).

Cognitive behavioural processes can also be subclassified into three major classes with different targets: (i) cognitive restructuring, which focuses on internal underlying beliefs and thoughts with the aim of challenging maladaptive thought patterns; (ii) coping skills therapy, which targets the identification and alteration of cognitions and behaviours that may increase the impact of negative external events; and (iii) problem-solving therapies, which combine cognitive restructuring and coping skills therapy to change internal thought patterns and optimise responses to external negative events (see the Cochrane website for further details).

Cognitive behavioural interventions are based on the proposition that behaviours are cognitively mediated, and that mental health and social problems are influenced by cognitions and resulting behaviours. Because cognitive activity may be monitored and altered, behaviours may be changed through cognitive changes. The underlying theory is that appraisal of fear involves activation of a trauma-induced "schema" that causes the individual to pay attention to information consistent with the schema and to ignore information that is inconsistent. This means that even benign or ambiguous events can trigger fear appraisal in people who have experienced trauma (Beck et al. 1985). Cognitive theory as applied to PTSD focuses on (i) changing a person's cognitive appraisal of the traumatic event or changing the process by which an individual attaches meaning to an event; and (ii) changing a person's attribution of the event.

Coping skills approaches aim to teach people skills to manage their anxiety and trauma. Some interventions are designed to be delivered within a short period of time following the incident (e.g. less than 3 months), whereas others are used over the longer term. Third-wave CBTs, such as acceptance and commitment therapy and mindfulness, attempt to change the function of psychological events and the individual's relationship to them through acceptance, being present in the moment, and committed action.

Stress Inoculation Training was adapted by Veronen and Kilpatrick (1983) from anxiety management procedures (Meichenbaum 1977). It uses three components: behaviourally based psychoeducation so that individuals can understand and normalise fear and avoidance behaviours; guided hierarchical *in vivo* assignments targeting event-related phobias; and training in behavioural and cognitive behavioural coping strategies: thought-stopping, guided self-dialogue, muscle relaxation, controlled breathing, covert modelling and role playing. The goal of SIT is to increase the person's awareness of conditioned stimuli to improve early detection of anxiety-provoking cues and to use coping skills early in the stress response in order to reduce anxiety.

Prolonged Exposure Therapy or flooding was developed from earlier treatments using flooding exposure techniques and emotion processing theory with anxiety disorders. It was proposed that it is the encoding of memories under extreme distress that leads to disjointed and disorganised memories, and that these impede natural recovery and lead to PTSD. The aim of PET is to decrease the anxiety associated with memories of the traumatic event and begins with psychoeducation, breathing training and the development of a fear and avoidance hierarchy for *in vivo* exposure (Foa et al. 1999).

Cognitive Processing Therapy (CPT) was developed from emotional processing theory to identify the parts of a traumatic narrative that cause the individual the greatest conflict (Nishith et al. 2005; Resick and Schnicke 1992; Resick et al. 2003). These are said to be the result of unsuccessful attempts to accommodate information about the stressful or traumatic event into pre-existing memory and belief structures. The goal of CPT is to help individuals integrate their issues into pre-existing schemas, and so to decrease avoidance and intrusions of unintegrated aspects of the event. Unlike PET, CPT tries to directly correct participants' misconceptions or misinformation about an event and includes psychoeducation, exposure and cognitive methods.

Behavioural therapies are based on the premise that all behaviours are learned and that unhealthy behaviours can be changed. Techniques such as systematic desensitisation and flooding are often used with people suffering from effects of severe stress and trauma to extinguish anxiety and reduce avoidant behaviours. Victims are taught to replace a fear response with relaxation responses. This can be done gradually, with systematic desensitisation, or more quickly, by flooding.

Eye Movement Desensitisation and Reprocessing (EMDR) was developed for the treatment of PTSD and uses exposure and cognitive techniques (Shapiro 1995). The person imagines a scene related to the event and recites words related to the scene while the therapist moves his or her fingers back and forth so that the person performs rhythmic, multi-saccadic eye movements by watching the therapist's fingers. This movement is hypothesised to facilitate the processing of trauma memory through the dual attention required to focus on attending to the therapist's finger movement (external stimulus) and the trauma scene (internal stimulus). When anxiety in the scene has decreased, a new adaptive belief is rehearsed until this new belief is thought to be "true" (Rothbaum 1997). EMDR is similar to the behavioural techniques of flooding and systematic desensitisation; studies comparing EMDR with and without eye movements show that EMDR without eye movements leads to equivalent outcomes as EMDR with eye movements (Pitman et al. 1996).

Counselling encompasses a range of interventions that may be used in many settings and is focused on the needs of the person. It can be based on a number of approaches and can be delivered by itself or in combination with other approaches.

Humanistic and supportive therapies include a mix of therapeutic techniques. Supportive therapy is almost always non-directive, that is, the person is empowered to guide the content and the therapist avoids offering direct advice. The focus is on developing a supportive, emotionally involved relationship between the therapist and participant. Supportive therapy can be conducted in either an individual or group format.

Other psychologically orientated interventions include a diverse range of therapies that aim to help people cope with, express and work through problems by, for example, expressive writing, drama or mindfulness. Equine-assisted therapy for anxiety and post-traumatic stress symptoms has been shown to reduce symptoms of post-traumatic stress, severe emotional responses to trauma, generalised anxiety, symptoms of depression and alcohol use (Earles et al. 2015).

Evaluation of interventions

Han and colleagues conducted an extensive review of psychological therapies for trauma-related problems. More than half of the 32 studies examined were randomised controlled trials, with child abuse, domestic violence or sexual assault being the most common types of trauma addressed. The interventions were largely focused on reducing symptoms of PTSD or anxiety, and were mostly delivered in an outpatient setting by healthcare professionals. Two of the most frequently used interventions were EMDR (6) and CBT (5). Trauma-informed interventions significantly reduced PTSD symptoms in 11 of 23 studies, while 15 studies found improvements in three main psychological outcomes, including PTSD symptoms (11 of 23), depression (9 of 16), and anxiety (5 of 10). CBT consistently improved a wide range of outcomes, including depression, anxiety, emotional dysregulation, interpersonal problems and risky behaviours (Han et al. 2021). The authors concluded that, overall, there is inconsistent evidence to support many of the interventions used to treat psychological problems and recommended that a wider range of stress and trauma-related outcomes should be studied. Similarly, in their extensive 2020 review, Asmussen and colleagues concluded that while overall the evidence for the treatment of psychological problems related to ACEs is limited and inconsistent, there are a number of effective interventions, including CBT as well as several interventions focusing on PTSD.

Due to the severity of some responses to traumatic events, which can result in prolonged problems in many psychological and physiological processes, interventions for PTSD are some of those most widely and thoroughly studied, including extensive reviews by the Cochrane and United Kingdom's National Institute for Health and Clinical Excellence [NICE (UK)] groups as by Asmussen and colleagues for the Early Intervention Foundation. These reviews are recommended to the reader as some of the best sources of information on this topic. Some of their main findings are included below.

The estimated lifetime prevalence of PTSD in adults in the United Kingdom is around 4.4%; in the United States, 6%; in Australia, 7.2%; in Canada, 7.7%; and in Europe, ranging from less than 1% to 7% depending on the level of problems related to WW2, worldwide 3.6% (WHO 2024). Approximately twice as many women as men are diagnosed with PTSD, with sexual assault being the most common traumatic incident.

PTSD includes re-experiencing the trauma (nightmares, flashbacks and intrusive, distressing thoughts), avoidance of reminders of the traumatic event, negative mood and symptoms of hyperarousal (feeling anxious or angry, being easily startled, sleep disruption, and problems concentrating). Reviews of the evidence have supported the use of individual trauma-focused CBT (TFCBT) and EMDR in the treatment of PTSD (Bisson et al. 2013; NICE 2018; Schrader and Ross 2021). TFCBT is a combination of cognitive therapy aimed at changing the way a person thinks about the event, and behavioural therapy, which aims to change the way a person acts. TFCBT helps an individual come to terms with a trauma through exposure to memories of the event. EMDR helps a person reprocess their memories of a traumatic event. TFCBT and EMDR are currently recommended as the treatments of choice by guidelines such as those published by NICE (UK).

A Cochrane review of treatment for PTSD in 2013 brought together evidence from 70 studies, including a total of 4,761 people (Bisson et al. 2013).

The review found there to be continued support for the efficacy of individual TFCBT, group TFCBT, EMDR and CBT in the treatment of chronic PTSD in adults. There was evidence that individual TFCBT, EMDR and non-TFCBT are equally effective immediately post-treatment in the treatment of PTSD. There was some evidence that TFCBT and EMDR are superior to non-TFCBT between 1–4 months following treatment, and also that individual TFCBT, EMDR and CBT are more effective than other therapies. Although the Cochrane review included a substantial number of studies, each study included only small numbers of people and some were methodologically poor. It was concluded that the overall quality of the studies was very low and that the findings of the review should be interpreted with caution. There were limited follow-up data, so the long-term effects of treatment could not be determined.

The NICE 2018 review of several hundred interventions focused on people who have persistent traumatic stress symptoms. It covered both those with PTSD, as defined by a diagnosis according to DSM or ICD criteria, and those with clinically significant PTSD symptoms as indicated by baseline scores above a threshold on a validated scale (NICE 2018). The outcomes assessed were:

- Efficacy (PTSD symptoms/diagnosis/response/remission /relapse)
- Acceptability of the intervention (discontinuation for any reason used as a proxy)
- Dissociative symptoms
- Personal/social/occupational functioning (including global functioning/ functional impairment)
- Sleeping difficulties
- Quality of life
- Symptoms of a coexisting condition (including anxiety, depression and substance misuse problems).

The key findings of the review were that much of the evidence was of low or very low quality, and that PTSD is a treatable condition with a range of interventions available. Interventions include psychological therapy: TFCBT such as CPT, NET, PET and EMDR; and drug therapy: venlafaxine or a selective serotonin reuptake inhibitor (SSRI), antipsychotics such as risperidone, in addition to psychological therapies for special cases (they recommend avoiding benzodiazepines or other sedative hypnotic medications, which can cause increased intrusive and dissociative symptoms).

The key recommendations stemming from the NICE review were:

- ensure that methods of access to services take into account the needs of specific populations of people with PTSD, including migrants and asylum seekers, people who are homeless or not registered with a general practitioner (GP), looked-after children and young people and preschool-aged children
- minimise the need to move between different services or providers
- provide multiple points of access to the service, including self-referral

- establish clear links to other care pathways, including for physical healthcare needs
- offer flexible modes of delivery, such as care in non-clinical settings such as schools or offices
- offer a choice of therapists that takes into account the person's trauma experience – for example, they might prefer a specific gender of therapist
- assess the need for further treatment or support for people who have not benefited fully from treatment or have relapsed.
- peer support groups with people with mental health training and supervision should be delivered in a way that reduces the risk of exacerbating symptoms, provides information and helps access services. Be aware of the risk of continued exposure to trauma-inducing environments. Avoid exposing people to triggers that could worsen their symptoms or stop them from engaging with treatment, for example, assessing or treating people in noisy or restricted environments, placing them in a noisy inpatient ward or restraining them.
- think about the impact of the traumatic event on other family members because more than one family member might have PTSD.
- pay particular attention to identifying people with PTSD in working or living environments where there may be cultural challenges to recognising the psychological consequences of trauma.

In the United States, treatment strategies for control of trauma-associated symptoms of PTSD have recently been updated by the Veterans Affairs (VA) and the Department of Defense (DoD). The most recent evidence shows that trauma-focused therapies such as CPT, PET, EMDR and others with significant trauma focus are the current "gold standard" for treatment. Additional medication use may be of assistance in the treatment of symptomology, with special avoidance of benzodiazepines or other sedative hypnotic medications, which are causal of increased intrusive and dissociative symptoms over time (Schrader and Ross 2021).

Examples of some specific approaches

Art therapy

Art therapy combines psychotherapy with artistic creativity, using imagery and colour and to express thoughts that would otherwise be very difficult to convey. It can be particularly useful with children and adolescents who have been abused. A chapter in this book by Deidre McConnell describes art therapy with a young girl from a very difficult background.

Sound or sonic therapy

The use of sound and vibrations for healing has been reported from cultures all over the world and dates back millennia, as does the search for the 'secret chord: Priests in Egypt used tones and sounds from instruments such as the rhombus in rituals which were passed on to the Greeks and into modern times with recreations of various mysteries. Pythagoras used the instrument called the kithara for calming people and animals, calling it "musical medicine'. Many cultures today still use the rhombus and similar devices in their ceremonies and healing. Like touch, sound can be an effective way to work with lower brain areas that are preverbal and preimagery.

Sound therapy uses sounds to promote relaxation both centrally and in the autonomic nervous system and has been associated with the production of brain waves associated with meditation and sleep. The therapy is delivered using instruments such as Tibetan and crystal singing bowls, gongs, drums, tuning forks and more.

Music therapy uses music and song to improve mood and well-being, especially for those with depression, anxiety and PTSD. It can involve playing, listening or creating music, singing or writing songs and dancing. Drumming is a popular healing technique for North American indigenous peoples. Cognitive behavioural music therapy combines CBT with music, where music is used to reinforce some behaviours and modify others (de Witte et al. 2022).

Because musical participation and response do not depend solely on the ability to speak, music therapy is a particularly effective clinical intervention for people who have difficulty communicating verbally. The approach appears to hold great potential for people on the autism spectrum, acquired brain injury and dementia; the evocative power of music and rhythm can help access memories and remember behaviours. A recent book by the musician and neuroscientist Daniel Levitin (2024) examines in detail the connections between music and the brain. He notes that music is part of our earliest memories, is connected to our emotional regulation and cognition and its rhythms and sounds are interwoven with our social behaviours.

Haptic therapy

Touch is the most fundamental of human experiences. Infants rely on touch to feel safe and loved; being rocked, held and soothed calms them and regulates the nervous systems and helps form attachment (see, e.g. the classic, groundbreaking work of Harlow and later of Bowlby on this, Bowlby 1988; Harlow and Zimmermann 1958; Harlow et al. 1965). Our societies today are word- and image-dominated, and the creation and processing of imagery develops much later than that of touch. As noted in the chapter by Nicholls, research supports regulation techniques such as touch as effective in the treatment of trauma, being based on a bottom-up approach such as that followed by Perry (Brummelman et al. 2019; Grandin 1992; Harlow and Zimmermann 1958; Harlow et al. 1965; Perry 2009; Perry and Winfrey 2022). As the work of Harlow and colleagues so clearly demonstrated, tactile stimulation is essential not only for ensuring proper attachment but also for preventing the development of high levels of anxiety and distress (Harlow and Zimmermann 1958; Harlow et al. 1965). Repetitive and rhythmic interventions such as touch, movement and sound help regulate the nervous systems and interventions involving drumming make use of this. Rhythmic movements reduce arousal and stress in children and adults, as seen with approaches such as yoga, meditation and heart-rate variability feedback (Khajuria et al. 2023; Pascoe et al. 2017; Payne et al. 2015; Seekircher et al. 2023).

Touch triggers the release of oxytocin, which regulates cortisol levels and overall arousal. Regulating overactivity in the lower brain regions helps ensure that there is more effective processing at the higher levels of cognitive activity. Without this, traditional cognitive-based therapies are often inadequate in addressing trauma and may increase inappropriate reactions, which can interfere with therapy, causing the individual to feel helpless.

A hug machine or a squeeze machine is a therapeutic device designed to calm hypersensitive persons, usually individuals with autism spectrum disorders. The device was invented by Temple Grandin to administer deep-touch pressure, a type of physical stimulation often self-administered by autistic individuals as a means of self-soothing. Grandin is herself on the autism spectrum and her work on autism and touch in humans and other mammals has been groundbreaking. Autistic people often have sensory processing disorder, which entails abnormal levels of stimulation of the senses (such as hypersensitivity). Because of difficulty with social interactions, it can be uncomfortable or impractical to turn to other human beings for comfort, including hugs. Grandin addressed this by designing the hug machine, in part to help her own anxiety and sensory sensitivity (Grandin 1992).

Preliminary results in the literature have demonstrated that haptic technology can support mental health and well-being by addressing associated risks, including abnormal levels of stress/anxiety as well as social isolation/exclusion. This includes games, toys and play, motion regulation, stimulation therapy, distributed touch therapy and haptics for social wellness. Several techniques can be applied at a distance using smart phones, computers and other devices (haptic interpersonal communication) (McDaniel and Panchanathan 2020; Pacheco-Barrios et al. 2024).

Education

The education of children who have experienced ACEs can be more problematic than working with children who have not experienced them. Because of their early experiences, they often do not do well in educational environments and can be labelled as naughty, underachieving or stupid, as having ADHD, ASD or being "on the spectrum" because their experiences have influenced their current behaviour.

Children who have experienced serious adverse experiences in their early lives often need either additional help at school or more empathy for their condition. Schools can contribute to negative experiences either by the abuse that we know occurs in some or merely because of the way teachers address them, implying that they are stupid or not capable of learning. In the past, schools used corporal punishment (smacking or caning) to discipline children, but this is no longer allowed in many countries, such as the United Kingdom,

Canada and the United States. Punitive rules or behaviourist or consequence-based management to enforce zero tolerance are still sometimes used today, with, for example, detentions used as punishments. ACEs will often lead to behavioural difficulties and unconventional responses from children, but punishing them serves no purpose as we know that punishment does not stop the behaviour and may lead to anger and aggression.

The inaccurate attachment of a label can lead to that child being treated differently and inappropriately. As Perry has noted, a traumatised child entering preschool will not act like a typical 5-year-old. They will have poorer language development and self-regulation, and they will shut down or act out and so fall further behind. In the United States, more children are expelled from school in pre-Kindergarten than at any other level; children of colour, especially boys, are expelled at rates three times that of white boys. The hypervigilance of the child resulting from a sensitised stress response can be mislabelled as ADHD, and their efforts at self-regulation, such as doodling, listening to music and tapping, are prohibited. If they break these rules, they will be labelled, medicated and perhaps expelled, and when they try to avoid school, they are charged with truancy. And "so they enter the school to prison pipeline" (Perry and Winfrey 2022, p. 222).

All children are required to go to school (unless they are being "home schooled"), so we need to ensure that there is equal opportunity for all children, regardless of their background and early experiences. If there are difficulties arising from their early experiences, then a flexible approach is needed which takes account of these and responses that have developed to these. In fact, school can be a normalising experience away from the difficulties that have arisen in their family of origin, so it is imperative that schools and teachers understand this and the role that they play.

In the past, it was not recognised that children with several adverse experiences could be severely affected by what had happened to them. They may have been labelled as troublesome or difficult children without any understanding of what they have been through. Clearly, it is unlikely that such children will immediately tell you what has happened to them, their problems and traumas will be deeply buried, and they will often have a history of being ignored, told off or accused of lying. One of the things that is crucial, as has been previously discussed in this book, is that we need to listen to children and give them time and opportunity to speak about their histories and we need to believe them and believe in them.

One thing that is essential in working with children, especially those with ACEs, is attunement, the ability to recognise and respond to another person's emotional needs and moods, or the understanding of what is happening to that child. We have already mentioned listening without interrupting or contradicting, and we also need to observe them, their body language and how they respond to stimuli. For example, a child who has been sexually abused may resist being touched even on non-intimate parts of their bodies, such as arms. They may dislike crowds because of previous experiences and stand away when there are crowds of people. We can learn from their body language that there are things they do not like from the way they react and respond or even a look in their eyes. As Bombér says, "The capacity for attunement of the people around the child or young person is the best predictor of favourable mental health and well-being" (2020, p. 128). She points out that it is not just about the warmth of care, or sensitivity to need, but how we respond, and the timing involved, sensitive timings based on the interpersonal cues from the child or young person. This is in agreement with findings such as those by Bowlby (1988), Bellis et al. (2017) and Perry and Winfrey (2022), which indicate the importance of an always available, supportive adult with whom secure attachment is formed.

In a study in a children's home in 2019 on children with several ACEs, Harris et al. (forthcoming) found in 46 children a difference of 12 points on average between the verbal IQ and the performance IQ, with the verbal IQ being the lower score. This may affect their communication skills and their ability to understand instructions and so forth. The authors suggested that this was due to these children missing a lot of education and coming from an unstimulating environment where normal communication between parents and children was often lacking.

One very effective approach to education that addresses the gap between a child's developmental age and their biological age was developed by Michael Maloney and a team of educators and academics in Canada. This program provides effective instruction and, at the same time, reduces the students' frustration and confusion by ensuring that they enter each subject at the level at which they are proficient, no matter the age gap (Maloney 1998).

Indigenous healing

Traditional indigenous healing refers to the health practices, approaches, knowledge and beliefs involved in First Nations healing and wellness. These practices include using ceremonies; plant-, animal- or mineral-based medicines, energy-based therapies and physical or hands-on techniques and are based on a holistic approach to the person and their community.

Indigenous healing practices follow the Medicine Wheel model and focus on the whole person – mind, body and spirit – and are based on cultural respect and understanding. Healing is often a communal activity, emphasising the importance of relationships. Indigenous healing practices are not just methods of treatment; they also have significant cultural value and help preserve cultural identity and foster a sense of belonging within communities, e.g. sweat lodge, drumming and dancing.

Psychedelic substances

Natural psychedelics have been used for millennia by people in several regions of the world for ceremonial and ritualistic purposes. The extent and nature of this use, however, appears to have been exaggerated in popular culture, perhaps by wishful thinking, with a tendency to portray shamans and similar figures as therapists focused on a modern interpretation of healing mental disorders rather than as people who dealt with problems in terms of the supernatural and good versus evil (Singh 2025).

SSRIs and trauma-focused psychotherapies, such as PET and CBT, are considered the most effective treatments for PTSD, but many people do not respond well to these treatments or continue to have significant symptoms, and dropout rates are high (Haagen et al. 2015; Krediet et al. 2020; Steenkamp et al. 2017; Watkins et al. 2018). Clearly, dealing with traumatic memories can be a very difficult experience for people with PTSD patients and this can mean that it is not possible to finish treatment (Goetter et al. 2015; Krediet et al. 2020; Mott et al. 2014). The introduction of psychedelic substances (hallucinogens or entactogens) in treatment is thought to be a way to reduce emotional difficulties faced by patients (Krediet et al. 2020; Kyzar et al. 2017).

The rationale behind the use of these substances is that they can increase the effectiveness of psychotherapy through a number of different neurobiological and psychological mechanisms, such as increased neuronal plasticity, diminished fear and arousal, altered memory consolidation, increased insightfulness or an improved therapeutic relationship (Cameron et al. 2014; Ney et al. 2019; Rucker et al. 2018; Zuj et al. 2016). There are still many questions about the effectiveness of these substances as well as mechanisms of action, but there is an increasing amount of research on them as well as clinical interest (Curran et al. 2018; Kyzar et al. 2017; Rucker et al. 2018).

The classical psychedelic drugs, including psilocybin, lysergic acid diethylamide (LSD) and mescaline, were used extensively in psychiatry before they were placed in Schedule I of the UN Convention on Drugs in 1967. Research prior to legal control found psychedelics to be ineffective or problematic with established psychotic disorders and in those liable to develop them. Individuals with 'psychoneurotic' disorders sometimes showed marked improvement by being able to change maladaptive patterns of cognition and behaviour, especially when the drugs were administered in a supportive, therapeutic setting. These studies were conducted in ways that render their results in need of replication. (For a detailed review of these issues, see the Special Issue of Neuropharmacology titled 'Psychedelics: New Doors, Altered Perceptions 2018').

More recently, several psychedelics have been investigated for the treatment of PTSD: some cannabinoids, 3,4-methylenedioxymethamphetamine (MDMA), ketamine and classical psychedelics (e.g. psilocybin and LSD). The use of psychedelics can result in a very broad range of physical, psychological, cognitive and emotional effects.

Cannabis has been used in some parts of the world for spiritual, medicinal, relaxation and other purposes for thousands of years (Haney and Hill 2018). In the West, medicinal use of cannabis began in the 19th century for the treatment of rheumatism, convulsions and other disorders. The endogenous cannabinoid (endocannabinoid) system was identified in 1990, which led to an increase in studies of medicinal use, especially pain relief, multiple sclerosis and epilepsy (Haney and Hill 2018; Whiting and Wolf 2015). Several countries, including Canada, have legalised medical cannabis in the past few decades, and the United Nations Office on Drugs and Crime (UNODC) and the World Health Organization (WHO) have proposed rescheduling cannabis to allow for medical applications (Cavalieri and Riley 2012; Mayor 2019; Pates and Riley 2012; Riley 1998).

Cannabis and synthetic cannabinoids act on the endocannabinoid system, which is involved in emotional memories and the hypothalamic-pituitary-adrenal response to stress (Ney et al. 2019). They differ from other psychedelic compounds in that they are used primarily for the temporary PTSD symptoms, although they may also be useful in a psychotherapy model. Studies have shown improvement in PTSD symptoms, especially nightmares and sleeping problems (Black et al. 2019; Cameron et al. 2014; Fraser 2009; Jetly et al. 2015). Cannabinoids are prescribed as a take-home medication for daily use to reduce PTSD symptoms.

MDMA reduces fear and anxiety in response to certain stimuli provoking, including traumatic memories and improves introspection and therapeutic trust (Bershad et al. 2019; Kuypers et al. 2017; Schmid et al. 2014). MDMA also increases oxytocin levels, which is a potential contributing factor to experienced increases in interpersonal trust (Vizeli and Liechti 2018). There are usually several non-drug sessions before and after each MDMA session, which is several hours long and involves two therapists whose role is to facilitate introspection about past experiences. MDMA-assisted psychotherapy showed higher effect sizes and significantly lower dropout rates than seen in data on SSRIs from the US Food and Drug Administration (FDA) (Feduccia et al. 2019). The FDA granted MDMA a breakthrough therapy designation for the treatment of PTSD.

Ketamine has been reported to have very rapid effects in the treatment of depression (Murrough et al. 2013) and for the symptoms of PTSD (Feder et al. 2014) when used in combination with psychotherapeutic interventions (Albott et al. 2018; Pradhan et al. 2017). More recent research using strict control procedures, however, has found that the observed effects are no better than placebo (Borgogna et al. 2024). The importance of the correct control procedures when elaborate, combination interventions are being used is demonstrated by the work on psychoactive drugs such as ketamine as an intervention because of the complications raised by the use of combination therapies.

Ibogaine is a psychoactive substance derived from plants, which affects several neurotransmitter systems. It has been investigated for the treatment of alcohol and other forms of substance dependence for several decades. Its use remains controversial because of dangerous side effects and variable results in terms of efficacy.

Classical, or serotonergic, psychedelics include psilocybin, LSD, and dimethyltryptamine (DMT). In the 1950s and 1960s, they were used in psychotherapy; more than 700 scientific articles were published, and a few thousand patients were treated for anxiety, trauma, alcohol dependence and other problems. PTSD was introduced as a psychiatric diagnosis in the third edition of the Diagnostic and Statistical Manual of Mental Disorders in 1980. Prior to that, LSD, psilocybin and ketamine were used in the Netherlands in the treatment of "concentration camp syndrome". During the intense period of the drug war in the 1960s to the 1990s, most psychedelic drugs were classified in a way that did not allow for their use in medicine and research on them was discouraged. Since the 2000s and the pioneering work of the late Amanda Fielding, the Beckley Foundation, which she founded, and the Multidisciplinary Association for Psychedelic Studies (MAPS) (2025), there has been a new wave of research and increased interest in the use of these substances in therapy. Psilocybin, which appears to have long-lasting effects, has received breakthrough designations from the FDA for use in depression, and several trials with psilocybin- and LSD-assisted psychotherapy are being conducted in Europe and the United States. Classical psychedelics are administered in a therapeutic manner similar to that of MDMA. They have also been used in interactive and group settings with small to moderate doses to lower psychological defenses as was done with psycholytic therapy.

The DMT-containing plant-based ayahuasca is being investigated as a treatment for PTSD (Gonçalves et al., 2023;, Inserra 2018; Labate and Cavnar 2014; Nielson and Megler 2014). The US Veterans Health Administration's Office of Research & Development is currently funding research on psychedelic compounds in veterans.

In summary, recent systematic reviews of unipolar mood disorders and alcoholism have found that some psychedelics are effective. The incidence of serious adverse events appears to be low. Since 2006, there have been several pilot trials and randomised controlled trials (RCTs) using psychedelics (mostly psilocybin) in various non-psychotic psychiatric disorders. Research suggests a potential role for classical psychedelics in the treatment of anxiety, depression and PTSD but there may be limitations to their use due to the heightened arousal and sensitivity induced by these substances (Berkovitch et al. 2021; Ghaznavi and Richter 2025; Mohamed et al. 2022; Morland and Woolley 2024; Muttoni et al. 2019; Rucker et al. 2018). As shown, when strict control procedures are used, at least some of the positive outcomes of these intensive treatments to date are due to the intensity of the interventions themselves. These interventions also require a great deal of resources in terms of therapist time and related costs, and that limits their cost-effectiveness. While some studies indicate initial evidence of safety and efficacy, as Rucker and colleagues have noted, there are formidable regulatory and legal hurdles to licensing psychedelics as medicines (Rucker et al. 2018). Considerably more research needs to be done on contraindications, side effects and other issues before these substances can be introduced for regular clinical use in dealing with mental health issues.

Substance use treatment

Interventions for substance use problems can generally be divided into outpatient and inpatient or residential treatment, although some combine both. They can also be used on an individual or group basis, and many are applied virtually as well as in person, especially since the COVID-19 pandemic limited personal contact.

Until the 1990s, the main aim of substance use treatment in North America was abstinence. In the United Kingdom and parts of Europe, the prescription of certain drugs to drug users was an accepted and effective practice and provided the basis for the development of harm reduction (Riley et al. 2012).

Harm reduction

The main characteristics or principles of harm reduction are:

Pragmatism: Harm reduction accepts that some use of mind-altering substances is inevitable and that some level of drug use is normal in a society.

Humanistic Values: The drug user's decision to use drugs is accepted as fact, as his or her choice; no 'moralistic' judgement is made either to condemn or to support use of drugs, regardless of level of use or mode of intake. The dignity and rights of the drug user are respected.

Focus on Harms: The extent of a person's drug use is of secondary importance to the harms resulting from use.

Hierarchy of Goals: Most harm-reduction programs have a hierarchy of goals, with the immediate focus on addressing the most pressing needs.

Harm reduction can be viewed as both a goal and a strategy. In both cases, the person's use of drugs is accepted as fact. This does not mean that harm reduction approaches preclude abstinence but only that there is acceptance of the fact that there are many possible approaches or strategies that can be taken to address drug-related problems, harm reduction and abstention being two of these. A harm reduction approach to a person's drug use in the short term does not rule out abstinence in the longer term, and vice versa. The following definition of harm reduction strategies is one that is now used by many organisations: 'A policy or program directed towards decreasing the adverse health, social, and economic consequences of drug use without requiring abstinence from drug use'.

With the HIV/AIDS pandemic and the spread of the virus through injecting, harm reduction became more popular and has been endorsed by the WHO and other UN agencies (Riley 1998; Riley et al. 2012). Despite the increase in popularity amongst workers in the field, many health and addictions agencies remain ambivalent about harm reduction as it pertains to alcohol and other drugs. Harm reduction raises some difficult questions, but it is evident that it is better to debate these openly rather than to ignore them as has been done all too often in the past. Comprehensive harm-reduction programs that are culturally sensitive are necessary: harm reduction must be multifaceted, not just a singular intervention.

The use of harm reduction for alcohol problems was studied at the Addiction Research Foundation (ARF) in Canada in the 1980s, and the controlled drinking approach has now become widely used as an intervention (Riley et al. 2012; Sanchez-Craig et al. 1984).

Psychological interventions

The following interventions have been found to be effective (that is, they have a documented clinical evidence base) in reducing problems with alcohol or other substances:

Brief interventions for alcohol use disorders involve screening, assessment and advice, and are effective in reducing alcohol use and CBTs and motivational interviewing (MI) have been found to be moderately effective compared to treatment-as-usual for a number of different substances (Jhanjee 2014; MacKillop et al. 2017; Magill and Ray 2009; Ray et al. 2020; Riper et al. 2014; Sherman and McRae-Clark 2016; Zamboni et al. 2021).

Contingency management (CM) involves reinforcing abstinence with money, vouchers or other rewards in exchange for drug-free urine screening or treatment compliance and improvements in measures of life functioning (Festinger et al. 2014; Prendergast et al. 2006). It has been found to be successful with cocaine and methamphetamine, combined opiate and cocaine use, alcohol use disorders and marijuana use disorders.

Couple- and family-focused treatments aim to change behaviour around substances by including partners, children and others to increase positive interactions and reduce aversive ones (Ariss and Fairbairn 2020). They have been found to increase abstinence, improve relationship functioning and decrease domestic violence in both male and female clients.

Other treatments, including inpatient or residential programs, and self-help programs such as Alcoholics Anonymous (AA), are effective for some people, but because many of these approaches have not been evaluated using appropriate scientific criteria, their level of efficacy cannot be determined (MacKillop et al. 2017).

Key factors in effective treatment

Comparing different psychosocial interventions, Rounsaville et al (2001) and McCrady and Nathan (2006) identified several common elements that need to be addressed: motivation, coping skills, conditioned responses and reinforcement contingencies, painful emotions, self-efficacy, interpersonal functioning, social supports and pharmacotherapy.

Standardized assessment

An assessment should include: nature of substance use and severity, psychiatric problems and severity, medical conditions, substance withdrawal potential, legal pressures, family/social relationships, motivational factors, recovery and support environment, treatment history and behaviour and cognitive capability. An individual's treatment and services plan should be assessed continually and modified as necessary to ensure that it meets his or her changing needs.

Duration of treatment

The appropriate duration for an individual depends on the type and degree of the patient's problems and needs. Research indicates that most individuals need at least 3 months in treatment to significantly reduce or stop their drug use and that the best outcomes occur with longer durations of treatment.

Problem-service matching

No single treatment is appropriate for everyone as treatment needs vary depending on the type of drug and the characteristics of the patients. Matching treatment settings, interventions and services to an individual's particular problems and needs is critical. Effective treatment attends to multiple needs of the individual, not just his or her substance use. To be effective, treatment must address the individual's alcohol and other drug use and any associated medical, psychological, social, vocational and legal problems. It is also important that treatment be appropriate to the individual's age, gender, ethnicity and culture. Many individuals dependent on substances also have other mental disorders, and patients presenting with one condition should be assessed for the other(s). And when these problems co-occur, treatment should address both (or all), including the use of medications as appropriate. When services are matched to problem areas and services for people with co-occurring substance use disorders and severe mental illness are integrated, outcomes improve (Drake et al. 1998; McClellan et al. 1991).

Availability

Treatment needs to be readily available. Because individuals may be uncertain about entering treatment, taking advantage of available services, the moment people are ready for treatment is critical. Potential patients can be lost if treatment is not immediately available or readily accessible.

Medications are an important element of treatment for many patients, especially when combined with counselling and other behavioural therapies. For example, methadone, buprenorphine and naltrexone are effective in helping individuals who are dependent on heroin or other opioids to stabilise their lives and reduce their illicit drug use. Acamprosate, disulfiram and naltrexone are medications approved for treating alcohol dependence.

Pharmacological therapies

Apart from alcohol and opioids, pharmacotherapy has not been proven efficient in treating substance use issues. When pharmacotherapy is used, it has to be combined with psychotherapy to be effective (Sarkar et al. 2021).

Pharmacotherapies for alcohol use disorders

Disulfiram inhibits aldehyde dehydrogenase and results in an aversive metabolic response to alcohol. In systematic reviews of controlled trials, the outcomes for disulfiram were inconclusive, and the type of administration, psychological deterrent factors and physician and patient choice are thought to account for the continued use of disulfiram.

Naltrexone has been shown to be more effective than placebo in reducing alcohol use and craving, time to first relapse and the severity of relapse. Acamprosate, alone and in combination with naltrexone, has been widely used in Europe and tested in North America with good outcomes (McPheeters et al. 2023).

Pharmacotherapies for opioid use disorders

Methadone treatment for heroin users dates back to the 1960s. It has been used for short- and long-term maintenance and has demonstrated many public health outcomes: decreases in illicit drug use, psychiatric symptoms, family problems and crime and increases in employment. Methadone is a long-acting opiate agonist that prevents withdrawal and reduces the effects and cravings for other opiates.

Levo-alpha-acetylmethadol (LAAM) is an opioid agonist analog. Like methadone, LAAM has demonstrated effects to prevent opiate withdrawal and block the effects of heroin use. LAAM has low abuse potential, but its use is rare because of some findings of potential adverse effects on the cardiovascular system, regulatory and insurance issues and clinic acceptance.

Buprenorphine hydrochloride is a partial agonist, semi-synthetic opioid analgesic. It is safe, long-acting and has a mild dependence potential and has been shown to reduce heroin use.

Naltrexone directly blocks opiate receptor activity and reduces the pleasurable, positive effects of opiates. In RCTs, it has been found to reduce substance use and the amount of illicit substances used per episode. Retention is an issue, with few patients remaining on naltrexone after a year.

Pharmacotherapies for other drug use disorders

No pharmacological agents have been approved by the FDA in the United States for treating cocaine (or other similarly acting stimulants), cannabis (marijuana, hashish) or benzodiazepine use disorders. Elsewhere, some pharmacotherapies are being tested on a very small scale. In the United Kingdom, for the past 30 years, dexamphetamine has been used to treat amphetamine dependence and has shown excellent results. A study by Pates et al. (1996) found that this substitution therapy not only greatly reduced the use of street-bought amphetamine but also reduced crime and sex work.

Trauma-informed approaches

The work by Felitti and colleagues on the effects of ACEs, the subsequent large body of research, and the experiences of individuals who have suffered from trauma have resulted in a huge number of research articles, books and websites dealing with trauma and interventions. This, along with evidence of iatrogenic harm and retraumatisation in psychological and psychiatric services based on coercion and control, has led to the development of trauma-informed approaches. This, in turn, has led a number of health facilities, organisations and even governments to develop policies and training that deal with such approaches. For example, in the United Kingdom, the National Health Service (NHS) has outlined its strategic direction for working with victims of sexual abuse and emphasises the need for services to be trauma-informed, making explicit the links between trauma and mental health, and some cities and even countries now claim to be "trauma-informed".

Trauma-informed approaches are system-wide approaches where staff are knowledgeable in referring on to trauma-specific services, where this is appropriate. These are different from trauma-specific services, which treat people experiencing the effects of trauma using, for example, CBT or EMDR. Trauma-informed approaches require change at the organisational level, and are processes focused on helping the client deal with trauma and on preventing further traumatisation whilst in therapy. Key principles and factors associated with success include (Asmussen et al. 2020; Sweeney et al. 2018):

- collaborative relationships based on trust and respect (trust is one of the most important components of therapy for those suffering from the effects of trauma but can be hard to establish)
- an understanding and acknowledgement of the links between trauma and mental health
- focus on what happened to the person, not what is wrong with them
- a broad definition of trauma extending beyond PTSD
- sensitivity and knowledge of how to respond appropriately
- referring people to evidence-based, trauma-specific support, where indicated
- addressing vicarious trauma and retraumatisation
- transparency in communications
- strengths-based approaches that reframe symptoms as coping adaptations
- prioritising emotional and physical safety for service users and providers
- support for therapists from management and organisations
- allowing sufficient time for effective therapy
- working in partnership with trauma survivors to design, deliver and evaluate services.

Trauma-informed approaches and related concepts suffer from a number of problems which have been examined in some excellent articles (e.g. Asmussen et al. 2020; Smith and Monteux 2023; Walsh et al. 2019). In brief, these approaches are often poorly defined, appear far too complex to be adopted in full or appear to duplicate services already provided but with a new packaging. While a number of clinicians and individuals claim that these approaches could lead to major changes in the way that mental health services are organised and delivered as well as in efficacy, this has yet to be demonstrated in the weight of evidence. There is concern that trauma-informed approaches will come to mean little more than treatment as usual in a new, trendier package, so that any rebranding of services needs to be accompanied by real systemic change. There is also inconsistent evidence to support trauma-informed interventions as an effective system-wide approach, as opposed to interventions for specific problems related to the effects of adversity and PTSD, where efficacy has been demonstrated, such as CBT and EMDR.

The trauma recovery model

The Trauma Recovery Model (TRM) (Skuse and Mathew 2015) was developed by two staff members working at a secure children's home in Wales, United Kingdom. Secure children's homes are homes that care for the most troubled children in the United Kingdom. These homes have locked doors because children who are referred to them are deemed to be in danger to themselves or others. Often seen by the public as very naughty children, these are the most damaged and abused children in society. The TRM model was developed by Dr Trisha Skuse, a clinical psychologist and Johnny Mathew, a social worker at the same home.

The model was developed for dealing with serious young offenders in a secure children's home. The model is also observed in non-secure children's homes as a model for children who need to recover from ACEs they have experienced. In this secure children's home, as was shown in the introduction, none of the children had zero ACEs, but 64% had experienced four or more ACEs compared with 13% of the general population. Nearly all ACEs have an impact on a child's life, and the more of them they have or the more serious they are, the greater the impact on the child and the adult they will become (See Figure 13.1).

The model goes through six stages of development, which should help a child recover (or partially recover) from their ACEs. This starts with recognition that the child's behaviour might be unstable and chaotic with challenging behaviour, for example, aggression, self-harm, absconding and the like, with an underlying need for structure and routine. Interventions would be regular meals and bedtimes, school attendance and clear boundaries. This can lead to a readiness to build relationships with adults.

At the next level of trust and relationship building, the need is to develop trusting relationships with appropriate adults and to develop a secure base. They need to maximise 1:1 time with adults, have clear boundaries and maintain structure and routine. They should smile more and build closer relationships (in a children's home with 1 or 2 staff member(s)) and be willing to comply with routines. There will be continuing peer relationship difficulties and maybe ongoing confrontational relationships and challenging outbursts.

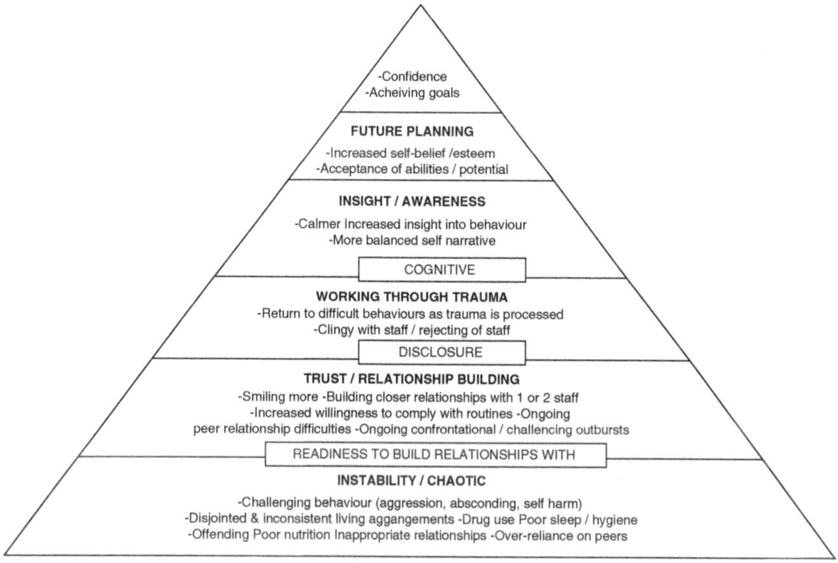

Figure 13.1 Trauma recovery model. Adapted from Skuse and Mathew (2015).

This can lead to disclosure of things like sexual abuse that they had been too frightened to mention.

Once they have made their disclosure, there can be a working through of the trauma, where there is a need to process their past experiences and grievances. This is where intervention is needed, such as counselling or more specialist interventions regarding their trauma, so that they may develop containment and grieve their losses. This means that while they are working through the trauma, it may bring a return of the trauma and lead to renewed difficulties with staff or close adults.

This leads to a cognitive threshold, which means that they can start gaining insight into their past behaviours and a more balanced self-narrative, leading to an integration of their old and new selves and developing confidence in thinking and planning skills. Cognitive interventions can now be used, which would have been inappropriate before, such as anger management, victim empathy and consequential thinking, restorative practice and a good lives approach.

Once this has been reached, it can then lead to Future Planning with an increase in self-belief and esteem and an acceptance of their abilities and potential. This is developed by adult-guided and supported planning with a sense of purpose and achievement and structured to maximise the chances of success. This uses guided goal setting and targets, a scaffolded structure, supports into education or a training placement, helps structure free time constructively and uses cognitive behavioural therapy where appropriate.

The top level is achieving goals and gaining confidence. They need autonomy within a supported context and increased self-determination. This is done by providing a supportive safety net for learning.

This is a model developed for helping young people who have got into trouble with the law and who are being held in secure environments. This model also has many things that can help children with ACEs in other environments. It provides a structure for helping the child recover from the traumatic events that they have experienced and develop self-help skills which will aid them through adolescence into adulthood.

It is important to recognise the level of the child's cognitive development so that any intervention is appropriate. As Skuse and Mathew say in the paper, "until young people have transcended through the first three stages of the TRM, they are not yet cognitively able to embrace their current situation, their behaviour or to address the impact or implications of their offences. Expecting a young person to use consequential thinking skills, have empathy for the victim/s and be able to plan and act differently when they are still in a state of trauma and survival is unrealistic and unattainable."

This is, of course, true of any intervention with a child, that we must understand them and use age-appropriate measures. We know that the human brain does not finish development until the 20s and this will influence the way a child will think and understand. We also know that there can be an impact on the development of brain function through ACEs, and therefore, need to be aware of this when working with children, especially those who have experienced a number of ACEs.

Developmental-age intervention

Bruce Perry has developed a developmental-age-appropriate form of trauma-informed therapy, which he and his colleagues have successfully applied in numerous cases. According to this approach, to effectively address trauma, it is essential to first regulate and stabilise the limbic system before engaging the neocortex. This is known as the 'Bottom-Up' approach to therapy (Perry 2009; Perry and Szalavitz 2007; Perry and Winfrey 2022). Perry's Neurosequential Model of Therapeutics (NMT) describes how trauma predominantly affects the brain's lower regions, such as the brainstem and limbic system, crucial for survival responses (Perry 2009). According to this, trauma-induced hyperarousal in these lower areas can hinder the development of higher brain regions like the limbic system and neocortex. According to Perry, the brain develops sequentially, with the brainstem laying the groundwork for more advanced functions, and trauma can interfere with higher cognitive functions and emotional and academic development (Perry and Szalavitz 2007; Perry and Winfrey 2022). Traditional therapies, such as CBT, may be ineffective for children in a heightened state of arousal. These approaches can unintentionally increase stress responses and emotional reactivity in the limbic system, which can lead to acting-out behaviours instead of encouraging thought. A child may then be labelled with ADHD, given detention and so forth, rather than given the support and understanding that they really need.

The following chapters address some specific forms of interventions at different levels, from the individual to the community level.

References

Albott, C.S., Lim, K.O., Forbes, M.K. et al. (2018). Efficacy, safety, and durability of repeated ketamine infusions for comorbid posttraumatic stress disorder and treatment-resistant depression. *The Journal of Clinical Psychiatry* 79 (3): 17m11634. https://doi.org/10.4088/JCP.17m11634.

Asmundson, G.J. and Afifi, T.O. (2019). *Adverse Childhood Experiences: Using Evidence to Advance Research, Practice, Policy, and Prevention.* New York: Academic Press.

Asmussen, K., Fischer, F., Drayton, E. et al. (2020). *Childhood Experiences: What We Know, What We Don't Know, and What Should Happen Next.* Early Intervention Foundation https://www.eif.org.uk/report/Adverse (accessed 31 March 2025).

Beck, A.T., Emery, G., and Greenberg, R.L. (1985). *Anxiety Disorders and Phobias: A Cognitive Perspective.* New York: Basic Books.

Bellis, M.A., Hardcastle, K., Ford, K. et al. (2017). Does continuous trusted adult support in childhood impart life-course resilience against adverse childhood experiences - a retrospective study on adult health-harming behaviours and mental well-being. *BMC Psychiatry* 17 (1): 110. https://doi.org/10.1186/s12888-017-1260-z.

Bershad, A.K., Schepers, S.T., Bremmer, M.P. et al. (2019). Acute subjective and behavioral effects of microdoses of lysergic acid diethylamide in healthy human volunteers. *Biological Psychiatry* 86 (10): 792–800. https://doi.org/10.1016/j.biopsych.2019.05.019.

Bisson, J.I., Roberts, N.P., Andrew, M. et al. (2013). Psychological therapies for chronic post-traumatic stress disorder (PTSD) in adults. *Cochrane Database of Systematic Reviews* 2013 (12): CD003388. https://doi.org/10.1002/14651858.CD003388.pub4.

Black, N., Stockings, E., Campbell, G. et al. (2019). Cannabinoids for the treatment of mental disorders and symptoms of mental disorders: a systematic review and meta-analysis. *Lancet Psychiatry* 6 (12): 995–1010.

Bombér, L.M. (2020). *Know Me to Teach Me.* Worth Publishing.

Borgogna, N., Owen, T., Vaughn, J. et al. (2024). So how special is special K? A systematic review and meta-analysis of ketamine for PTSD RCTs. *European Journal of Psychotraumatology* 15 (1): 2299124.

Bowlby, J. (1988). *A Secure Base: Parent-Child Attachment and Healthy Human Development.* New York: Basic Books.

Brummelman, E., Terburg, D., Smit, M. et al. (2019). Parental touch reduces social vigilance in children. *Developmental Cognitive Neuroscience* 35: 87–93.

Cameron, C., Watson, D., and Robinson, J. (2014). Use of a synthetic cannabinoid in a correctional population for posttraumatic stress disorder-related insomnia and nightmares, chronic pain, harm reduction, and other indications: a retrospective evaluation. *Journal of Clinical Psychopharmacology* 34 (5): https://doi.org/10.1097/JCP.0000000000000180.

Cavalieri, W. and Riley, D.M. (2012). Harm reduction in Canada. In: *Harm Reduction in Substance Use and High Risk Behaviour: International Policy and Practice* (ed. R. Pates and D.M. Riley). Oxford: Wiley/Blackwell Publishing.

Curran, H.V., Hindocha, C., Morgan, C.J. et al. (2018). Which biological and self-report measures of cannabis use predict cannabis dependency and acute psychotic-like effects? *Psychological Medicine* 4: 1–7.

Drake, R.E., Mercer-McFadden, C., Mueser, K.T. et al. (1998). Review of integrated mental health and substance abuse treatment for patients with dual disorders.

Schizophrenia Bulletin 24 (4): 589–608. https://doi.org/10.1093/oxfordjournals.schbul.a033351.

Earles, J.L., Vernon, L.L., and Yetz, J.P. (2015). Equine-assisted therapy for anxiety and posttraumatic stress symptoms. *Journal of Traumatic Stress* 28 (2): 149–152.

Feder, A., Parides, M.K., Murrough, J.W. et al. (2014). Efficacy of intravenous ketamine for treatment of chronic posttraumatic stress disorder: a randomized clinical trial. *JAMA Psychiatry* 71 (6): 681–688.

Feduccia, A.A., Jerome, L., Yazar-Klosinski, B. et al. (2019). Breakthrough for trauma treatment: safety and efficacy of MDMA-assisted psychotherapy compared to Paroxetine and Sertraline. *Frontiers in Psychiatry* 10: 650.

Festinger, D.S., Dugosh, K.S., Kirby, K.C. et al. (2014). Contingency management for cocaine treatment: cash vs. vouchers. *Journal of Substance Abuse Treatment* 47: 168–174.

Foa, E.B., Dancu, C.V., Hembree, E.A. et al. (1999). A comparison of exposure therapy, stress inoculation training, and their combination for reducing posttraumatic stress disorder in female assault victims. *Journal of Consulting and Clinical Psychology* 67 (2): 194–200.

Fraser, G.A. (2009). The use of a synthetic cannabinoid in the management of treatment-resistant nightmares in posttraumatic stress disorder (PTSD). *CNS Neuroscience & Therapeutics* 15 (1): 84–88.

Ghaznavi, S. and Richter, S.G. (2025). Classic psychedelics for the treatment of depression: potential benefits and challenges. *Drugs* 85 (5): 609–626. https://doi.org/10.1007/s40265-025-02172-2.

Goetter, E.M., Bui, E., and Ojserkis, R.A. (2015). A systematic review of dropout from psychotherapy for posttraumatic stress disorder among Iraq and Afghanistan combat veterans. *Journal of Traumatic Stress* 28 (5): 401–409. https://doi.org/10.1002/jts.22038.

Gonçalves, J., Luís, Â., Gallardo, E., and Duarte, A.P. (2023). A Systematic Review on the Therapeutic Effects of Ayahuasca. *Plants (Basel)*. 12 (13): 2573. https://doi.org/10.3390/plants12132573.

Grandin, T. (1992). Calming effects of deep touch pressure in patients with autistic disorder, college students, and animals. *Journal of Child and Adolescent Psychopharmacology* 2 (1): grandin.com/inc/squeeze.html.

Haagen, J.F.G., Smid, G.E., Knipscheer, J.W., and Kleber, R.J. (2015). The efficacy of recommended treatments for veterans with PTSD: a metaregression analysis. *Clinical Psychology Review* 40: 184–194.

Han, H.R., Miller, H.N., Nkimben, M. et al. (2021). Trauma informed interventions: a systematic review. *PLoS One* 16 (6): e0252747. https://doi.org/10.1371/journal.pone.0252747.

Haney, M., Hill, M. (2018) Cannabis and cannabinoids: from synapse to society. Neuropsychopharmacology 43, 1–3. https://doi.org/10.1038/npp.2017.255

Harlow, H.F. and Zimmermann, R.R. (1958). The development of affective responsiveness in infant monkeys. *Proceedings of the American Philosophical Society* 102: 501–509.

Harlow, H.F., Dodsworth, R.O., and Harlow, M.K. (1965). Total social isolation in monkeys. *Proceedings of the National Academy of Sciences of the United States of America* 54 (1): 90.

Harris, R., Pates, R.and Barratt, H. (forthcoming) Differences in verbal and performance IQ in a group of traumatised children.

Inserra, A. (2018). Hypothesis: the psychedelic Ayahuasca heals traumatic memories via a Sigma 1 receptor-mediated epigenetic-mnemonic process. *Frontiers in Pharmacology* 5 (9): 330. https://doi.org/10.3389/fphar.2018.00330.

Jetly, R., Heber, A., Fraser, G. et al. (2015). The efficacy of nabilone, a synthetic cannabinoid, in the treatment of PTSD-associated nightmares: a preliminary randomized, double-blind, placebo-controlled cross-over design study. *Psychoneuroendocrinology* 51: 585–588. https://doi.org/10.1016/j.psyneuen.2014.11.002.

Jhanjee, S. (2014). Evidence based psychosocial interventions in substance use. *Indian Journal of Psychological Medicine* 36 (2): 112–118. https://doi.org/10.4103/0253-7176.130960.

Khajuria, A., Kumar, A., Joshi, D. et al. (2023). Reducing stress with yoga: a systematic review based on multimodal biosignals. *International Journal of Yoga* 16 (3): 156–170. https://doi.org/10.4103/ijoy.ijoy_218_23.

Krediet, E., Bostoen, T., Breeksema, J. et al. (2020). Reviewing the potential of psychedelics for the treatment of PTSD. *The International Journal of Neuropsychopharmacology* 23 (6): 385–400. https://doi.org/10.1093/ijnp/pyaa018.

Kuypers, K.P., Dolder, P.C., and Ramaekers, J.G. (2017). Multifaceted empathy of healthy volunteers after single doses of MDMA: a pooled sample of placebo-controlled studies. *Journal of Psychopharmacology* 31 (5): 589–598. https://doi.org/10.1177/0269881117699617.

Kyzar, E.J., Nichols, C.D., Gainetdinov, R.R. et al. (2017). Psychedelic drugs in biomedicine. *Trends in Pharmacological Sciences* 38 (11): 992–1005. https://doi.org/10.1016/j.tips.2017.08.003.

Labate, B.C. and Cavnar, C. (ed.) (2014). *The Therapeutic Use of Ayahuasca*. Berlin/Heidelberg: Springer-Verlag.

Levitin, D. (2024). *I Heard There Was a Secret Chord*. New York: Penguin.

MacKillop, G., Kenna, L., and Ray, L. (ed.) (2017). *Integrating Psychological and Pharmacological Treatments for Addictive Disorders an Evidence-Based Guide*. New York: Routledge https://doi.org/10.4324/9781315683331.

Magill, M. and Ray, L.A. (2009). Cognitive-behavioral treatment with adult alcohol and illicit drug users: a meta-analysis of randomized controlled trials. *Journal of Studies on Alcohol and Drugs* 70 (4): 516–527. https://doi.org/10.15288/jsad.2009.70.516.

Maloney, M. (1998). *Teach Your Children Well!* Cambridge: Cambridge Center for Educational Studies.

Mayor, S. (2019). WHO proposes rescheduling cannabis to allow medical applications. *BMJ*. 364: l574. https://doi.org/10.1136/bmj.l574.

McCrady, B.S. and Nathan, P.E. (2006). Treatment factors in treating substance use disorders. In: *Principles of Therapeutic Change That Work* (ed. L.G. Castonguay and L.E. Beutler). New York: Oxford University Press.

McDaniel, T. and Panchanathan, S. (2020). Therapeutic haptics for mental health and wellbeing. In: *Haptic Interfaces for Accessibility, Health, and Enhanced Quality of Life* (ed. T. McDaniel and S. Panchanathan). Cham: Springer https://doi.org/10.1007/978-3-030-34230-2_6.

McPheeters, M., O'Connor, E.A., Riley, S. et al. (2023). Pharmacotherapy for alcohol use disorder: a systematic review and meta-analysis. *JAMA* 330 (17): 1653–1665. https://doi.org/10.1001/jama.2023.19761.

Meichenbaum, D. (1977). *Cognitive-Behavior Modification: An Integrative Approach*. New York: Plenum Press.

Mohamed, A., Touheed, S., and Ahmed, M. (2022). The efficacy of psychedelic-assisted therapy in managing post-traumatic stress disorder (PTSD): a new frontier? *Cureus* 14 (10): e30919. https://doi.org/10.1007/978-3-030-34230-2_610.7759/cureus.30919.

Morland, L. and Woolley, J. (2024). Psychedelic-assisted therapy for PTSD. https://www.ptsd.va.gov/professional/treat/txessentials/psychedelics_assisted_therapy.asp (accessed 18 May 2025).

Mott, J.M., Mondragon, S., Hundt, N.E. et al. (2014). Characteristics of U.S. veterans who begin and complete prolonged exposure and cognitive processing therapy for PTSD. *Journal of Traumatic Stress* 20 (3): 265–273. https://doi.org/10.1007/978-3-030-34230-2_610.1002/jts.21927.

Multidisciplinary Association for Psychedelic Studies (2025). https://www.maps.org (accessed 21 June 2025).

Murrough, J.W., Iosifescu, D.V., Chang, L.C. et al. (2013). Antidepressant efficacy of ketamine in treatment-resistant major depression: a two-site randomized controlled trial. *The American Journal of Psychiatry* 170 (10): 1134–1142. https://doi.org/10.1176/appi.ajp.2013.13030392.

National Institute for Health and Care Excellence (NICE) (2018). Post-traumatic stress disorder. NICE guideline. nice.org.uk (accessed 23 April 2025).

Ney, L.J., Mathhews, A., Bruno, R. et al. (2019). Cannabinoid interventions for PTSD: where to next? *Progress in Neuro-Psychopharmacology and Biological Psychiatry* 93: 124–140.

Nielson, J.L. and Megler, J.D. (2014). Ayahuasca as a candidate therapy for PTSD. Psychiatry & Behavioral Sciences. In: *The Therapeutic Use of Ayahuasca* (ed. B. Labate and C. Cavnar), 41–58. Springer Verlag.

Nishith, P., Nixon, R.D., and Resick, P.A. (2005). Resolution of trauma-related guilt following treatment of PTSD in female rape victims: a result of cognitive processing therapy targeting comorbid depression? *Journal of Affective Disorders* 86 (2–3): 259–265.

Pacheco-Barrios, K., Ortega-Márquez, J., and Fregni, F. (2024). Haptic technology: exploring its underexplored clinical applications – a systematic review. *Biomedicine* 12 (12): 2802. https://doi.org/10.3390/biomedicines12122802.

Pascoe, M., Thompson, D., and Ski, C. (2017). Yoga, mindfulness-based stress reduction and stress-related physiological measures: a meta-analysis. *Psychoneuroendocrinology* 86: 152–168. https://doi.org/10.1016/j.psyneuen.2017.08.008.

Pates, R. and Riley, D.M. (ed.) (2012). *Harm Reduction in Substance Use and High Risk Behaviour: International Policy and Practice*. Oxford: Wiley/Blackwell.

Pates, R.M., Coombes, N., and Ford, N. (1996). A pilot programme in prescribing dexamphetamine for amphetamine users – successes and problems. *Journal of Substance Misuse* 1 (2): 80–84.

Payne, P., Levine, P.A., and Crane-Godreau, M.A. (2015). Somatic experiencing: using interoception and proprioception as core elements of trauma therapy. *Frontiers in Psychology* 6: 93. https://doi.org/10.3389/fpsyg.2015.00093.

Perry, B.D. (2009). Examining child maltreatment through a neurodevelopmental lens: clinical applications of the neurosequential model of therapeutics. *Journal of Loss and Trauma* 14 (4): 240–255. https://doi.org/10.1080/15325020903004350.

Perry, B. and Winfrey, O. (2022). *What Happened to You? Conversations on Trauma, Resilience, and Healing*. New York: Flat Iron Books.

Pitman, R.K., Orr, S.P., Altman, B. et al. (1996). Emotional processing during eye movement desensitization and reprocessing therapy of Vietnam veterans with chronic posttraumatic stress disorder. *Comprehensive Psychiatry* 37 (6): 419–429.

Pradhan, B.K., Wainer, I.W., Moaddel, R. et al. (2017). Trauma interventions using mindfulness based extinction and reconsolidation (TIMBER) psychotherapy prolong the therapeutic effects of single ketamine infusion on post-traumatic stress disorder and comorbid depression: a pilot randomized, placebo-controlled, crossover clinical trial. *Asia Pacific Journal of Clinical Trials: Nervous System Diseases* 2 (3): 80. https://doi.org/10.4103/2542-3932.211589.

Prendergast, M., Podus, D., Finney, J., et al. (2006). Contingency management for treatment of substance use disorders: a meta-analysis. *Addiction* 101(11):1546–60. /https://doi.org/10.1111/j.1360-0443.2006.01581.

Ray, L.A., Meredith, L.R., Kiluk, B.D. et al. (2020). Combined pharmacotherapy and cognitive behavioral therapy for adults with alcohol or substance use disorders: a systematic review and meta-analysis. *JAMA Network Open* 3 (6): e208279. https://doi.org/10.1001/jamanetworkopen.2020.8279.

Resick, P.A. and Schnicke, M.K. (1992). Cognitive processing therapy for sexual assault victims. *Journal of Consulting and Clinical Psychology* 60 (5): 748–756. https://doi.org/10.1037//0022-006x.60.5.748.

Resick, P.A., Nishith, P., and Griffin, M.G. (2003). How well does cognitive-behavioral therapy treat symptoms of complex PTSD? An examination of child sexual abuse survivors within a clinical trial. *CNS Spectrums* 8 (5): 340–355.

Riley, D.M. (1998). *Drugs and Drug Policy in Canada: a Brief Review and Commentary*. Ottawa: Senate of Canada.

Riley, D.M, Pates, R, O'Hare, P. and Monaghan, G. (2012). A brief history of harm reduction. In Pates, R, and Riley, D.M. (eds.) *Harm Reduction in Substance Use and High Risk Behaviour: International Policy and Practice*, Oxford: Wiley/Blackwell.

Riper, H., Andersson, G., Hunter, S.B. et al. (2014). Treatment of comorbid alcohol use disorders and depression with cognitive-behavioural therapy and motivational interviewing: a meta-analysis. *Addiction* 109 (3): 394–406. https://doi.org/10.1111/add.12441.

Rothbaum, B.O. (1997). A controlled study of eye movement desensitization and reprocessing in the treatment of posttraumatic stress disordered sexual assault victims. *Bulletin of the Menninger Clinic* 61 (3): 317–334.

Rounsaville, B.J., Carroll, K.M., and Onken, L.S. (2001). A stage model of behavioral therapies research: getting started and moving on from stage I. *Clinical Psychology: Science and Practice* 8 (2): 133–142. https://doi.org/10.1093/clipsy.8.2.133.

Rucker, J.J., Iliff, J., and Nutt, D.J. (2018). Psychiatry & the psychedelic drugs. Past, present & future. *Neuropharmacology* 142: 200–218. https://doi.org/10.1016/j.neuropharm.2017.12.040.

Sanchez-Craig, M., Annis, H., Bornet, A. et al. (1984). Random assignment to abstinence and controlled drinking: evaluation of a cognitive-behavioral program for problem drinkers. *Journal of Consulting and Clinical Psychology* 52 (3): 390–403.

Sarkar, S., Tom, A., and Mandal, P. (2021). Barriers and facilitators to substance use disorder treatment in low-and middle-income countries: a qualitative review synthesis. *Substance Use & Misuse* 56 (7): 1062–1073. https://doi.org/10.1080/10826084.2021.1908359.

Schmid, Y., Hysek, C.M., Simmler, L.D. et al. (2014). Differential effects of MDMA and methylphenidate on social cognition. *Journal of Psychopharmacology* 28 (9): 847–856. https://doi.org/10.1177/0269881114542454.

Schrader, C. and Ross, A. (2021). A review of PTSD and current treatment strategies. *Missouri Medicine* 118 (6): 546–551.

Seekircher, J., Burgard, T., and Bošnjak, M. (2023). The effects of clinical meditation programs on stress and well-being: An updated rapid review and meta-analysis of randomized controlled trials (RCTs) with active comparison groups. *Zeitschrift für Psychologie* 231 (1): 16–29. https://doi.org/10.1027/2151-2604/a000510.

Shapiro, F. (1995). *Eye Movement Desensitization and Reprocessing: Basic Principles, Protocols, and Procedures*. New York: Guilford.

Sherman, B.J. and McRae-Clark, A.L. (2016). Treatment of cannabis use disorder: current science and future outlook. *Pharmacotherapy* 36 (5): 511–535. https://doi.org/10.1002/phar.1747.

Singh, M. (2025). *ShamanismL The Timeless Religion*. Knopf.

Skuse, T. and Mathew, J. (2015). The trauma recovery model: sequencing youth justice interventions for young people with complex needs. *Prison Service Journal* 220: 16–25.

Smith, M. and Monteux, S. (2023). Trauma-informed approaches: a critical overview of what they offer to to social work and social care. Institute for Research and Innovation in Social Services, Insight 70.

Steenkamp, M.M., Schlenger, W.E., Corry, N. et al. (2017). Predictors of PTSD 40 years after combat: findings from the National Vietnam Veterans longitudinal study. *Depression and Anxiety* 34 (8): 711–722. https://doi.org/10.1002/da.22628.

Veronen, L.J. and Kilpatrick, D.G. (1983). Stress management for rape victims. In: *Stress Reduction and Prevention* (ed. D. Meichenbaum and M.E. Jaremko). New York: Plenum Press.

Vizeli, P. and Liechti, M.E. (2018). Oxytocin receptor gene variations and socio-emotional effects of MDMA: a pooled analysis of controlled studies in healthy subjects. *PLoS One* 3 (6): e0199384. https://doi.org/10.1371/journal.pone.0199384.

Waite, R., Ryan, R. (2019), Adverse Childhood Experiences: What Students and Health Professionals Need to Know. London: Routledge.

Watkins, L.E., Sprang, K.R., and Rothbaum, B.O. (2018). Treating PTSD: a review of evidence-based psychotherapy interventions. *Frontiers in Behavioral Neuroscience* 12: 258. https://doi.org/10.3389/fnbeh.2018.00258.

de Witte, M., da Silva Pinho, A., Stams, G. et al. (2022) Music therapy for stress reduction: a systematic review and meta-analysis, Health Psychology Review, 16:1, 134–159, https://doi.org/10.1080/17437199.2020.1846580

World Health Organisation (2024). PTSD. https://www.who.int/news-room/fact-sheets/detail/post-traumatic-stress-disorder (accessed 18 April 2025).

Zamboni, J.A., Centoni, L., and Fusina, F. (2021). The effectiveness of cognitive behavioral therapy techniques for the treatment of substance use disorders: a narrative review of evidence. *The Journal of Nervous and Mental Disease* 209 (11): 835–845. https://doi.org/10.1097/NMD.0000000000001381.

Zuj, D.V., Palmer, M.A., and Lommen, M.J. (2016). The centrality of fear extinction in linking risk factors to PTSD: a narrative review. *Neuroscience and Biobehavioral Reviews* 69: 15–35. https://doi.org/10.1016/j.neubiorev.2016.07.014.

Chapter 14

TRAUMA AND ACE-INFORMED APPROACHES: WHY IT'S EVERYONE'S BUSINESS

Andrew Bennett

Merseyside Violence Reduction Partnership, Liverpool, UK

Introduction

Adverse childhood experiences or ACEs are an increasing international concern. There is a growing body of evidence that adults who were physically or sexually abused as children or brought up in households with domestic violence, problematic alcohol or drug use and other prolonged and extreme stressful occurrences are more likely to adopt health-harming behaviours and experience poorer physical and mental health.

Despite trauma being prevalent in the lives of young people and adults, health, education and criminal justice services rarely ask about adversity in childhood and sometimes struggle to work in a trauma-informed way. Understanding the causes and consequences of trauma in people's lives is essential. For example, avoidance, hyper-vigilance and aggression are common responses to trauma. Problematic drinking and drug-taking and violence are often survival strategies. By reframing individual characteristics and action, we enhance our ability to engage with people in a more empathetic and helpful way.

A trauma-informed approach refers to how individuals and organisations think about and respond to people who have experienced trauma.

This chapter documents my experience of implementing trauma and ACE-informed approaches in Wales and Northwest England and considers the importance, relevance and feasibility of working in a trauma-informed way. It will examine how emotionally stable and supportive actions, relationships and environments can prevent or help reverse damage caused by trauma and improve health and well-being.

The Intergenerational Effects of Adverse Childhood Experiences: Ripples on a Pond, First Edition. Edited by Richard Pates and Diane Riley.

Published 2026 by John Wiley & Sons Ltd.

'What are ACEs?'

On June 18th, 2015, I was in Lisbon attending the 9th International Conference on Nightlife Substance Use and Related Health Issues. Mark Bellis, Director of Research, Policy and International Development, Public Health Wales, asked if I would produce an animation about ACEs. My response was, *What are ACEs?* From that moment onwards, ACEs have been part of my work.

ACEs are a major cause of non-communicable disease. The relationship between health risk behaviour and disease in adulthood and exposure to childhood abuse, neglect or household dysfunction during childhood was first described in the academic literature in late 1998 (Felitti et al. 1998).

In 2016, Mark Bellis and colleagues published the *Adverse Childhood Experiences and their impact on health-harming behaviours in the Welsh adult population* report. The Wales ACE survey identified that a substantial proportion of the Welsh population suffered abuse, neglect and other ACEs during their childhood, with 47% reporting having experienced at least one ACE and 14% experiencing four or more ACEs (Bellis et al. 2016).

I was astounded by the findings. Like many others, I asked why I had not recognised the importance of underlying root cause issues in the young people and adults I had supported directly or as part of a population health programme. With hindsight, the signs of adversity and trauma are obvious. Poor decision-making heightened startled response, avoidance of people and places, memory problems, aggression, heightened stress response that focuses on short-term survival at the expense of long-term well-being, alcohol and other drug use and violence, for example.

I am a former drug worker. In the mid-1980s, I helped establish one of the first syringe exchange programmes in the United Kingdom. I was the Managing Director at HIT, a national agency providing drugs and other public health interventions, from 1994 to 2006. Since then, I have addressed several public health concerns, including alcohol and other drugs, smoking, death, dying and loss, overweight and obesity, sexual health, childhood immunisation and youth violence. The public health programmes from 2015 onwards, to a lesser or greater degree, incorporate ACEs and trauma-informed approaches. Before 2015, they did not.

ACEs animation

Following the national ACEs study in Wales and regional studies in England, it was recognised that more needed to be done to provide information about ACEs to professionals and the public. With the help of a graphic designer, animator, translator, actors, public health colleagues and funding from Public Health Wales and Blackburn with Darwen Local Authority, the ACEs animation was piloted and published online in 2017. Three language versions were produced (English language and accent, English language with Welsh accent and Welsh language).

The film lasts 5 and a half minutes and provides the narrative of a young boy growing up with ACEs. The film suggests the impact his exposure to ACEs may have on his physical health, including the early onset of cancer, heart disease and early mortality; mental health problems resulting in impulsivity, anxiety and school truancy and expulsion; and involvement in health-harming behaviours, including substance use, violence and imprisonment. Importantly, the film also highlights how support can provide resilience to help individuals follow different life course trajectories.

An evaluation of the ACEs animation explored attitudes and sentiment towards the film among professionals and the public and associations between attitudes and personal experience of ACEs. Attitudes to the film were positive. Ninety-four percent of professionals and the public, respectively, agreed that the film provided a helpful explanation about ACEs and trusted that the film was credible. Of those who reported ACE exposure, 89% agreed that those with ACEs would benefit from watching the film (Ford et al. 2017).

Developing ACE-informed policy and practice in a North Wales local authority

Following the publication of the ACEs and their impact on health-harming behaviours in the Welsh adult population report, a Local Authority in Wales asked me to help make the case for ACEs-informed practice and develop individual and organisational capacity and capability across the local authority.

Potential areas of work were discussed, and it was agreed that the work should focus on the development of individual and organisational capacity and capability in relation to ACEs across the local authority. Ten half-day training courses were delivered to 154 attendees. In addition, a Health Visitor ACE routine enquiry pilot programme was delivered.

Asking parents about ACEs

Although there is persuasive evidence of the impact of childhood adversity on later health and well-being, wider determinants of health are often not the focus of healthcare provision. Health practitioners report feeling ill-prepared to discuss childhood trauma, not having the time to devote to these discussions and fearing re-traumatising service users by opening a 'can of worms' when there are limited or no resources to then support identified needs (Flanagan et al. 2017).

The most influential people to prevent ACEs are parents and carers. To do this, it is important that parents and carers have the opportunity to learn about ACEs, what they are and how they can be prevented or the impact reduced. Knowing about ACEs can help parents give their children the best start in life. Health visitors provided new parents with the opportunity to find out more about ACEs. After much discussion among stakeholders, including parents, an ACE's enquiry during routine contact was piloted by all Health Visitors across a Local Authority with mothers aged 18 years and above and in 2017/2018.

Training for all Health Visitors took place over a 3-and-a-half-hour session and introduced Health Visitors to the purpose and rationale of ACE enquiry before outlining the delivery of the four-stage enquiry process: explain, ask, listen and close. One week prior to starting the programme, a further 1-and-a-half-hour refresher session to support and build confidence going in to the pilot and respond to any queries or concerns. A feedback session took place after the first month of delivery to address any challenges arising.

A short leaflet for service users was to be provided that explained the concept of ACEs and explained the rationale for the enquiry. A practitioner guide was produced to support the information provided in training and summary information was condensed into a brief prompt card for health visitors to refer to. A directory of local and national support services that Health Visitors could use to signpost families was also provided. Understandably, the Health Visitors had concerns, including the time it might take and the limited availability of talking therapies. One Health Visitor was very reluctant to take part, citing the risk of triggering the Mums.

Over a 6-month period, Mums were invited to complete an ACE questionnaire at either 6 weeks or 6 months post-delivery Health Visitor home visit. Nine out of 10 Mums who were asked agreed to take part in the ACEs enquiry ($n = 321$) (Hardcastle and Bellis 2017). Most Mums agreed strongly or agreed that the routine enquiry was acceptable (91%) and important (81%).

After the Mum had completed the questionnaire, a number of reflective questions were asked, including *'I see you have had some difficult childhood experiences. How have these experiences positively or negatively affected you?'*.

Many Mums spoke about their ACEs. Initial concerns about time, capacity, the need for onward referral and causing upset were not realised during the pilot. Some Mums said they had never spoken about their ACEs because they had never been asked. Waiting to be asked can result in individuals delaying disclosing adversity and trauma, and some never disclose.

Overall, Health Visitors were competent and confident to deliver ACE enquiry when provided with training and support. Initial reservations that were cited during the engagement and training phase did not materialise and were replaced with positive experiences. Health Visitors reported that delivering ACE enquiry was not time-consuming and did not markedly increase the need for support and referral to specialist services. The 'very reluctant Health Visitor' became one of the strongest advocates of the routine enquiry.

Early action together programme, Wales

Increasingly, the Police are the frontline for a range of vulnerabilities, violence and anti-social behaviour. Nowadays, just 20% of police time is crime-related.

In November 2017, the Home Office awarded £6.87 million to the four Police Forces and Police and Crime Commissioners, Public Health Wales, Barnardo's and Criminal Justice partners for the Wales National Adverse Childhood Experiences (ACEs) Approach to Policing initiative. I joined the North Wales Early Action Together team. My role included delivering training to the police and partner agencies and establishing referral processes in each local authority.

Primarily, the programme trained frontline police to provide them with the knowledge and confidence to work with other partners and offer support to vulnerable people who have experienced trauma. The demand on police is complex welfare, public safety and vulnerability issues so they are well placed to intervene more effectively and reduce the impact of ACEs and trauma. See Table 14.1 for more information.

During an 18 month period almost all the North Wales Police officers attended the 1-day course. A quarter of attendees on each course worked in statutory and voluntary organisations. This helped to foster understanding about responses and roles and potential referral pathways.

During my career, I have often been involved in the delivery of training programmes. At time I have been sceptical about the long and sometimes

Table 14.1 ACE TIME (trauma informed multi-agency early action together) training package (Adapted from Ace-time 2021)

The ACE TIME training had the following objectives:

- To support the workforce to increase awareness of ACEs, related trauma and impact across the life course.
- To enable individuals to competently and confidently respond using an ACE informed approach.
- To support a whole system approach with partners to prevent and mitigate trauma,

The training was developed as a 1 day package for delivery to frontline police. The aim was to introduce ACEs and trauma to further develop police officers' tactical skills and to enable an ACE and trauma informed response to vulnerability. Partner agencies were also invited to attend the training alongside police to provide the opportunity for cross agency learning. The training content included the following:

- Working with vulnerability
- Impact of toxic stress on the brain
- Understanding the impact of trauma on brain development behaviour and responses to threat
- Understanding ACEs and their impact on life outcomes
- Secondary and vicarious trauma
- Promoting personal well-being
- Applying an 'ACE LENS '(*Look, explore, needs, signpost, support, safeguard*)
- Tactical skills, communication and effective responses to trauma
- Working together for a trauma informed early intervention approach
- Promoting resilience to mitigate ACEs
- Local and national resources and pathways

short term impact. This has not been the case with ACEs and trauma. There is something about ACEs and trauma that captivates most course attendees. I wonder if it's because half the population has experienced at least one ACE and at least 10 percent of us experienced four or more ACEs. When we run a training course or deliver a lecture, we can be sure that our audience will include people who have experienced adversity and trauma.

The Early Action Together training programme was well received. Prior to the start of a course, a police officer had a quiet word with my co-trainer. *'If you think that you'll turn police officers into social workers, you can fuck off'*. By mid-morning, the officer apologised and said, *'I get it'*.

Resilience: the biology of stress and the science of hope film

> You are invited to attend a screening of the internationally acclaimed film, Resilience: The Biology of Stress and the Science of Hope. The 1-hour documentary explores the science behind how Adverse Childhood Experiences (ACEs) can affect brain development and lead to lifelong health and social problems but importantly provides solutions to the problem. The screening will be followed by a discussion, exploring what we can all do to prevent and alleviate ACEs and strengthen individual and community resilience. We all need to be ACE aware. Are you?
>
> (Advertisement to attend the internationally acclaimed Resilience film)

The *Resilience* film chronicles the beginning of a new movement among paediatricians, therapists, educators and communities in the United States to prevent cycles of violence, addiction and disease. Published in 2016, the internationally acclaimed 1-hour film that examines the science about prolonged and extreme stress and how it negatively alters the brains and bodies of children if left untreated.

I first watched the film when I started work in North Wales. The impact was such that the Early Action Together programme purchased a license to show the film in North Wales.

During 2017 and 2019, the Early Action Together programme provided at least 30 screenings of the *Resilience* film in cinemas, workplaces and community settings in North Wales.

Audiences included a wide range of professionals, volunteers and members of the public. Depending on the venue size and promotional activity, audience numbers ranged from 10 to 150. In most cases, the film was followed by a question and answer session.

Having watched the film many times, I am able to recite several standout sentences including, *'If you place knowledge about ACEs and trauma into the hands of the public they will create wise decisions'*.

Placing knowledge about ACEs and trauma into the hands of young people

Knowledge about the importance and relevance of ACEs and trauma among health, education and criminal justice organisation was taking hold in Wales and other parts of the UK in the late 2010s. I was intrigued how we include young people in the conversation. My instinct was that it is important, relevant and feasible to do so.

I delivered short sessions with teenagers aged 16 to 18 that began by discussing what resilience is, how it can help deal with adversities and support others. I summarised the Wales ACEs research findings including that one in two adults have experienced one ACE and 14% four adversities. Understanding the extent of ACEs and trauma, how prolonged or extreme stress affects our health and well-being and what we can do to prevent and reduce harm including reducing stigma was discussed.

We discussed how our mind and body respond to positive, tolerable and prolonged and extreme stress and how '*Resilience Top Tips*' including belonging, learning, coping and understanding of our core self can help us keep us safe and well. The young people also recognised the importance of talking with trusted adults and friends.

What's the power within your crown?

> You see the golden cracks, the scar and jewels. Each was made from breaks and missing pieces from the ACEs from my childhood. My crown is more beautiful than before.
>
> (Artist, aged 12)

Merseyside Youth Association (MYA) is a charity dedicated to providing innovative support and opportunities for young people across Merseyside. Their headquarters are in my home city of Liverpool. With leadership and guidance from Damian Hart, the organisation were incorporating ACEs and resilience into their programmes and approaches. MYA were especially interested in how ACEs and resilience can be explored with children and young people despite hesitancy among some clinicians who were '*terrified*' by this '*irresponsible*' prospect that '*children and young people will be overwhelmed*'.

My first meeting with Damian included a visit to the Tate Liverpool to view *The Power to Break Free* exhibition, inspired by the Japanese artwork Kintsugi – the Japanese art that repairs and strengthens broken pottery with gold. Visitors were invited to see a Kintsugi-inspired display created by pupils from a Primary School in Liverpool, which explored how negative experiences can lead to positive outcomes.

Kintsugi is the Japanese art of repairing broken pottery by mending the areas of breakage with powdered gold, silver or platinum, which adds value to damaged objects. The young people and visitors to the Tate were prompted to compare this to how we think about health and well-being. Working with MYA and artist Julie Mitchell, the young people and adults created a series of large-scale sculptural crowns, decorating them with jewels and prints to symbolise the power they had gained to break free from adversity.

The artwork on display explored ACEs and resilience among children, parents and carers from the Windsor Primary School, Liverpool. Their artwork illustrated that adversity doesn't shape a negative future. A broken piece of pottery is stronger and more resilient than something that has stayed pristine. The imperfections are what make it more beautiful, valuable and stronger.

The children and adults explained that their crowns show the power that can be gained through adversity and resilience and visitors to the Tate were prompted to compare this to how we think about health and well-being. A broken piece that is put back together has more of a story, seems more authentic and real, is stronger and more resilient than something that has stayed pristine.

NOW festival

The NOW Festival is an annual performing arts event that brings children and young people aged 8–16 years from across the city region to amplify their voices through performances that tackle issues that are important and relevant to them.

The festival takes place over three evenings and is held in prestigious theatres in Liverpool. Each evening, six to eight schools deliver a performance not exceeding 15 minutes. Typically, performances include music, dance, drama, film and spoken word. Depending on the schools that take part and the subject matter of the performances, one night may be reserved exclusively for children aged 8–11.

Since 2016, the annual event has established itself as a unique and inclusive opportunity for young people to collaborate and share creative ideas about a wide range of mental health issues, including Social media and technology, Belonging, Mental health, Listening to the voices of children and young people during COVID-19, Violence and Resilience.

In 2019, the theme was *'Rise Up – Adverse Childhood Experiences (ACEs) and Resilience'*. Under the guidance and support of teachers, youth workers, mental health and well-being staff, young people curated performances exploring the potential life-long effects of ACEs, including physical and mental health and violence, separation and substance use. Performances also examined what enables some people to be resilient.

The theme in 2024 focused on ACEs again. With a 3-year strategy launched to transform the way Liverpool City Council responds to violence against women and girls, St Julie's School students explored this issue.

The young women delivered a powerful performance titled '1 in 4' that explored the concept of men giving flowers to women as an apology for acts of violence. The girls stood strong, spoke out and vowed not to become women 'silenced by flowers'. The performers exclaimed, *'We are Liverpool's women and girls, and we can buy our own flowers'*. The audience and judges were moved by the students' performance and praised the important message they shared. They were awarded 'Best ACEs Message' of the festival and the overall 'Winners of Now Festival 2024'.

Why weight to talk?

In the early scenes of the Resilience film, Dr Vincent Felitti describes his frustration when patients with severe obesity frequently relapse or drop out of programmes. Felitti goes on to say that follow-up interviews with these patients reveal that the majority (55%) had experienced some form of childhood sexual abuse. Many women indicated that they believed their physical size helped ward off sexual advances from men. For these women, excess weight was protective.

Health Equalities Group is a UK public health charity working to improve the health and well-being of local communities. Based in Liverpool, I have worked with and for the organisation during the last decade. *Why weight to talk?* is a training intervention developed in 2023 that takes a whole systems approach to obesity that enables collective efforts and alignment of actions across a range of stakeholders to address obesity, promote healthy weight and empower professionals to have conversations about healthy weight, including ACEs and trauma.

Extreme or prolonged exposure to stress can lead to changes in the structure and function of parts of our brain that can cause cognitive, emotional and behavioural dysfunction that ultimately affects our decision-making and behaviour. Many people smoke tobacco, drink alcohol and consume other drugs to help manage their stress and cope. Individuals who have experienced trauma may also turn to food to cope with difficult emotions, leading to overeating and weight gain.

The training course sets out to raise awareness of the complex range of factors that are associated with weight gain, including the impact of adversity and trauma as well as stigma and stress-induced emotional eating.

ACEs occur more frequently in communities experiencing poverty and deprivation. ACEs can compound challenges associated with ensuring healthy and affordable food and nutrition. Those experiencing food insecurity are at risk of experiencing greater levels of stress. Trauma may limit people's ability to effectively participate in behaviour change interventions and necessitate targeted approaches in weight management.

We should aim to create weight-inclusive, welcoming environments that empower people to be healthy rather than reinforcing societal shame or stigma. Training knowledgeable and compassionate professionals who are trauma-informed will help achieve healthy weight outcomes and reduce the negative effects of weight bias.

Merseyside violence reduction partnership

Violence Reduction Units are multi-agency teams that bring together police, local government, criminal justice agencies, health providers, community leaders and other organisations to address violent crime by understanding its root causes and providing a coordinated response. Established in 20 of the most populated parts of England and Wales in 2019, I joined the Merseyside Violence Reduction Partnership (MVRP) as a public health lead for 3 years, commencing in 2022.

In 2024, the MVRP commissioned Liverpool John Moores University to undertake a representative household survey of adults to understand community safety and cohesion, violence victimisation and ACEs in Merseyside (Quigg et al. 2025). In line with other findings, adults who had experienced four or more ACEs in childhood, compared to adults with no childhood ACEs, were more likely to have ever been arrested and incarcerated and a victim of violence since the age of 18. For example, individuals with 4 or more childhood ACEs or those with none were 9.7 times more likely to have been a victim of violence since the age of 18 years.

Violence is not something that just happens or something that we should accept. Because violence is predictable, it is preventable. Recognising, preventing and mitigating ACEs is a key component of a public health, life course approach to youth violence.

Taking trauma-informed training to another level

My colleague at the MVRP, Jane Pepa, explains that trauma cannot be a tick box activity.

> I wanted to create a course that met the neuroscience of how we learn with activities that lasted no more than 20 minutes (our maximum attention span) and that took people on a journey of understanding, hope and healing. With a subject matter that can be re-traumatising, rushing through the content cannot be an option – it's not Trauma-Informed! When you slow down and make it about connection, safety and trust, you bring your audience with you. I also wanted delegates to sleep between the courses to consolidate the learning, embed and retain the knowledge.

Over the past 3 years, the MVRP has trained over 3,000 public service and 3rd sector staff in Merseyside, including schools, the National Health Service, Fire Service, Social Care, Local Authority, Housing and GPs. In addition, 2,000 Police officers have attended the courses. Each attendee completes a pre-survey using a nationally recognised Trauma-Informed survey tool. Six months later and a follow-up survey assessed the impact.

Inevitably, public and 3rd sector organisations work with individuals who have high rates of trauma. It's vital to equip the workforce with the knowledge, understanding and language to support themselves and avoid compassion fatigue or chronic stress.

Jane says, '*When organisations understand the impact of trauma and vicarious trauma, they can create organisations with greater resilience to stress and challenges. I'm really proud we've become statutory training for the police in Merseyside, I just hope it becomes compulsory for all schools – not just the ones that welcome us with open arms*'.

Back to the late 1980s

> All substances whether they are opiates, cocaine or anything else are actually pain killers either physical or emotional. All addictions are an attempt to smooth the pain.
>
> Gabor Maté, Physician

Local authorities in England eventually received funding to establish drug services in response to the heroin endemic, the likes of which had not been seen before. The tools at our disposal to help people were limited.

I had undertaken a 10-session counselling course, a 2-day Motivational Interviewing course and sought advice from other drug services about how to assess risk and prevent harm. The emergence of HIV among drug users resulted in a dramatic shift in Government policy, whereby the spread of HIV infection was recognised as a greater threat to individual and public health than drug misuse. The measures put in place, including syringe exchange schemes, safer injecting advice and methadone prescribing undoubtedly saved many lives.

During the intervening 40 years, heroin users have stopped but others are still using drugs or have died. What factors determine these outcomes? Is it poor decision-making, strength of character, supportive family and friends, bad luck or something else? In many cases, that 'something else' is trauma. My friend and colleague Mark Gilman says, '*There's a difference between people who choose to take drugs because they enhance their life and those who need to take drugs because their lives are unbearable taken neat*'.

It's everyone's business

Clinical care and talking therapies are essential treatment options for people suffering from trauma. But many people are unable or unwilling to access help and support. Given the extent of trauma, organisations and communities comprising health and social care workers, youth workers, teachers, sports coaches, parents, friends and many others can and must play a role in preventing childhood adversity and helping people recover from trauma. Every interaction made with someone affected by trauma is an opportunity to support their recovery.

There are effective ways to promote recovery by utilising existing assets within individuals, families, organisations and communities. Safe environments, positive adult relationships and creating opportunities for people to connect with each other can prevent and mitigate trauma. Being listened to and treated with empathy and respect by others is so important.

References

ACE-TIME (2021). An evaluation of the adverse childhood experience trauma informed multi-agency early action together (ACE-TIME) training: national roll out to police and partners. https://phwwhocc.co.uk/wp-content/uploads/2021/08/PHW-EAT-ACE-TIME-evaluation-1.pdf (accessed 1 November 2023).

Bellis, M.A., Ashton, K., Hughes, K. et al. (2016) Adverse childhood experiences and their impact on health-harming behaviours in the Welsh adult population.

Felitti, V.J., Anda, R.F., Nordenberg, D. et al. (1998). Relationship of childhood abuse and household dysfunction to many of the leading causes of death in adults: the Adverse Childhood Experiences (ACE) Study. *American Journal of Preventive Medicine* 14: 245–258.

Flanagan, T. et al. (2017). Feasibility and acceptability of screening for adverse childhood experiences in prenantal care. *Journal of Women's Health* 27 (7): 903–911.

Ford, K., Bellis, M.A., Isherwood, K.R. et al. (2017). Perceptions of a short, animated filmon adverse childhood experiences: a mixed methods evaluation. *BMJ Open* 11: e050398.

Hardcastle, K. and Bellis, M. (2017). Asking about adverse childhood experiences (ACEs) in health visiting. Findings from a pilot study. https://phwwhocc.co.uk/wp-content/uploads/2020/07/Asking-about-adverse-Report.pdf (accessed 1 November 2023).

Quigg, Z., Butler, N., Wilson, C. et al. (2025). *The Merseyside Violence and Community Safety. A Representative Household Survey of Adults to Understand Community Safety and Cohesion, Violence Victimisation, and Adverse Childhood Experiences.* Liverpool: Liverpool John Moores University/Merseyside Violence Reduction Partnership.

Chapter 15

SYSTEMATIC CAPACITY BUILDING IN CHILD AND ADOLESCENT CLINICAL CARE IN THE CZECH REPUBLIC: A CASE STUDY

Michal Miovský

Prague, Czech Republic
Department of Addictology, First Faculty of Medicine, Charles University, Prague 2, Czech Republic

Introduction: unique specialised care for children and adolescents with SUDs in the context of ACEs

The majority of existing mental health services have broader profiles and integrate complications related to adverse childhood experiences (ACEs). International experience suggests that the concept of a fully autonomous model of specialised addiction services for children and adolescents with substance use disorders (SUDs) is not very common and that this type of service tends to be viewed as an add-on to mental health facilities. Such a definition of services and understanding of addiction science have their parallels in education, where the 'specialisation model' (e.g. addiction psychiatry, addiction nursing, addiction psychology, addiction social work, etc.) seems to have become predominant as the mainstream in many countries. In this context, 'a specialisation model' refers to a system of education and training in which traditional professions can attain specialisation in addiction science in the existing courses (Miovský et al. 2021). Sporadic instances of a 'qualification model' have also occurred recently. This concept perceives addictions as a new type of qualification involving a new autonomous and unique profession. Despite the unprecedented expansion of such academic degree university study programmes in Europe (Pavlovská et al. 2017) and, in particular, in the United States, this trend does not seem to be reflected (Miovský et al. 2021)

The Intergenerational Effects of Adverse Childhood Experiences: Ripples on a Pond,
First Edition. Edited by Richard Pates and Diane Riley.

Published 2026 by John Wiley & Sons Ltd.

in solid legal grounding of these professionals in national legislation. This also applies to specialised services for children and adolescents with SUDs. Therefore, this chapter addresses particularly the aspect where the development of a new, unique professional group of addiction professionals correlates closely and positively with the emancipatory process, leading to the rise of new health and social services for children and adolescents with SUDs. This process has multiple underlying causes, including, as in many other countries, a dramatic long-term shortage of the psychiatrists, psychologists and nurses needed to facilitate the development of SUD services. In addition to the shortage of these professions in healthcare generally, their lack of interest in SUD patients has also been an issue. It has some specific clinical links towards ACEs, where SUD symptoms and complications can be typically overestimated or underestimated. Both extremes have a negative impact on developing an adequate treatment plan and strategy. The development of a new health profession with a narrow specialisation in SUD is thus a technically feasible and economical solution that can provide additional benefits for the system of services. Highlighted in our study, this particular aspect is demonstrated through the way specialised services for children and adolescents with SUDs are being developed and their capacity scaled up and what advantages it brings towards dealing with ACE issues. It has turned out that in the long term, the quality of specialised addiction services is growing remarkably and so, generally, is the interest in addiction science and work in specialised services, including specific modalities such as harm reduction. In this respect, the Czech Republic offers an interesting example of practice where a national specialised network of services for people with SUDs is being built hand in hand with the development of an addiction science-specific educational model. This gives rise to a hitherto rare national model that enjoys firm legislative grounding in the general system of health and social care, a clear conceptual framework, and sources of funding. In addition, this model seems to appeal to the emerging generation of professionals and, as a result of a massive increase in the need for such services in the post-COVID period, it is also receiving strong political backing and support from health insurers and other key stakeholders. The point of producing and discussing a Czech Republic case study thus gains additional dimensions. As a country situated in the very heart of Europe, it offers a number of geographical and political parallels, including aspects associated with the drug policy. The country represents a bridge between Western and Eastern Europe. It is a country where the first dedicated alcohol treatment services came into being under the same historical circumstances and with similar urgency as in Germany or English-speaking countries (Sejvl et al. 2019). It also became the first country in Europe to account for addiction professionals in the legislation regulating health professions and created a brand new regulated profession with high competencies, including the authority to run healthcare facilities and enter into contracts with health insurers. What makes this case study noteworthy from an international perspective is the development of specialised services for children and adolescents, including relevant policy-making in this segment of health and social care. This process continually changes a broader perspective on ACEs, including, e.g. direct impact on national network of orphanages and services for children with special needs (including specialised detention centres for youngsters). Finally, the impact of this process was powerful enough to initiate the development of unique national clinical guidelines for work with this target population.

Before a short overview on the epidemiology of SUD, we should start with recent figures representing ACEs in the Czech Republic using standard methodology. Veliminsky's team (Veleminsky et al. 2020) recently reported 20.7% of emotional abuse, physical abuse by 17.1%, sexual abuse by 6.4% and physical neglect by 8.0%. Household dysfunction was also high, with household street drug use reported by 4.9%, alcohol misuse by 15.3%, mental disorder by 13.4%, parental violence by 22.1% and parental separation by 23%. These numbers are lower because of the sampling of university students. The very reason for considering, discussing and initiating the development of such narrowly specialised addiction services/facilities should be sought in the epidemiological situation of the last decade. The alarming levels recorded in the Czech Republic during that time resulted in great pressure on clinical services, as well as initiating a wide-ranging debate within the field. The European School Survey Project on Alcohol and Other Drugs (ESPAD) conducted at the end of the decade, in 2019, showed that 24% of the adolescents who took part had smoked conventional cigarettes in the past 30 days and 10% had smoked daily (Chomynová et al. 2020). The extrapolation of the survey results onto the population of adolescents aged 15–19 indicated that approximately 40 thousand Czech adolescents had smoked conventional cigarettes on a daily basis. The decline in the use of conventional tobacco products is associated with the growing popularity of new forms of use of tobacco and nicotine products, such as e-cigarettes and heated tobacco. While the rates of smoking conventional cigarettes among 16-year-olds in the Czech Republic are comparable to the European average, the lifetime use of e-cigarettes among Czech adolescents is above that average. The level of alcohol consumption among adolescents in the Czech Republic was relatively stable prior to the COVID-19 pandemic (Chomynová & Kážmér 2019). According to ESPAD 2019, 63% of the 16-year-olds had drunk alcohol in the past 30 days, and the frequent use of five or more drinks on a single occasion (at least weekly or more) was reported by 12% (Chomynová et al. 2020). The 2022 HBSC study showed that alcohol had been consumed in the past 30 days by 48% of the 15-year-olds who took part and 23% had experienced drunkenness repeatedly. In comparison to other European countries, the level of alcohol consumption among Czech adolescents is high and approximately 45 thousand adolescents engage in frequent binge drinking.

Data on illegal substances can also be presented for comparison. In the long term, cannabis has been the most common illicit drug used among children and adolescents in the Czech Republic. According to both ESPAD 2019 and a study conducted by Palacky University Olomouc in 2021, lifetime cannabis use was reported by 28% of the adolescent participants (Chomynová et al. 2020). In 2022, the second most frequently used substance was kratom; it had been repeatedly used in the past 12 months by 1.5% of the adolescents. Cannabis had been used repeatedly by more than 50 thousand adolescents. The misuse of prescription sedatives and sleeping pills in the Czech Republic is above average in comparison to other European countries, particularly as regards their mixing with alcohol.

Naturally, the rise in behavioural addictions is a major issue. The rates of gambling among Czech adolescents remain relatively stable. Gambling in the past 12 months was reported by 9–10% of 16-year-olds (Chomynová et al. 2020) and 15% of the adolescents in the 15–19 age category. The gambling activity reported with the highest frequency was lotteries, engaged in both online and via land-based outlets. It has been shown that a large proportion of adolescents do not consider playing cards or dice for money, or participation in lotteries, a gambling activity. The excessive use of digital technology among children and adolescents has become a phenomenon of major concern, particularly in the context of the effects of the COVID-19 pandemic. According to HBSC 2022, the problematic gaming criteria were met by an estimated 13% of the boys and 5% of the girls and 5–7% of the boys and 7–13% of the girls came under the problematic use of social media category (Kalman and Baďura 2023). No less than 34% of the 16-year-old students were classified as being at risk in relation to their time spent on social media (Chomynová et al. 2020). When extrapolated, this data suggests that almost 70 thousand adolescents may be at risk of problematic gaming and no less than 180 thousand are at risk of problematic use of social media. The transfer of adolescents' activities into the online setting and the related reduction in time spent with their peers in the real world is one of the arguments used to explain a decline in the use of some substances among adolescents (Chomynová and Kážmér 2019).

The first large debates in the last decade made it clear that, given the estimated number of substance users among children and adolescents and the number of adolescents receiving treatment from outpatient addiction facilities, the availability of outpatient specialist care for children and adolescents in the Czech Republic falls dramatically short of the needs of this population. It became evident that there is a critical need for scaling up school- and community-based prevention and a greater emphasis should be placed on early diagnosis and brief intervention. In this respect, however, it is necessary to conceptualise the phrase 'specialised care for children and adolescents' in the context of SUDs and behavioural addictions. Such a concept lacks both an unequivocal understanding and a firm grounding in our field. For the purposes of this Czech Republic case study and the context in which such services are embedded, we invoke policy documents which the Czech professional associations pushed forward as integral parts of their professional and field identity:

> The concept of specialised and unique addiction services integrates multidisciplinary specialist services designed, operated and intended primarily for

people with SUDs and people with disorders along the behavioural addiction spectrums, including individuals who are at risk of such disorders and complications and their families and loved ones. Specialised and unique addiction services for children and adolescents are defined as services intended primarily for clients and patients with SUDs in the under-18 age group and pregnant women with SUDs, including their families and loved ones. In both groups, of course, the concept encompasses people with disorders along the behavioural addiction spectrum, with all relations towards ACEs.

The shaping of a perspective on addiction-specific services for children and adolescents is becoming ever more sophisticated. Naturally, comprehensive manuals for work with adolescent patients are becoming important milestones (e.g. Kaminer and Winters 2011). Extensive materials summarising the latest evidence base for effective strategies, tools and methods (e.g. NHS 2009), including documents dealing specifically with clinical evaluation (NHS 2007), are also available. It is therefore inevitable that the pros and cons of specialised services have become the centre of attention globally. A sensitive question has thus arisen as to whether to build specific services intended primarily for patients with SUDs and conceived strictly on an interdisciplinary basis (which we are becoming used to referring to as 'specialised addiction services') or, instead, increase the capacity of child psychiatry and child clinical psychology and mental health services in general. Their relationship is a crucial topic, not only in terms of healthcare in itself, but also, of course, in terms of the provision of medical care within a service conceived and staffed on an interdisciplinary basis (Kaminer and Winters 2011). Importantly, the key aspect is respect for specific needs associated with age, social roles, developmental aspects and the need for community-based programmes that are accessible and acceptable to the target group under consideration (NICE 2007). In this sense, the Czech experience is encouraging, as it has demonstrated pragmatism and motivation to address these challenges in spite of the high level of stigma and bias that persists in Czech society.

Historic development of a perspective on specialised care for children and adolescents

Specialised treatment institutions for alcohol dependency emerged quite early in central Europe. The first such facility in what is today the Czech Republic came into existence as early as 1908 and remained in operation until World War I. Another attempt at an inpatient specialised operation occurred in 1923 and lasted towards the end of World War II (Šejvl et al. 2019). Both these institutions were strongly influenced by ELLIKON, a Swiss treatment programme opened in 1887 by Auguste Henri Forel and Jakob Bosshard. By the start of the 20th century, alcohol use had become a major social issue, which began to draw attention from the first generation of practitioners engaged in services for people with alcohol-related problems. This initial movement had a major bearing on the generation of professionals that emerged after World War II. In 1948, they found their 'base camp' at a clinical facility known as 'U Apolináře'[1], established by the psychiatrist Jaroslav Skála as part of the largest hospital in Prague at the time (the General Hospital). While formally being a 'mere' remote site of the Department of Psychiatry at the time of its establishment, for the next 50 years, Apolinar became a hub and incubator of ideas and new approaches and concepts in addiction science in central Europe. Quite unexpectedly, as early as the late 1950s, it was here that the idea was conceived of creating a specialised outpatient facility for adolescents and juveniles, which was finally opened in 1957 (Mečíř 1989). This accomplishment should be credited to a prominent child psychiatrist, Professor Jan Mečíř, who had a significant impact on the development of approaches to working with young drug users throughout the second half of the 20th century.

Clinical interest on the part of several experts, spearheaded by Professor Mečíř, then initiated a debate about substance use among children and adolescents and clinical facilities for them. Despite this early recognition of the need to address alcohol dependency among children, including concerns about the growing use of drugs other than alcohol among this population, the intention of creating a new clinical concept and new treatment sites did not seem to engage the wider professional community beyond the narrow circle of the Prague team. However, in Prague, the influence was strong enough for two additional specialised facilities to be incorporated into the Apolinar clinical operation. First, in 1967, the Centre for Children and Adolescents at Risk of Alcohol Dependence came into existence and, in 1971, the Drug Addiction Centre was opened. Following their model, similar facilities were established in other regions of what was then communist Czechoslovakia (Brno, Opava, Liberec and Teplice), giving rise to the first wave of dedicated professional services (Mečíř 1989, p. 140). For reasons which remain unclear, the first specialised outpatient clinic (established in 1957) ceased to exist, despite its successful operation and publication activities. Nevertheless, the leading figure of the emerging clinical field of addiction science at the time, Jaroslav Skála, took account of the rising clinical interest in children and adolescents and, in the 1970s and 1980s, which saw major development of outpatient services, incorporated components aimed at children and adolescents into their profile (Rubeš et al. 1973). From today's point of view, the international isolation of the entire project may seem peculiar. It can hardly be explained by the simple fact of the division between Western and Eastern Europe referred to as the 'Iron Curtain'. The

[1] Its name was derived from its location in the former chapterhouse of the nearby Church of St. Apolinar. Today the building houses the Department of Addictology of the First Faculty of Medicine (Charles University), with its clinical branches being part of the General University Hospital.

aforementioned process did not seem to meet much response from the professional community within the former 'Soviet Bloc' either and was even left almost unnoticed by mainstream practitioners in Czechoslovakia itself. With this legacy and experience, addiction services for children and adolescents entered a new decade and new economic and political circumstances following the 'Velvet Revolution' in 1989.

Quest for identity of specialised services for children and adolescents

The first two post-revolution decades (1990–2010) in the Czech Republic were marked by experimenting. Typically, during this period, various models of services for children and adolescents in different segments of care and institutional settings were tested and were very close to ACE concept (using a more integrative perspective), with no deep focus specifically on addictions. The first attempts at sharing clinical experience then were far from any coordination or standardisation of services in terms of quality policy. The models employed during that period remained more or less isolated endeavours pursued by various teams and service providers, although some of them were very original and clinically innovative and valuable. Unfortunately, the vast majority of the evidence they produced was reported in local anthologies and national journals, i.e. in the Czech language only. For this reason, all these models, with few exceptions, went almost unnoticed outside the Czech Republic. The exception in this respect is the school- and community-based prevention of addictions.

After the first attempts at its conceptualisation and institutionalisation and not fully successful efforts to create a consistent policy, school- and community-based prevention was given a major impulse in 1999. In that year, a governmental project, Phare Twinning 2000, was launched, with the assignment being to carry out needs assessment and inform the development of a national prevention policy including ACEs. In 2003, a body of documents was adopted as part of a governmental task and the Ministry of Education was commissioned to implement it. Despite the implementation being sometimes chaotic and lengthy, it led to the development of a single concept, which, however, faced major challenges in being put into practice at the time (Miovsky 2015).

Unsurprisingly, the origins of interest in screening and working with pregnant women and mothers with SUDs were difficult and burdened with strong stigma. Nevertheless, even then, the first efforts were made to address this agenda, place it within a theoretical framework (Binder and Vavřínková 2006), and engage in systematic monitoring and clinical support and assistance (Sedláčková and Žižková 2007b). In addition, the first works dealing specifically with births given by drug-dependent mothers were published (e.g. Čihař 2009). Although these published works have a missing terminological focus on ACEs, this phenomenon was logically integrated because of the clinical perspective. All related problems in families cannot be separated. In this context of different target groups, special attention was focused on patients in opioid maintenance treatment (Vavřinková and Binder 2007) with their special needs.

The first inpatient detoxification unit intended specifically for children and adolescents (admitting no patients above 19 years of age) was established (Koranda 2016). At the same time, other ambitious treatment programmes aspired to go beyond the boundaries of healthcare and introduce a robust modality reflecting these clients' wide-ranging and complex needs, taking into consideration the perspective of both the parents (especially mothers) and the children, including children of very young age (e.g. Sedláčková et al. 2016). Another promising project was a treatment programme for young people aged over 15, launched as part of a therapeutic community (NGO White Light) and the effort to integrate it into the standard system. One inspiring programme was a model developed by Dr. Preslová's team for the SANANIM NGO (Preslová et al. 2011) in the context of outpatient programmes followed up by a therapeutic community programme designed specifically for mothers with children. In addition, a programme originally developed in 1967 was transformed into a new model under the Centre for Therapy and Family Counselling, operated as part of the Department of Addictology of the First Faculty of Medicine at Charles University and the General University Hospital. Thanks to the Anima NGO, a unique model of family care and therapy was developed, which gave rise to a successful educational and training model. Throughout the period under consideration, a range of counselling and therapeutic programmes for children and adolescents came into existence and were successful in reflecting on frequent ACE problems in families and adopting their therapeutic strategies. However, many of them experienced sustainability issues and difficulties in evolving into an integrated working system, which would be critical for further development and growth.

Autonomous conceptual framework for services dedicated to children and adolescents with SUDs

The turning point for addiction services for children and adolescents in the Czech Republic was the 2010s. The creation of a system was facilitated by school- and community-based prevention efforts, which were eagerly followed by screening and brief interventions together with outpatient modalities. While almost unnoticed in its initial phase (until 2015), the process saw dramatic acceleration in its second phase, and during the COVID-19 pandemic and shortly after, it gathered full momentum, demonstrated by a rapid increase in new services and engagement of health insurers and other stakeholders. Finally, structural changes in the education and training of addiction professionals worked as a significant impulse.

Prevention, early diagnosis and brief intervention

Encouraged by a series of EU projects, the first major headway was made by the prevention domain, as reflected by a special issue of the Addictology journal[2]. Growing pressure from the professional community and frustration caused by slow implementation, receiving poor support (from key stakeholders) resulted in the formulation of a bottom-up implementation plan. While not having the desired effect on practice, this initiative led to the development of independent projects promoted by some of the most proactive prevention providers and academic institutions. This entire emancipatory process was analysed and described in an account of the development and shaping of the national quality assurance and quality standards system. This system has become a part of a robust project in support of the infrastructural development of school- and community-based prevention involving a catalogue of preventive interventions and implementation support, structural support for graduate and lifelong education in prevention, quality policy and the promotion of evidence-based approaches in general. This gave rise to IPREV[3], a national platform bringing together professionals and prevention providers. Additionally, an independent prevention-specific professional association, OSPRCH (Professional Society for Prevention Professionals), affiliated with the movement represented in Europe by European Society for Prevention Research (EUSPR), was established.

The second line of measures in this area is represented by early diagnosis and brief interventions. Similarly, to many other countries, the Czech Republic has adapted and localised screening tools such as AUDIT, ASSIST and CRAFT. The availability of the tools, however, does not necessarily ensure that they are consistently used in practice. Therefore, a major structural step was the adoption of a statutory responsibility[4] for all health practitioners to apply these tools effectively. To facilitate such a strategy, the first series of online training courses for paediatricians, gynaecologists and nurses was launched thanks to a donation from the Sirius Foundation. It was also critical for a deeper reflection of ACE-related issues, including increasing sensitivity of these professional groups towards this phenomenon. In association with the Government Council for Addiction Policy Coordination, in 2024, Charles University launched a long-term project[5] of structural support for the training of health and social workers aimed at implementing early diagnosis and brief

[2] The full text of this issue is available in English at https://www.addictology.cz/journal-archive/2012-2/3-2012/

[3] The objective of this open interactive platform is to foster mental health and prevent risk behaviour. It is operated as a non-commercial public service at www.iprev.cz (available in the Czech language only).

[4] Special Act No. 65 approved by the Czech Parliament in 2017.

[5] NPAS, a national project for supporting health, social and education professionals in screening and brief interventions. It provides online training and methodological support and tools at www.npas.cz (available in the Czech language only).

intervention tools, including freely available instruments and support for their use and innovations.

Specialised outpatient clinics and day centres

The general group of service providers comprises a wide range of counselling facilities and centres, typically affiliated with schools, children's homes and institutions for juvenile delinquents and children with behavioral disorders. Some of them have begun to adapt their services to address the needs of children and adolescents with SUDs. Nevertheless, it soon became clear that comprehensive care, ranging from assessment and diagnosis to all the general types of interventions, including family support, can hardly be possible without a new interdisciplinary model of services. To inform the Government Council for Addiction Policy Coordination, the Ministry of Health and health insurers, the existing services for children and adolescents with SUDs were subjected to extensive needs assessment and evaluation (Miovský et al. 2014). Their results were convincing enough for the largest Czech health insurer (VZP) to support in 2014 the idea of developing and testing a new child outpatient clinic model. This made it possible to put such a new facility into operation and conduct its 12-month pilot testing, including an evaluation study (Miovský and Popov 2016). The new model, operated in a university hospital setting, has proved effective in both clinical and economic terms. Following this template, similar services came into being in other regions. There are currently eight of them and others are in the making with support from health insurers and regional authorities. From the beginning, however, these facilities have been faced with the critical question as to whether they can actually reach out to their target population and retain it in the programme (e.g. Pinto et al. 2011). With regard to the latter, another question is to what extent they are currently using effective tools for reducing dropout rates, such as case management, a method which is increasingly being employed in these facilities but requires more attention.

Residential programmes

A unique facility by nature, the Prague-based inpatient detoxification programme dedicated specifically to children and adolescents (Koranda 2016) has become a stable component of the network of services for the entire Central Bohemia region. The first attempts to adapt this model in other regions have been made in response to a dramatic increase in the number of young people admitted to hospital with acute conditions (Miovský et al. 2014). The issue is becoming socially and politically sensitive. Unfortunately, even the second attempt to replicate the detoxification facility in Brno (the second-largest Czech city) has failed. The inpatient detoxification facility in Prague thus remains the only project of its kind nationally. Interestingly, the critical parameter is human resources rather than funding; the lack of staff has repeatedly posed a threat even to the existing programme.

It was eventually the reason for moving it from a small healthcare facility to a large university hospital to prevent the service from being discontinued.

It has been difficult to conduct any formal evaluations, specific investigations or monitoring of other residential programmes for children and adolescents with SUDs. Thus, the only update that can be provided on them is that they remain in operation. Some of them work under specialised institutions for juvenile delinquents and children with behavioural disorders, non-healthcare establishments managed and funded by the Ministry of Education. The first therapeutic community-based programme for adolescents (from 14 years of age) has been opened and there are other therapeutic communities run by non-governmental organisations, which accept adolescents from the age of 16 (however, none of these programmes is integrated into the network of health services).

Policy documents and strategies

The Czech Republic formulated 'National Strategy for the Prevention of Child Abuse and Neglect in 2008–2018' and specifically defines fundamental categories of abuse: emotional, physical and sexual abuse, including non-contact abuse, as well as systematic abuse or commercial sexual abuse (i.e. child prostitution, pornography and trafficking) (Vanickova 2009). This strategy is linked to different governmental key documents, including National Drug Policy of the Czech Republic, where this issue has a completely new reflection. In 2019, the Sirius Foundation provided a unique grant to support the development of services for children and adolescents with SUDs. This project made it possible to found the Section for Child and Adolescent Addiction Treatment, DADA[6], a platform bringing together all four Czech professional associations concerned with addictions. One of the first outcomes of its activities is a regular training programme introduced as part of the long-term task of supporting professional training in work with children and adolescents with SUDs, formulated as a founding principle of the Section's mission. The first-ever policy document was also articulated to define the domain of working with children and adolescents with SUDs as an autonomous segment of addiction studies (referred to in the Czech Republic as 'addictology'). The document defines the network of specialised health and social services for children and adolescents with SUDs, including a plan for its further development (Policy Document 2020). Four years later, the document was successfully incorporated into the national drug policy. In March 2024, it was formally adopted by the Government Council for Addiction Policy Coordination, which proceeded to commission all the relevant ministries with the implementation of all the tasks set out in the policy document.

[6] https://dada.snncls.cz (in Czech only).

Sustainability of the system and its implications for clinical practice

Sustainability is becoming a sensitive topic and a mantra across mental health services. The Czech Republic is not the only country where the workforce is a critical parameter in terms of the sustainability of specialised services, especially in the health sector. In order to address this issue, the Czech team have taken several steps aimed at fostering the sustainability and development of services for children and adolescents with SUDs. The objective of these services becoming firmly embedded in healthcare was at the core of a unique project leading to the development of specialised clinical guidelines for treating children and adolescents with SUDs and behavioural addictions. Indeed, in both the Czech healthcare system and in others, there is an unwritten rule that in medicine, 'only a field with its own clinical guidelines can exist and survive'. It should therefore be seen as a success that special guidelines for work with children and adolescents with SUDs were incorporated into general clinical guidelines for SUDs and behavioural addictions developed as part of a national project[7]. The financial support, which made it possible to finalise and introduce the original national guidelines, caused the desired shift and enhanced respect for this area of specialised care. Naturally, major international guidelines (e.g. Gilvarry et al. 2012; Kaminer and Winters 2011; NHS 2007, 2009) are the subject of intensive discussions and interest on the part of Czech professionals.

The aforementioned agreement of all four major professional organisations concerned with addictions has made it possible to ensure targeted support for cooperation among service providers and the activities of the joint DADA Section. The Section has quickly become promoted even by two rather small but very sensitive professional groups – child clinical psychologists and child psychiatrists, including links and a significant increase in sensitivity generally towards ACEs. The entire process facilitated a surprising and positive shift during the post-COVID period. All the major health insurers support the development of new health services for this target population and virtually all new service providers can secure contracts with these health insurers almost immediately. This has never before happened in any other segment of addiction-specific health services. Its positive impact is, however, hampered by the previously mentioned shortage of a qualified workforce. This is the reason this issue was identified as the top priority for professional education in addictions. This intention was reflected in the key vision and proposed framework (see also Miovský et al. 2021) for the education and training of addiction professionals ('addictologists'). It was agreed that a two-level model of qualification and specialist education and training will apply to addiction professionals. The first level is associated with the profession of an addictologist and the second level with the profession of a clinical addictologist. Set out

[7] Initiated by professional organisations and the Government Council for Addiction Policy Coordination, this project was funded by the Technology Agency of the Czech Republic.

in the special Act No. 96 approved by the Czech Parliament, this two-level model integrates the full profile of professional education and training, ranging from prevention, treatment, rehabilitation and recovery to harm reduction. This profile does not differentiate between age groups: it is generic in this respect, spanning all the age categories of the target population, topics and types of specialised services for patients with SUDs. The subspecialisation in services for children and adolescents will follow up on this model. This approach is highly beneficial for the system and attractive to professionals, as it paves the road for them to receive bonuses from health insurers and special competencies warranting their work positions.

References

Binder, T. and Vavřínková, B. (2006). *Návykové látky v těhotenství [Substance Abuse in Pregnancy]*. Prague: Triton.

Chomynová, P. and Kážmer, L. (2019). Leisure-time socializing with peers as a mediator of recent decline in alcohol use in Czech adolescents. *Journal of Substance Abuse* 24 (6): 630–637. https://doi.org/10.1080/14659891.2019.1640304.

Chomynová, P., Csémy, L., and Mravčík, V. (2020). Evropská školní studie o alkoholu a jiných drogách (ESPAD) 2019. [European School Survey Project on Alcohol and Other Drugs (ESPAD) 2019]. *Zaostřeno* 6: 1–20.

Čihař, M. (2009). Novorozenec drogově závislé matky [Newborn of a drug-dependent mother]. In: *Ženy a drogy: sborník odborné konference* (ed. I. Preslová and V. Maxová), 51–54. SANANIM: Prague.

Gilvarry, E., McArdle, P., O'Herlihy, A. et al. (ed.) (2012). *Practice Standards for Young People with Substance Misuse Problems*. London: Royal College of Psychiatrists.

Kalman, M. and Baďura, P. (2023). *Online svět patří (k) mladé generaci! HBSC studie v ČR [The Online World Belongs to the Young Generation. HBSC Study in the Czech Republic]*. Olomouc: Univerzita Palackého v Olomouci.

Kaminer, Y. and Winters, K. (2011). *Clinical Manual of Adolescent Substance Abuse Treatment*. London: American Psychiatric Publishing.

Koranda, M. (2016). Dětské a dorostové detoxikační centrum (DaDDC) [Child and Adolescent Detoxification Centre (CaADC)]. *Adiktologie* 16 (4): 342–351.

Mečíř, J. (1989). *Zneužívání alkoholu a nealkoholových drog u mládeže [Alcohol and Drug Abuse among Youth]*. Prague: Avicenum.

Miovský, M. (2015). The development of the National System of School-based Prevention of Risk Behaviour in the Czech Republic: reflections on the outcomes of a 15-year process. *Adiktologie* 15 (1): 62–87.

Miovský, M. and Popov, P. (2016). Planning and process evaluation of an outpatient addiction treatment clinic for children and adolescents as a pilot project. *Adiktologie* 16 (4): 292–318.

Miovský, M., Čablová, L., Šťastná, L. et al. (2014). Analýza potřeb dětí a mladistvých z hlediska užívání návykových látek a souvisejícího rizikového chování v kontextu institucionální sítě služeb na území hl. města Prahy a Středočeského kraje [Needs analysis of children and adolescents in terms of substance use and related risk behaviour in the context of the Institutional Network of Services in Prague and the Central Bohemia Region]. *Adiktologie* 14 (1): 10–21.

Miovsky, M., Volfova, A., Johnson, K., Peters, R., Koutsenok, I., Heaps, M., & Lososova, A. (2021). New trends in education and training programs in addictions at the higher education and university levels. Adiktologie, 21(4), 201–209. https://doi.org/10.35198/01-2021-004-0005

NHS National Treatment Agency for Substance Misuse (2007). Assessing young people for substance misuse. www.nta.nhs.uk (accessed 14 December 2016).

NHS National Treatment Agency for Substance Misuse (2009). Exploring the evidence. www.nta.nhs.uk.

NICE Public Health Guidance 4 (2007). Community-based interventions to reduce substance misuse among vulnerable and disadvantaged children and young people. www.nice.org.uk/nicemedia/ live/11379/31939/31939.pdf.

Pavlovská, A., Miovský, M., Babor, T.F., and Gabrhelík, R. (2017). Overview of the European university-based study programmes in the addictions field. *Drugs: Education, Prevention and Policy* 24 (6): 485–491. https://doi.org/10.1080/09687637.2016.1223603.

Pinto, R., Campbell, A., Hien, D. et al. (2011). Retention in the National Institute on Drug Abuse Clinical Trials Network Women and Trauma study: implications for posttrial implementation. *The American Journal of Orthopsychiatry* 81: 211–207.

Policy Document (2020). Child and adolescent clinical services in addictions. Working document of the Professional Society on Addictions. Prague.

Preslová, I., Černohorská, K., and Konečná, V. (2011). *Manuál práce s dětmi drogově závislých klientů [Manual for Work with Children of Drug-dependent Parents]*. Prague: o.s. Sananim.

Rubeš, J., Urban, E., Jenýšková, D., and Šípová, B. (1973). Program a činnost střediska drogových závislostí v Praze [Programme and activities of the Drug Addiction Centre in Prague]. *Československá Psychiatrie* 69 (5): 322–327.

Sedláčková, S. and Žižková, B. (2007b). Jeden ze systémů péče o těhotné uživatelky drog, drogově závislé ženy a jejich děti v České republice [A system of care of pregnant drug users and drug-dependent women and their children]. *Prevence úrazů, otrav a násilí* 3 (1): 45–50.

Sedláčková, S., Dobrinič, K., and Hamplová, L. (2016). Metodika péče o matky užívající návykové látky a jejich děti v projektu Slunečnicová zahrada [Methodology of the care of drug-using mothers and their children in the "Sunflower Garden" project]. *Adiktologie* 16 (4): 352–359.

Šejvl, J., Gavurová, B., Barták, M. et al. (2019). First alcohol treatment institutions in today's Czech Republic and Slovak Republic. *Central European Journal of Public Health* 27 (Suppl): S55–S65. https://doi.org/10.21101/cejph.a5812.

Vanickova, E. (2009). *Národní strategie prevence násilí na dětech v ČR na období 2008–2018 [National Strategy for the Prevention of Child Abuse and Neglect in the Czech Republic in 2008–2018]*. Praha/Prague: Úřad vlády ČR/ Governmental Office.

Vavřinková, B. and Binder, T. (2007). Vliv substituční terapie na porodní hmotnost novorozence, poporodní adaptaci, trofiku a průběh abstinenčního syndromu novorozence [The effect of substitution therapy on the birth weight of the newborn, its postpartum adaptation, trophic and course of the neonatal abstinence syndrome]. *Česká gynekologie* 72 (4): 247–253.

Velemínský, M., Dvořáčková, O., Samková, J. et al. (2020). Prevalence of adverse childhood experiences (ACE) in the Czech Republic. *Child Abuse & Neglect* 102: 104249. https://doi.org/10.1016/j.chiabu.2019.104249.

Chapter 16

A FAMILY AFFAIR! FIXING ADULTS TO BREAK THE INTERGENERATIONAL TRANSMISSION OF SUFFERING

Eric Breton[1,2], *Elodie David*[1,2], *and Line Caron*[3]

[1] Department of Humanities and Social Sciences, EHESP School of Public Health, Rennes, France
[2] Arènes Research Unit (UMR CNRS 6051: INSERM U1309 team), Rennes, France
[3] Independent Consultant, Baie-Comeau, Canada

Introduction

When Françoise entered the room that morning, she didn't really know what to expect. Maria, the addiction nurse at the drug treatment centre, had encouraged her to join the group. She wasn't really into groups, but at least it would get her out of the house, away from her problems with her alcohol-dependent son, who hardly spoke to her anymore! Anyway, Maria had told her that she didn't have to talk and that she was totally free to leave whenever she wanted. She had even decided to keep her backpack on her back, just in case!

Stepping in, she was greeted by the smell of coffee and the two smiling facilitators. They introduced themselves: Julie, daughter of Jean and Claudine, mother of Camille, Léon and Liam, and her colleague Ana, daughter of Marie and Jacques, mother of Clément. Both facilitators had been through the programme before delivering it and seemed to understand how hard it could be to attend the first meeting. The other members of the group looked at each other. Françoise didn't mix too much with them; she wasn't interested in making friends.

Then came the 'What do I do as my parents' workshop. In small groups, everyone was sharing ideas. Some of the participants seemed so comfortable talking about their families! Françoise didn't want to talk about herself; she had been estranged from her parents for years. She just sat there listening, her backpack still on her back. But then, when all the groups were writing their ideas on the flipchart, it hit her! She froze, petrified: 'I cook like my father!' The words came out of her mouth as she was still stunned by the idea. So, there are certain things she does just like her parents! Was it possible that other behaviours had been passed on to her without her being aware of it? Could this have influenced

The Intergenerational Effects of Adverse Childhood Experiences: Ripples on a Pond,
First Edition. Edited by Richard Pates and Diane Riley.

Published 2026 by John Wiley & Sons Ltd.

> what she was going through today? These were the questions she was to explore by taking part in 'A Family Affair!'.
>
> Over the course of the 8 'A Family Affair!' meetings she attended, Françoise dropped her backpack. She discovered that certain behaviours in her family were passed down from generation to generation, and that she had the power to break this pattern. She learned to express her feelings, to take a step back from the situations she experienced in her daily life and to listen to others. She was able to reconnect with her parents and siblings and have pacified conversations with them. Her relationship with her son has also improved. He is being monitored by the drug addiction treatment centre, and since she joined the programme, he has been attending all his appointments, as if Françoise's repositioning in the family and her appeasement had had an influence on him too.

This is the story of Françoise who experienced the 'Une affaire de famille !' (A Family Affair! (AFA)) programme. The programme was created in the 1990s by Line Caron, a public health professional who was in charge of the addiction unit of the Quebec Regional Public Health Directorate of the Côte Nord, when she realised that they could only do so much with some users of addiction treatment centres without addressing the broader issue of family functioning. In this chapter, we present the theoretical roots of the programme, its main components and impact. Since 2020, we have been conducting a research project (the PATTERN project) to identify AFA's causal model and theories of change and to evaluate the impact and effects of the programme on its beneficiaries. Most of the material presented here comes from the PATTERN project. Readers can find out more about this research project in our research report (David et al. 2023).

Assumptions underpinning the programme

The programme is based on three main assumptions. The first is that dysfunctional families are characterised by a hyper-organisation of their relationships, resulting in rigidity in their functioning.

On this issue of rigidity, the facilitator's guide explains that problematic behaviours appear to be attempts to regulate the family system. These patterns of behaviour then create a state of distress that families alleviate by adopting a set of rules and by confining their members to certain roles. To maintain the stability of the family, these rules and roles remain unchallenged, preventing the family from adapting its functioning. Interestingly, dysfunctional families could be seen as actually well-organised but locked into a rigid mode of functioning that can lead to the reproduction of the same patterns of suffering and behaviours across generations. These families often impose secrets and loyalties that are passed down from one generation to the next.

The second assumption is that individuals from troubled families, such as those affected by substance use disorders (SUDs), have a low degree of *differentiation of self*. This concept (Bowen 1978; Calatrava et al. 2022) refers to the degree to which an individual's emotional and intellectual functioning are distinct, which influences their ability to remain emotionally objective in stressful situations.

Finally, the third assumption, derived from the systemic perspective, is that by bringing about changes in one family member, the programme is likely to change the whole family system. The programme adopts an intergenerational perspective of the family as 'the prevention of psychosocial functioning problems must take into account the relational models of previous generations in order to have an impact on the present' (Caron and RRSSS Côte-Nord 2003: our translation).

Aims and main features of the programme

A Family Affair! aims to prevent the intergenerational transmission of the difficulties faced within a family. It enables participants to:

- avoid the transmission of suffering related to family dysfunction to the next generation.
- free themselves from the suffering associated with their family of origin (Caron 2020).

The programme consists of a structured sequence of activities, the framework of which is set out in a facilitator's guide (Caron and RRSSS Côte-Nord 2003; Caron 2020). Its main features are the following:

- It targets adults from families affected by SUDs, but can also address other intra-family problems, such as violence, depression and emotional dependence.
- It consists of 12 modules unfolding over a period of 6 months, in 8 3-hour sessions.
- It includes a variety of activities such as role-plays, questionnaires, group discussions, presentations and applications of learning in real-life situations.
- Specially trained professionals facilitate groups of up to 12 people, none being from the same family.

In France, the programme is run by a national NGO, *Association Addictions France*, which provides free-of-charge prevention, care and harm reduction services. *Addictions France* has been implementing the programme in the regions of Normandy and La Réunion since 2012 and 2017, respectively. A Family Affair! is currently being rolled out in other regions of France.

The 12 modules cover different aspects of family functioning. The first one builds a sense of trust in the group and asks participants about the family in which they grew up. An activity around family and addictions can also be added, depending on the issues that brought the participants to the programme.

The second and third modules deal with roles and rules within the families. From the fourth module on, the participants seem to be sufficiently equipped to deal with more sensitive topics such as the survival strategies put in place when one goes through ACEs and the phenomenon of emotional dependency. They will then start working on the intergenerational transmission by addressing concepts such as abandonment, attachment and relationship with their children. They never talk about their history, but only about the emotions felt. They will also build their own genogram, a family map showing the relationships between family members and draw up action plans for the future. Finally, it is worth noting that the activities follow a logic of gradation of emotional intensity, allowing the participants to tackle increasingly more difficult issues without activating defence mechanisms as their ability to cope with difficulties increases.

All the modules follow the same pattern. Participants are greeted with coffee and biscuits and asked how they feel and have felt over the past few days. The facilitators are really part of the group. They accompany the participants, not so much as professionals but as members of a family themselves and as former participants in 'A Family Affair!'. In small groups, the participants take part in experiential workshops and after realising that their emotions are also shared by other members of the group, they learn the core concepts related to the workshop. For example, they are asked how they reacted when there was a conflict between their parents and reflect on this in small groups. Then, one group member will share his/her reflections with the whole group. This helps participants distance themselves from their emotions by learning to analyse their own reactions. The facilitators then explain what a survival behaviour is, which helps participants further distance themselves from their emotions and to improve their understanding of what they are experiencing on a daily basis. In between sessions of the programme, they are asked to pay attention to what they see from their new understanding and to try to experiment with solutions they can implement. The facilitators also make themselves available to participants who may need support between the sessions.

Main transformations generated by the programme

Figure 16.1 shows the logic model we inferred from the material analysed in the PATTERN project. In order to identify the key transformations generated by the programme, we explored the link between the activities carried out and the changes reported by the participants and facilitators. With the guiding question, 'What is happening in the minds of people exposed to the activities?', two types of impacts emerged: (1) cognitive impacts related to participants' learning about family systems, the suffering they can cause and the process of intergenerational transmission; and (2) impacts on their vision of and connection to the programme.

Participants showed a particularly good understanding of the concepts of roles and rules, which were the most spontaneously mentioned topics when

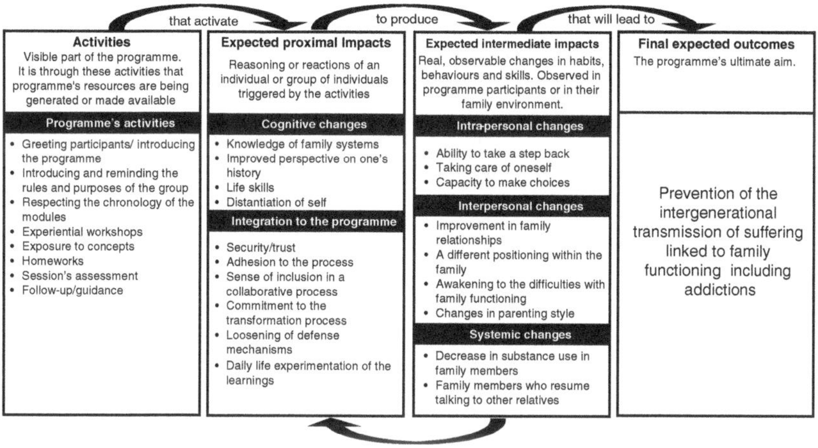

Figure 16.1 Logic model of the 'A Family Affair!' programme.

asked about what they had learned from the programme, especially after the genogram exercise. Roles and rules are covered in the first three sessions, with the third session being described by the facilitators as a 'pivotal session'. According to them, this session marked a change in both the beneficiaries and the group dynamics.

The programme's activities also foster in participants a more positive view of their life history. In particular, through the genogram, they are invited to 'retrace their family history and understand it to enable them to differentiate themselves from their family of origin' (Caron and RRSSS Côte-Nord 2003: our translation). Participants reported an ability to reflect on their past without feeling the pain associated with it, and they demonstrated a remarkable ease in sharing their family history, even when it included difficult episodes.

An important change for participants is their vision of the programme; a positive vision being a *sine qua non* condition for successful integration into the process. They had come to believe that the programme could help them and that their participation would be risk-free. Several participants expressed a sense of security and confidence during the sessions.

> When we started the training, when the conditions were set out, we were reassured that we were safe, that we could talk to each other, and then it was off we went [...]. What I remember most was the feeling of togetherness. We were united enough, respectful enough to share and listen to each other.
>
> (PA03)

Group dynamics play an important role in the integration process in the programme. Participants reported that the group atmosphere supported them throughout their journey. The fact that they no longer felt alone in their situation enabled them to take a step back. Several respondents mentioned that working in small groups made them feel useful, as they appreciated not only receiving support but also helping others.

> The group is good because we help and support each other, and we're better able to open up and find the right words to say things.
>
> (PA09)

> The [programme] facilitators really had this ability to put us at ease [...] the rules were set and the way they were set, why we were there, and the point of sharing together, in the end, it came naturally.
>
> (PA13)

The homework recommended by the programme helps embed learning in participants' daily lives.

> I really appreciated the preparatory work that had to be done between the sessions. The day before or a few days before, I'd go back to my folder [containing all the documents distributed by the facilitators] to prepare something.
>
> (PA08)

Impact on the participants' lives

We identified three types of transformations experienced by the participants and their families. We categorised them as intrapersonal, interpersonal and systemic changes. Participants clearly emphasised the need to distance themselves from their family history. They reported being able to step back from family situations to reflect on the situation rather than react intensely.

> We were given the keys to get rid of the big suitcases we were carrying. [...] It goes to the heart of things, our childhood, our family, our relationships with others.
>
> (PA09)

Participants testified that they had become the protagonists of their lives again and that they were able to make their own choices. For example, some had changed jobs and attributed this change to their participation in the programme. One participant resumed driving her car after feeling unable to do so following a traumatic event. Although most of the changes reported were modest, such as adjusting the timing of calls to a relative or having a spouse pick up their children from school, these changes had a meaningful impact on their daily lives.

> I no longer hang out with my friends outside the boutique [...]. I've even sorted out my relationships. (In La Réunion, a 'boutique' is a shop somewhere between a grocery store and a bar, where men traditionally gather to socialize.)
>
> (PA10)

Some participants also confided that they were taking better care of themselves and had rediscovered the pleasure of taking care of their appearance. This is also emphasised by the facilitators, who reported cases of participants who have undergone changes from one programme session to the next, which they liken to a metamorphosis.

> It's incredible, we say this every time with our colleagues, how we can see this person transform over the course of the sessions. Transformed in what they tell us but also transformed in their behaviour, the way they dress, the way they carry themselves.
>
> (FA01)

Taking care of oneself also means stopping prioritising the needs of others over one's own.

Interpersonal relationships are a locus of change mentioned by all participants. They reported improved relationships with family members, whether with partners, parents or siblings, or even with their own adult children. Some participants were able to make peace with one or other of their parents or discuss their family's past, which they attributed to the program.

> The results of the programme that I've felt are mainly in my relationship. [...] I feel that my partner is more loving, attentive, and supportive. We share... he's more supportive, more polite. [...] We're quite close, and we manage to do more and more things together, we have more and more to share.
>
> (PA04)

> I'm closer to my children. I had to cut the umbilical cord to let them live.
>
> (PA07)

> I was able to get closer to my father at the end of his life. I saw his love.
>
> (PA08)

Our respondents also reported changes in their attitudes towards their family. For example, they decided to no longer take responsibility for organising family meals, or to stop being 'the one who always looks after the parents' or stop solving their siblings' problems, or they regained the choice to do so and are no longer confined to a role.

> In my family I've been given a role [...] now that I know I've been given that role, it's easier for me to say it's your problem, it's not mine.
>
> (PA01)

> I do a lot of things for my 75-year-old father, and I couldn't say no to him [...] I was the one I always put behind, and there was a change in my stance.
>
> (PA09)

Participants also credited the programme with increasing their awareness of their family situation. This was particularly evident in the case of substance use-related issues, where several beneficiaries only became aware of a recurring family problem of addiction after participating in AFA.

> I had an alcoholic uncle who died of liver cancer. Talking about him in 'A Family Affair!' with the genogram [i.e. a family tree featuring information about critical family events] reminded me of my uncle. I told myself I don't want to end up like him.
>
> (PA08)

> I've noticed that it [the alcohol problem] goes back to my great-grandfathers, my great-grandmothers [...]. I wouldn't have thought it was almost hereditary.
>
> (PA10)

Parenting practices were also identified as a locus of change triggered by the programme. Parents reported that they had adopted a more communication-based approach, had stopped hitting their children, had become more assertive in their choices, and had ceased intervening in disputes.

> When it comes to my daughter's education, I've decided to change things. To stop talking about certain subjects the way I used to.
>
> (PA09)

> We've got a pretty tough upbringing here. The whip, the slaps, and all that. For me, that's all over. [...] Just because my dad and I went through that doesn't mean my son has to.
>
> (PA10)

In addition to changes in interpersonal relationships, we have documented a number of changes (referred to as systemic changes) within the wider family system that cannot be directly linked to the programme participants themselves. For example, they report improvements in relationships between other family members, such as between a participant's spouse and their daughter, or the opening up of dialogue about family secrets between a participant's father and his extended family.

> There was little dialogue with the children when my husband was suffering from alcoholism. [...] my daughter now wants to have this dialogue, and so does my husband. And all this started to happen in the months after [the programme].
>
> (PA04)

We also documented one case where a participant reported a reduction in her partner's substance use (PA13).

> I've changed my position towards my partner. As soon as my anxiety comes back or I absolutely want to help and support him [...] I reposition myself. [...] He too is doing his job and is really freeing himself from his addiction.
>
> (PA13)

General observations on a family affair!

An implicit aim of 'A Family Affair!' is to 'repair' the adults in order to stop the intergenerational reproduction of suffering, which can take the form of various problems such as addictive behaviours. The aim is to 'protect' the next generation. In this sense, AFA is a prevention programme in the truest sense of the term.

We have documented several elements that make this programme stand out. One is that the transformations it generates in its participants can reverberate over a large spectrum of individual and family problems, such as SUDs, violence and depression. This is something that is less likely to happen when focusing on a specific problem and not its root causes as we sometimes see in therapies focusing on specific addictive conduct.

Interestingly, we found both young childless adults and grandparents in the participant groups. And in both cases, it can be argued that their inclusion in the programme is an investment in the well-being of future generations. The reported improvements in quality of life experienced by a grandmother, who was well into her 60s, suggest a potential trickle-down effect to her grandchildren. This example, and the others mentioned above, also show that the programme can have a ripple effect through a single family member on a large group of non-participants from the extended family.

Another important feature of the programme is the way changes are brought about through a collective process. The participants interviewed for the PATTERN project all insisted on the fact that 'A Family Affair!' was not a therapy. And the reason for this has to do with two elements of the programme. Firstly, the facilitators make sure that they introduce themselves as members of a family, like anyone else at the table. They also confide that they have been through the programme and are therefore familiar with the different emotional states the participants will go through. Secondly, each session includes a small group activity in which participants reported that they felt they were helping other participants. We had a number of testimonies from participants who looked forward to the debrief session, which takes place 6 months after the end of the programme, saying that they were curious to see whether X's or Y's life had improved.

> They have a theme, and we let them work on it and discuss it [...] the facilitators make the link with the topic of the day. That's the fundamental difference with [clinical] interviews: we listen and don't interpret.
>
> (FA03)

Many questions are left unanswered with this first phase of our interventional research project. Firstly, we do not know for sure whether the programme has a significant and positive impact on people's lives. In PATTERN 2, our first prospective evaluation of the impact of the programme on a small sample of participants, we found no effect on psychological well-being but a significant effect on family adaptability and cohesion. This evaluation was performed primarily to field test our recruitment strategy and data collection instruments.

Our next step will be to carry out a more ambitious evaluation, recruiting participants over a longer period to achieve sufficient statistical power.

Secondly, we still ignore what makes participants drop out of the programme and who they are. We need to test at least three hypotheses. One that participants simply do not see the point of continuing the session. Either they feel that the programme is not for them, or they feel that the few sessions they attended were good enough to improve their lives. Two, that the programme made them experience something quite negative, which could have been harmful. Three, that the programme does not account for some of their constraints and lack of resources (e.g. childcare, transport and literacy levels). If confirmed, this last hypothesis would suggest that the programme may be contributing to increasing inequities in access to these types of resources. With PATTERN 2, we have been able to collect data on the profile of participants, and we have found that low socioeconomic status people are under-represented. However, we still need to collect data on those participants who do not complete the programme.

Conclusion

At this stage, our evaluation of 'A Family Affair!' suggests that this programme has the potential to address adverse childhood experiences and, in so doing, break the cycle of transmission to the next generation. The logic model which we inferred from our interviews with participants and facilitators and from the documents describing the programme shows a coherent construct linking the theory underpinning the programme, its mode of action and the outcomes reported by participants. This leads us to conclude that 'A Family Affair!' is promising and has great potential for addressing adverse childhood experiences.

References

Bowen, M. (1978). *Family Therapy in Clinical Practice.* New York: Jason Aronson.

Calatrava, M., Martins, M.V., Schweer-Collins, M. et al. (2022). Differentiation of self: a scoping review of Bowen Family Systems Theory's core construct. *Clinical Psychology Review* 91: 102101. https://doi.org/10.1016/j.cpr.2021.102101.

Caron, L. (2020) Une affaire de famille!: Programme de prévention de la transmission générationnelle: Guide de l'animateur (3e éd.). Baie-Comeau: Régie régionale de la santé et des services sociaux de la Côte-Nord.

Caron, L. and RRSSS Côte-Nord (2003). Une affaire de famille!: Programme de prévention de la transmission générationnelle: Guide de l'animateur (2e éd.). Baie-Comeau: Régie régionale de la santé et des services sociaux de la Côte-Nord.

David, E., Couderc, C., Bellegarde, J. et al. (2023). *Construire la preuve de l'efficacité d'un programme de prévention des addictions: rapport sur le 1er volet du projet de recherche interventionnelle PATTERN sur le programme «Une affaire de famille!».* Rennes: EHESP et Laboratoire Arènes (UMR CNRS 6051: équipe RSMS INSERM U1309) https://hal.science/hal-04213607.

Chapter 17

ART THERAPY: SAFE (ENOUGH) SPACES TO EXPRESS CREATIVELY WHAT WORDS CAN'T SAY

Deirdre McConnell

School of English, Faculty of Arts and Humanities, Sheffield University, Sheffield, UK

Anchoring bubbles

Inspirational poet and activist Audre Lorde described her childhood thinking process and how it differed from others. She wrote: 'When I was in high school ... I saw the way other people thought, and it was an amazement to me – step by step, not in bubbles up from chaos that you had to anchor with words' (Lorde and Rich 1981, p. 715). Her phrase 'bubbles up from chaos' is a striking image that chimes with the expression of the unutterable that art therapy facilitates. Releasing bubbles of emotion that take on tangible, visual forms in art therapy helps anchor emotional experience and then, possibly, find words.

Art therapy exists in many countries and has been adapted in different ways. In the United Kingdom, it was born during the Second World War, with an artist providing an art studio as a 'dynamic form of treatment' in a psychiatric hospital (Adamson 2014, p. 1). Art therapy (also known as art psychotherapy) is an allied health profession regulated by the Health and Care Professions Council. Literature on art therapy with children who have experienced trauma is extensive. It includes case studies on complex family trauma (O'Brien 2004), early relational trauma (Chong 2015), working with children in schools (Markland 2011) and a synthesis of research and practice when treating trauma through the expressive arts (Malchiodi 2020). In my 40 years as a teacher and art therapist, I have seen the effects of inter-generational ACEs and have witnessed changes that art therapy can bring. Later in the chapter, I will share the work that a child and I did together.

The Intergenerational Effects of Adverse Childhood Experiences: Ripples on a Pond, First Edition. Edited by Richard Pates and Diane Riley.

Published 2026 by John Wiley & Sons Ltd.

Becoming an art therapist

In the mid-1980s, after having taught in high schools, I worked for several years as an art teacher in a residential centre for teenage girls who had experienced difficulties at home and breakdowns of foster placements and were permanently excluded from school. These girls were victims but also survivors of abuse. Keen to learn how to understand these children better, I asked for a secondment from my teaching post to train as an art therapist. My trainee placement was in the children's inpatient unit in the local psychiatric hospital. The course introduced me to practical methods and theoretical frameworks integrating art-making with psychotherapy. Art materials serve as a fluid, creative medium, offering children a sense of freedom, control, achievement and an outlet for non-verbal expression. I like Diane Waller's advice to art therapists about playfulness in art therapy: 'We should be like our materials, inviting, exciting and easy to use!' (Walker 1978, quoted in Waller 1991).

Teacher-therapist in a children's home

After my art therapy training, I worked in a teaching service that mediated between social services and schools to serve the city's looked-after children. My formal role was as an art teacher since the local authority could not create an art therapy post; the health department would need to fund that. I worked during the decade of the 1990s in a residential children's home for primary-aged pupils who needed long-term support before being considered for a foster placement or adoption. My newly gained art therapy skills helped me as a teacher/advocate for children. Our small, tightly knit team worked with children on-site and then coordinated school placements for them. In my direct work with children as an art therapist, my first goal was to establish a 'safe enough' environment where children could use art materials at their own pace. I say safe enough because children who have had only dangerous and ambiguous spaces to play in (where love, trust and abuse overlap in complex layers) need time for a more profound sense of safety to develop in later sessions. The art therapist has to prove their reliability, metaphorically 'holding' the space and 'containing' the child, the work and their own experiences in response. The child's expression and engagement are encapsulated in the art, which may communicate something, perhaps unintended or unconscious. The children's trauma, stored in preverbal spaces, may resonate in the therapist's somatic experience, which becomes a medium of expression for the child.

Art therapy in schools – Olive's story

In the early 2000s, education and social policy changed, and in some parts of the country, arts therapies were introduced into schools. I was seconded to set up school art therapy interventions as part of coordinated services for refugee children arriving from war-torn countries. Within 3 years, the referral criteria broadened to include all children affected by traumatic experiences, whatever their circumstances. A multidisciplinary team referred a 7-year-old child to me for art therapy support; she was at risk of permanent exclusion from school. I call her 'Olive'; this is not her real name.

The behaviour support services stated that the range of Olive's behaviours 'appeared to vary from mildly disruptive, shouting out, calling names and wandering off, to very challenging behaviours of kicking, screaming, biting and punching. Sometimes, she was dominant and threatening in her play with other children'. The clinical psychologist had found that Olive had 'significant difficulties in many areas of learning comprehension and processing' and a 'pattern of over-familiarity and aggression with adults'. The educational psychologist who assessed Olive's needs said she was 'a child with complex emotions and complex adult relationships' and that 'the trigger for a difficult behaviour may, at times, to staff, be difficult to fathom, as it emerges from Olive's internal emotional environment'. It was hoped that art therapy would help Olive with her emotional inner life.

Olive's big inner-city school in the North of England was culturally diverse, with over thirty languages spoken. Professionals adopted a supportive approach when working with the school's children and families. In Olive's case, they were aware of the need to be reflexive about intergenerational trauma experienced by the Afro-Caribbean community, pressures of racism and socio-economic difficulties and urban violence that contributed to Olive's family's difficulties (Pillow 2019). Olive had witnessed the shooting of her oldest brother, who was injured and in prison. Education home support personnel reported a 'nuclear and extended family tradition of bullying', from adults to children, especially towards Olive's other brother, a few years older than her, of whom her mother 'was sometimes scared'. Olive's mother 'managed her punitively, under pressure from her [Olive's] father', who acted with what we would now call coercive control. He spent half his time with his other family on the opposite side of the city. When Olive and her brother were placed on the Child Protection Register for several months, their family no longer accepted contact with the health services who had reported the child abuse. Trusted by Olive's parents, the school staff and the 'team around the child' worked with her father and mother to change home chastisement patterns and improve family dynamics. The relationship between the health services and the family was gradually rebuilt.

Olive and I worked together for 15 months alongside the ongoing systemic family support. Our weekly 1-hour sessions had firm space and time boundaries. Olive was a delightful, lively and curious child. Her energy was sometimes like a whirlwind of rapidly changing emotions, driving her mood and movements. At the start, she explored all aspects of the physical space of the art therapy room. I knew she needed non-judgemental spaciousness, where anything could be expressed uncensored. We worked with what arose, amplifying and expanding ideas like riffs or musical variations of tunes. The space between us became rich with associations and evolving rhythms as themes developed. Together, we gradually created the 'feel' of the time that was our weekly 1-hour meeting. In the early sessions, Olive sometimes wandered out of the room. Perhaps, I thought, she was testing me to see what I would do. Would I follow her or maybe insist that she return? I gently explained that if she left the room, I would wait for her to return when she was ready. But how would she know I would be there for her when she came back? Would I accept her as she was? Would I scold her for running out, rummaging in the room or falling asleep? She always returned. Our journey together was long and adventurous, sometimes intense, often fun and everything in between. After a year, Olive's anxiety had reduced significantly; she could focus and create art more typical for her chronological age (in widely understood child development terms). This lengthy process required trust and risk-taking on both sides. The following seven pictures, selected from the many she made and reproduced with permission, show how our work evolved through several phases over the 35 sessions.

Sensory experimentation

Session 3

This artwork is representative of the work Olive made in her first sessions. She became absorbed in sensory experimentation and played with the art materials for short periods. Here, there are fragments of everyday life, a football pitch in red on the middle-right, a barely perceptible sun in the centre, two plates of food (including 'relation-chips') on the left – (she asked me to guess which foods) – and fringes cut round the edges which symbolised 'home'.

There was also the 'Fire of London' in orange felt pen and a bomb above it.

'... and a plate of relation – chips'

While making this piece of art, Olive gave me glimpses of her self-image in words: 'I want to get run over by a car, I'm bad, I've been bad!' She knew she had 'been bad' because of a consequence she had been given; she had been denied a treat outing at a takeaway restaurant. When I asked Olive what 'bad' was, she said she didn't know. In some moments, I felt she had a global sense of being 'badness' itself. Her desire to self-harm was worrying.

During the sessions, I noticed my feelings arising in the moment in response to Olive's words, actions, choices and emotions, including intense distress. When she was physically present in the room, I remained relaxed yet alert, staying attentive to her 'being': to what she paid attention to and how she focused that attention. I did not (and could not) know what was going on within her mind, but I could allow her the spaciousness for her mind to wander and follow any lines of enquiry she desired. Providing an opportunity to play (which is work for children) in a safe space, I welcomed her expressions and aimed to affirm her intentions by responding to her choices and sometimes mirroring them. This way of working kept us both interested and engaged in what was happening in the present moment.

Relational problem-solving

Session 4

When I collected Olive for this session, she was standing with the deputy headteacher: she had kicked her teacher (a trainee) in the morning. Olive gingerly touched the paints in the art therapy room and painted a little with her fingertips. She said it was like 'poo, blood and eggs' and washed her hands several times to clean and rid herself of any trace. Then she created the piece below, engrossed in experimenting with how glitter glue glows on paper.

She liked the different textures and the shininess of the sequins.

'The soft feathers and shiny sequins'

As Olive worked, she did not talk about the image, but once relaxed, she started talking about the morning's events that were on her mind. She told me how angry she had been with her teacher, who was not her 'proper teacher'. She did not want to do her work and didn't want to attend school anymore. She stopped working on her picture and told me she would get her brother to come and 'beat the teacher up'. I wondered out loud about how upset she was. We talked about her feelings around the incident, before and after. We were sitting near each other, and when our speaking got close to her complicated feelings, all mixed and muddled up, she leaned her shoulder on me gently and became very quiet. After some moments of silence, she asked, 'How can I tell Miss I'm sorry?' We discussed possible ways of letting Miss know and the idea of creating a card arose. Olive liked this, made a card, and gave it to Miss at the end of our session.

'I needed this'

Session 13

This was the first session after the Summer holiday. We had been given a different room. The first thing Olive did was reach for the paints and brush. She sat at the table, declared, 'I needed this!' and proceeded to paint her left hand and print with it. Then she asked me to paint her right hand, and she printed both hands in turquoise, then brown.

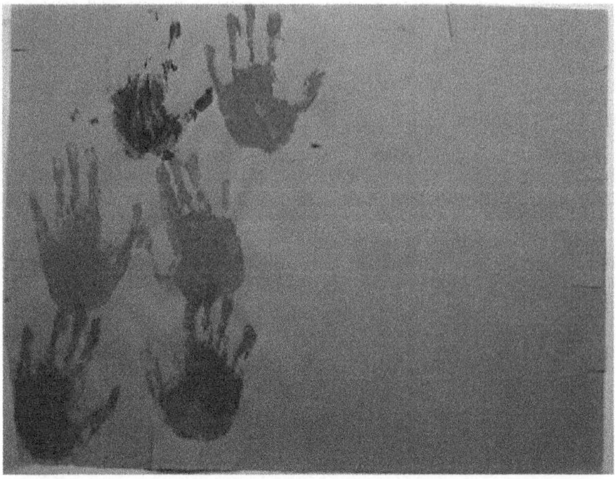

'Olive's hand prints'

There are at least two points of interest here. Firstly, it was as if Olive needed to 'make her mark' in this new room at the start of Year 3 and her move up to Key Stage 2, a significant transition for all pupils. She was reclaiming her art therapy space, investing in it in a new way. Able to stay without darting out of the room, she engaged with the materials, using her body as an identity stamp – her handprint. Secondly, Olive could tolerate the paint on her hands. What had been partly disgusting to her before, associated with bodily excretion and the unclean, was now a valued material for creating art, which she embraced, expanding creative possibilities. The unpainted half of the page seems to signify potential. A new development emerged; we played mirroring games, taking turns to lead. Olive mirrored slow movements for a few seconds. There was also time for free play with toys in the room and role-playing scenes of cooking at home and buying at the shops and the post office.

'I'm the teacher – you're the bad girl'

Session 18

The room had a flipchart, which stimulated a new phase in our work from the 14th to the 20th sessions. This started with Olive creating a classroom environment. The flipchart simulated a whiteboard: she gathered some books and packets of pastel crayons as rewards. Olive played the role of teacher, first collecting ideas from the class (me) on how to keep the room clean for a science lesson. She told a story about a bully, 'reading' from a book held sideways, describing and turning each page. Using her script, she wrote the children's names on the flipchart, with corresponding ticks for good behaviour and crosses for bad behaviour, as her teacher did. This was the assertive discipline method of classroom management. I switched roles, representing different children. Olive enjoyed this very much. Her teaching style was strict, but she rewarded those who did as told. This continued, with variations, for seven sessions. In the image below, the behaviour of all 'her pupils' was good.

She gave us both ticks. Her name, spelt correctly, is deleted on the top left.

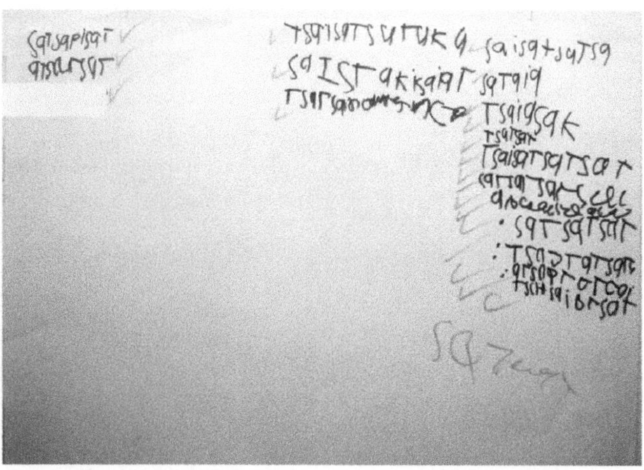

'Assertive discipline in action'

Olive appeared to be exploring what 'good' and 'bad' are, the nature of boundaries in school, what a sense of order in the classroom means, why it exists and how it is created. It seemed she was interested in understanding something about the feelings of the teacher managing a class of thirty children. Gradually, she appeared to be gaining positive ideas about relationships in school, respect and fairness. However, at this stage in her play, she usually needed to gain control in an authoritarian way. Simultaneously, the theme of her father's authoritative role in the home, which she showed in earlier sessions, started to diminish, and she also started talking more fondly about her mother.

Six sessions later, at the beginning of the 24th session, Olive told me that she liked working with me. At the end of that same session, she announced, 'I hate you!' I wondered aloud, suggesting it might be difficult for her when the sessions ended. She agreed. The sessions could contain strongly opposing complex feelings, and that was alright.

Symbiosis

Session 28

During the seven-session phase of Olive being a teacher, she had not been able to tolerate the idea of us taking turns. But in this next phase, there was a change. We started to take turns being the teacher. In this session, towards the end of the art therapy intervention, after a warm-up period of some turn-taking role play and doing an initial drawing, Olive settled thoughtfully at the table with paper and pastels. She delighted in the colours and let associations form in her mind. Pink was for happiness.

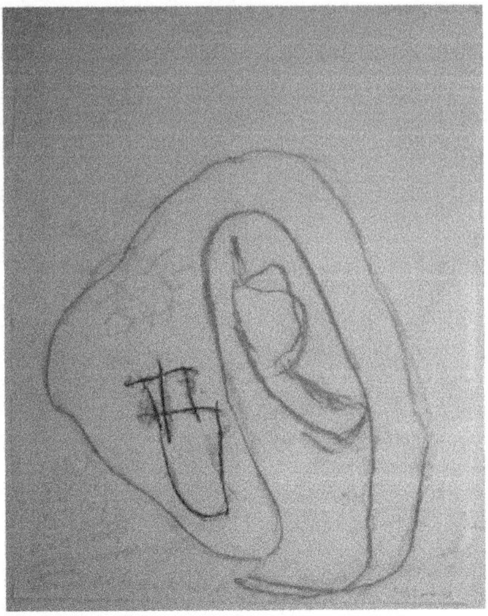

'Olive and Deirdre's home'

The drawing, she said, was a home for her and me. While writing in her script, she narrated a story about our work together, some of what we had done, and how good it felt to be in the art therapy room. Her verbal and visual eloquence touched me. She was accepting me in a new way, inviting me into the picture. The outer shape holds the forms within it: the sun, a drink and us in the house. It seemed a moment of symbiosis, where she and I were metaphorically merged. The drawing resonates with the image of a foetus, conveying the newness of growth and flourishing of potential which I perceived in Olive.

A narrative of the farm

Session 29

Springing from confidence in her abilities in the art therapy room, in image making and imaginative work, Olive started to bring wider socio-cultural themes into her artwork. In this picture, she created a scene from a television programme about a farm. She first drew a rainbow with several colours woven on each other and extended it to make a circular shape. She added her name in large letters at the bottom of the circle (deleted) and wrote more letters, which she asked me to read out. She wrote 'Mom' in a speech bubble.

'The Farm – looking after the animals'

Olive then used sequins, chalk and pastels to represent parts of the story while she told it. Sequins suggested a hotel near the farm. She added cows, green grass for their food and a pond of blue water for them to drink, with fish in it. She was nurturing these farm animals. Olive delighted in the process of communicating and developing ideas and a theme. This picture marked a significant shift from the sensory, fragmented associations in the images she had made a year earlier, and the chart markings of classroom role-play. Increasingly, she found words to accompany her images; her verbal and emotional vocabulary grew. She had anchored 'bubbles up from chaos' with her play, role-play, artwork and words.

The gift

Session 32

Our ending process began by reviewing what we had done together over the 15 months and how much Olive had learned. She was now growing up, attending full-time lessons with her school class, and was much happier. She was more positive in her language about mum, dad, school and school staff; her difficulties in school were rarer, and her vulnerability to permanent exclusion from school seemed a distant past. Olive's internal emotional environment, which the educational psychologist had said may have been the source of triggers that led to Olive's behaviours, had changed significantly.

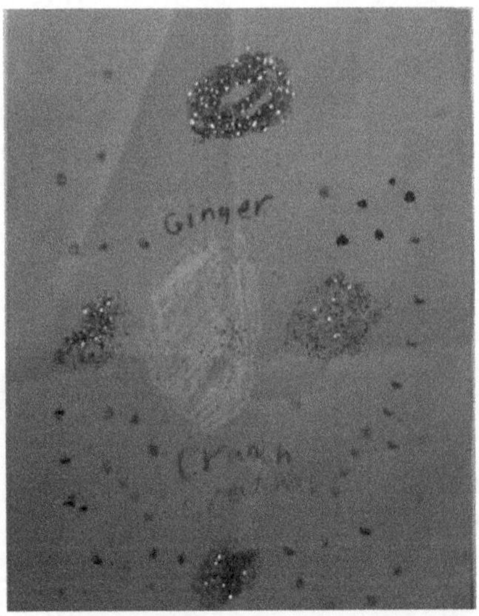

'Ginger biscuit gift'

In this session, Olive extended her drawing skills to include observational inquiry. There was a packet of biscuits in the room; she used this as a resource to make a drawing for a new person who was becoming special to her in school. She was careful with the lettering and enjoyed using the glitter glue, and she had fun with the decorative colour dots and creating symmetry. This piece is about relationality. Made within our therapeutic relationship when we had three sessions left, it was destined for the skilled teaching assistant who had started to build a relationship with Olive. At the time, the local authority's process for deciding what provision was best for each child with complex needs involved collating assessments completed by professionals in the multidisciplinary team around the child and the parents' views. A casework team considered all the advice and issued an Educational Statement identifying how best to meet the child's needs. Olive's case resulted in the recommendation of full-time support from a suitably matched teaching assistant. The local authority funded the post, which, bespoke to Olive's needs, facilitated her remaining in mainstream school.

Olive's decision to make and gift this picture demonstrated her positive feelings. The teaching assistant warmly appreciated Olive's gift. These interactions contributed to a smooth and healthy transition from my work with Olive to the following professional, who would provide Olive with steady support in school in the future. When the time came for our work to end, 3 weeks later, the closing process was careful and sensitive on both sides. I was happy that 'bubbles up from chaos' had been anchored in our work with Olive's sensory and visual experimentations, her play, artwork, words and all this meant.

Thoughts on my work with Olive

I could not know how Olive would respond to my ideas and presence from 1 week to the next. But I got to know her 'way of being' in the world, or at least her way of being with me. I needed to accept 'not knowing for certain' and work towards 'new knowing'. Immediately after each session, I reflected on what had taken place and what I felt and thought was happening between us and within me (known as transference and countertransference). Drawing on my practical experience and theoretical training, I formulated hypotheses about what might have been happening, informing how I prepared the room and my mind for the next session. I found the work of Melanie Klein, Carl Jung and Donald Winnicott to be helpful resources in my work with Olive. On occasions when perplexed, I would discuss my feelings and thoughts with my clinical supervisor, also an art psychotherapist.

Olive's intuitive 'knowing' was immense: she knew what she liked and didn't like and what she needed to do. This challenged me to hear, see, feel or sense what she was telling me or showing me: to hold it in mind, reflect on it, make connections and search for meaning. Olive's 'knowing' required a reliable space that welcomed it warmly. Over time, Olive developed longer periods of focused attention and absorption. Though an increased concentration span was essential for engaging in mainstream classrooms, many other relational changes helped her expand her 'window of tolerance' and were also vital (Siegal 2020, p. 341). She started by expressing emotions through her play and artwork, then used mark-making to explore themes of control and cooperation. Finally, she communicated verbally what her artwork meant to her. Art therapy processes enabled connection and communication with Olive's visual and nonverbal expressions. She discovered many things joyfully, taking pride in her creations. In doing so, she started to take pride in herself.

Note on art psychotherapy communication processes

Art therapy involves complex individual and interpersonal learning processes that can later be transferred into broader social situations. Crucially, this work must be done at the child's pace. The creative process, combining play and emergent art-making, helps integrate thoughts and feelings and generate new ones. Researchers have defined three communication processes intrinsic to effective psychotherapy, whatever the modality (Fonagy and Allison 2014). Looking at art therapy with Olive through this lens is helpful. The first process involved Olive feeling that her emotional states were convincingly recognised. Her emotional states were 're-presented' by the images she made, which 'stood for' her emotions. The art-making and artwork spoke for her emotions when she had no words. Through a range of responses to her and her work, I showed her that I recognised her emotional states. My body language and facial expressions showed her that I could recognise her emotion. If I did not, I sought clarification from her to understand better, signalling that she was the expert in her feelings.

This first communication process connected Olive's internal emotional environment with my 'felt' responses. The second communication process was built on this. It involved Olive being able to imagine what I might be thinking. I kept her artwork carefully and securely, which initially surprised her. She gradually felt understood and knew that she was held in mind over time; she understood that her images and the feelings they contained were worthy of respect. She started to trust my thinking, anticipating how I would respond. The third communication process was built on the previous two. It involved Olive transferring the trust she had developed within the therapeutic relationship and her positive self-image into the world outside the therapy room. This could happen because the school responded to her with understanding. The gift Olive made in session 32 exemplifies this. The teaching assistant reciprocated Olive's gesture with warmth, acknowledging her art and action, as well as her effort and kind thoughts. This response reinforced Olive's self-image of being worthy. Rather than a slippery slope downward towards permanent exclusion, the school community and the art therapy together had brought Olive back from the brink, transforming her life and educational trajectory into one of incremental upward change.

Endnote

I am deeply grateful to Olive's school for allowing me to work freely, to Olive's parents, to my supervisor, and most of all to Olive herself for sharing her way of being and innate wisdom with me. With support, Olive stayed in her primary school for the next 3 years and transitioned to mainstream high school with her peers.

References

Adamson, E. (2014). *Art as Healing. Originally Published in 1984*. London: Coventure Ltd.

Chong, J. (2015). Why art psychotherapy? Through the lens of interpersonal neurobiology: the distinctive role of art psychotherapy intervention for clients with early relational trauma. *International Journal of Art Therapy* 20 (3): 118–126.

Fonagy, P. and Allison, E. (2014). The role of mentalizing and epistemic trust in the therapeutic relationship. *Psychotherapy* 51 (3): 372–380.

Lorde, A., & Rich, A.(1981). An interview with Audre Lorde. *Signs, JSTOR*, 64, 713–736. University of Chicago Press. http://www.jstor.org/stable/3173739 (accessed 15 June 2022).

Malchiodi, C. (2020). *Trauma and Expressive Arts Therapy: Brain, Body and the Imagination in the Healing Process*. USA: Guildford Publications.

Markland, F. (2011). Effectiveness of school based art therapy for children who have experienced psychological trauma. [Doctoral dissertation, University of Manchester]. University of Manchester Digital Archive. https://www.research.manchester.ac.uk/portal/files/54513305/FULL_TEXT.PDF.

O'Brien, F. (2004). The making of mess in art therapy: attachment, trauma and the brain. *Inscape* 9 (1): 2–13. https://doi.org/10.1080/02647140408405670.

Pillow, W. (2019) Epistemic witnessing: theoretical responsibilities, decolonial attitude and lenticular futures, *International Journal of Qualitative Studies in Education*, 32:2, 118–135, https://doi.org/10.1080/09518398.2019.1576938

Siegal, D. (2020). *The Developing Mind: How Relationships and the Brain Interact to Shape Who We Are*. New York: Guildford.

Walker, C. (1978). *The Inner Eye. Exhibition Catalogue. Oxford. Quoted in Waller, D. (1991) Becoming a Profession: The History of Art Therapy in Britain 1940–1982*. London and New York: Tavistock/Routledge.

Chapter 18

SOLUTIONS: TOUCH THERAPY AND OTHER THERAPIES

Adam Nicholls

Independent Researcher & Statistical Analyst, Wales, UK

This chapter advocates for the vital reclamation of physical touch as a therapeutic tool for children affected by trauma, particularly in residential childcare settings. By thoughtfully integrating touch into daily interactions, we can significantly enhance emotional regulation and foster healing in those whose experiences have left them profoundly affected.

Traumatic experiences are often stored in the body in ways that bypass verbal expression. This understanding is crucial when addressing the needs of children who have experienced Adverse Childhood Experiences (ACEs), Complex Developmental Trauma, or Post-Traumatic Stress Disorder (PTSD) – conditions arising from overwhelming early experiences before the child's cognitive abilities enable them to articulate their emotions.

Trauma and persistent stress, particularly during foetal and early childhood periods, profoundly alter biological systems in the brain, impacting a child's life long after the trauma has ended (Dalvie and Daskalakis 2021; National Scientific Council on the Developing Child 2014). Gabor Maté and Maté (2022) highlights that early trauma becomes engrained in the nervous system, affecting a child's biology and relationships throughout their life:

McCrory et al. (2011) highlight the profound impact of trauma on brain function by comparing brain scans of traumatised children with those of soldiers before and after combat. His comparisons of the two reveal that children who have experienced maltreatment and domestic violence show increased activation in brain regions linked to threat detection and hypervigilance, resembling patterns seen in soldiers with combat trauma. While this heightened state of alertness can be adaptive in dangerous environments, it often hinders their ability to engage in cognitive tasks, achieve emotional growth, and form healthy relational bonds.

This can give rise to latent vulnerability (McCrory and Viding 2015), which suggests that childhood trauma can create hidden changes in the brain that

The Intergenerational Effects of Adverse Childhood Experiences: Ripples on a Pond, First Edition. Edited by Richard Pates and Diane Riley.

Published 2026 by John Wiley & Sons Ltd.

elevate the long-term risk of developing mental health issues. Even if a psychiatric disorder does not manifest immediately, early adverse experiences can predispose individuals to future problems.

Given this understanding, traditional therapies, such as Cognitive Behavioural Therapy (CBT) and its denominations, may be ineffective or even detrimental for children in a heightened state of survival. These approaches can unintentionally worsen a child's stress responses, reinforcing heightened emotional reactivity and vigilance within the limbic system. This may lead to acting-out behaviours instead of encouraging mind–body control and reflective thought.

Research supports body-based regulation techniques, such as touch, as effective methods within the Bottom-Up approach to trauma treatment. Field (2002) notes that touch stimulates the central nervous system, promoting relaxation and focus in children. Brummelman et al. (2019) found that parental touch alleviates children's fears, regulates anxiety and fosters trust, which is crucial for those affected by trauma. Similarly, Owen and Gillentine (2011) emphasised touch's role in soothing emotions and providing reassurance.

Recognising trauma's impact on children's biological regulation and the therapeutic benefit of touch highlights the need for nurturing interventions. Unfortunately, therapy often lacks physical touch and is limited to 1-hour sessions, which is inadequate for trauma symptoms. Children in care frequently have unmet emotional and physical needs. If their experiences of touch are limited to harm or abuse, they miss learning appropriate, nurturing, therapeutically beneficial touch. Touch should not be limited to scheduled sessions; instead, it should be offered naturally and as frequently as instinct suggests, while remaining genuine and authentic, based on the child's comfort and willingness.

Children need to learn co-regulation of their emotions before they can achieve self-regulation, particularly after experiencing trauma. The instinctive responses of parents are essential in guiding children through this process. For example, when a baby cries, a parent instinctively picks them up, rocks them gently and provides soothing touch to offer comfort. If the baby is hungry, the parent feeds them; if the baby feels cold, the parent provides warmth. These actions, including the parent's slower breathing, rhythmic motions and close physical proximity, create a sense of safety for the child, helping lower their physiological arousal. Additionally, touch triggers the release of oxytocin, which mitigates cortisol levels, calms the amygdala and assists in regulating the child's overall arousal state.

As Silver (2024) explains, if a child has not experienced an adult who can regulate themselves and assist the child, the child cannot manage their fight/flight/freeze response until the neurochemical messengers subside. Reasoning or imposing consequences will not suffice; thus, caregivers must assist the child in recognising, calming and controlling their emotional states. Silver notes, 'Children who have not experienced physical affection may find touch unfamiliar or uncomfortable, but without it, they may never learn to regulate their bodies and emotions without resorting to physical outlets such as running or fighting' (pp. 70–73).

In summary, touch and body-based regulation strategies are essential for supporting children affected by trauma. They help reduce stress, enhance emotional and cognitive processing, teach regulation and promote healthy development.

Prioritising interventions that target a child's survival responses and restore balance to the lower brain regions is essential for establishing a foundation for more effective cognitive and emotional processing later. Without this crucial step, traditional cognitive-based therapies are often inadequate in addressing the root trauma and may reinforce maladaptive survival mechanisms. This can hinder therapeutic progress, leaving the child feeling helpless, unable to control their body and viewing themselves as a victim, rather than understanding they have the power to address and manage their trauma.

This leads to the question: Why are we not touching children more?

To answer this, the following discussion will examine how the UK care system has arrived at its current stance on physical touch, providing a basis for advocating for change grounded in first principles. We will then explore pragmatic solutions to address these issues, with the goal of integrating touch more meaningfully into the care and support of traumatised children.

'Care' in the United Kingdom

In many childcare environments, touch has become increasingly restricted, with staff and caregivers apprehensive about the potential for accusations of misconduct if their actions are misinterpreted. As a result, some settings, like residential care settings, have effectively become 'no touch' zones, significantly limiting opportunities for nurturing physical contact that could benefit children, particularly those who have experienced trauma.

Piper et al. (2006) contend that this widespread fear is driven by two key discourses: the more overt concern about violence, and the more hidden, yet equally powerful fear of sexual misconduct. Together, these fears have shaped the strict regulations in the United Kingdom, which tend to prioritise the protection of staff from potential allegations over the emotional and developmental needs of children. These regulations fall under the guise of 'Child Protection', but they often do more to safeguard adults than to care for vulnerable children.

Although the literature on physical touch is extensive – highlighting its benefits (Packheiser et al. 2024) and warning of its risks (Zirkel 2000) – few sources focus on the confusion and contradictions surrounding this issue, as noted by Piper et al. (2006). This confusion has led to policies advising caregivers to avoid physical touch unless necessary, such as during restraint to prevent harm (Piper and Smith 2003). Consequently, supportive touch, crucial for a child's emotional well-being, has been sidelined in favour of crisis management interventions.

The professionalisation of touch has transformed it from an instinctive, caring gesture into a clinical act focused on protecting staff.

Johnson (2000) attributes this shift to moral panic, where fear influences professional behaviour. Green and Day (2013) note that professionals often feel uneasy about using supportive touch due to concerns over false abuse allegations and crossing boundaries. For example, Lynch and Garrett (2010) found that social workers deemed touch initiated by children or necessary for their safety acceptable, but were hesitant to use touch to express empathy and reassurance because of fears of allegations. However, the fear of accusations of abuse has been disproportionate to actual occurrences (Green 2017), resulting in professionals developing defensive and distorted thinking (Owen and Gillentine 2011).

This paradox creates a distorted dynamic in professional settings: appropriate touch – when given by the right person, at the right time, and in the right manner – is discouraged. In contrast, restrictive or aggressive physical interventions are often deemed acceptable. The fear of accusations can skew caregivers' perceptions, shifting their focus from genuinely supporting children to protecting themselves (Stanley and Goddard 2002). This issue is particularly acute for male staff, who face even greater scrutiny when providing physical comfort, such as a hug, to a child in distress (Piper and Smith 2003).

Phelan (1997) critiques the approach, noting that caregivers often rely on cognitive strategies to manage children's physical behaviours, expecting the children to self-regulate eventually. This approach is unrealistic for children with trauma, who often operate from their limbic system or brainstem, leaving them with little control over their bodily responses.

Ultimately, this moral panic has led to guidelines favouring adult protection over children's emotional needs. Physical touch has become a cautious act, driven by reputation concerns rather than children's well-being. Reclaiming its therapeutic value is essential for improving care for traumatised children.

None of this is helped by the legislative shifts that have occurred within the field of care. Despite its intended purpose of providing healing environments for children affected by trauma or neglect, the concept of 'care' in residential childcare remains poorly defined (Smith 2009). Legislation, such as the 1989 Children Act, the 1995 Children (Scotland) Act, and the Social Services and Well-being (Wales) Act, 2014, rebranded children from being 'in care' to 'looked after and accommodated', with the state assuming the role of 'corporate parent'. Yet, despite these changes, there is still no clear definition of what care should entail.

Residential settings often prioritise safety over relational support, such as love and emotional connection, which are more common in family environments (Cameron et al. 2020). This emphasis on risk management leads to viewing children as 'at risk' or 'dangerous', resulting in excessive assessments for simple activities like picnics (Milligan and Stevens 2006). Consequently, strict regulations on physical contact between staff and children hinder the formation of meaningful therapeutic relationships and the ability to co-regulate children's biological responses to trauma.

The policy shift towards 'caring about' children from a distance, rather than 'caring for' them through direct interaction, undermines the nurturing relationships crucial for their growth (Noddings 2002). Brown et al. (2019) highlight that true care extends beyond rules, advocating for moral and relational engagement. Care should be reciprocal, with staff meeting children's emotional and physical needs through consistent, engaged interactions, rather than through a transactional or bureaucratic lens. The increase in regulations has led to a shift from nurturing relationships towards procedural justice, weakening the relational foundation necessary for children's development.

Bowlby (1969) and Harlow and Zimmerman (1958) highlighted the vital role of touch, stressing that it is not solely about meeting basic needs such as food but also about the feelings of love and comfort that individuals experience. Harlow's experiments demonstrated that emotional connection and physical comfort outweigh material provisions. This reveals a significant issue within the current structure of the care system, which, while capable of addressing physical needs, often fails to provide the love and affection that children deeply desire. Consequently, this lack of emotional nurturing can lead children to disrupt their placements and seek to reunite with their families despite the trauma they have experienced at the hands of the family they were removed from.

Smith (2009) suggested that workers' fears are produced through policies and procedures that attempt to 'impose certainty and order on acts and relationships that are irredeemably uncertain and ambiguous [and where] there are consequences for the slightest breach. In daily residential care practice, this can result in workers' 'fear of touching' young people, of 'emotional intimacy' with them and reluctance to confront challenging behaviour through a fear of allegations being made against them' (p. 95). Piper and Stronach (2008) concluded that the concrete guidelines and the fear of wrongful allegations have impoverished practice and relationships with children and staff.

Del Prete (1998) cautions that the lack of physical contact with children might be viewed as a type of neglect, which can lead to significant issues as they navigate their understanding of acceptable social behaviour. When adults adopt a distant and detached approach, they risk sending the message that aggressive or violent forms of touch are permissible, while affectionate gestures like hugs and gentle pats are not. This disconnect can create confusion for children regarding the nature of healthy relationships.

Piper and Smith (2003) support this, describing that affectionate or supportive touch becomes interpreted as extraordinary and abusive, whereas aggressive touch is regarded as ordinary. This is a stark warning because, as Steckley (2011) says, the clarity given by restraint and 'no touch' policies becomes far preferable to the unprescribed territory of, for example, a young person who simply wants to be held.

While safeguarding is essential, the main objective of residential childcare should be to encourage the development and well-being of children, rather than just ensuring their safety. Existing systems often reserve touch and care for exceptional situations, implying that physical comfort and regulation are only accessible during crises. When such crises arise, caregivers frequently depend on verbal communication, even though they recognise that, in moments of heightened emotional arousal, a child's limbic system – responsible for emotional responses – can overpower their capacity to process verbal cues.

Unfortunately, this situation presents significant challenges for children who have endured trauma, the staff members who strive to support them and the services dedicated to fostering their healing and development. The difficulties stem from the fact that essential components for aiding traumatised children – such as biological, emotional, social, psychological and physical intimacy – are fundamentally at odds with the practices and policies prevalent in residential care homes and 'therapeutic' settings.

Imposing certainty and order in care environments is not feasible; when attempts are made to do so, it leads to negative consequences for both children and staff. This phenomenon can be described as the 'great entropy of care,' where rigid structures imposed on an inherently complex and unpredictable human system result in increased dysfunction and harm. Like natural systems, where entropy signifies a tendency towards disorder, care systems become overwhelmed when inflexible policies disrupt the fluid and personalised needs essential for trauma recovery.

The iatrogenic consequence of the United Kingdom's current approach is that it reinforces the very neglect and trauma it intends to resolve. The irony is that if these same standards were applied to typical parenting (Winnicott 1953), the legal threshold for 'good-enough parenting' would not be met.

Call for change

The solution is clear: reintroduce physical touch as a fundamental part of care and reclaim its therapeutic value. Physical touch should not be seen as a last resort or used only in restraint situations. Instead, it should be integrated into everyday interactions, helping children develop trust and regulation. Understanding the therapeutic benefits of providing the right type of touch, by the right person, at the right time, is far more effective for these children than expecting them to control their bodies cognitively through conversation alone.

Recommendations for practice

Three key principles can guide practice.

1. **Follow the Child's Lead**
   It is essential for caregivers to recognise the brain state of the child and respond appropriately. Engaging with a child cognitively is ineffective if they are in a more reactive, emotional (limbic) state. Children often communicate their needs through their words or behaviours, such as acting out or dissociating. Understanding these signals is crucial.

2. **At the Very Most, Do Something; At the Very Least, Do No Harm**
   The guidelines outlined here are intentionally flexible, as caregiving shouldn't be rigid. This flexibility allows caregivers to connect with each child in a way that supports healing, while giving staff the autonomy to build their skills, confidence and reflective practice. The application of psychology in real-world settings is a nuanced process, and staff should be encouraged to develop their own approach without fear of repercussions when things inevitably go wrong.
3. **Emphasise Fairness and Accountability**
   It is vital that staff are not punished for honest mistakes but are held accountable for any harmful behaviour. If investigations are deemed appropriate, they must be thorough, yet fair, distinguishing between errors and misconduct. Implementing restorative practices, such as facilitated dialogues, can help repair relationships and rebuild trust between staff and children. It's unlikely that a caregiver would worsen a child in care's situation through benign touch. If they were going to worsen a child's life whilst in care, it would most likely be through betrayal (Gobin and Freyd 2009).

Leadership support is essential, ensuring transparency in handling incidents and fostering a culture of trust. Ongoing evaluation, including tracking allegations and feedback from both children and staff, helps refine guidelines and ensure the environment remains safe.

Taken together, these three principles could effectively counteract the 'entropy of care' by promoting a system that is adaptive, responsive and attuned to the real-world complexities of trauma-informed care.

Interventions

Interventions should be based the least intrusive, yet most effective, methods for regulating a child that align with the bottom-up approach and fit within the three principles outlined in this chapter.

Individuals should offer sensory-rich, therapeutic interactions through physical touch, aiming to soothe the nervous system, foster connection, and help children regulate their emotions and engage in higher cognitive processing. Each activity should be rhythmic, repetitive and relational. With this understanding, I encourage readers to explore innovative ways to support children on their journey towards healing and resilience.

Throughout this chapter, I have laid the groundwork for justifying these approaches, drawing upon evidence that underscores the importance of nurturing interventions. Children who have endured unbearable, cumulative traumas are not responsible for what has happened to them; however, they are responsible for managing their trauma – an unjust reality. It is, therefore, our responsibility to apply the knowledge gained in this paper to teach them co-regulation and control over their bodies.

Let us put the care back into 'care'.

References

Bowlby, J. (1969). *Attachment and loss.* In: *Attachment*, vol. 1. New York, NY: Basic Books.

Brown, R., Alderson, H., Kaner, E. et al. (2019). "There are carers, and then there are carers who actually care": conceptualizations of care among looked after children and care leavers, social workers, and carers. *Child Abuse & Neglect* 92: 219–229. https://doi.org/10.1016/j.chiabu.2019.03.002.

Brummelman, E., Terburg, D., Smit, M. et al. (2019). Parental touch reduces social vigilance in children. *Developmental Cognitive Neuroscience* 35: 87–93. https://doi.org/10.1016/j.dcn.2018.05.002.

Cameron, C., Höjer, I., Nordenfors, M., and Flynn, R. (2020). Security-first thinking and educational practices for young children in foster care in Sweden and England: a think piece. *Children and Youth Services Review* 119: 105523. https://doi.org/10.1016/j.childyouth.2020.105523.

Children (Scotland) Act 1995 (1995). *Children (Scotland) Act 1995.* https://www.legislation.gov.uk/ukpga/1995/36/contents (accessed 30 August 2025).

Children Act 1989 (1989). *Children Act 1989.* https://www.legislation.gov.uk/ukpga/1989/41 (accessed 30 August 2025).

Dalvie, S. and Daskalakis, N.P. (2021). The biological effects of trauma. *Complex Psychiatry* 7 (1–2): 16–18. https://doi.org/10.1159/000517236.

Del Prete, T. (1998). Getting back in touch with students: should we risk it? *Professional School Counselling* 1 (4): 62–65.

Field, T. (2002). Violence and touch deprivation in adolescents. *Adolescence* 37 (148): 735–749. PMID: 12564826.

Gobin, R.L. and Freyd, J.J. (2009). Betrayal and revictimization: preliminary findings. *Psychological Trauma: Theory Research Practice and Policy* 1 (3): 242–257. https://doi.org/10.1037/a0017469.

Green, L. (2017). The trouble with touch? New insights and observations on touch for social work and social care. *The British Journal of Social Work* 47 (3): 773–792. https://doi.org/10.1093/bjsw/bcw071.

Green, L. and Day, R. (2013). To touch or not to touch? Exploring the dilemmas and ambiguities associated with touch in social work and social care settings. In: *Practical Social Work Ethics: Complex Dilemmas Within Applied Social Care* (ed. M. Carey and L. Green). Dorset: Ashgate.

Harlow, H.F. and Zimmermann, R.R. (1958). The development of affective responsiveness in infant monkeys. *Proceedings of the American Philosophical Society* 102: 501–509.

Johnson, R.T. (2000). *Hands off!* New York: Peter Lang.

Lynch, R. and Garrett, P.M. (2010). More than words: touch practices in child and family social work. *Child & Family Social Work* 15 (4): 389–398. https://doi.org/10.1111/j.1365-2206.2010.00686.x.

Maté, G. and Maté, D. (2022). *The Myth of Normal: Trauma, Illness, and Healing in a Toxic Culture.* Avery.

McCrory, E.J. and Viding, E. (2015). The theory of latent vulnerability: reconceptualizing the link between childhood maltreatment and psychiatric disorder. *Development and Psychopathology* 27 (2): 493–505. https://doi.org/10.1017/S0954579415000115.

McCrory, E.J., De Brito, S.A., Sebastian, C.L. et al. (2011). Heightened neural reactivity to threat in child victims of family violence. *Current Biology* 21 (23): R947–R948. https://doi.org/10.1016/j.cub.2011.10.015.

Milligan, I. and Stevens, I. (2006). Balancing rights and risks: the impact of health and safety regulations on the lives of children in residential care. *Journal of Social Work* 6 (3): 239–254.

National Scientific Council on the Developing Child (2014). Excessive stress disrupts the development of brain architecture. *Journal of Child Service* 9 (2): 143–153. https://doi.org/10.1108/JCS-01-2014-0006.

Noddings, N. (2002). *Starting at Home: Caring and Social Policy*. Berkeley: University of California Press.

Owen, P. and Gillentine, J. (2011). Please touch the children: appropriate touch in the primary classroom. *Early Child Development and Care* 181 (7): 857–868. https://doi.org/10.1080/03004430.2010.497207.

Packheiser, J., Hartmann, H., Fredriksen, K. et al. (2024). A systematic review and multivariate meta-analysis of the physical and mental health benefits of touch interventions. *Nature Human Behaviour* 8: 1088–1107. https://doi.org/10.1038/s41562-024-01841-8.

Phelan, A.M. (1997). Classroom management and the erasure of teacher desire. In: *Making a Place for Pleasure in Early Childhood Education* (ed. J. Tobin). Yale University Press.

Piper, H. and Smith, H. (2003). 'Touch' in educational and child care settings: dilemmas and responses. *British Educational Research Journal* 29 (6): 879–895. https://doi.org/10.1080/0141192032000137358.

Piper, H. and Stronach, I. (2008). *Don't Touch! The Educational Story of a Panic*. London: Routledge.

Piper, H., Powell, J., and Smith, H. (2006). Parents, professionals, and paranoia: the touching of children in a culture of fear. *Journal of Social Work* 6 (2): 151–167. https://doi.org/10.1177/1468017306066742.

Silver, M. (2024). *Child Trauma and Attachment in Common Sense and Doodles. A Practical Guide*, 2e. Jessica Kingsley Publishers.

Smith, M. (2009). *Rethinking Residential Child Care: Positive Perspectives*, 165–176. Policy Press https://doi.org/10.1332/policypress/9781861349088.003.0011.

Social Services and Well-being (Wales) Act 2014 (2014). *Social Services and Well-being (Wales) Act 2014*. https://www.gov.wales/sites/default/files/publications/2019-05/part-4-code-of-practice-meeting-needs.pdf (accessed 30 August 2025).

Stanley, J. and Goddard, C. (2002). *In the Firing Line: Violence and Power in Child Protection Work*. Chichester and New York: Wiley.

Steckley, L. (2011). Touch, physical restraint and therapeutic containment in residential childcare. *British Journal of Social Work* 41 (2): 322–340. https://doi.org/10.1093/bjsw/bcq024.

Winnicott, D.W. (1953). Transitional objects and transitional phenomena; a study of the first not-me possession. *The International Journal of Psychoanalysis 34*: 89–97.

Zirkel, P.A. (2000). Don't touch! *Principal* 79 (4): 77–79.

Chapter 19

LIVED-EXPERIENCE LEADERSHIP IN TWO TRAUMA SERVICES: CHIME TO THRIVE AND STAYWELL DERBY CIC

Lauren Jones

Long Eaton, UK

Introduction

I am Lauren, a 37-year-old woman from South Wales, the United Kingdom. I love travelling, reading, connecting with people and equally enjoy both the Arts and Sciences. I now live in the East Midlands with my beautiful family: my husband (my rock), toddler (my light) and dog (constant companion). I hold a Master's in Language Pathology (Speech Therapy) as well as in Psychology. Although adverse childhood experiences (ACEs) are a significant part of my history, they do not define me. They are the papers on which the rest of my story has been written, and so, while I will not go into these experiences here, this chapter would not be here without them.

Despite the challenges of ACEs, I recognise the privileges I have had: being a White British citizen, having a middle-class upbringing, access to excellent education and a supportive network of family, friends and mentors.

In this chapter, I will briefly discuss my mental health journey following ACEs. I will also share how I used the experiential knowledge gained from trauma and recovery to co-/establish two lived experience-led services: CHIME to Thrive and Staywell Derby CIC, which ran from 2019 to 2024. I will reflect on how these services were designed and the insights I gained from working in these roles.

My gratitude goes out to all who have supported me along the way.

Background

I experienced periods of mental ill-health from around age 13, ranging from mild to severe. These included anxiety, depression, eating disorders, self-harm and suicidal ideation. Over the years, I attempted multiple times to get help

The Intergenerational Effects of Adverse Childhood Experiences: Ripples on a Pond, First Edition. Edited by Richard Pates and Diane Riley.

Published 2026 by John Wiley & Sons Ltd.

for the symptoms I was experiencing. I was first prescribed antidepressants at around age 14–15, following the first experience of suicidal intent, self-harm and disordered eating. At that time, the medical recommendation was for me to be hospitalised, to which both my parents had strongly objected. I cannot blame my parents for this and will never know what the alternative outcome would have been had I been admitted. I did very briefly see a child psychologist, but he did not see what was happening. I was advised by people who loved me that admitting my mental health difficulties would make me less employable. I tried to suppress my mental-illness identity, physically, with medication (which I still use), as well as socially. My symptoms were undesirable and something for which I should be deeply ashamed. These symptoms were difficult to separate from who I was, particularly before any trauma-related causes had been identified for my symptoms, and also before I had been diagnosed with attention-deficit hyperactivity disorder (ADHD) as an adult. I felt like I had a lot to be ashamed of.

At age 28, I experienced a severe depressive episode and, following failed, desperate attempts to access help, I eventually attempted suicide. I was in a crisis house the night Trump was elected in 2016 – the external chaos a macrocosm for my inner turmoil. I attempted suicide again in early 2017. Recovery has been long, painful and non-linear; undoubtedly the hardest thing I have ever done. I spent weeks in a day hospital, worked with a community psychiatric nurse, saw several psychiatrists and attended therapy, including trauma-informed eye movement desensitisation and reprocessing (EMDR) therapy with a compassionate clinical psychologist. It was then that I was diagnosed with complex post-traumatic stress disorder (CPTSD), stemming from childhood trauma, and later ADHD, which I had lived with undiagnosed for my whole life.

During my recovery, I ordered a 'Buddy Box'[1], a self-care package designed to bring a smile with small items and messages. The shame I felt after ordering it was intense – a visceral heat surged from my stomach to my face, leaving me physically and emotionally paralysed. Hours later, my husband found me still in the same spot, dissociated. This was a wake-up call. I realised my response was not rational, so I committed to practising self-care like an athlete training to increase fitness. I had to start small and practise regularly, especially when I did not feel deserving.

A few years after that, in Winter 2019, just before the coronavirus hit the United Kingdom, I contracted a viral infection which developed into myalgic encephalomyelitis (ME), otherwise known as chronic fatigue syndrome. In the meantime, I have completed a Master's in psychology and started and, because of health reasons, had to leave, a PhD exploring whether some mental health diagnoses are more helpful or harmful than others in people who have a history of trauma. I have also had a son and found happiness that I did not think was possible.

[1] From the Blurt Foundation CIC no longer in existence.

Going into crisis and leaving speech and language therapy (SLT)

In 2016, under considerable stress after moving house and jobs, I reached a crisis point. My new role at a large teaching hospital had a different ethos from those I had previously worked in and enjoyed. Speech and language therapists were not based in wards as part of the multidisciplinary team, communication between professionals was poor, and the tone was 'stay in your lane'. While I saw some good care, I also saw a lot of bad care and a general failure to see patients as human beings. When I raised concerns about institutional abuse, such as withholding food for days from a diabetic man with a learning disability who was begging to be fed and had no alternative source of nutrition, I was told to 'pick my battles'. This affected me deeply. My core values of empathy, advocacy, compassion and safeguarding were no longer valued, and my identity became conflicted. My anxiety skyrocketed. I could not focus, and I felt completely isolated.

In 2017, following my second, and final, suicide attempt, I woke up on a ward where I had occasionally worked. After a prolonged period of sick leave, I eventually returned to work in a lovely neurorehabilitation unit. I was still in early recovery from trauma, including the trauma from having reached the stage of deciding to end my life, seeing no other future and no other options. My neurodivergence had not yet been recognised. It was more convenient at this point for the National Health Service (NHS) for me to be a patient rather than an employee in recovery. The strict, black-and-white sickness policy – whereby you are either sick and off, or you cannot have more than two periods of absence in 6 months without being placed on a 'sickness target' – created a cycle of hyperarousal, pushing through, stopping sleep, triggering emotional flashbacks and resulting in suicidal ideation. The sickness policy was making me sicker. Early on in my return to work, a close friend of mine, who I had met in a crisis house and who had post-traumatic stress disorder (PTSD), ended his life following systemic discrimination. Sitting in the car park after the funeral, I received a voicemail and text message from my service lead, who knew where I was, saying I needed to renew my sick note – this was her concern that day.

After my CPTSD diagnosis, at work, my compassion and acts of kindness (something which had never been a cause for concern in previous settings and had been seen as a strength) were now viewed as poor boundaries. I was shut down when I began discussing patients' past trauma within 1:1 supervision because it was outside my remit – despite the patient having cried about past traumatic memories (ACEs) following a traumatic brain injury, in a joint session with a clinical psychologist. My diagnosis limited how I was viewed by others, which impacted my confidence and my view of myself. Experiential knowledge, especially from those labelled 'mentally ill', is often devalued in favour of rationality, a phenomenon called epistemic injustice (Faulkner 2017).

My employers' responses framed my mental illness as an issue solely for me to deal with. This reflects the medical model of mental illness, which overlooks the external factors contributing to trauma (ACEs). When I suggested mental health first aid training for colleagues, my manager dismissed it, implying that it was 'my problem, not theirs'. The solution was for me to better conceal my distress, even in a hospital attached to a mental health unit. As I was forced to hide my illness, I became increasingly isolated, stigmatised and unable to function. Nightmares plagued me, and my anxiety was overwhelming. I had to drop my hours to part-time and use annual leave as a reasonable adjustment. I could no longer afford food at work and lacked the energy to prepare meals, which further affected my ability to focus and meet job demands.

Feeling trapped exacerbated my trauma, triggering responses of hyperarousal and shutdown, I realised I had to prioritise myself over fighting the system. A memory of my late friend, who had also faced systemic discrimination, sparked a shift in me. My sadness turned to anger and I found strength in this. I knew I could not risk my life for an unjust sickness policy. While leaving the job was painful, I gained invaluable lessons in leadership and service management and in how to design services that truly meet the needs of both staff and service users.

Personal recovery

Approximately 1 year into my recovery journey, I encountered a Research Assistant position focused on the CHIME model of recovery. This model, grounded in William Anthony's definition of personal recovery, significantly reshaped my understanding of the process. Anthony (1993) defines recovery as 'a deeply personal, unique process' involving transformations in attitudes, values, feelings, goals, skills and roles, enabling individuals to lead meaningful lives despite ongoing illness challenges'.

This definition was pivotal in my own conceptualisation of recovery. Prior to this, I adhered to a traditional view of recovery, which emphasised the complete eradication of symptoms or a return to pre-illness functioning. However, Anthony's definition reframes recovery not as the removal of illness or trauma, but as a process of learning to live a fulfilling life with these challenges. This perspective prompted a profound shift in how I perceived mental illness and my own identity. Recovery was not necessarily about achieving an absence of illness but about cultivating a meaningful life despite its presence.

The Research Assistant role, which focused on lived-experience research, became an extension of this newfound understanding. Although I was not successful in securing the position, the experience deeply impacted me, sparking an interest in pursuing postgraduate studies in Psychology and exploring career pathways centred on lived experience – a field I saw as essential in the context of the growing patient revolution and survivor research (Sweeney et al. 2009).

The CHIME model of recovery

The CHIME model, developed by Leamy et al. (2011), identifies five key elements that promote recovery: Connectedness, Hope, Identity, Meaning and Empowerment. These elements are grounded in Anthony's conceptualisation of personal recovery and provided a structured framework for my recovery process. I found these elements particularly resonant and integrated them into my life through goal-setting and reflection.

For example, in relation to Connectedness, I developed a Likert scale to assess my daily sense of connection to others. This tool enabled me to track fluctuations in social interactions and set goals to enhance my sense of connection, such as reaching out to a friend or engaging in small social activities. These actions facilitated tangible progress, reinforcing the idea that recovery is an incremental process nurtured through concrete steps.

Additionally, I embraced a flexible approach to recovery, acknowledging that it is not linear but involves both progress and setbacks. During challenging periods, I focused on a 'could-do' list, breaking down tasks into achievable components. This strategy helped manage the anxiety associated with complex PTSD and ADHD by reframing tasks in ways that felt more manageable.

More routes to personal recovery

As my recovery progressed, I began to reframe what I had perceived as impairments – such as dissociation and hypervigilance – as survival strategies that had served me well in navigating past trauma. This shift in perspective was empowering and led to a deeper understanding of my lived experience. Further exploration of trauma neurobiology and somatic experiencing provided insights into how my body and brain adapted to adversity. With the therapeutic guidance of my Clinical Psychologist, I developed greater self-compassion and reduced the internalised shame that had previously marked my experience of mental illness.

Basic education on neurology and trauma became an essential aspect of my recovery. I believed it could help people whose symptoms had been framed negatively, rather than recognising them as adaptive responses to trauma that had become maladaptive when safety was restored. Importantly, not everyone is currently safe; many people still experience very real threats, including abusive relationships, financial stress, social disadvantage, discrimination and isolation.

CHIME to Thrive

CHIME to Thrive was a social enterprise I founded in 2019 to support individuals in their recovery journeys from mental health challenges. Drawing on my own experiences of recovery, which I have shared earlier, alongside my healthcare training in areas such as communicating with people with varied needs, evidence-based practice, goal-setting and progress evaluation, I aimed to provide a supportive service tailored to the unique needs of each individual. My work was further informed by my ongoing Master's studies and personal research into trauma embodiment, personal recovery, peer support and patient leadership.

Before launching CHIME to Thrive, I recognised the need for regular supervision, both for my own protection and to safeguard my clients. At the time, there were no established guidelines or governance requirements for user-led services like mine, so I contacted the British Psychological Society to highlight this gap and offered to help develop these guidelines. Unfortunately, I did not receive a response, but I did arrange for supervision with Professor Richard Pates, a Clinical Psychologist (and one of the editors of this book). His guidance proved invaluable, and I strongly recommend supervision for anyone engaged in similar work.

The individuals who came to CHIME to Thrive often had complex histories of trauma, including ACEs. My initial service model focused on private, one-to-one sessions, providing a therapeutic hour (50 minutes) where the emphasis was placed on reducing power imbalances. I believed that clients were more likely to feel these imbalances acutely, so I aimed to create an environment of safety by giving them as much control as possible, allowing them to decide how and when to share their stories, set their goals and determine how long they wished to work with me.

The service was highly flexible: clients were never penalised for being late or missing sessions. I provided forms where clients could share emergency contact details and specify their preferences for action in case of an emergency. This was done with the understanding that recovery was possible for them and that, in emergencies, contacting services might be necessary. While most clients agreed to this, one chose not to share this information, and I respected their autonomy, continuing to work with them.

I trusted my clients and their stories, and I actively worked to reduce barriers between us. This required me to make myself more vulnerable than would typically be expected in professional settings. I believed that by sharing relevant parts of my own experiences, I could help reduce stigma and foster a sense of shared social identity. This approach was informed by the Social Identity Approach to Health (SIAH) (Haslam et al. 2019), which emphasises the importance of shared identity in recovery. Survivor research also highlights the benefits of peer support and lived experience, while cautioning against tokenistic or disempowering uses of such support. I saw my work as sitting between clinical practice and peer support.

My approach was trauma-informed, compassion-focused and rooted in unconditional positive regard. I recognised the power of the therapeutic relationship to either support or hinder recovery. I was deeply person-centred, believing it was essential to be 'on the side' of the person seeking help, as many clients had never experienced this or had not in a long time.

Clients had control over what they chose to share, and I made it clear that I assumed there was much I did not know. I was mindful of how exhausting it had been in my own recovery to repeatedly answer irrelevant questions from professionals, only to have those answers lead to inadequate or no support. Ironically, by avoiding prescriptive questioning and sharing a salient social identity as someone who had also experienced trauma and mental health challenges, I often became the first person to whom clients felt they could fully open up. Many shared profound trauma – some of it recent, some buried for decades. Often, these traumas were layered and interwoven. Being trusted in this way was both a privilege and a tragedy. It underscored the question: how had these clients, with such significant needs, come to me – traumatised, mentally ill me – as their best available support? They deserved far better and much sooner.

The impact of the pandemic

I launched CHIME to Thrive in April 2019. I was still refining the service delivery model when, in January 2020, I became aware of a new virus in China. My history of trauma helped me tune into the warning threats on social media from clinicians seeing the deadly impact firsthand in their countries. This was urgent, they said. I kept checking for information about what we were going to do to prevent it, but our government's response was reactive rather than proactive. Apart from the physical threat, I quickly recognised the threat posed to the thousands already struggling with inadequate or inaccessible mental healthcare. It felt like I was watching a tsunami approach, and I had a little boat which might be able to help a tiny proportion of people who lacked life jackets.

My lived experience of personal recovery has helped me recognise the threat and problem-solve quickly and creatively. I adapted my service delivery model to online sessions and launched a free COVID-19 response, open to anyone affected physically, emotionally, socially or financially by the pandemic. The response was subsidised through small grants, pay-what-you-can options and commissioned work like webinars and courses. Although the income barely sustained me, I would not change this period of work. I met so many incredibly resilient, wonderful humans, who trusted me to support them in their recoveries. The feedback I received was that I had supported their recoveries and made a difference in some way.

Evolving the service model

Initially, CHIME to Thrive focused on the CHIME recovery model, using solution-focused approaches and SMART goals, which I had employed in my own recovery. However, I soon realised this model was too reductive. In reality, systemic and societal barriers played significant roles in clients' struggles, and the service became more trauma-informed, e.g. incorporating polyvagal theory (Porges 2011).

I also expanded my model to include The CHIME-D model (Stuart et al. 2017), which incorporates 'difficulties' as a core component of personal recovery. I noticed that clients often needed to address trauma, adversity and systemic barriers before they could even begin to think about problem-solving, which makes sense; if they are hyperaroused and amygdala is in over-drive, then their frontal lobes are essentially going to be offline, disabling executive function. I also recognised the power of the therapeutic relationship in facilitating this process and understood that some people would come to internalise the compassion and unconditional positive regard with which I spoke to them as their inner voice when they needed support. This was fed back to me directly by several clients.

As the work evolved, in light of the pandemic, I expanded my role to support not just individuals but also their spouses, parents, siblings, personal assistants and healthcare professionals. This expanded approach shifted from simply focusing on recovery goals to crisis prevention and response, including advocacy.

I supported clients with a wide range of challenges – from suicide prevention to domestic abuse, to housing situations and workplace difficulties, I supported people to identify and seek assessment and support for long-overlooked conditions, including Autism, ADHD, pathological demand avoidance, bipolar and OCD, and supported people in recovery, including people with anorexia. The majority of clients were navigating complex layers of trauma, abuse, systemic failures, grief, addiction, neurodivergence, social deprivation and harm caused by the very services meant to help them. Where they had been just about surviving before the pandemic, now they were hanging on for dear life.

I eventually shifted my focus from CHIME to Thrive to Staywell Derby CIC as I felt that through this community-based approach, I had the potential to have a greater impact than I could give working 1:1 with people, even though I love this work.

Access to services

Over the past few decades, stigma surrounding mental illness has somewhat reduced, particularly with the help of public figures who openly discuss their mental health challenges. However, stigma still persists, especially for those facing severe, persistent and complex mental health difficulties often linked to ACEs. This group is underrepresented in the media and typically portrayed in a negative light, either as villains or as cautionary tales.

The stories that tend to receive attention are of individuals who have experienced milder forms of mental health challenges, such as temporary anxiety, depression or stress, and have had access to resources that helped them recover. While these stories are valid, they do not reflect the experiences of those whose mental health difficulties are deeply rooted in ACEs and continue unresolved. This gap in representation misrepresents the true breadth of mental health struggles, leading to a skewed public understanding.

Campaigns like Mind's 'It's OK to not be OK' aim to raise awareness, but they perpetuate the idea that support is readily available if individuals simply ask for help. In reality, accessing services, particularly for those with complex emotional, social and cognitive needs, including ACEs, can be incredibly difficult. The barriers to accessing help are significant, and many individuals become lost within systems designed to support them.

The third sector – social enterprises and charities – often steps in to fill the gap left by overstretched public services. However, years of funding cuts, particularly under Conservative governance, have stretched these services thin.

Staywell Derby

Staywell Derby aimed to provide a community approach to well-being within one setting, which offered support for people with addiction, mental health difficulties and social difficulties, including trauma and neurodivergence, and offered opportunities for creative and spiritual outlets.

It was a well-being and recovery service in Derby's Cathedral Quarter, which ran from May 2020 to June 2024. We aimed to prevent people with complex biopsychosocial needs, including dual diagnosis, from 'falling through the net' and to improve outcomes for people with combinations of needs, including people who have experienced trauma, addiction, mental ill-health and neurodivergence. We aimed to prevent preventable harm and build resilience by providing a safe community space which included regular support groups, a café, 1:1 support and community collaborations and producing and supporting user-led research. We aimed to offer the opportunity for people to increase the number of multiple meaningful groups people belonged to, but without the additional barriers of these being spread geographically in different locations. This could increase their social capital and social identities, supporting their well-being. We also wanted people to feel ownership over the organisation itself through a shared sense of being 'part' of Staywell.

All directors had lived experience of ACEs, trauma, mental ill-health, addiction, neurodivergence, stigmatised identities and homelessness (different combinations of experiences). There were changes in leadership over the duration of the service, but Rosa Pary, Pippa Nayer and I were there at the beginning as well as the end. Special thanks to all the wonderful humans who helped us along the way, including other directors, peer supporters, lived-experience coordinators, volunteers and partners. The people who used our service were amazing.

Our experiences led us to recognise crucial gaps in existing services for people vulnerable or at risk of becoming vulnerable. We integrated our personal knowledge of ACEs and their impact.

We understood how early trauma shapes emotional, cognitive and behavioural responses. From our experiences, we understood experientially, for example, how neurodivergence, such as ADHD and autism, could exacerbate and interact with the effects of ACEs. Two out of the three of us directors received diagnoses of neurodivergence while running the service, despite having sought help for mental health challenges throughout our lives.

We had multiple ways of measuring how effective our service was and saw, consistently and holistically, that we were doing what we sought to do, that is that people were using our services to support their well-being and that they were finding that as a result of the support they received from people with lived experience of things which they could relate to including trauma and related mental health and addiction challenges, they felt more connected, hopeful and empowered. We saw people find meaning and improve self-confidence through volunteering and working with us, and people would regularly refer to feeling as though Staywell were a 'family'. We believe that what we did demonstrated 'proof of concept' in that the service, fully led by people who had 'been there', worked. Staywell Derby sadly closed on May 31st, 2024, through a lack of funding.

Insights

Following are some of the insights I took from leading these services:

Harm from existing systems

Most but not all people who found themselves accessing CHIME to Thrive or Staywell had attempted to access a range of mental health services in the past. Many reported unhelpful, or even harmful experiences, which is why they were pursuing other methods of support. Many had disengaged from traditional services as a means to protect themselves; this included crisis services. For many people, CHIME to Thrive and Staywell Derby CIC allowed them to talk about ACEs/trauma for the first time.

Neurodivergence

A significant proportion of clients had neurodevelopmental differences such as ADHD or autism spectrum disorder (ASD), which may or may not have been recognised as a child. These difficulties were discussed in relation to high levels of reactivity and more punitive and stigmatising methods in home, school and society more broadly as a means to control the child's behaviour. In addition, caregivers themselves may have been struggling with emotional dysregulation from generational trauma and/or overstimulation from undiagnosed conditions, which are only more recently being recognised.

Borderline personality disorder

Several women diagnosed with borderline personality disorder (BPD) accessed the services. Many of these women were highly traumatised and neurodivergent. They often reported, and I occasionally saw, that their distress was dismissed as manipulative, with false attributions made about the causes of their behaviour and a focus on the need to take responsibility. Taking responsibility is all well and good, but when a person does not have access to the most basic of needs, has severe untreated PTSD, and responds to threats by dissociating, it is not that the person is not taking responsibility, but they cannot and need help to get to that point. This lack of trauma-informed care, which is pervasive, violates NICE guidelines, which stress the importance of patient choice and individualised treatment. Many women with this diagnosis were denied essential support, and their distress was minimised. Some of the most egregious examples of neglect and mistreatment I witnessed involved women bearing this label, which often further compounded their suffering.

Trauma, neurodivergence and systemic factors were frequently overlooked, mirroring the treatment of men and women with substance addictions, where underlying issues were ignored.

Highly intelligent women who challenged authority or questioned gender and power norms were often silenced by this diagnosis and the stigma it created. Neurodivergence was rarely recognised before the BPD label, and by the time it was diagnosed, it became the primary lens through which others perceived and treated them. Treatment often defaulted to dialectical behaviour therapy (DBT), which, while beneficial for some, failed to address their complex trauma or individual needs.

The need for supervision

This work is by far the most complex and emotionally demanding I have undertaken. In terms of impact on the people my colleagues and I supported, I believe it has, overall, been incredibly successful. In order for it to be successful, I have had to actively work to reduce barriers between me and the people I have worked with and to embrace vulnerability. This openness has allowed me to connect deeply with people, share social identities, reduce (but not eliminate) power imbalances and support stigma reduction.

Regular support and supervision are essential to sustain our well-being and effectiveness. For me, working with a clinical psychologist who was an ally – someone who genuinely understood and valued this work – was ideal. What would not have been helpful, however, is rigid oversight from those in positions of power who lack insight into the lived-experience model or, worse, have contributed to harm in the past. The other thing which would not be helpful would be supervision from somebody claiming to have lived experience of, e.g. severe mental illness, because they had a family member who experienced severe mental illness if the service was not for family members, but for people experiencing this directly. Clinicians would need to be aware of the power they hold within the dynamic and the differences in their experiences. The ideal would be someone with lived experience.

Supervision in these contexts must empower rather than constrain, supporting lived experience–led services in ways that prioritise understanding, collaboration and healing. Red tape and imposed hierarchies risk undermining the unique strengths of this approach, reinforcing the very dynamics we seek to dismantle.

Need for racial diversity

A large majority (90%) of people who accessed both services were White British. Minority racial groups face greater barriers to service access and are at higher risk of mental ill-health due to systemic racism and its intersection with socioeconomic disadvantage. Research indicates that systemic racism increases stress and mental health risks, while socioeconomic factors like poverty further exacerbate these disparities (Patel et al. 2020). Refugees and asylum seekers face additional challenges linked to trauma, identity and lack of support, with higher rates of PTSD and anxiety often observed (Blackmore et al. 2019). The social identity approach to health highlights the importance of belonging and shared identity in promoting well-being, particularly for individuals recovering from trauma (Kellezi et al. 2019). This underscores the need for leadership from individuals who share the lived experiences of minority groups and can foster trust and connection. Representation not only builds trust but also ensures services are culturally competent and effective (Saha et al. 2016).

There were some people we could not support in spite of our best efforts, e.g. a Deaf asylum seeker from Africa, who communicated to me about extreme childhood trauma. I can use conversational British Sign Language, but this person was using another Sign Language. I could only follow approximately 30% of his signs. This person seemed desperate for help and totally alone in a foreign country. A volunteer came to try and interpret for us twice, but both times the person did not show up, I am sure for a valid reason.

Systems

We learned that we cannot operate outside existing systems. Some of the problems which I had experienced within the NHS both as a member of staff and as a patient, I had assumed were specific to the NHS including because of its size and being systematically stripped of money; however, while some problems were able to be avoided in a smaller user-led organisation, e.g. our sickness policy actually supported well-being rather than led to making people more likely to become sick and not only helped retain staff but helped them thrive in their positions, there were other problems which turned out to be part of a broader problem in how funding is allocated. Complex, intersecting needs can present a challenge for models of funding which prioritise short-term, highly specific and novel projects.

We understood that the people who used our service wanted long-term communities and the feeling of safety that comes from this. We observed this, and we were told this by people who used our service. We worked so hard to show the funders why this was a project worth continuing through our user-led outcome measures, including a community cafe that served as an interactive focus group, following which action was taken on feedback, written and electronic feedback, observations and informal. However, what we failed to understand until too late was the importance to funders of money in the bank in order to reduce perceived risk.

Tokenism

'Lived Experience' has become a buzzword, just like 'recovery' and 'peer support'. Even when this criterion was listed as essential, and when people claimed to support this work, it was not always the case. 'Everyone has lived experience' was one misconception of how our work was not just about having this experience but working through this lens to create systems designed to be user-led.

These user-led services supported hundreds of individuals in their personal recoveries and it was a privilege to be involved with them. I now have a toddler whom I want to nurture and spend time with, as well as a chronic physical health condition which takes a lot of time managing. For the time being then, I am stepping away from lived-experience leadership to focus on my physical recovery and my little family.

References

Anthony, W.A. (1993). Recovery from mental illness: The guiding vision of the mental health service system in the 1990s. *Psychosocial Rehabilitation Journal 16* (4): 11–23. https://doi.org/10.1037/h0095655.

Blackmore, R., Boyle, J.A., Fazel, M. et al. (2019). The prevalence of mental illness in refugees and asylum seekers: a systematic review and meta-analysis. *Frontiers in Psychiatry 10*: 517. https://doi.org/10.3389/fpsyt.2019.00517.

Faulkner, A. (2017). Survivor research and Mad Studies: the role and value of experiential knowledge in mental health research. *Disability & Society 32*: 1–21.

Haslam, S.A., Jetten, J., and Haslam, C. (2019). Social scaffolding: applying the lessons of contemporary social science to health and healthcare. In: *The Social Identity Approach to Health* (ed. R. Williams, S. Verity Kemp, A. Haslam, et al.), 31–39. Cambridge: Cambridge University Press https://doi.org/10.1017/9781911623069.004.

Kellezi, B., Bowe, M., Wakefield, J.R.H. et al. (2019). Migration, social identity, and psychosocial well-being. In: *The New Psychology of Health: Unlocking the Social Cure* (ed. S. Jetten, K. Mols, and T. Haslam), 96–111. Psychology Press.

Leamy, M., Bird, V., Le Boutillier, C., Williams, J., & Slade, M. (2011). Conceptual framework for personal recovery in mental health: systematic review and narrative synthesis. The British Journal of Psychiatry, 199(6), 445–452. https://doi.org/10.1192/bjp.bp.110.083733

Patel, K., Kouvonen, A., Close, C., and Väänänen, A. (2020). Systemic racism and mental health of ethnic minorities in the UK. *Lancet Psychiatry* 7 (9): 754–755. https://doi.org/10.1016/S2215-0366(20)30381-1.

Porges, S. (2011). *The Polyvagal Theory: Neuropsychological Foundations of Emotions, Attachment, Communication and Self-regulation*. WW Norton and Co.

Saha, S., Beach, M. C., & Cooper, L. A. (2016). Patient-centeredness, cultural competence, and healthcare quality. *Journal of the National Medical Association, 108*(6), 123–131. https://doi.org/10.1016/j.jnma.2015.12.013

Stuart, S.R., Tansey, L., and Quayle, E. (2017). What we talk about when we talk about recovery: a systematic review and best-fit framework synthesis of qualitative literature. *Journal of mental health (Abingdon, England)* 26 (3): 291–304. https://doi.org/10.1080/09638237.2016.1222056.

Sweeney, A., Beresford, P., Faulkner, A. et al. (ed.) (2009). *This Is Survivor Research* 200 pp. Ross-on-Wye: PPCS Books.

Part 4
Discussion

Chapter 20

DISCUSSION

Richard Pates[1] *and Diane Riley*[2]

[1] Independent Consultant, Wales, UK
[2] Independent Consultant, Ontario, Canada

The material in this book shows that there is a high rate of harmful mental and physical health problems as a result of maltreatment, natural disasters, and other adverse childhood experiences (ACEs). These problems are seen in many countries, in very different cultures, and cut across lines of income, education and social class, although they are greatly exacerbated by poverty, discrimination and community violence. We are starting to better understand the mechanisms of these problems, but the level of public awareness is still low, policies and laws remain inadequate, and interventions for prevention and treatment are still woefully few, of limited efficacy and often based more on popularity than on evidence.

This book has examined the problems related to childhood adversity both from the individual perspective and from a societal perspective, and covered many different causes and correlates of ACEs and long-term effects. As discussed, the concept of ACEs as used widely today was first detailed by Felitti and colleagues in 1998, who identified ten individual factors relating to ACEs. With further research over the years by many investigators, our understanding of negative childhood experiences and the impact of them had increased. It is clear that ACEs are not only caused by individual events but also by major societal events such as warfare and natural disasters, and that poverty and violence are responsible for a considerable amount of childhood adversity. These events can be related to serious mental and physical health problems in later life, and intergenerational effects are also evident.

In the nearly 30 years since Felitti's original work, a huge number of papers on the subject have been published, so there is a greater academic understanding of ACEs. This understanding, however, has in many cases not been shared by services, especially those that work with children. For example, an 8-year-old girl who arrived at a children's home with a terrible history of abuse and unsettled living conditions behaved with great difficulty when she arrived, shouting and screaming, and not being able to settle. After 6 months,

The Intergenerational Effects of Adverse Childhood Experiences: Ripples on a Pond,
First Edition. Edited by Richard Pates and Diane Riley.

Published 2026 by John Wiley & Sons Ltd.

she had formed relationships with staff and had begun to disclose abuse, and it was clear she had formed attachments which had been missing all her life. At this point, she needed to stay where she had formed attachments for at least 2 years, but Social Services decided to move her, probably because they had found cheaper solutions. In the next year, she had six different placements and was then referred back to the original home. If the person who made the original decision to move her had thought about the impact of constant moving, she should have remained where she was. The people working directly with these children understand this, but not all the managers understand the impact of their decisions.

It is also clear that there are many other societal events that have been ignored in terms of their effects on an entire community, especially children. These include the tragic events such as the disaster at Aberfan in Wales in 1966, the impact of certain religious practices and beliefs, for example, Fletcher's experience in an orthodox Jewish community who did not want her sexual abuser taken to court (Fletcher 2025), institutional cruelty, such as in the Magdalene laundries, forced marriage in some cultures, the impact of residential schools on Indigenous peoples in certain countries, the effects of adoption across cultures, the increasing evidence of sexual abuse in residential schools and in religious environments, and many other events. While this book has discussed a number of these issues, there are many, many which affect children all over the world. The current situation in Gaza, which has been viewed on screens across the world, will produce some serious and long-term effects on those people, especially children, who have seen their family shot and starving. If they survive, the impact of these experiences will be lifelong.

Some common themes

Evasion of responsibility

When a catastrophic event takes place, which results in the loss of many lives and there are inevitably long-term impacts on the children involved, it is notable that responsibility is frequently denied by those who should have taken responsibility for the events. Examples of this are the pit disaster at Aberfan in 1966 and the Grenfell fire in 2017. The Grenfell fire broke out in the 24-storey Grenfell Tower block of flats in North Kensington, in London, in the very early morning and burned for 60 hours. Seventy people died at the scene and two people died later in hospital, with more than 70 injured and 223 escaping. The fire was caused by an electrical fault in a refrigerator in a fourth-floor flat, but block of flats was covered in a cladding which was highly inflammable. A subsequent enquiry found that the building's exterior did not comply with regulations and was the central reason why the fire spread, and that the fire service was too late in advising residents to evacuate. There have been a number of enquiries and as of February 2025, seven organisations are under investigation for professional misconduct. Little responsibility was initially taken for the large number of deaths and injuries caused by this avoidable fire.

The Aberfan disaster described in her chapter by Gaynor Madgwick, who was present during the disaster, was probably the biggest in the United Kingdom outside of wartime, certainly in the 20th century. Thousands of tons of coal waste slid down a hillside and engulfed Pantglas Primary School in the Welsh village of Aberfan; 116 children and 28 adults were killed. As Gaynor describes, she was in the school when this happened, but she survived with serious injuries. She had a sister and brother in the same school, both of whom were killed. This area of Wales was the major coal-producing area in the United Kingdom in the early 20th century, with many villages and small towns built around the coal mines, known to be high-risk environments because of collapsing infrastructure, gas explosions and the like. Every coal mine had to dump the waste (non-coal products) near the pits and these could be unstable and unreliable. Merthyr Vale, which was the colliery that was using this tip, had seven waste tips, six of them no longer in use. Four of these tips were perched on hillsides, including number seven, and they were also built on water, in the case of number seven, on two underground springs. Prior to 1966, when this disaster happened, there had already been two tip slides related to this pit, one in 1944 and one in 1963. No one, including the National Coal Board (NCB), which owned the mine, took responsibility. At a meeting of the Town Planning Committee for the borough in which Aberfan existed in 1964, 2 years before the disaster, a counsellor, Mrs Williams, said, 'There are dangers from surface tipping. We had a lot of trouble from slurry causing flooding, but if the tip moved it could threaten the whole school' (Kane, in Madgwick 2016, p. 14).

As Kane says, 'Lord Robens (head of the NCB) and the Coal Board betrayed the Aberfan community continuously. Robens fought tooth and nail to limit the cost of Aberfan to the NCB. The opening offer to each bereaved family was £50 and it wasn't increased to £500 until 1970 when Robens' 10-year stretch was over' (p. 23). Even the Charity Commission was hostile to the community; at one stage, they insisted that compensation should only be paid to those parents of whom it could be established that 'they had been close to their child or children'. And this is when a generation of children had been wiped out by a preventable disaster. On reading Gaynor's chapter in this book, one can see the enormous long-term impact these events have had on her psychological wellness. People will still say to her, 'Get over it, it was 60 years ago', but the reality is that one does not ever get over such events. Would you?

Individual responsibility is important too. One hears of teachers and other people working with children making casual negative comments that they will immediately forget, but the child will remember for many years. Many, many ACEs are caused either individually by violent, abusive or careless behaviour by individuals or by lack of responsibility in organisations and this needs to be considered when working with people who have suffered the consequences. The chapter on Lived Experience showed the long-term impact of behaviours that were, in some cases, not physically abusive or not directed at the person they affected. In that chapter, Alf has to hear his parents fighting from a very young age and see the impact of their violence on each other. This was the start of a long series of problems for his mental health. In the same chapter, Gwyneth Lewis, a talented poet, had to suffer emotional abuse from her mother from a very young age, which affected her throughout her life. The perpetrators of the harm done to both Alf and Gwyneth probably did not recognise what they were doing, but they were causing serious problems.

Extent of institutional abuse

While institutional abuse has not been the subject of an individual chapter in this book, it is clear that it is a major problem. There has been a history of sexual and physical abuse in boarding schools in the United Kingdom for many years. These schools were popular for the upper classes from the time of the Empire onwards and were seen as developing the right character for running the Empire. The irony is that these schools are very expensive, far more than what most of the population of the country can afford, but children, mainly boys, did, and do, suffer abuse in some of them. The schools, when children were sent there at a young age, also destroyed the attachment process considered so important in raising children. Some of these issues were mentioned in the introductory section of this book when young boys such as Charles Spencer and James Rhodes describe being seriously abused despite coming from a privileged background. Certainly, in the past 15–20 years, reports of these abuses have become more common. We know it was not just these privileged children who were abused in institutions. In a number of countries, including Canada, as detailed in a chapter in this book, thousands of Indigenous children were abused in residential and day schools established by the government and run by the church.

In one case recently reported (Guardian, 11/08/2025), a teacher was found guilty of frequent abuse. John Young, now 91 and a former international rugby referee, carried out a 'harrowing' assault on a boy whom he kicked and punched repeatedly while the child was recovering from a spinal injury. The boy, who was 12 and walked with a visible limp because of the injury, pleaded with Young during a PE class that he was unable to pick up some weights as ordered, prompting Young to lash out at his head and kick him, causing 'substantial pain'. In other cases, Young's assaults, which took place between 1966 and 1993, included twisting and squeezing boys' genitals, striking them with a cricket bat, a wooden implement or a clipboard, and looking at their genitalia under their shorts. As is typical in such cases, many victims were not believed at the time. The case had shown that Young 'committed acts of cruelty and had physically and mentally terrified many boys that he was entrusted to look after'. 'The fact that numerous men came forward, many decades later, shows the severity and lifelong impact that childhood abuse has had throughout their lives, with many waiting over 50 years for justice to be served'.

This is yet another case of severe abuse in a boarding school and it makes one ask: why did it take so long for these cases to come to court, as they must have been known about for so long, and why were the victims not believed?

Institutional abuse also occurred in various denominations of the church and was often covered up. The resignation of the Archbishop of Canterbury, the most senior cleric in the Church of England, was, as a result of his not acting more decisively when dealing with the case of John Smyth, who systematically abused boys at Christian Holiday Camps. The Indigenous residential and day schools in Canada and a number of other countries were run by the church. The Magdalene Laundries in Ireland were run by the Catholic Church, taking in unmarried mothers and other young females, and the children who were born into that environment suffered terrible consequences of their mothers' supposed bad behaviours.

We know all too well that abuse of various sorts has happened in numerous institutions of all kinds, many of which were central in the Establishment or culture of the society in which they operated. These are often the organisations that should be calling out that abuse but fail to do so, probably because of a fear of damaging their reputation, without regard to the damage that is done to the victim.

The abuse in these institutions is, of course, all the more awful because they are made up of the very people who are expected to be trusted. One of the most appalling examples is being revealed as this book is being finished. In the town of Rotherham in the North of England, a 'grooming' gang was grooming young girls aged 12–15. Up to 1,400 girls were involved who were abused and raped by gangs of up to 20 men. These were already very vulnerable girls, mostly from children's homes; this continued until 2013. What has just been revealed is that four police officers who were investigating the crimes have also been accused by five girls of sexually assaulting them too. One girl who was raped in a marked police car by a serving police officer was told that if she did not comply, he would return her to the grooming gangs and she said, 'It was better to be raped by one man than by 20 in a grooming gang' (The Guardian, 30/7/2025).

The importance of communication

Two of the chapters in this book show the enormous impact of a lack of communication as a form of neglect. These are very different chapters and are highly unusual stories, but show what the impact of a lack of communication has on children who do not receive information from their responsible adults. The two chapters, Letter to Breslau by Maya Lasker-Wallfisch and Writing as therapy for my deep personal trauma by Alison Knight, tell of two heartbreaking situations which both have good outcomes after much turmoil.

Maya Lasker Wallfisch is a psychoanalytic psychotherapist and author. Her story, of her early days, describes her alienation in school, stealing money from her mother's purse, using drugs, and even being expelled from one of the most progressive schools in London. She tells us where these problems stemmed from and describes in the opening of her chapter, 'There were two languages spoken in our house, one was music, and the other was German. I didn't speak either of them'. Maya's description of her early years was of a child not communicating with her parents, being alienated in school for being Jewish, and for being different. All of this was linked to the most vile act of genocide seen in this world. Maya's mother, Anita Lasker Wallfisch, was a renowned cellist, a founder member of the English Chamber Orchestra. What Maya did not know was that her mother had been in Auschwitz, the notorious Nazi concentration camp, and being a musician had saved her life as the camps used musicians to play to the prisoners as they went to work. Her mother, who is still alive and 100 years old at the time of writing, recently had a film made about her and her fellow musicians in the Women's Orchestra of Auschwitz titled 'The Last Musician of Auschwitz', a deeply horrifying and troubling film showing some victims of the Nazi holocaust.

Maya's father was a pianist who played for 8 hours a day, and the children were forbidden to interrupt him. Her parents had met after Anita had been liberated from Bergen-Belsen and moved to London, where she eventually met Peter, Maya's father, whom she married. Maya knew nothing of her mother's history or times in Auschwitz and Bergen Belsen (where her grandparents were also murdered) until she was 12 or 13 in about 1970, 25 years after the war. She went to try to find some cigarettes in her mother's cupboard, but found instead a set of photographs of corpses, piled high and being bulldozed into a grave. This was a total shock to Maya, who knew nothing about the Holocaust (it was not taught in British schools then), but because she was not supposed to be going through her mother's cupboard, she just put them back and said nothing.

Maya writes that her mother wanted to raise her and her brother Raphael in a 'normal' atmosphere at home, but as Maya says, how can a home be normal, given what her mother went through? She never wanted to talk about their grandparents and neither Maya nor her brother asked about them. These experiences clearly had a major impact on Maya's life. Both parents were professional musicians and spent considerable time on this, and they also spoke to each other in German, which Maya did not speak. She grew up in an isolated environment. We know that when people have been through horrific experiences, as Maya's mother did, they do not want to talk about it, but children like to know about where they came from, about their grandparents and parents' earlier history. Maya clearly did not go through any of the awful experiences her mother did, but she had a confusing childhood, which made making sense of the world very difficult. She left school with minimal qualifications, but despite this, she has made a great success of her life and she must be admired for this.

Interestingly, there is also a short chapter in the book written by a German woman, Sabine Bode. She describes the grandchildren of people who lived in Germany during the Nazi era and whom she calls War Grandchildren: the children of the children who were living in Germany during the horror of war. The effects on these children were profound, as were those on their children growing up in an emotionally difficult environment, but Sabine found that nobody would talk about it. War has victims on all sides; ACEs are part of this and can be passed on to the next generation.

A chapter by Alison Knight describes the awful events of when her father killed her mother and then threw himself out of the window, thus making her an orphan. She heard her father jump out of the window as she was in the same building at the time. She describes that she had a happy childhood and was loved by her parents, but when her mother decided to leave to live with another man she could not understand, at the age of 6, why she was leaving her beloved daddy. Though she was adopted by a family, her father's brother and his wife, who had been her mother's best friend, nobody talked about what had happened, and nobody ever mentioned her parents. She writes, 'When it was decided that I couldn't go to their joint funeral, I began to wonder whether they had really died or not. Maybe, I thought, they were really alive and just needed some time together away from me and my eighteen-year-old sister in order to work out their problems. I began to look for them everywhere I went, expecting to see them open their arms to me the moment we were reunited'. This is a 10-year-old girl who finds that not only have her parents disappeared and she heard her father falling from the building but also that no one would talk about it. She was left without the parents she really loved and who had loved her, but what had happened became a mystery. She felt that she had to behave, or she might be sent to an orphanage.

Alison developed post-traumatic stress disorder (PTSD) and has suffered the consequences of what happened all her life, not only of her parents' deaths but also of the silence maintained around the subject. There was no such thing as counselling for her then. One hopes that had this occurred now, she would have had a completely different course, not only psychological help to deal with the trauma of her parents' deaths but also hope that the family into which she had moved had been able to talk to her and help her understand more about what had happened.

These chapters remind us of why it is important to keep children informed as to what has happened, even when it becomes difficult. Awful events should not be avoided even when they are painful. In both these cases, the impact of not knowing was probably worse than having to talk about the events. Similarly, for Gaynor Madgwick, the disaster that had claimed the lives of her siblings and friends and caused her serious injuries was never talked about and she was not given therapy until many years later. She was never given the chance to begin to heal.

Effects of adoption

The chapter written by Diana Lesme Romero on adoption is very interesting because adoption is potentially an area of much confusion for adopted children. There are major issues of attachment, potential secrecy about a child's origins and, if the child's birth family had been neglectful or violent, this is something a child may bring with them to the new family. As Diana says,

'They can become an adverse factor in childhood, potentially triggering trauma, stress and psychological suffering in the adoptee, as well as in adoptive and biological parents, leaving subjective marks of suffering, pain, abandonment, frustration and guilt'.

This chapter reports on a study on people who were adopted to a country different from their birth country in international adoptions of Paraguayan children to the United States. The connection between international adoption and ACEs has not yet been extensively researched and this chapter presents some very important work on the direct experience of some of the people interviewed for the study. As described, there are a lot of difficulties relating to attachment both with birth parents and the adoptive parents. Many people adopted by families from a different cultural context experience ACEs before and during the adoption process. Adoption can be a lifeline for children who have lost parents or who have come from an abusive home but, as the chapter explains, it can also make things more difficult. This must be especially so when the adopted child was adopted at an age when they had already known and formed attachments with their birth families.

Sociodemographic and cultural factors

The universality of ACEs has been acknowledged, but two chapters in this book highlight problems in countries with different cultures and sociodemographic issues. Anna Tsiboukli's chapter focuses on Greece and the problems that exist there. As Anna explains, Greece went through economic turmoil for over a decade, then experienced, as every country did, the COVID-19 pandemic. Austerity measures were introduced, which had a significant socioeconomic impact on the population, increased unemployment rates and risk for poverty and social exclusion. This also resulted in major cuts to healthcare and mental healthcare services, which left the population without adequate support. These events led to an increase in illicit drug use, including the arrival of a new drug known as the 'cocaine of the poor', and an increase in the illegal trade in alcohol. Additionally, the number of children at risk for poverty and social exclusion in Greece is amongst the highest in the European Community, exceeding 30%, thus compounding the problems of young people. At the peak of the financial crisis, the number of adolescents and young people facing adversities in Greece increased, with 20% of all young people and 30% of young women out of training, education or employment, a devastating impact on so many.

Athens is a major tourist destination containing some of the most well-known architecture and buildings in the western world, but Anna describes Athens as a city with two facades. This was a theme from a discussion group of adolescents in the city, 'the tourist façade, where the real part of the city is hidden and the façade of misery they perceive in people's sad faces, in the dirty streets, the ruined playgrounds and the air pollution where people's health issues seem to get worse or relationships with old friends broken'. The chapter describes some of the interventions both in Athens and the second city, Thessaloniki, and the adverse experiences of some of the young adults who have survived the turbulent times in the past 40–50 years in Greece.

The other country described in detail in the book is Mexico, in the chapter written by Liliana Templos-Núñez, another country with very high levels of crime and drug use. As Liliana points out, most of the data on ACEs comes from more developed higher-income countries and yet in low- and middle-income countries, conditions of poorer economic levels and difficult social and political situations make a potentially greater environment in which ACEs may occur. For example, she quotes from a report from the United Nations Children's Fund in 2022 that reported that over 60% of children between the ages of 1 and 14 in Latin America and the Caribbean were subjected to violent discipline at home and that the death rate from homicide among children and adolescents is 4 times higher than the global average.

Liliana highlights the very high levels of poverty and extreme poverty, lack of access to social security, health services, nutritious food and education. She also highlights the very high levels of violence and crime, often related to the drug trade. These are, of course, the situations where children will experience great difficulties in growing up and exposure to many adverse experiences. The number of ACEs is evidenced in the chapter as a result of the aforementioned difficulties, with men reporting more childhood adversity than women, but women reporting more exposure to childhood sexual violence. As these two chapters show, ACEs are evident in different societies, and the impact of poverty and high levels of violence exacerbates these problems.

Whilst strictly speaking not a separate country, the living conditions of many Indigenous people in Canada make it seem as though they are in another, much poorer, country. One irony of this is, of course, it is **their** country and not that of the invading colonizers who, for the most part, live much wealthier lives. The chapter on Indigenous peoples in Canada describes a situation in many ways similar to the conditions of countries such as Greece and Mexico, with high levels of poverty and substance use, as well as levels of violence generated by years of abuse at many levels.

Racism and discrimination

Another recurrent theme throughout this book is the role of racism and discrimination in either causing adverse experiences or exacerbating them. The chapter on Indigenous people by Diane Riley and Mike DeGagné shows the appalling way people in the colonies were treated. In this case, it was by the British and French in Canada, but as the authors point out, the case was the same in all such colonies and probably in those of other European nations as well. These people were treated as 'savages', a word used at the time when speaking of them, their religion, culture and language were eroded, and their children often forcibly removed to abusive institutions. This had lifelong effects not just on them but also on their families and their offspring. While most of these appalling measures have stopped, in most of the former colonies, many of the Indigenous people are still living in a disadvantaged state and suffer daily racism and discrimination.

As Perry has noted in his work, black, brown and Indigenous children are more likely to be over-/wrongly diagnosed and overmedicated in mental health systems, removed from their homes, suspended or expelled from school, charged with assault and to enter the juvenile justice system (Perry and Winfrey 2021). As healthcare professionals, we have to remember that our interactions with our clients, especially children, are built on a difference in power, and that this includes racial, ethnic and gender issues.

In her chapter on the Aberfan disaster, Gaynor Madgwick describes the attitude of the NCB to the residents of the Welsh mining towns. Interestingly, in one part of the United Kingdom, in Wales, between 1840 and 1940, the use of the native language, Welsh, was forbidden in schools, even though this was the language they spoke at home. A child who was heard speaking Welsh was made to wear a wooden badge with WN on it and the child who wore it at the end of the school day was caned by the headteacher. This was known as the 'Welsh Not'.

Intergenerational and historic trauma

The chapter on Indigenous people in Canada outlines how a long history of invasion, disease, death and incarceration of various forms, including in residential schools where all forms of abuse were common, has led to generations of ill health and mental and social problems. These problems have been passed from one generation to the next in intergenerational or historic trauma, a form of trauma common to many Indigenous people who have been colonized. There are examples of intergenerational trauma in many of the lives that are described in this book. Though the precise mechanisms for this are still far from clear, it is so important that we acknowledge that this occurs and do what we can as healthcare professionals and society to break the cycle.

What is also remarkable is the ability of people to rebuild their lives when given social and financial support and the crucial role of education in this rebuilding.

Origins of violent behaviour

As has been discussed previously, ACEs are often intergenerational, passing down from one generation to the next either through learned behaviours and norms or epigenetic mechanisms. Working with troubled children and investigating their pasts, it can often be seen that the sort of behaviour perpetrated on the child was also experienced by the perpetrator. In the Lived Experience chapter, the story of Gwyneth Lewis tells of how she was abused by her mother, and her mother was abused in a similar way. These stories of repeated behaviour can be found frequently and are no more clearly set out over generations than in the chapter on Indigenous people and historic trauma.

In the chapter on violent offenders and the origins of their violence, Gwen Adshead and her colleagues describe studies that are related to violent offending and ACEs. For example, studies in prisons have shown that people with four or more ACEs are 8 times more likely to become perpetrators of violence compared to offenders who have no ACEs but also 8 times more likely to become victims of violence and 30 times more likely to attempt suicide. They point out that only a minority of those exposed to ACEs will go on to commit violence in adulthood and that rates of violence are dropping in the United Kingdom. They cite a review study that found that the greatest historical risk factor for committing violent acts was witnessing or being the victim of violence as a child. Among the risk factors, the most influential were neuropsychiatric disorders, substance use, schizophrenia, personality disorders and traumatic brain injuries, all of which are more common in individuals with high ACE scores.

The chapter concludes by explaining how the exposure to ACEs and the link to violence commission is currently limited and requires further research. Interventions, regulation and reducing substance misuse and addiction, improving mental health and emotional regulation, and studying offending history to understand what led a person to cause such harm will help them desist from violence in the future. Understanding their experience of victimisation as children and how this affected their sense of self-worth, inner security and perception of others is a worthwhile intervention. Contrary to popular opinion, many offenders may need compassionate support, and group work in prisons has been found to be effective, as has drama therapy (the excellent film *Sing Sing* covers one such program).

As Adshead and colleagues write, we do not yet know the best way to mitigate the effects of extensive traumatic events in young children whose brains are still developing. Providing children with attachment figures who can soothe and comfort them may prevent them from suffering from trauma or perhaps supporting the adults who care for the children may be effective. They conclude with an important statement: 'The question is urgent as children around the world are exposed to a variety of ACEs, including war, and the financial cost of those ACEs becomes unaffordable'.

How do we intervene most effectively?

The third part of the book is about interventions with descriptions of a wide range of therapies that have been used in dealing with mental health problems, especially PTSD. These range from psychological and psychosocial therapies to pharmacological therapies and include such approaches as art and music therapy and interventions with psychedelic drugs. In addition, there are a number of chapters from different countries describing different interventions ranging from the individual to the group and societal level. Education, in many forms, is clearly central to many successful interventions.

Training

The chapter written by Andrew Bennett is titled 'Everybody's Business' because, of course, it is if we are to have a society which will be safer and healthier for children and the adults that they become. Andrew's chapter focuses on the development and delivery of a training programme about ACEs, both for a police force in North Wales and a local authority. These are very important because they are aimed at many of the people who routinely deliver help to those with ACEs and not just some specialist staff. Interestingly, he describes when one policeman was introduced to the course, he spoke with one of the trainers and said, 'If you think you can turn police officers into social workers you can f*** off' but by the middle of the programme, he apologised and said, 'I get it'. This illustrates how people think it is not their issue, but come to realize that it *is* everybody's responsibility.

The chapter also points out that the most influential people to prevent ACEs are parents and carers, the people who interact most with children and who can see problems and identify needs. The chapter also describes training for health visitors (healthcare workers in the United Kingdom who work with mothers and young children). All the health visitors in the area were trained, although one expressed reluctance initially, citing the risk of triggering the mothers. This is clearly a very important sector of health provision for people who may see the consequences of ACEs but do not understand the origin of the problems. A survey of mothers was also undertaken, in which some disclosed that they had never been asked about ACEs.

Once the health visitors had been trained, they were able to ask their clients about ACEs and found that their initial reservations were not borne out. They reported that delivering the ACE enquiry was not time-consuming and did not increase the need for onward referral for specialist services. Training police officers and health visitors is a vital part of delivery to a group of public service workers who will confront these problems as part of their everyday work.

The chapter also describes working with children through art with the Merseyside Youth Association (MYA) is a charity dedicated to providing innovative support and opportunities for young people across Merseyside. This involved working with the Tate Gallery in Liverpool, working with children, mending broken pottery as an analogy for broken relationships and the like, and the NOW festival, an annual performing arts event that brings in children and young people from across the city region through performances that tackle issues that are important to them. Andrew also joined the Merseyside Violence Reduction Programme, which commissioned Liverpool John Moores University to undertake a representative household survey of adults to understand community safety and cohesion, violence victimisation and ACEs in Merseyside.

Substance use and ACEs

In his chapter, Michal Miovský describes how services developed in a different culture, the Czech Republic. He points out that the concept of a fully autonomous model of specialised addiction services for children and adolescents with substance use disorder (SUD) is not very common and tends to exist as an add-on to adult mental health services. In the Czech Republic, there are now substance use services dedicated to young people with specialist psychiatrists, psychologists, social workers and others. There is often a clear link between substance use and ACEs. As Michal points out, the lack of specialist services for young people with SUD means that, in general, adolescent services for ACEs are often overlooked or SUD can often be over or underestimated, with negative effects on treatment programmes.

'Une affaire de famille!' (a family affair!) programme

This programme was developed in the 1990s in Quebec by Line Caron. The programme aims to prevent the intergenerational transmission of the difficulties faced within a family and to free people from the suffering associated with their family of origin. Using a structured sequence of activities, it targets adults from families affected by SUDs and can also address other intra-family problems such as violence, depression, emotional dependence and so forth. It consists of 12 modules unfolding over a period of 6 months, in 8 3-hour sessions and includes a variety of activities such as role-plays, questionnaires, group discussions, presentations and applications of learning in real-life situations. The program is run by specially trained professionals who facilitate groups of up to 12 people, none being from the same family.

The programme covers different aspects of family functioning and may include addiction depending on the people involved. It deals with roles and rules within families and talks about the survival strategies put in place when experiencing adversity and the phenomenon of emotional dependency. They work on the intergenerational transmission by addressing concepts of abandonment, attachment and the relationship with children. They do not talk about their own histories but only how the emotions felt, building up 'genograms' of their families and drawing up plans for the future. Over the 12 sessions, participants tackle increasingly more difficult issues without activating defence mechanisms as their ability to cope with difficulties increases. To quote a woman who went through the programme: *She discovered that certain behaviours in her family were passed down from generation to generation, and that she had the power to break this pattern.*

This is an excellent programme highlighting the need to intervene with the intergenerational patterns of behaviour and how to cope in the future. It has been introduced in France as well as Canada and is now being evaluated. The evaluation of 'A Family Affair!' suggests that this programme has the potential to address ACEs and, in so doing, break the cycle of transmission to the next generation.

Art therapy

Deidre McConnell contributed a chapter on art therapy with children with ACEs. Deidre became an art psychotherapist and worked at a residential home for children whose foster placements had broken down, who had been permanently excluded from school, and had experienced difficulties at home. These girls were victims and survivors of abuse. The child's expression and engagement are encapsulated in the art, which may communicate something, perhaps unintended or unconscious. The children's trauma, stored in preverbal ways, may be expressed through art. Deidre describes in detail her work with one girl (Olive) who came from a very difficult family, her brother had been shot (in front of her) and was in prison, her father was only partially available and very coercive, and there was a long history of bullying and of societal racism. Trusted by Olive's parents, the school staff and the 'team around the child' worked with her father and mother to change home chastisement patterns and improve family dynamics. The relationship between the health services and the family was gradually rebuilt.

She describes the process of working with Olive, the ups and downs of therapy over 32 sessions and illustrates this with pictures she drew. She concludes: 'Rather than a slippery slope downward towards permanent exclusion, the school community and the art therapy together had brought Olive back from the brink, transforming her life and educational trajectory into one of incremental upward change'. This is a very useful addition to the range of therapies that can be used with children from difficult backgrounds who cannot express themselves verbally.

Trauma care

The chapter by Lauren Jones describes the work of two organisations she ran to help people who had experienced trauma, including ACEs. Lauren had her own experiences of ACEs and mental health issues, and so can provide perspectives from both sides. Her description of some of the difficulties in providing help raises some of the key issues in dealing with the effects of childhood adversity, both in terms of specific therapies and also within the broader context of what we think of as trauma-informed care. What is best for whom and when, and what is the difference between trauma-informed care and what practitioners should be doing already? We have tried to address these issues as we have moved through this book, but there are some pertinent points that still need to be addressed and, if not solved, then at least raised for the reader to think about and pursue.

Issues raised

Some problems with ACEs

As we have seen, ACEs have provided researchers with many useful ways to link childhood adversity to problems later in life. ACE screening is also used by many frontline agencies to increase public awareness of childhood adversity and to help individuals access appropriate support. In some cases, this screening is used to produce an 'ACE score', which reflects the number of ACEs experienced before the age of 18. Yet they are not without their problems and their detractors. Researchers and practitioners using ACE instruments for screening have noted unacceptably high levels of both false positives and false negatives, as emphasised in a comprehensive review by the Early Intervention Foundation into ACE research to date (Asmussen et al. 2020). Some suggest that we look for new ways of conceptualising and measuring ACEs since the expanding area lacks a clear definition and a coherent theoretical framework. Others have criticised the fact that the interest in and use of ACE screening had become a movement, a fad, at the expense of other factors that need to be considered for dealing with childhood. This has included criticism of the neglect of sociodemographic factors as a correlate of later ill health, especially poverty, violence and discrimination, with some pointing to this as a way to absolve society, and politicians, of responsibility by targeting the individual and family as the problem. The increasing focus on the role of genetic mechanisms has similarly raised the issues of a narrow focus on genetic determinism rather than on broader social, political and, increasingly with climate change, environmental factors.

There are also concerns about the ethics of some ACE screening practices (Asmussen et al. 2020). ACE screening is increasingly being used to identify children with symptoms of trauma, but there is little research based on whether such screening is an effective method for identifying vulnerable children and making treatment decisions. ACE screening could retraumatise children and screening may not be ethical if there is no referral to effective treatments. Screening tools cannot replace empathetic interviews and counselling with trained professionals. Asmussen and colleagues recommend that guidelines for the implementation of ACE screening practices must be developed and tested as most ACE screening practices do not comply with the World Health Organization's standards for screening implementation.

It is clear that ACEs are prevalent and that we need to improve the quality of our data in order to identify those likely to be in need of interventions. At the moment, there are few places in which there is a comprehensive, evidence-based approach to care and the emphasis has been on routine screening and trauma-informed care. Felitti and colleagues recommended that universal, selected and targeted interventions were necessary to prevent and reduce ACEs. These included intensive home visiting interventions for vulnerable families, school-based programmes aimed at preventing health-harming behaviours and targeted psychotherapeutic treatments designed to help children and parents cope with ACE-related mental health problems. The evidence to date suggests that this should be part of a system-wide public health approach at the community level.

Some problems with interventions

Cognitivism is a pervasive paradigm that has gained widespread popularity in the past several decades and has confused the true understanding of the human brain and body. Thus is the view that all human psychological activity is mediated by cognition and that it is subject to the principles of contingency and not just contiguity. A number of factors have led to the rise and imperialism of cognitivism over the last several decades: the advances in digital computing, the reliance on computer models of the brain and nervous system, the rise of the Information Age, the lack of attention to the importance of emotion, feeling and lower brain functions and a desire to distance from our animal characteristics. Yet, as TS Eliot so wisely put it: 'Where is the wisdom we have lost in knowledge? Where is the knowledge we have lost in information?' (TS Eliot, The Rock).

While it may be true that many human psychological processes are cognitive in nature, by no means all of them are. The rise of cognitive psychology corresponded with the rise of artificial intelligence, where indeed cognition and contingency are the chosen model. Nonetheless, we are analogue, not digital, creatures composed of bodies and minds that are intimately linked and where cognition is but one process that has evolved after many others on which the organism depends for survival in a real, not artificial, world. We are psychophysiological beings, not just cognitive machines. As Damasio noted, in describing Descartes' Error, rationality is built on top of and from the apparatus of biological regulation. The workings of the homeostasis and emotional structures of our brains and bodies, developed long before the thinking cortex, are the scaffolding of our thoughts and conscious feelings and actions. What an infant feels before they can think is a determinant of what they will later think, feel, believe and how they act and self-regulate (Damasio 1994). This is not intended to endorse a tripartite theory of the mind, which has been shown not to be based on sound science. It is intended to recognise the levels of development of the brain and nervous systems, and to call attention to the level and which stimuli are input to the organism. It is also important to recognise to importance of non-cognitive, non-contingency-based processes, especially the operations of the autonomic nervous system (ANS) and lower brain centres, and the role of Pavlovian conditioning in human learning, especially of fears and phobias. The popular Rescorla-Wagner model of learning emphasised the importance of contingency and cognition, but it did not deal with the activities controlled by the ANS and, as a result, left gaps in the understanding of emotional behaviours.

Once we understand the importance of the role of the ANS in stress-related behaviours, phobias and traumatic reactions, we can understand why so many interventions fail and why the data on some interventions appear so inconsistent, depending on the measures used to assess them. These interventions focus too much on the cognitive and on contingency-based approaches when assessing extinction of responses. The rates of extinction are different in different nervous systems as they operate according to different principles. The ANS is not under direct cognitive control and for extinction to occur in the sympathetic branch (the SNS), there has to be allowance for multiple sessions, with the focus being on contiguous, not contingent, pairings of stimuli. Cognitive-behavioural approaches are based on the assumption that behaviours are cognitively mediated, but that is not always so.

Attention to the ANS also highlights the need to assess the level of arousal of an individual. Hence, the need to measure heart rate and, if possible, sympathetic nervous system activity in particular, when assessing a client who appears to be distressed and aroused. The state of the ANS can give us a good indication of this, especially that of the SNS (the T wave of the EKG is a particularly good measure of this). We need to help lower this arousal so that the higher, cognitive, brain levels are better able to operate rather than being overwhelmed by the lower, emotional and motivational levels and by stress-related activity that can interfere with therapy.

Less emphasis on cognitive processes and more on other processes, especially of the lower brain, is so important in tapping into basic healing mechanisms such as rhythm and rocking, which are regulating and soothing. This is especially so for the young, for the developmentally delayed and for those who are overwhelmed by feelings. Perry has incorporated this into his neurosequential model of education (Perry and Winfrey 2021). All such models emphasise regulation and connection and reliance on somatosensory activation using a bottom-up approach.

When dealing with intense trauma, what is tolerable for the individual may be very brief indeed, as the person may simply want to shut down or to leave the situation and the level of arousal. It is better to have multiple, brief sessions that the client can control and feel safe in, and where they have the sense that they are being really listened to and believed.

Some problems with trauma-informed approaches

Trauma-informed care

Trauma-informed care is aimed at increasing healthcare and social workers' awareness of trauma and its effects. The rationale is that this will enable them to reduce any trauma individuals might experience in using routine services and to increase the level of trust felt by the individual. It also involves changes in services to increase transparency and a client's sense of control, choice and safety.

Research on the efficacy of trauma-informed care has yielded mixed results and an improved definition of the approach, along with more testing, is needed (Asmussen et al. 2020). As we have pointed out above, there are a number of concerns with this approach, including that the concept of trauma remains ill-defined, training is often exceedingly brief and that the focus on trauma is too narrow and can limit alternative approaches. Others argue that trauma-informed care is really no different from current models of good professional care and is just a new name for it.

Another criticism is that trauma-informed approaches are another form of reductionism, one more way of medicalising human responses to traumatic events. Others claim that epigenetics continues the dogmatic dominance of the disease model by reducing psychosocial factors to subsidiary, modifying or mediating influences. There is concern that an emphasis on trauma and mental health will place clients in the position of victims and vulnerable, with all of the attendant risks of labelling and self-fulfilling identity.

The overall assessment seems to be that trauma-informed care has potential to be helpful if its shortcomings are addressed, but it is by no means enough to address the problems raised by childhood adversity and its effects.

The medical model and labelling

We live in a time when a lot of 'isms' have combined to provide a perfect environment for labelling and medicalising individuals. Mechanism, materialism, determinism, reductionism and cognitivism have combined with the rise of pharmaceutical companies and a new age of brain imaging techniques. The desire to pigeonhole and to look for a neuroscientific basis to a condition is widespread and fuelled by insurance systems that require diagnostic labels to be applied to a client before they will guarantee funding of treatment. It is also fuelled by healthcare systems that are stretched beyond breaking point and our desire for simple solutions and magic bullets in the form of a pill.

The widely popular medical or disease paradigm separates mind from body, seeing the brain in purely biochemical terms and mental health and addiction as part of these processes. The approach to treatment then becomes focused on medications and pharmaceuticals. Yet there are no physical markers of mental illness other than dementia, only those which are subjective and behavioural.

The reality of the human organism is much more complex than the simple and reductionistic disease model describes. We are biopsychosocial beings and explanations and interventions need to address the complexity of the multiple systems that compose our lives. While there is a new emphasis on holistic approaches to health, there is still a reliance on the search for a neuroscientific basis, as with brain imaging, as though this somehow conveys real meaning and status to a condition. The search for a neuroscientific basis also reinforces the reification of diagnoses that have no real bases in fact.

The disease model is still the current most prominent approach to mental health and addiction, even though there has been a rise in the popularity of harm reduction approaches to drug use in the past few decades. Again, there is the search for the quick fix, with the surge in the use of selective serotonin reuptake inhibitors (SSRIs) for depression, even though, in most cases, they are no better than a placebo.

Labelling

Medical diagnoses are a vital part of working with and the treatment of people with problems. They can help us understand the nature of a problem, why a person is behaving or reacting in a certain way and how to respond to them. For example, if we meet a person who is hard of hearing, we might say that they are 'partially deaf' and if they have no hearing, we would describe them as 'completely deaf'. When correct diagnoses are made and shared, the people working with a person with this label will know what to expect and how to treat and respond to them.

In the area of mental health, however, the role of diagnoses is much less clear than in that of medicine. For some mental health problems, understanding and diagnosing conditions appears to be improving. For example, 50 years ago, the terms autism spectrum disorder (ASD) or attention deficit hyperactivity disorder (ADHD) were not known or used. Hyperactivity was described in some children, but not with the associated attention deficit that we know about now or the fact that adults may present with this condition. This labelling, however, can cause problems where there is not a full understanding of a person or what their history may be. It also becomes a problem when 'experts' provide labels in documents. Many professionals may use a label in a letter to other professionals or in case notes and this then becomes 'fact'. Working in children's homes (RP), where the majority of the children have had traumatic backgrounds and often experienced several ACEs, the children would come in with these labels of ADHD or ASD, but when they had settled, had security and began to form attachments with trusted adults, their difficult behaviours would often disappear. We need to be very careful before we apply labels to children, which other professionals, on reading the notes or letter, may not question.

ASD is an important diagnosis of a problem which can present in a wide variety of forms. What we do not need, however, is the application of the label to young people based on only brief contact and quick observations. This may then have serious consequences for the child. The inaccurate attachment of a label can lead to that child being treated differently and inappropriately. As Perry notes, a traumatised child entering preschool will not act like a typical 5-year-old; they will have poorer language development and self-regulation and so will shut down or act out and fall further behind. A British Columbia study of one million schoolchildren over 11 years found that children born in December are 39% more likely to be diagnosed with ADHD than classmates born in the previous January, 11 months behind in brain development (Perry and Winfrey 2021). Hypervigilance from sensitized stress response can be labelled ADHD. Efforts to self-regulate, such as doodling, listening to music and tapping, are prohibited in schools; the children will be labelled, medicated and perhaps expelled. When they try to avoid school, they are charged with truancy and so they enter the school-to-prison pipeline. The children themselves assume that they must be stupid (Perry and Winfrey 2021). Perry and his colleagues do not use labels in their clinics as they claim that these tell them nothing about what is underlying what they are seeing in the client.

Children brought up in families with lots of conflict may dissociate because they can't flee the situation, and this may become labelled as a dissociative disorder. Children with Oppositional Defiant Disorder usually lack sufficient connection with nurturing adults and resist being controlled by people they don't trust; there is nothing disordered in that form of behaviour in those circumstances.

Self-diagnosis or diagnosis by an unqualified person through social media or the web has become very popular over the past few years, with the result that there are many people who wrongly believe that they have conditions that they do not have. For example, rates of ADHD, especially in adults, have increased markedly in recent years. While it is true that neurodiversity has been underestimated and too often stigmatised, there is also a risk of swinging too far to the other side and overdiagnosing if this is not done by qualified professionals. What we need to do with children with 'problems' is either not to apply 'labels' or diagnoses at all, or at least wait until the children have been properly observed and understood, and the consequences of that diagnosis may be determined.

One of the most serious effects of labelling is stigma; we see the label, not the person, and respect and understanding are removed and possibilities for intervention, if needed, are reduced. People who use drugs are called addicts or drug users rather than people, removing any sense of the individual and the heart of the issue (Canadian HIV/AIDS Legal Network 2005).

Rosenhan's 1973 study of being sane in insane places (where researchers entered psychiatric institutions as patients in order to see what diagnoses and labels they would be given) spurred new attempts to 'standardise' diagnostic practice after he demonstrated that psychiatrists were often unable to discriminate between sane and psychotic people. Formal diagnostic systems like DSM (Diagnostic and Statistical Manual of Mental Health lDisorders) and ICD (International Classification of Diseases) attempted to address these problems by imposing diagnostic standardisation of criteria through the use of symptom checklists. This approach, however, has led to numerous problems:

- Many serious mental health conditions mimic the symptoms and diagnostic criteria of each other; diagnostic labels can be incorrectly applied.
- The frequency with which patients are given more than one diagnosis raises a concern about the specificity of diagnostic categories.
- Factors such as developing a strong therapeutic alliance are much more important than therapeutic technique in determining outcomes.
- Biases can inflate diagnosis rates of mental health conditions, particularly among disadvantaged minority communities.
- Labelling can strongly influence negative academic evaluations, behavioural evaluations, evaluations of personality and overall assessments of the child.
- Diagnostic-based frameworks are unable to either improve our scientific knowledge or improve outcomes in clinical practice.
- Psychiatric diagnoses are only descriptors, not explanations; they are abstractions and summaries, and are often circular, like the definition of bipolar disorder.
- Other evidence-based models for organising mental healthcare are available.
- Diagnoses (apart from dementias) listed in the diagnostic manuals have not been associated with any sort of physical test or biological marker and there are no physiological correlates.
- In some cases, reliability in making diagnoses has improved for research purposes, but not for clinical practice, and validity remains poor.
- Use of psychiatric diagnostic categories does not significantly improve treatment outcomes and evidence suggests they cause significant harm.

- Since the first edition in the 1980s, the DSM has widened its scope considerably, and many conditions that are not typically thought of as medical have become medicalised.
- Labels such as Borderline Personality Disorder become a grab bag in which to put people who don't seem to fit anywhere else.
- Diagnoses reveal nothing about the underlying events and dynamics of a person's life, about what happened to them.
- We create a self-fulfilling category; once given a label, the person is considered to be that way and can start to think of themselves in that manner, as a label rather than an individual.

As first set out by Plato, for a diagnostic system to be a good, useful taxonomy, it should show that there are natural places to cut when dividing the world into categories, and it should not just use arbitrary distinctions based on symptoms. To be clinically useful, diagnostic labels should help treatment decisions that effect outcomes, but this seldom happens (Timimi 2014). Labels raise many problems and shift the focus from where it should be: the psychophysiological individual in their complex environment. Alternative evidence-based models for organising effective mental healthcare are available.

One serious overarching problem with the medical model and diagnostic approaches is that many of the conditions diagnosed are considered to be genetic and that the best that can be done for the person is to control symptoms. Again, this can become a self-fulfilling label. Psychiatric diagnoses are also criticised as setting standards for 'normality', by categorising what emotional and behavioural traits and experiences should be considered disordered (Timimi 2014). We also impose Western medical-model approaches to mental health on the rest of the world, which can undermine local cultural approaches and increase the incidence of disorders common in the West, as well as the use of Western pharmaceuticals (Watters 2009; Whitaker 2010).

What we can learn from indigenous cultures

One of the many important points raised by the Indigenous chapter in this book and related materials is that Indigenous cultures have a great deal to tell us about raising children, not to mention our relationships with our communities and with our land and nature. In Canada, it was the colonisers who brought brutal forms of physical punishment and discipline and imposed a patriarchal system on what were, in many cases, matriarchal communities. Children were raised by the extended family and the community as a whole in an environment rich with people and different forms of stimulation, relieving the burden on the mother, a burden that we see all too often today being carried by a single parent.

This has been the pattern of many cultures for millennia, as many writers on social anthropology and psychology have pointed out. The individual was strongly connected to family and clan or tribe (and indeed the sense of 'individuality' was very different from our current, Western, sense of it), reciprocity or sharing was the norm, community and cultural meaning was deeply instilled as a way of explaining the world, and people were grounded through dance, drumming, singing and other forms of rhythm. These are, of course, what have been found through the research reported in this book and elsewhere to be the foundations of good mental and social health.

We are not calling for a return to a tribal life, but only for a recognition that we are human beings who have, in many ways, barely evolved since leaving the trees. We are not simply cognitive machines and need to respect and understand our fundamental and biopsychosocial natures. Our technology and other inventions are evolving at a much faster rate than we are; we are all aware of where this might take us in the next few decades, and this should alert us even more to the need to adopt approaches that attend to our humanity and our real needs.

Listening, understanding and believing: why the difference matters

As Delap notes in her review of attitudes towards sexual abuse, although the late twentieth century appeared to be much more open than previous times in its sexual politics, disclosures about abuse were still ignored, misheard, discouraged and suppressed (Delap 2018). This began to change in the 2010s with the number of cases involving high-profile figures and the Me-Too movement, but, alas, as we have seen, many of the most powerful figures continue to escape appropriate censure or justice. Children and adolescents continue to be seen as liars and seducers, even in courts of law, as seen in the case of Jack Mount, the headmaster of Brookside school, who was acquitted on several occasions of multiple charges of abuse and the abused children labelled as obsessed with sex by the defence.

Listening properly is something all professionals involved in providing therapy must learn to do at the very beginning of their careers. This may sound obvious, but unfortunately, it is often the case that people are not really listened to, not understood or not believed. This is especially so for women and children; for women, this is particularly true as applied to the menstrual cycle and menopause, which are often dismissed as 'women's problems'. For example, one young client would feel quite suicidal just before her period started. She was admitted to a psychiatric facility because of this, but her GP had dismissed it as a non-serious menstrual problem; she had a condition known as premenstrual dysphoric disorder (PMDD).

It is also clear that many people ignore children's complaints. When working with troubled children, you learn that they have often reported abuse but were not believed. A common theme is that if a child tells their mother about sexual abuse by a man close to the mother (such as a stepfather), they are told, 'Oh, he wouldn't do that!' A 58-year-old female client reported that she had been sexually abused in her childhood by her clergyman father, an experience that had a long-term impact on her life. The conversation started by asking her about the problem, and she talked for an hour and a half without being interrupted. When she was offered another appointment the following week, she said that there was no need; the session had been wonderful. She had met someone who listened to her talk about the abuse for the first time in 50 years, and they had believed what she said.

One girl of 14 years of age had drawn pictures which clearly showed abuse of women and girls. During the third session, she stated, 'I think I had better tell you about the pictures', then proceeded to discuss her experience of abuse. When RP met the girl's social worker, the girl said to the social worker, 'You don't listen to me, but he (RP) does'. The child needs to express in their language what has happened, and when they tell us, we should believe them or give them the benefit of the doubt. As therapists, we understand that not all information shared by clients may be entirely accurate. However, it is crucial to allow clients to express themselves in their own words and to listen attentively to what they are telling us.

Listening to children is vital, especially as they may have been told, 'This is our secret, don't tell anyone', or they may be being threatened. When trust is established, individuals may become more communicative, though this process could require multiple sessions with minimal dialogue and include activities such as drawing or painting. It is also true that the more abuse they may have experienced, the harder it will be to express, and periods of disclosure may be very brief.

Listening is part of the process of dialogue, and it is very important that the listener shows that they are following the conversation by maintaining eye contact, if that is culturally or otherwise appropriate or possible, by not interrupting, by not asking questions until a suitable break in the conversation, and by not asking questions which appear to doubt the speaker's veracity (note that some children on the autism spectrum find eye contact threatening). Once a person, particularly a child, trusts the person they are talking to, they are more likely to reveal abuse or other traumatic events, but this should not be forced as the client has to feel safe and may only be able to reveal a little at a time. Once they do begin to talk, this may only be in very brief disclosures at a time as the alternative may be emotionally overwhelming. It is then important to be able to help the client calm down and to be able to function in the present. In this way, we can better focus on the complex, psychophysiological individual in their real context, and not just a label or a diagnosis. As Perry notes, it is essential to understand what happened in the life of the individual to bring them to where they are today, and not to focus on what is wrong with them.

Conclusions and recommendations

ACEs have probably occurred throughout history all over the world, with some cultures no doubt being worse than others in terms of their occurrence and how they were dealt with. Some societies were matrilineal and tended to use less physical punishment with children than did Western ones, such as that used by colonisers and oppressors. Interestingly, most of the incidents of domestic and other violence in Western society are carried out by men, although not all. Some of the old ways of bringing up children based on 'spare the rod and spoil the child' led to physical abuse, which was not uncommon in some of the most expensive private schools in the United Kingdom and Indigenous school systems in colonies. The subject of ACEs is difficult to discuss because of the impact of these experiences on individuals. It is encouraging that childhood adversity is being talked about more and that research is increasing our knowledge of its effects and effective interventions for these. In the United Kingdom, for example, physical punishment is now banned in schools. There is also a greater awareness of Institutional abuse, given the wide reporting of it and the numerous scandals about people in responsible positions failing to take action against perpetrators.

As has been shown throughout this book, these events experienced in childhood can be extremely damaging, with effects lasting a lifetime, and at times being passed on to offspring. So, whose responsibility is it to make these changes? As the title of Andrew Bennett's chapter states, it's everyone's business. People working with children need to be educated thoroughly so that they can spot signs of distress and the impact of what has happened. They need to be aware of the long-term damage and the potential for contributing to the distress by careless handling of situations and by retraumatising the child. It is not only the staff dealing directly with the young people who need training but also the people who manage the services. Some of the most damaged children are put into care in children's homes and the selection of that home can be very important. In the case mentioned at the beginning of this section about the girl who was frequently moved, the managers of Social Services had only thought of the money saved and not about the girl. Social Services were responsible for continuing this girl's stress and making it worse.

All services which deal with children and their families should train their staff, including managers, on the effects of ACEs. Dealing with ACEs is not just about dealing with individuals but also about the circumstances of, and risk conditions for, adversities as well as the consequences, short- and long-term. This should include the educational system, staff of social, health and probational services, law enforcement and the legal system, including those in courts.

People working in all religious organisations need to be aware of ACEs and their effects and to understand the role that such organisations play in these. As has been described earlier, abuse has occurred in churches and other religious institutions, with abuse being carried out by religious staff and not reported by senior staff who knew of the abuse. There are also some religions and cultures whose practices are abusive, as with, for example, female genital mutilation and forced marriage for very young girls.

Improving laws, regulations and protections around child abuse, especially regarding online abuse and bullying, is imperative. This will also involve the control of online influences for children and adolescents, and the control of screen time for very young children in favour of other forms of sensory input, including touch. Part of this process is the awareness that we are being bombarded by stimuli of all kinds from so many different sources, which in itself can be stressful.

Policy changes are needed at a number of levels to deal with the causes and effects of childhood adversity. Strategies are needed to deal with social and economic factors such as poverty, discrimination, unemployment, housing and crime, and to increase a sense of supportive community, with a social safety net.

More support is needed from a range of services for those who are most vulnerable, including social, psychological, medical and law enforcement, with strong leadership for coordination. These services require good supervision and an understanding of how to carry out interventions in an effective and safe manner with trusted practitioners. This is something that we need to remember amidst all the negative information about adversity: there are good interventions that are known to work for prevention of ACEs and for treatment of their effects, including trauma and PTSD.

In our stimulation-filled, climate change-challenged future, we must recognise that we are complex psychophysiological beings who are not just cognitive machines. For this, the best we can do is to listen more and be more patient and supportive. It is worth noting that the best predictor of current mental health is our relationships with others, and that we need rhythm, rocking and touch in order to decrease stress levels and to be well-balanced. And perhaps most important of all, we should remember that the single most effective therapeutic intervention remains the trusted relationship between a client and a healthcare practitioner who has the time to provide the care and support needed to help the individual to heal.

References

Asmussen, K. Fischer, F., Drayton, E. et al. (2020). Adverse childhood experiences: what we know, what we don't know, and what should happen next | Early Intervention Foundation https://www.eif.org.uk/report/ (accessed 31 March 2025).

Canadian HIV/AIDS Legal Network (2005). *Nothing About Us Without Us*. Toronto: Canadian HIV/AIDS Legal Network.

Damasio, A. (1994). *Descartes' Error: Emotion, Reason, and the Human Brain*. New York: G.P. Putnam & Sons.

Delap, L. (2018), "Disgusting details which are best forgotten": disclosures of child sexual abuse in Twentieth-Century Britain, Journal of British Studies, 57, https://doi.org/10.1017/jbr.2017.181

Fletcher, Y. (2025). *Chutzpah, A Memoir of Faith, Sexuality and Daring to Stay*. New York: Doubleday.

Madgwick, G. (2016). *Aberfan, A Story of Survival, Love and Community in One of Britain's Worst Disasters*. Cardiff: Y Lofla.

Perry, B.D. and Winfrey, O. (2021). *What Happened to You? Conversations on Trauma, Resilience and Healing*, 2021. London: Bluebird.

Rosenhan, R. (1973). On being sane in insane places. *Science* 179: 251–258.
Timimi, S. (2014). No more psychiatric labels: why formal psychiatric diagnostic systems should be abolished. *International Journal of Clinical and Health Psychology* 14 (3): 208–215.
Watters, E. (2009). *Crazy Like Us: The Globalization of the American Psyche*. New York: Free Press.
Whitaker, R. (2010). *Anatomy of an Epidemic*. New York: Crown.

INDEX

The Intergenerational Effects of Adverse Childhood Experiences: Ripples on a Pond, First Edition. Edited by Richard Pates and Diane Riley.

Published 2026 by John Wiley & Sons Ltd.